# Art and History

# Art and History

## Texts, Contexts and Visual Representations in Ancient and Early Medieval India

*Edited by*

R. Mahalakshmi

BLOOMSBURY

NEW DELHI • LONDON • OXFORD • NEW YORK • SYDNEY

BLOOMSBURY INDIA
Bloomsbury Publishing India Pvt. Ltd
Second Floor, LSC Building No. 4, DDA Complex, Pocket C – 6 & 7,
Vasant Kunj New Delhi 110070

BLOOMSBURY, BLOOMSBURY ACADEMIC INDIA and the Diana logo are trademarks of Bloomsbury Publishing Plc

First published in India 2020
This edition published 2020
This paperback edition published 2025



Bloomsbury Academic
An imprint of Bloomsbury Publishing Plc



ISBN: PB: 978-93-69522-99-6; eBook: 978-93-88414-31-9

2 4 6 8 10 9 7 5 3 1

Typeset in Minion Pro by Manipal Technologies Limited
Printed in India by Manipal Technologies Limited, Manipal

*For my father, Shri K.S. Ramakrishnan, who passed away while this book was in press, and my sons Ramakrishna and Vishnuvardhan*

# Contents

# List of Images, Tables and Figure

## Images

## Tables



## Figure

# Acknowledgements

All the papers in this volume were presented at the two workshops that I had organised at the Centre for Historical Studies (CHS), Jawaharlal Nehru University (JNU), New Delhi, in 2015 and 2016. The first was organised in collaboration with Professor Eva Ehninger, Professor of Modern Art History, Humboldt University, who, at that time, was with the Institute for Art History, University of Bern. The focus there was on photography, cinema and painting in South Asia, and we planned to put together a volume based on the conference papers—a project which has not materialised yet. The second workshop, from which the sub-theme of this volume draws its title, was more focused in its chronological sweep. The financial support received from the Centre for Advanced Study of the CHS, and the International Collaboration unit of JNU, allowed for the smooth organising of these collaborative events.

I am indebted to Eva for inviting me over to Berlin and providing me with the academic space to present my ideas on the interface between art and history, and reflecting on the generalised understanding of the relationship between the two as it developed in the colonial Indian context. The workshop on 'Working through Colonial Photography' held during my time at the Humboldt University was illuminating, and the comments on my own paper offered by Eva and other scholars in Humboldt have contributed significantly to my fashioning of the themes for this volume.

This volume is the result of academically rich interactions and lively discussions with several colleagues, students and learned friends. Professor B.D. Chattopadhyaya had been the first to encourage me in the study of art in historical contexts, and I am extremely grateful for his insights and comments on various aspects of the themes, which are focused on in the introductory essay. My colleagues at the CHS—Mridula Mukherjee, Aditya Mukherjee, Ranabir Chakravarti, Kunal Chakrabarti, Sucheta Mahajan and Kumkum Roy—have indulged my requests to read and comment on drafts of articles, chair seminar sessions on the theme, and share their views on art and aesthetics in specific temporal frames. Professors C.P. Bhambhri,

K.M. Shrimali, Avijit Pathak, H.S. Shivaprakash, Shyam Narayan Lal, P.K. Basant, Sarvani Gooptu, Suchandra Ghosh, Susmita Basu Majumdar, Y.S. Alone and Anamika Roy have on different occasions discussed their disciplinary perspectives and academic insights, and enriched my understanding of art and/in history. The talented and engaged research scholars who have worked under my supervision, and the master's students I have taught at the CHS over the years, have questioned, critiqued and discussed many of the assertions presented in the volume.

The India International Centre (IIC) library, the JNU library, the CHS-CAS library and the Humboldt University library were important repositories that I made use of, and the IIC, in particular, has been my refuge over the past year.

My dear friends V.K. Karthika, Antony Thomas, Ravi Singh, Susmita Dasgupta and Vivek Menon have been an enormous source of support and encouragement through the years. Rushda Siddiqui, Swapna Liddle, Ravindranathan, Sameer Thomas, Sujit Thomas, Resmi and Sarabjit have responded with affection and kindness upon receiving academic and other requests.

My parents, Rajeswari and K.S. Ramakrishnan, deserve special thanks for pitching in when required, as do my siblings. Krishna and Vishnu have been generous and accommodated my absences and absent-mindedness. Rakesh Batabyal, my partner, a much published and respected scholar, has been my greatest critic as well as a sounding board and adviser, whose valuable opinions have shaped my academic understanding.

The contributors to this volume have responded to my frantic emails and WhatsApp messages with alacrity. Without their wonderful essays and their support, this book wouldn't have seen the light of day. I am grateful to Deepna, Menka, Nirupama, Prerana, Dev Kumar, Devdutta, Rajalakshmi and Sneha, who helped in various ways during the final stages of the publication. I am particularly indebted to Professors B.D. Chattopadhyaya, Irfan Habib, D.N. Jha and Hermann Kulke for giving their valuable endorsements for the volume. Last but not least, the capable team at Bloomsbury—Chandra Sekhar, Shreya Chakraborti and Arnab Karmakar—deserve full credit for their involvement at every stage, and ensuring that this volume would reach bookshelves as scheduled.

# Visual Representations as Historical Source in Ancient and Early Medieval India: An Introduction

R. Mahalakshmi

Art history as a discipline has carved a distinctive niche for itself, with a focus on objects and monuments and their material, contextual, aesthetic and philosophical dimensions. History has tended to be viewed as having a larger methodological and analytical framework, and given its incompatibility with that which is static or unchanging, an exclusive focus on materiality is automatically discounted. The tendency amongst historians, therefore, has been to treat visual elements as supplementary sources at best, and more commonly as not having any real significance on historical contexts. The challenge of integrating broader historical issues within art history has been undertaken with some degree of efficiency and sensitivity, but the reverse is not quite true. This volume is an attempt at redressing the lack, by focusing on visual representations as sources and signifiers that emanate from specific contexts, which can be illuminated through a range of textual, epigraphic and other material. The visual, here, is not just a supplement, nor is it the prime focus of analysis; it is the integrating of the interpretation of the visual material with socio-economic and politico-cultural concerns in relation to a specific historical context that constitutes the core of this book. In the introduction, we will discuss some concerns that are essential for historians studying visual representations, with regard to the rendering and signification of the visual, before discussing historical studies on art and the institutionalisation of art history.

## Unravelling the Visual

The *Viṣṇudharmottara Purāṇa*, a seventh-century text inserted as an appendix to the *Viṣṇu Purāṇa*, narrates an illuminating dialogue between

King Vajra, a seeker of knowledge, and his preceptor, Mārkaṇḍeya.[1] On being asked how to make images of deities, Vajra is instructed that only one who understands painting would know the art of sculpting images. When he wishes to learn the rules of painting, Mārkaṇḍeya advises him to first learn dancing. Vajra then asks to be instructed in dancing, upon which the sage comments that only with a thorough knowledge of music can the art of dancing be mastered. Visual representations, thus, are conceptualised as an important component of what is designated as art, and are closely linked to performative traditions as creative expressions of the human mind. That such expressive traditions are rooted in specific historical contexts, but their value, appreciation as well as relevance may carry across temporal locations, is widely recognised by scholars studying art.

To understand why and how art emerges in societies, philosophies of art in the Western scholarly traditions hark to the great Greek thinkers Plato and Aristotle. The latter emphasised the mimetic elements—what may be understood as the imitational qualities of a work of art—and both were of the opinion that by stretching the limits of representation, art attempted to mediate with reality.[2] While these thinkers were largely concerned with drama, their understanding of the representative quality of art can be applied to the visual forms, such as sculpture and painting, as well. But rather than see art as simply representational, we may also look at its self-expressive quality and extra-representational aspects. The latter would include the creation of illusion and abstract forms. Art cannot be understood as mirrors, according to the well-known art scholar E.H. Gombrich, but 'they share with mirrors that elusive transformation, which is so hard to put into words'.[3] Although the expressive idiom cannot be disentangled from skill acquisition and formation, for Gombrich, the attempt to imitate or replicate the perfection of nature by the ancient Greeks was a highly individualised act, and the claim of reproducing the 'image on the retina' itself was an illusion.[4] Despite this, there are likenesses, fashions and tastes that reveal the 'social forces on our attitude towards representation in art'.[5] To decipher the 'cryptograms' of art, we need to understand the 'mental set' or horizon of expectation that influences our perceptions of nature and society, and likewise is influenced by it.[6] This view is reminiscent of Immanuel Kant's understanding of aesthetics as subjective since the beauty of an art object is neither intrinsic nor universally accepted.[7] The object is seen here as having an identity outside of the cognitive range marked by sensuous intuition, having an 'intelligible existence' by its own right.[8] Hence, meaning cannot be understood in an objective framework, as it is ultimately the individual who offers an interpretation and appreciation. However, Ananda Kentish Coomaraswamy deemed it 'pure nonsense' to understand art through disinterested aesthetic contemplation, and preferred to use the early Greek notion of rhetoric—'giving effectiveness to truth'—to categorise artistic experience.[9]

The unitary, monolithic construction of artistic expression from an individualistic or psychological perspective has been criticised in recent times.[10] Instead, emphasis is given to the social dimensions of art, particularly the production process, patronage and intended use of the artwork.[11] It has been argued that what is understood as the artistic expression was almost never individual preference because invariably the artist was commissioned to execute a work of art. Similarly, premodern art cannot be understood completely as a free expression because it is within certain parameters of style and taste the artist works. Locating the ideological roots of art, Walter Benjamin argues:

> Even the most perfect reproduction of a work of art is lacking in one element: its presence in time and space, its unique existence at the place where it happens to be. This unique existence of the work of art determined the history to which it was subject throughout the time of its existence. This includes the changes which it may have suffered in physical condition over the years as well as the various changes in its ownership. The traces of the first can be revealed only by chemical or physical analyses, which it is impossible to perform on a reproduction; changes of ownership are subject to a tradition, which must be traced from the situation of the original.[12]

The evocation by Benjamin of the intrinsic value of art in the premodern period as linked to its extrinsic worth was embedded in the idea of its uniqueness and its individual character, suited to specific contexts. Although liable to reproduction, for Benjamin, the distinctiveness of the work of art was due to its temporal location. The claim of authenticity of the 'original' artwork conferred authority on it, and the development of modern techniques of mechanical reproduction denuded that authority or 'aura'. Benjamin's ultimate purpose is to laud the deconstruction of the art object located within a time–space continuum in the modern period. But his interpretation of the iconic status of European works of art in the premodern period as rooted in the religious and the cultural value bestowed on it is of importance to the understanding of Indian art as well. This Marxist understanding of art as camouflaging social realities has an uncanny resemblance to Plato's distrust of artistic mimesis. Despite the insights offered in such studies, there are limitations imposed by the monolithic constructs of art and aesthetics on which these are premised.

The issue of aesthetics and beauty being incumbent on context, and that even within contexts there can be differences in tastes and expression that relate to social hierarchies has been raised.[13] Here, issues of class and other social identities as impinging upon these conceptual categories are given importance. This, in a sense, contradicts Benjamin's analysis of premodern art as cutting across social differences and hierarchies, and acting as an ideological tool as well as reflecting the hold of the elites in particular social contexts. Political motivations, social aspirations and cultural tastes motivate specific forms and themes of artistic production. It appears that if philosophies of the (visual) arts have privileged the art themselves, votaries of the social dimensions of art have tended to submerge works in political, economic and social structures.

What is striking in the critical analysis of art and aesthetics is that there is an almost-complete negation/ignoring/marginalising of art that is non-European. Gombrich makes passing references to Oriental art, and pays slightly more attention to the Egyptian traditions; neither is seen as contributing significantly to a serious understanding of art. This is indeed surprising because some of the noteworthy studies on the non-Western traditions were already well known in the first half of the 20th century. Christopher Pinney, in the context of the theoretical analysis of photography, suggests there is a neo-colonial, new imperialist design by which what emanates from the West, with a focus on Europe and North America, is considered as contributing to a 'theoretical' understanding, while what emerges from, say, India provides a 'locational' focus—a case study.[14] The 'ex-nomination' principle used by Roland Barthes to describe 'the process through which an ideological fact disappears', according to Pinney, can be used as a frame to understand the marginalisation or erasure of India-centric studies on photography. This comment is as true for studies on critically understanding premodern art.

The collection of essays in this volume seeks to redress this 'ex-nomination' of premodern Indian art traditions in analytical works that contemplate answers to crucial questions in the philosophy of art—why and how did it emerge and develop?[15] How central was prescription, technique and skill to its production? Who were the makers and patrons of art? What were the purposes served by art? Are meanings emanating from art literal, or derivative and symbolic? And most crucially, how and why do certain forms, meanings and symbols retain a valence across context? The thematic thread that runs through these essays is on the relationship between texts, contexts and visual representations.

## Pioneers of Indian Histories of Art

Indian art as a subject of study received its impetus in the 19th century as a result of colonial efforts at retrieving the lost historical past of the land now under their control. The development of archaeology as a discipline, on the one hand, and the 'picturesque' form of painting as a mode of representation as well as photography, on the other, dovetailed with imperialist expansion and the social accumulation of wealth in Europe.[16] Knowledge production was one of the key elements behind the efforts at reconstructing the historical past in different parts of India, and providing a chronological order and interpretation was the stated intention of some of the pioneers in this regard. Questions of preservation, conservation and restoration were at the same time being debated in Europe and the Indian subcontinent, with its rugged landscape dotted with ruins, harking to an evocative past, provided the arena for the playing out of these arguments.

Monica Juneja and Michael Falser argue that notions of heritage and preservation stemmed from an understanding of the historical value and aesthetic attainments that were rooted in European sensibilities.[17] In Asia, these ideas were put into practice as a result of the colonial projects of the European states. Romanticism dominated the efforts at conservation and preservation of 'overgrown, deserted and forgotten sites'.[18] The creation of the archaeological site itself was an offshoot of this enterprise, and the idea of the picturesque dominated the manner in which the monument as an object came to be construed. It is argued that there was also a transposing of these theoretical concepts and their transcultural circulation in such a manner so as to allow for their reconfiguration in the new colonised setting. Hence, the binary in recent scholarship between the colonial 'universalist' claims and intentions, and the native culturally localised values may be misplaced and even misleading.[19] The participation of native scholars and enthusiasts in the documentation and archaeologising endeavour is well known.

However, it would be simplistic to disaggregate individual intentions and general contexts of this enterprise; as Tapati Guha-Thakurta has shown, the ordering of the wilderness afforded by the archaeological projects of preservation, conservation and restoration had their roots in the colonial surveys of the landscape that were started in India from the early 19th century.[20] These surveys were to provide a sense of topography, the extent of political territories, prevalent socio-economic structures and the existing systems of revenue settlement. The English East India Company with its acquisition of territories and extension of military and administrative control, both directly and insidiously, sought to finance its establishment from within the colony.[21] James Renell was the first Surveyor-General of Bengal, appointed by Robert Clive in 1757, soon after the East India Company established administrative and military control in India. Colin Mackenzie, the first Surveyor-General in the Madras Presidency in 1810, extensively recorded the art and architectural remains he encountered, providing sketches detailing features, which continue to serve as important documentation even today.[22] This was possibly the first of such endeavours, and while Mackenzie's intention was not to provide an archaeological record but a topographical survey, monumental architecture, in particular, served for him as a scientific register of altitude and terrain. It is only incidental, or as a secondary exercise, that he and other officials sought to present an account of monuments and antiquities that served as a record for later institutionalised academic studies.[23]

The Orientalist interest in the history and culture of Asia had already led to the ferreting of valuable details through textual analysis in the

18th century, facilitated increasingly from the end of that century by the presence of administrators and the colonial machinery in different parts of the continent. This was especially so in the Indian subcontinent, where armchair scholarship was gradually supplemented by field knowledge.[24]

Two individuals in colonial India in the mid-19th century who deserve special mention in any discussion on the documenting of monuments and iconography are James Fergusson and Alexander Cunningham.[25] The former was initially employed in a private firm in Calcutta and later went on to become an indigo plantation owner,[26] while the latter, a contemporary, was an engineer who entered military service under the East India Company.[27] Both travelled extensively across the country, were interested in the documentation of antiquities, and developed techniques suited to their purpose. While Fergusson was primarily interested in cataloguing architectural details and maintaining a record of monuments across the vast Indian countryside, Cunningham began to undertake field surveys of monuments and sites, and reading meanings into the art and architecture through textual analysis. Both petitioned the colonial administration to formalise institutional surveys to facilitate colonial knowledge production. It is because of a letter petitioning the government that the primary purpose behind such an exercise would be to know and understand the natives and their culture better—which, in turn, would facilitate the British rule—that the colonial Indian government, now under the British Crown, appointed Cunningham as the archaeological surveyor in 1861. His task was to undertake surveys of the vast dominions of the empire, from the mountainous terrain of the Himalayas, through the north and central Indian plains, eastern and western India, the Deccan plateau and South India.

The first major work that Fergusson wrote was delivered originally as a lecture at the Royal Asiatic Society of Great Britain and Ireland, and a list of 18 plates of rock-cut temples with brief descriptions preceded the text.[28] The plates affixed at the end were tinted lithographs and meant to be the primary focus of the publication, which was brought out as a folio. Fergusson mentioned that the sketches were made by him while studying and making notes within the caves, and was hopeful that through the intervention of the government, which had acceded to the memorandum of the Royal Asiatic Society, there would be, in the future, 'competent persons to draw and copy the antiquities and paintings in each district, and thus we may at last hope to have these caves illustrated in a manner worthy of their magnificence and great historical interest. I only hope the subject will not now be allowed to drop till every monument of ancient India has been thoroughly examined and detailed, and we may thus escape the hitherto too merited reproach of having so long possessed that noble country, and done so little to illustrate its history or antiquities.'[29]

Fergusson was not the first person to take an interest in art and architecture. A number of illustrated works had begun to be written in the early 19th century focusing on specific cities and regions, partly because of colonial requirements, but also because of the increasing numbers of European visitors to the subcontinent.[30] From the late 18th century, paintings in the picturesque mode had been collectors' items, published and circulated widely, the most famous of these being Hodges's *Select Views in India* (1786), and the two collections of Thomas and William Daniells—*Oriental Scenery* (1785–1808) and *Twenty-Four Views in Hindostan* (1805).[31] The role of the Asiatic Society, established in 1784 by William Jones, cannot be understated, with its interest in texts and antiquities that would throw light on Oriental civilisations. In 1834, an Indian scholar, who had risen from the ranks in government service and reached the position of a judge and magistrate in Bangalore, wrote the first treatise that exclusively focused on Indian architecture.[32] Ram Raz made a number of extremely accurate hand-drawn illustrations of various temple sites in South India, although unlike Fergusson's sketches, there was no attempt at providing scales. For Raz, the purpose of such an undertaking was to highlight the 'state of arts and sciences in India in the early days … deserving the attention of the antiquarian and philosopher'.[33] He further states:

> Some of the western authors have traced a certain resemblance in the leading features of the buildings in Egypt and India, and have thence concluded that there has very early been a communication of architectural knowledge between the two countries. But it is not altogether improbable that the resemblance may be merely owing to accident … I will not venture to affirm anything with certainty, until I have collected sufficient information to form

> an opinion ... that until the *Śilpa Śāstras* of the Hindus is correctly illustrated and laid before the public, the question as to whether the art owes its origin to the one or the other of the two countries must remain problematical.[34]

Fergusson's own stated intention was to bring to public notice the earliest-known Indian antiquities, although at this stage neither the comparative method nor frames of comparison with other regions of the world, alluded to in Raz's work, seem to be the motivating force. In fact, he constantly alluded to the cost of publication, and whether the effort required for this would prove its worth in terms of sales, suggesting personal pecuniary gain as the motivating factor.[35]

In a later publication, *The Cave Temples of India*, Fergusson informs us in the preface of the efforts made towards documentation of cave temple art and architecture since his own work, and concluded that 'a great deal has been done since by new discoveries and further investigations to fill up the cartoon I then ventured to sketch in, but the correctness of its main outlines have never been challenged and remain undisturbed'.[36] He draws attention to governmental institutions such as the Bombay Cave Temple Commission in 1848, which acknowledged his role in the process: 'The Royal Asiatic Society of Great Britain and Ireland having, on the suggestion of James Fergusson, Esq., to whom we are so much indebted for the artistic and critical illustration of the architectural antiquities of India, represented to the Court of Directors of the East India Company the propriety of taking steps for their preservation, as far as possible, of the Cave Temples and other ancient religious memorials of this country, and for their full delineation and description... It has determined to appoint a general Commissioner of Orientalists to direct its accomplishment in the way which may best tend to the illustration of the history, literature, religion and art of ancient India.'[37] Thus, in his own view as well as in the views of others, apparently, it was his emphasis on visual documentation that was seen as most valuable. This, then, may be seen as the first clear instance of a methodology for the study of Indian art and architecture being laid out. Secondly, the institutionalisation of the documentation and reporting of the art and architectural specimens may also be attributed to his efforts, along with others. The numerous ground plans with elevation and features demarcated according to scale, signifying the scientific methods employed in documentation, may also be attributed to Fergusson.

In fact, in the preface to a work written in 1876, Fergusson refers to more than 3,000 photographs in his possession that served as his primary sources, and which he pored over, day in and day out.[38] He says:

> For the purpose of a work such as this, however, photography has probably done more than anything that has been written. There are now very few buildings in India—of any importance at least—which have not been photographed with more or less completeness; and for purposes of comparison such collections of photographs as are now available are simply invaluable. For detecting similarities, or distinguishing differences between specimens situated at distances from one another, photographs are almost equal to actual personal inspection, and when sufficiently numerous, afford a picture of Indian art of utmost importance to any one attempting to describe it.[39]

Thus, the comparative methodology raised by Raz also becomes significant in Fergusson's study. He, in fact, comments on the lack of any evidence to connect the histories of Egypt and Assyria with the subcontinent, and attributes the earliest knowledge of the region to Alexander's invasion: 'It was just when the old Vedic period was passing away, to give place to the new Buddhist epoch; when that religion was rising to the surface, which for nearly 1,000 years continued to be the prevailing faith of northern India, at least.'[40]

While the temporal-spatial analysis of architecture remained the primary focus, Fergusson began to focus on issues of geography, historical chronicling (or its lack), ethnographical accounts and religious traditions of the country, bringing in current racial prejudices and simplistic understanding of migration and sociopolitical contexts. For him:

> in the midst of all these perplexities and uncertainties there is still one thread which, if firmly grasped, will lead us with safety through the labyrinth and land us on firm ground, on which we may base our explorations in search of further knowledge. India is covered with buildings from north to south, and of all ages, from the first introduction of stone architecture in the third century BC down to the present day. With scarcely an exception, these are marked with strongly developed ethnographic peculiarities, which are easily read and cannot be mistaken. Many of these have inscriptions upon

> them, from which the relative dates, at least, can be ascertained, and their chronological sequence followed without hesitation. In addition to this, nearly all those before the Moslem conquest have sculptures and paintings, which give a most vivid picture of the forms of faith to which they were dedicated, and of the manners and customs, as well of the state of civilisation of the country at the time they were erected.[41]

Thus, for Fergusson, despite the dubious nature of literary evidences, it was the monumental remains that provided a firm footing and aided the understanding of the Indian past. The fundamental contribution of Fergusson for the student of early Indian art is his focus on style, religious orientation and period of composition, although he himself revised his ideas in later works.

Cunningham presents a similar understanding of the need to visually document with precision in his first major publication, *The Bhilsa Topes*. He says:

> The plans and sections which accompany this work are all drawn from careful measurements on the same scale (of 40 feet to an inch) to preserve the relative proportions of the different Topes. The top of each drawing is the north, by which the relative positions of gateways, staircases, and other parts, may be determined at a glance. The plans of the different hills on which the several groups of Topes are situated, are all taken from my own surveys on the same scale of 400 feet to an inch. The eye can thus compare the disposition of one group with another. Lastly, the drawings of all the relic-boxes and caskets are one half the original size, sufficient (I have reason to think) for the delineation of the different shapes and various mouldings.[42]

This book also provides numerous hand-drawn sketches and privileges detailing through observation. In another book on the *stūpa* at Bharhut that he had excavated, we find plates of lithographs produced by the famous British firm Vincent Brooks, Day and Son.[43] What is also distinctive about Cunningham's method was that he stressed the larger historical context by taking recourse to mythology, travel accounts and sacred texts to link monuments and histories.

The 1862 minute of Lord Canning, the Governor General of India, in response to the memorandum of Cunningham in 1861, refers to the latter's appointment to undertake archaeological surveys so that 'an accurate description, illustrated by plans, measurements, drawings or photographs, and by copies of manuscripts' of the numerous remains in India could be provided.[44] Cunningham himself, in the first volume of the Archaeological Survey of India (ASI) Report, mentions, 'It would be desirable also to have photographic views of many of the remains, both of architecture and of sculpture, but to obtain these it would be necessary to have the services of a photographer.'[45] We find photozincographs used in the series of reports published by the ASI. Cunningham's method of data collection on the basis of field archaeology, his search for textual references to space, monument and icon, and his preoccupation with Buddhist remains need to be placed in the context of other researches that were being carried out by agencies such as the Asiatic Society, with which he had been closely associated.

There were other efforts being carried out to understand Indian art and architecture, all of which borrowed from and contributed to the methodological base established by these pioneering scholars with regard to fieldwork, scientific recording and cataloguing, and interpretation based on chronology and regional context. These methods continue to dominate studies emanating from the disciplinary perspectives of art history and archaeology even today. What is significant in these pioneering studies is the emphasis on the retrieval of historical contexts through an understanding of art forms, although it is in a very limited sense that the context is explored.

## Spirituality and Art

Vajra: '*Rūpagandharasehīnam śabdasparśavivarjita, puruṣastu tvayā proktastasya rūpamida katham.*'

Mārkaṇḍeya: '*Pravṛtivikṛtistasya dve rūpa parmātmana, alakṣya tasya tadrūpa prakṛti sā prakrītitā.*'[46]

Coming back to the *Viṣṇudharmottara Purāṇa* mentioned earlier, Vajra's thirst for knowledge leads him to a new line of questioning of the sage Mārkaṇḍeya. He asks how one who is formless does not emanate any smell, is devoid of taste, and cannot be discerned through words or touch, can possibly be known? Mārkaṇḍeya replies that the form which is difficult to perceive through specific characteristics is *prakṛti* or original nature; thereby the whole universe itself is to be understood as *pravṛti* or manifestation through *vikṛti* or modification, thus providing *rūpa* or form.

On the basis of this and other textual inferences, scholars working on early Indian art have emphasised the spiritual content of art, where deep philosophical ideas and meanings are seen as embedded in visual representation. Two noteworthy names are Coomaraswamy (1877–1947) and Stella Kramrisch (1896–1993), both of whom stressed the larger cultural framework within which Indian art would have to be viewed. For Coomaraswamy, the idea of 'art for art's sake' was alien to Indian craftspeople, and the lack of distinction between the sacred and profane marked their understanding of their creations.[47] He saw a distinction between medieval Mughal art and the earlier traditions, because in the latter, individual aesthetic directed by patronage structures predominated. Earlier, he argued, the common people and the elites shared a collective religious and aesthetic culture, and this is what made Jaina, Buddhist and Hindu art distinctive. For Coomaraswamy, all art of this period was religious, and there is no essential contradiction between this and the aesthetic or scientific elements in any production.[48] Deeply influenced by the '*philosophia perennis*' theory of René Guénon, Coomaraswamy identified an everlasting, continual flow of ideas and symbols in premodern artistic traditions that were intuitively recognised by artists and spectators.[49] Hence, while technique and form were important markers of artworks, their true meanings emanated from the cultural significance attached to aniconic, anthropomorphic and ornamental representations, which, in turn, drew upon the deep philosophical ideas and spiritual understanding imbuing Indian culture.[50] His famous and most cited essay on the dance of Śiva, visually exemplified in the bronze icons of Naṭarāja belonging to the Cōḻa period, analyses its cosmic significance, symbolising the creation, maintenance and destruction of the universe, and ultimately its rejuvenation. On the basis of a variety of philosophical treatises, Coomaraswamy interprets the dance of Śiva as the signifier of cosmic activity envisaged in five aspects (*pañcakṛtya*): *sṛṣṭi* or creation, *sthiti* or maintenance, *saṁhāra* or destruction, *tirobhāva* or disappearance/concealment and *anugraha* or grace. In fact, the *pañcākṣara* (five syllables) in Śiva's name—*na-ma-*śi-*vā-ya*—are seen as representing this five-fold creative activity of the deity.

What Śiva creates is the manifest and unmanifest world; what he destroys are the illusory bonds that fetter not only the world at large, but every individual soul in the cosmos. The symbolism of fire, a visual connect between the earth and sky, the perceived and intuitive, and the tangible and intangible, is analysed through the association of Śiva's dance with the burning grounds. This is then represented in the beautiful circle of fire—the *tiruvāci*—that encompasses the icon of Śiva as Naṭarāja in the Indic imagination. The *ānanda* or bliss of Śiva's dance, ultimately, is to meditate upon the breaking of *māyā* (illusion), the trampling of *mala* (impurity), which manifests as *āṇava* (miniscule) and *avidyā* (ignorance), and the freeing of the soul from the bonds of *karma* (causality/rebirth).[51]

Kramrisch, drawn to Indology and art history because of her chancing upon a translation of the *Bhagavad Gītā*, was also attracted to the spiritual element in Indian art and architecture.[52] She focused primarily on the Buddhist and Brahmanical traditions, and to hone her understanding, she studied Sanskrit and Pali language and literature, and even took *dīkṣa* from an Aghori in Kalighat.[53] Rather than identify linear artistic developments alone, Kramrisch emphasised the transcendental element in visual representations; the notion of the formless/unmanifest and the form/material aspect intrinsically interwoven in art and architecture separated by time and space. In the introduction to the catalogue *Manifestations of Śiva*, with reference to the aniconic phallic representation of the deity, she says:

> The concrete shape of the Śiva *liṅga*, of stone, wood, metal, sand, or clay, is understood to be a concretisation of subtler stuff, of light or sound—of a light stronger than eyes can see, of a sound in which reverberates the primordial stress of creation. Light and sound are manifestations of movement. It was in a Liṅga of Flames that Śiva was seen by the gods in a cosmic night between the destruction of one universe and the creation of another.
>
> The *liṅga* is also looked upon as the visible form of mantra, that is, of sound before it has become word, of sound forms and of words. The ontology of the cosmos together with that of man's mind and body inhere in the concrete shape of the Śiva *liṅga*. Descending from its apex in the four directions of space to its bottom, the *liṅga*, in a complex system of analogical categories, is understood symbolically as the embodiment of the five elements (ether or space, air, fire, water, and earth), the five sense data (sound, touch,

> form, taste, and smell), and the five sense faculties (hearing, feeling, seeing, tasting, and smelling). Analogous to the categories of the physical world and of sentiency, higher categories comprising mentation and transcendency have, in ontological order, their symbol in the *liṅga*, the principles of essence (*puruṣa*) and substance (*prakṛti*), universal intellect (*buddhi*), personality (*ahankāra*), and mind (*mānas*). Of these and further categories comprising the entire realms of existence and transcendence, the *liṅga* is the pivot.[54]

In both Coomaraswamy's and Kramrisch's analysis, the visual representation becomes the signifier of a shared cultural universe, which mediates form, meaning and symbol. The Vedic, Puranic and *Śaiva Siddhānta* traditions are invoked to demonstrate the layers of accretion, to be unravelled through mythology and philosophy. Such an interpretation continues to be relevant in the study of visual representations, although historical studies have emphasised the political and social contexts that determine the choice of icons from the wide range available in the cultural spectrum. Secondly, by focusing on religious iconography in particular as being imbued with cultural valence, non-religious contexts of artistic production, while acknowledged, get swamped. The third problem is that with a view to establishing religious and spiritual content in art, the emphasis is given to textual material that belongs to very different time periods, thereby obfuscating the contextual dimensions of artistic endeavour. Hence, while the underlying of symbolic content and signification of the art form are very important, the social and economic determinants also need to be prioritised.

## Artistic Prescription and Execution

Textual authority and its bearing on ancient and early medieval art and architecture have been the focus of a number of critical studies in relation to the Indian subcontinent. A wide range of treatises pertaining to art and architecture, generally known as the *Śilpa Śāstra*, form the prescriptive corpus; some prominent works are the *Bṛhat Saṁhitā* (fifth/sixth century CE), *Viṣṇudharmottara Purāṇa* (seventh century CE), *Mānasāra* (eighth to twelfth century CE), *Mayamatam* (eighth to twelfth century CE), the 28 *Śaiva Āgama* (such as the *Suprabheda*, *Kāmika*, *Karaṇa*, etc.), *Samarāngaṇa*

*Sūtradhāra* of King Bhoja of Dhāra (eleventh century CE), *Aparājitapṛcchā* of Bhuvanadevācārya (thirteenth century CE), *Rūpamaṇḍana* of Maṇḍana (fifteenth century CE), etc. Some of the *Purāṇas*, such as the *Matsya Purāṇa* (seventh century CE) and *Agni Purāṇa* (ninth/tenth centuries CE), contain references to *tīrthas*, prescriptions regarding temple building and iconography, and have also been valuable in reconstructing early art and architectural traditions. Buddhist and Jaina liturgical texts, as well as popular narratives, have similarly been used to understand visual representations within these traditions, such as the Buddhist Pāli *Piṭaka* and *Jātaka*, and the Jaina *Aṅga*. Other texts like Kautilya's *Arthaśāstra* (third to first century BCE), Megasthenes' *Indica* (fourth century BCE) and Bharata's *Nāṭya Śāstra* (third century CE) have also been studied because of the copious information on art and architecture found in them.

Many scholars, such as T.A. Gopinatha Rao, J.N. Banerjea and N.K. Bhattasali, have tried to trace the evolution of Brahmanical iconography through a study of the prescriptive textual traditions, while also referring to mythologies and descriptions in Vedic, Puranic and Tantric literature.[55] For instance, Rao, in his discussion on Brahmanical goddesses, refers to prescriptive texts like the *Viṣṇudharmottara Purāṇa* with regard to the iconographic features of Mahiṣāsuramardinī and Kātyāyanī. He, thereafter, provides an elaborate discussion of her mythology from the *Varāha Purāṇa*, *Vāmana Purāṇa* and *Padma Purāṇa*, indicating the rich textual tapestry that provides the prototype for the visual representations.[56]

However, it has been found in several regional contexts in the subcontinent that deviations from the norm, as well as innovations in representation, existed. With regard to the icon of Mahiṣāsuramardinī, for instance, D.C. Sircar discusses the correspondence between the prescriptive and mythological descriptions, and the iconographic specimens in parts of the subcontinent.[57] In my own work on the iconography of goddesses in the Tamil region, I have pointed out the anthropomorphic representation of the demon with a buffalo head to indicate his identity as a form-changer.[58] The depiction of the demon as a powerful figure, almost as if he were a worthy adversary of the goddess, indicates other processes at work. D.D. Kosambi points out the assimilation of the pastoral communities who worshipped a buffalo-god with the hunting-gathering ones, who had their own distinctive mother goddess cults, in the western Deccan. The conflict of the demon and the goddess reflected the clash of these two traditions, with the goddess emerging as the victor in the narrative and ritual traditions.[59] Brenda Beck in the context of Tamil Nadu, and M.L.K. Murthy in the Andhra region noted similar myths and ritual practices indicating conflict and contestation between the local goddess and the buffalo-god.[60] While for the art historian, the primary concern would be documenting the different versions and emphasising stylistic developments, the historian is concerned with explaining the reasons for the differences, particularly in the form of depictions. Hence, while the prescriptive texts are invaluable as a source, they may be understood as essentially providing a referent, as often the icons differ significantly from the text.

## Artists and Patronage

The identity and status of artists has been a concern in studies on art and architecture. It has been argued that the idea of freedom of expression is inappropriate when referring to premodern art traditions. This is primarily because art was seen as reflecting certain spiritual and cultural values, and hence even though artistic excellence with reference to individual artists was recognised, this did not reflect creativity. Rather, it was part of a production process—the training of artists, nature of patronage, consumption of a finished piece (whether it was for a religious, public or domestic context), the existence or evolution of a market, the technology that was used and its modifications/transformations, etc., become significant.[61] It appears that in the Western context, there was a distinction made between the artist and craftsperson.[62] This does not seem to be the case in the Indian context, although the idea of specialisation was quite clearly enunciated in treatises related to art and architecture, specifically in the context of architectural knowledge and technique.[63] While there has been a tendency to club art and artists under the generic terms *śilpa* and *śilpin*, R.N. Misra argues that there are a variety of connotations of these very terms, and also that there were several other terms that were in circulation to refer to these categories.[64] Specific material on which the artist worked was one way of distinguishing them: the *śilākarmanta/śailakarma* were those engaged in stonework, the *daṁtakāra* were ivory workers, and the *vardhakī* worked on wood.[65] Texts and inscriptions refer to the *rūpakāra* (sculptor), *citrakāra* (painter), *pustakāraka* (plasterers), *lepaka* (decorators), etc. Terms such as *āveśana* and *akṣaśāla* indicate workshops of artists.[66] We hear of lineages of artists at Mathura—Nandibāla as the chief among the Candaka brothers, and Kuṇika and his pupils Gomataka and Nāga. We also know there were itinerant artists whose mobility was linked to the commissions they received—Nākacaṁda (Nāgacandra) was the *āveśani* at Naḍatūra, in Kammaka *viśaya*, while his son Sidatha (Siddhārtha) was a resident of Mahākāṁḍarūra, who was the sculptor at the *mahācaitya* of Velagiri.[67] The famous Maṇḍana, author of the śilpa text *Rūpamaṇḍana*, is reputed to have built the Kīrtistambha at Chittor (1440–1448); his descendants, we are told in an inscription from the Udaipur Jagannātha Rāya Temple, were the architects of the latter structure in 1653.[68] What is most interesting in the Kīrtistambha, is the carving of the images of Maṇḍana and his sons on either side of the patron of the arts and knowledge—the goddess Sarasvatī—thereby commemorating their excellence and also giving them divine legitimacy.[69]

Samuel Parker points out that given the nature of apprenticeship and workshop-based training, the importance of artisans in art production has been underrated and undervalued; together with the texts, transmission of art traditions, which are context-sensitive, fluid and transforming, is defined as part of a 'ritual mode of production' that is premised on improvisation and innovation.[70] On the basis of an ethnographic study in Tamil Nadu, Parker argues that the architects and artisans worked almost completely without any textual reference per se, in that it was not by reading texts that they transmitted knowledge; the *sthapati* was considered the living embodiment of the *śāstras*, and it was through his direction and training that artistic and architectural knowledge was transmitted.[71] This is possibly what led to the tall claims and self-glorification of the *sthapati* we find in early medieval inscriptions; for instance, Naraśobha, the *sthapati* of the Cālukya period temple at Aihole, is referred to as the greatest *vidvān* in the entire Jambudvīpa, unsurpassed in the art of building temples.[72] We find a backhanded compliment in the *Samaraṅgaṇasūtradhāra*, where the architect is enjoined to propagate the tradition of the celestial architect

Viśvakarma, and thereby to imbue his work with aesthetic and magical properties.[73] There is also a dire warning—he who didn't carry the proper knowledge and built monuments and images contrary to prescription would bring ruin to the state itself; he would be given the death penalty by the ruler, and his ghost would wander the earth as he would be denied redemption. While class differences and hierarchies are quite visible in relation to the artists, caste is never explicitly stated but alluded to in ancient and early medieval texts. Interestingly, women as artists did find a place in historical records, although this was rare; the example of the daughter-in-law of the well-known *citrakāra* Śrī Sātana, whose husband was also a sculptor, is found from an inscribed image of the Buddhist goddess Tārā from central India.[74] All in all, the evidence from ancient and early medieval India suggests the importance of artists as creators, particularly of religious images, and brings to light the hierarchies and differences amongst various categories of artists. We also see that while anonymity was the norm, there is visibility accorded to the master craftsman and architect in inscriptions and literature by naming and assigning attributes and status.

The historical dimensions of art are best illuminated through an analysis of patronage structures, which facilitated their development. The artist was commissioned and depended on the largesse of the patron for his survival. We can trace the movement of the families of architects and artists during the Cōḻa period, where the availability of resources and the royal building enterprises facilitated the move.[75] Romila Thapar, denying a simplistic economic association with regard to patronage, argues that it can be understood as a cultural transaction. She states:

> The definition of patronage is popularly treated as a restricted one: the wealth given by a person of superior status to an artist to enable the latter to produce a work of art. But the act of patronage is neither so restricted nor so simple. It implies a variety of social categories which participate in the making of the cultural object; implicit also is the understanding of the institution which is created from the act of patronage and has social manifestations. It becomes the legitimiser of the patron and in addition to a possible role of authority, may take on other social roles. Not least of all is the consideration of the audience to which the act of patronage is directed, which may operate as the arbiter of the patronage in question. Patronage therefore can act as a cultural catalyst.[76]

Devangana Desai, in a bid to understand art in society, emphasises the social contexts in which art is produced, thereby implying that patronage itself could not be understood as an unchanging element in art production.[77] Different contexts would result in different categories of patrons, which, in turn, would affect the nature of art production. Using a dynastic chronology to distinguish broad phases, the emergence of trade and urbanism are seen as the bedrock of patronage in early times. However, unlike the Mauryan phase where the ruler was the patron, the post-Mauryan phase is seen as one dominated by collective patronage.[78] While the latter view has been challenged in more recent studies, the fact of ordinary folk in large numbers contributing to the erection of monumental structures is striking.[79] The gender disparity in gift-giving has been brought out by several studies, and specifically, the role of royal women in religious donation in the development of the institutional base of the religious traditions through monumental activity has been shown.[80]

For the historian, patronage is a reflection of social affluence, access to economic resources, religious piety and political legitimisation. Thus, iconographic choice and placement in the religious monument have to be understood within a larger context of socio-economic change, embedding of normative values and reflecting politico-religious ideologies. For instance, images of Kālī dancing at the feet of Śiva occur not so infrequently in monuments across early medieval temples of Tamil Nadu. At one level, this may be understood in terms of the identification of Kālī with the rapturous hordes following Śiva and dancing in step with him; at another, in the Puranic myth of the contestation of the two deities in a dance competition, we may identify an attempt at patriarchal control and order of the male over the female, portrayed visually by the grand dancing figure of Śiva and the diminutive Kālī dancing image. A third interpretation rests on the analysis of a wide range of literary descriptions, which indicate that Kālī/Durgā became a generic figure through whom the absorption of various local female deities was achieved—the towering Śiva then represented the cultic and territorial integration of these deities/localities through a central authority.[81] The fact that such a representation was chosen at a time of imperial expansion of the Cōḻas in temples patronised by the royalty indicates that this was a deliberate choice, and not incidental or innocent.

# Texts, Contexts and Visual Representations

The papers in this collection reflect a contextual analysis of society, economy, political structure and religious culture as gleaned from visual representations in ancient and early medieval India, corroborating these with literary and other evidence. Some focus on a singular aspect, as enunciated earlier, while others bring in different dimensions and lenses into the study. The concern in all these, however, is uniform: understanding historical context from visual material.

Power is construed, refined and reconstituted beyond coercive state apparatuses, or the self-proclamations and eulogies of rulers; the media used for such purposes by the state, such as inscriptions, monuments and coins, invoke symbolic elements that reinforce notions of power and prestige. Suchandra Ghosh, in her essay 'Power of Image and Image of Power in the Indo-Iranian Borderlands: Case Studies of Bactrian Greeks and the Indo-Greeks' focuses on the period from second century BCE to third century CE. This era witnessed the presence of several competing powers in the Indo-Iranian borderlands, which denoted a wide geographical expanse extending from Afghanistan to north-west India. The Bactrian Greeks, the Indo-Greeks, Indo-Scythians, Indo-Parthians and the Kuṣāṇas found the space to enter the subcontinent because of the porosity of the borderlands, resulting in political coexistence marked by regular contestations, as well as the periodic dominance of a single power. What is striking about the region was the evolution of what may be called pluralistic and/or multicultural traditions here. Ghosh examines royal coins to understand how imageries of power were communicated to the multiethnic and culturally diverse subjects. Royal coinage was carefully designed by the Greeks to enhance the image of a courageous king, giving the public a chance to see the king's portrait, and identify the gods or heroes whose powers the king was depicted as sharing and wielding. In the case of the Kuṣāṇas, they chose symbols that reflected, to some extent, their nomadic character, and hence the fast horse rider was a common imagery of their power and might. Ghosh's work draws us to a period of history that has generally been overlooked by scholars of early Indian history because of the difficulty posed by sources. With her knowledge of numismatics as well as Prākṛt, Brāhmī and Kharoṣṭhī scripts,

Ghosh is able to present fresh insight into how the Bactrian Greeks, Indo-Greeks and Kuṣāṇa rulers were able to exert their influence over north-western and northern India for a substantial period of time towards the end of the first millennium BCE and the beginning of the first millennium CE. Dev Kumar Jhanjh also focuses on this time period and region, and is also concerned with numismatic evidence. He examines the Ābhīraka coins found in the north-west, which have typical imagery and legend. He critically evaluates existing scholarship, which attributes this piece of coin to a satrap ruler Ābhīraka on the basis of the Kharoṣṭhī legend on it. Using other contemporary numismatic evidence as well as epigraphic material, he presents a revision of existing understanding.

Niharika Sankrityayan and R. Mahalakshmi shift the temporal focus to early medieval South India, and both use temple-based sculptural representations as their primary source of study. Sankrityayan analyses the significant transformations in economic, social and political spheres in western Deccan in the early medieval period, which led to the emergence and establishment of powers like the Cālukyas of Badami. She focuses on patronage to temples as an integral part of the expansion of state power. The temples built during the Cālukya rule were richly carved with divine imagery, and often a parallel between divine images and the kings were made. She focuses on the significance of the projection of Viṣṇu as Varāha, Trivikrama or Narasiṁha, and Śiva as Gaṅgādharamūrti and Tripurāntakamūrti, in the embedding of the authority and power of the Cālukya kings. Mahalakshmi focuses on a single image—that of Śiva as Gaṅgādhara, or the one who bears the river Gaṅgā. This is a well-known icon in the Tamil region and finds a place in the iconographic plan of early medieval Śiva temples in this region, and others as well in a less systematic manner. The paper looks at theoretical, mythic, iconographic and inscriptional evidence that underscore the importance of water, and the implications of the association and management of water resources for kingship and state power in the early Indian context, specifically in the context of state formation. It is obvious from various sources that control over flowing waters, literally and figuratively, signified power and authority. In many early Indian sources, it is the river Gaṅgā who is venerated, and in different regional contexts, local rivers are seen as forms of her. By focusing on the image of Gaṅgādhara, the semiotic interplay of power and benevolence reflected in the representations of Śiva in this form is highlighted, in the context of the literary and visual culture of the Tamil region.

Sneha Ganguly, Megha Yadav and Virendra Singh Bithoo discuss the psycho-analytical, philosophical and symbolic content in visual representations of goddesses in different religious traditions—the Tantric and Puranic Brahmanical, Buddhist and Jaina ones. Ganguly's concern is with representations and associations of the fierce blood-thirsty goddess; in her study, the focus is on a single deity—the goddess Kālī, popularised through Puranic mythology and early medieval temple sculptures. Yadav examines the doctrine of emptiness and selflessness as expounded in the Mahāyāna Buddhist tradition, through the concept of *Prajñāpāramitā*. By the end of the fifth century CE, the transformation of the philosophical concept of *Prajñāpāramitā* into a deity, an object of worship, is enquired into, with a particular focus on the physical form ascribed to her. Bithoo unravels the representation of the category of female deities called Mahāvidyā in the Jaina temples constructed in thirteenth/fourteenth centuries CE at Dilwara in modern Rajasthan. He situates the philosophical and iconographical dimensions of the sixteen Mahāvidyā and one *śruta devī* in terms of the transformations occurring within Jainism.

Archaeology provides us with another entry point to understand visual representations as historical sources. V. Selvakumar brings to our notice images that are not found within structural remains—often labelled 'loose sculptures' in archaeological parlance—in many parts of Tamil Nadu, especially in remote villages, fields, along village boundaries, and near tanks or lakes. Several images of Puranic and local deities such as Ayyaṉār, Durgā, Jyeṣṭhā Devī, Gaṇeśa, Kaṇṇappar, as well as hero stones, fall in this category. On the basis of these, he argues for the possibility of reconstructing the diversity of the early medieval iconographic (and cultic) landscape, which may allow us a glimpse of the religious life of people at the margins. Umakant Mishra uses a plethora of epic and Puranic references for the region called Jajpur/*Virajā-kṣetra*, a prominent religious *kṣetra* (centre) of Odisha since the fifth century CE. Corelating this with archaeological evidence, he seeks to understand how and why the polyreligiosity evident in the region, where

Vaiṣṇava, Śaiva and Śākta elements coexisted with Buddhism, appears to have eroded by the fourteenth century, and this *kṣetra* became a primarily Vaisnavite centre. Sayantani Pal draws us towards the microanalysis of a single site, to enable an institution-wise study of the background of donors of inscribed images, to further an understanding of patterns of patronage, the social base of a sacred establishment and the nature of its interaction with outsiders. Pal's site of study is the monastery at Kurkihar in Bihar, which shows certain interesting features regarding the pattern of donation of images. For several centuries, it had hosts of monk and nun visitors from different parts of South India, indicating the vibrant monastic networks and connections in early medieval India, a period conventionally associated with the decline of Buddhism in the country.

Normative ideas related to gender hierarchies and relationships can be gleaned from visual representations. Neha Singh takes up for analysis the divine icon of Kalyāṇasundaramūrti, a euphemistic allusion to Śiva as the bridegroom. Through the representation typically portraying the marriage ceremony of Śiva and Pārvatī, with the gods officiating and divinities surrounding them, Singh points out how Brahmanical notions of the good, ritually sanctioned marriage are conveyed, reinforcing patriarchal notions of the husband as the taker and controller of the woman as his wife. She reads this through prescriptive texts that specify the ideal forms of marriage, as well as literary descriptions of this specific marriage. Sujata Rakshit, on the other hand, focuses on depictions of a category of women known in architectural treatises variously as *nāyikā*, *surasundarī* and *alasā kanyā*, who epitomise eroticism and beauty. Malavika Binny undertakes a survey and analysis of the hero stones found across South India to probe into the manner in which men and women are commemorated in death, and what could be the social purpose behind the erection of these. The use of *vīrakal* for hero stones in general, and *satikal* for those marking a woman's demise, is scrutinised by her in iconographic terms, as reflecting a gendered perspective even in/on death.

Two papers present the art historical perspective in terms of understanding motifs and theories of representation respectively. The first by Anisha Saxena is a reflection on motifs and symbols in Indian art as not merely being aesthetic designs, but being deeply rooted in religious philosophy and having layered meanings and associations. The *kīrtimukha*, one such decorative motif whose origins can be traced to Puranic texts, is examined on the basis of a detailed literary and art historical survey from the fifth to the tenth centuries CE, mapping its transformation from a mythical character into an architectural motif. Y.S. Alone examines the Buddhist theory of representation and art, which has often been marginalised and even ignored in traditional art history discussions. That the philosophical dimension and specific Buddhist concepts are very integral to this theory of artistic representation brings home to us the importance of thick description while examining any historical context.

This bouquet of essays presents a diverse array of ideas and analysis, which provide an entry point into an area that has traditionally been neglected by historians. While the discipline of art history has opened up important and interesting ways of looking at the past through an examination and appreciation of visual material, there are certain limitations that stem from the disciplinary focus. Our attempt here has been to draw upon the insights afforded to us by art history while charting a course for the better understanding of visual representations in the analysis of historical contexts. The literary sources used here belong to different language traditions, and hence, different transliteration methods and system of diacritical marks have been used by various authors.

## Endnotes

1 Priyabala Shah, ed., *Viṣṇudharmottara Purāṇe Tritiya Khaṇḍaha*, Ch. 2 Verses 1–9 (Baroda: Oriental Institute, 1958), 3; *The Vishnudharmottara Part III: A Treatise on Indian Painting and Image-Making*, trans. Stella Kramrisch (Calcutta: University of Calcutta, 1928), 31–32.

2 Noël Caroll, *Philosophy of Art A Contemporary Introduction* (New York: Routledge, 1999), 21–22.

3 E.H. Gombrich, *Art and Illusion: A Study in the Psychology of Pictorial Representation* (London: Phaidon Press, 1984 [1960]), 5.

4 Ibid., 8–12, 19.

5 Ibid., 23.

6 Ibid., 32, 50–1.

7 Tom Rockmore, 'Kant on Art and Truth After Plato,' *Washington University Jurisprudence Review* 6, no. 1 (2013): 47.

8 Immanuel Kant, *The Critique of Pure Reason*, trans. J.M.D. Meiklejohn, Ch. 3: Of the Ground of the Division of All Objects into Phenomena and Noumena, (1781), http://www.gutenberg.org/files/4280/4280-h/4280-h.htm.

9 Ananda K. Coomaraswamy, *Figures of Speech or Figures of Thought? The Traditional View of Art* (Bloomington: World Wisdom, Bloomington, 2007 [1946]), 2–3. Coomaraswamy's views will be discussed in detail later.

10 Austin Harrington, *Art and Social Theory* (Cambridge: Polity Press, 2004), 2.

11 Harrington, *Art and Social Theory*, 41–75. The works of various scholars relevant to the theme are discussed by Harrington: John Berger, *Ways of Seeing*, (UK: Penguin, 1990 [1971]); Janet Wolff, *The Social Production of Art*, (New York: NYU Press, 1984); Robert Witkins, *Art and Social Structure*, (Cambridge: Polity Press, 1995).

12 Walter Benjamin, 'The Work of Art in the Age of Mechanical Reproduction,' last accessed 21 January 2019, https://www.marxists.org/reference/subject/philosophy/works/ge/benjamin.htm.

13 Harrington, *Art and Social Theory*, (Cambridge: Polity Press, 2004), 45.

14 Christopher Pinney, 'Seven Theses on Photography,' *Thesis Eleven* 113, no. 1 (2012): 142.

15 The term 'ex-nomination' is borrowed from Roland Barthes, who uses it to 'describe the process through which an ideological fact disappears'. Pinney, 'Seven Theses', 2.

16 Tapati Guha-Thakurta, *Monuments, Objects, Histories: Institutions of Art in Colonial and Postcolonial India* (New Delhi: Permanent Black, 2004), viii–ix, 3, 8.

17 Michael Falser and Monica Juneja, '"Archaeologizing" Heritage and Transcultural Entanglements: An Introduction,' in *'Archaeologizing' Heritage? Transcultural Entanglements Between Local Social Practices and Global Virtual Realities*, eds. Falser and Juneja (Springer, 2013), 1.

18 Ibid., 3.

19 Ibid., 2.

20 Guha-Thakurta, *Monuments*, 10–11.

21 Bipan Chandra, *Nationalism and Colonialism in Modern India*, (Calcutta: Orient Longman, 1979), 203–206.

22 Guha-Thakurta, *Monuments*, 11.

23 A tangential discussion on this aspect is found in Katharina Weiler, 'Picturesque Authenticity in Early Archaeological Photography in British India,' in *'Archaeologizing' Heritage? Transcultural Entanglements Between*

*Local Social Practices and Global Virtual Realities*, eds. Falser and Juneja (Springer, 2013), 45.

24 Ibid., 43.

25 Guha-Thakurta, *Monuments*, 5.

26 Ibid. Also see, Takeo Kamiya, 'James Fergusson and Indian Architecture,' http://www.kamit.jp/08_fergusson/ferg_eng.htm.

27 Guha-Thakurta, *Monuments*, 5, 27.

28 James Fergusson, *Illustrations of the Rock-Cut Temples of India, Text to Accompany the Folio Volume of Plates* (London: John Weale, 1845).

29 Ibid., 63.

30 C.M. Naim, 'Syed Ahmad and His Two Books called "Asar-al-Sanadid"', *Modern Asian Studies* 45, no. 3 (2011): 680–682.

31 Guha-Thakurta, *Monuments*, 8.

32 Captain Harkness, 'Preface,' in *Essay on the Architecture of the Hindus*, Ram Raz (London: John William Parker, 1834), iii–ix.

33 Ibid., xiii.

34 Ibid., xiii.

35 Fergusson, *Illustrations of the Rock-Cut Temples*, v–vii.

36 James Fergusson, 'Preface,' in *The Cave Temples of India*, Fergusson and James Burgess (London: W.H. Allen and Co., 1880), xiv.

37 Ibid., xiv–xv.

38 James Fergusson, 'Author's Preface to the First Edition,' in *History of Indian Eastern Architecture*, Vol. 1 (London: John Murray, London, 2nd revised edition, 1910), ix.

39 Ibid., vii.

40 Ibid., 3. Also see James Fergusson, 'Introduction'.

41 Ibid.

42 Alexander Cunningham, *The Bhilsa Topes: Or, Buddhist Monuments of Central India: Comprising a Brief Historical Sketch of the Rise, Progress, and Decline of Buddhism: With an Account of The Opening and Examination of The Various Groups of Topes around Bhilsa* (London: Smith, Elder and Co., 1854), ix.

43 Alexander Cunningham, *The Stupa of Bharhut: A Buddhist Monument Ornamented with Numerous Sculptures Illustrative of Buddhist Legend and History in Third Century* BC (London: W.H. Allen and Co., 1879).

44 Alexander Cunningham, *Four Reports Made During the Years 1862–63–64–65* Vol. I (Simla: Govt. Central Press, 1871), iii.

45 Ibid., viii.

46 *The Vishnudharmottara*, chapter 46, vv. 1–2, 162.

47 Ananda K. Coomaraswamy, *The Arts and Crafts of India and Ceylon* (London: T.N. Foulis, 1913), vii.

48 Ibid., 17.

49 Mircea Eliade, 'Some Notes on "Theosophia Perennis": Ananda K. Coomaraswamy and Henry Corbin,' review of *Coomaraswamy* by Roger Lipsey, *History of Religions* 19, no. 2 (November 1979): 169–171.

50 For a discussion on this aspect, see Phillip B. Wagoner, 'Ananda K. Coomaraswamy and the Practice of Architectural History,' *Journal of the Society of Architectural Historians* 58, no. 1 (March 1999).

51 R. Mahalakshmi, 'Introduction,' in *The Dance of Shiva*, Ananda K. Coomaraswamy (New Delhi: Rupa, 2013).

52 Barbara Stoler Miller, ed., *Exploring India's Sacred Art: Selected Writings of Stella Kramrisch* (Philadelphia: University of Pennsylvania Press, 1983), 3–33.

53 Ibid., 15.

54 Stella Kramrisch, *Manifestations of Śiva* (Philadelphia: Philadelphia Museum of Art, 1981), xvi.

55 T.A. Gopinatha Rao, *Elements of Hindu Iconography*, Vol. 1 Parts 1 & 2, Vol. 2 Parts 1 & 2 (New Delhi: Motilal Banarsidass, 1968 [1914]); J.N. Banerjea, *The Development of Hindu Iconography* (Calcutta: University of Calcutta, 1956); Nalini Kanta Bhattasali, *Iconography of Buddhist and Brahmanical Sculptures in the Dacca Museum* (Dacca: Dacca Museum, 1929).

56 Rao, *Elements* Vol. 1 Part 2, 345–354.

57 D.C. Sircar, *Studies in the Religious Life of Ancient and Medieval India* (New Delhi: Motilal Banarsidass, 1971), 229–237.

58 R. Mahalakshmi, *The Making of the Goddess: Koṟṟavai-Durgā In The Tamil Traditions* (Delhi: Penguin, 2011), 256, 260.

59 D.D. Kosambi, *Myth and Reality: Studies in the Formation of Indian Culture* (Mumbai: Popular Prakashan, 1994 [1962]), chapter 3.

60 Brenda E.F. Beck, 'The Goddess and The Demon: A Local South Indian Festival and Its Wider Context,' *Puruṣārtha* 5; M.L.K. Murthy and Gunther Sontheimer, 'Prehistoric Background to Pastoralism in the Southern Deccan in the Light of Oral Traditions and the Cults of Some Pastoral Communities', *Anthropos*, 75, 1980.

61 Janet Wolff, *The Social Production of Art* (St. Martin's Press: New York, 1981).

62 Stella Kramrisch, 'Artist, Patron and Public in India,' *The Far Eastern Quarterly* 15, no. 3 (May 1956): 335. However, it has been pointed out that in early Greek thought such a distinction did not exist—for instance, Plato uses the term *techne* to refer to the work of the artist, which in Greek meant craft/skill. Such a distinction appears to be a late medieval/early modern development, once

the market became the driving force behind art production. See Harrington, *Art and Social Theory*, 9.

63 See, *Arthaśāstra*, trans. R.P. Kangle (New Delhi: Motilal Banarsidass Publishers; Eighth Reprint edition (2010); *Mānavadharmaśāstra*, trans. Patrick Olivelle (Oxford: Oxford University Press, 2005); *Mānasāra*, trans. P.K. Acharya (reprint New Delhi: Motilal Banarsidass, 1980 [1934]); *Mayamatam*, ed. Bruno Dagens, (Delhi: Indira Gandhi National Centre for the Arts and Motilal Banarsidass Publishers, 2007)

64 R.N. Misra, *Ancient Artists and Art Activity* (Simla: IIAS, 1975), 1–5.

65 Ibid., 10–11, 16.

66 See *āveśana*: 'a house in which work is carried on, a workshop, manufactory,' in Monier Williams, 'Sanskrit-English Dictionary (2008 Revision),' accessed 21 January 2019, http://www.sanskrit-lexicon.uni-koeln.de/monier/. In the *Arthaśāstra*, *āveśana* is given as a synonym of *akṣaśāla*, hence, also indicating a manufacturing unit; Misra, *Ancient Artists*, 20–21.

67 Misra, *Ancient Artists*, 16. For a full translation of the inscription dated to third/fourth century CE, see, J.A.S. Burgess, *The Buddhist Stupas of Amaravati and Jaggayyapeta in the Krishna District, Madras Presidency* (Madras: Archaeological Survey of Southern Indịa, 1886), 110–111.

68 Kramrisch, 'Artist, Patron,' 336.

69 Ibid., 340–341.

70 Samuel K. Parker, 'Text and Practice in South Asian Art: An Ethnographic Perspective,' *Artibus Asiae* 63, no. 1 (2003): 8–13.

71 Ibid., 10.

72 Kramrisch, 'Artist, Patron,' 338–339. Other examples are cited in Misra, *Ancient Artists*, 44–46.

73 Kramrisch, 'Artist, Patron,' 336–337.

74 Misra, *Ancient Artists*, 52.

75 Baldev Raj, C. Rajagopalan, C.V. Sundaram, *Where Gods Come Alive: Bronze Icons of South India* (New Delhi: Vigyan Prasar, 2000)

76 Romila Thapar, 'Cultural Transaction,' *Social Scientist* 15, no. 2 (1987): 3–31, 18.

77 Devangana Desai, 'The Social Dimensions of Art,' *Social Scientist*, 18 no. 3 (1990): 3–32.

78 Desai, 'The Social Dimensions,' 9.

79 For a critique of the collective patronage argument, see M.D. Milligan, *Of Rags to Riches: Indian Buddhist Patronage Networks in the Early Historic Period*, PhD Dissertation submitted to the Graduate School, The University of Texas at Austin, August, 2016: 248–264, http://hdl.handle.net/2152/41539.

80 Vijay Nath, *Dana: Gift System in Ancient India, c. 600* BC—*c.* AD *300: A Socio-economic Perspective* (New Delhi: Munshiram Manoharlal, 1987); Upinder Singh, 'Sanchi: The History of the Patronage of an Ancient Buddhist Establishment,' *IESHR* 33, no.1 (1996): 1–35; Leslie C. Orr, *Donors, Devotees and Daughters of God: Temple Women in Medieval Tamilnadu* (New Delhi: OUP, 2000); Ellison Banks Findly, 'Women's Wealth and Styles of Giving: Perspectives from Buddhist, Jain and Mughal Sites,' in *Women, Patronage and Self-Representation in Islamic Societies*, ed. D. Fairchild Ruggles (Albany: SUNY, 2000), 91–120; Kumkum Roy, 'Women and Men Donors at Sanchi,' in *The Power of Gender and the Gender of Power: Explorations in Early Indian History* (New Delhi: OUP, 2010), 38; Seema Bawa, *Gods, Men and Women: Gender and Sexuality in Early Indian Art* (New Delhi: D.K. Printworld, 2013).

81 Mahalakshmi, *The Making of the Goddess*, Ch. 2 & 5.

# I

# Visualising Power: Sacred and Temporal

1

# Power of Image and Image of Power in the Indo-Iranian Borderlands: Case Studies of Bactrian Greeks and the Indo-Greeks[1]

Suchandra Ghosh

The Indo-Iranian borderlands extending from Afghanistan to the north-west of India helped in providing regular linkages with West and Central Asia on one hand and regions to the south of Hindu Kush on the other. The borderland was porous enough to make it a polyethnic zone.[2] This porosity of frontiers helped powers like the Bactrian Greeks, the Indo-Greeks, the Indo-Scythians, the Indo-Parthians and the Kuṣāṇas to enter the subcontinent. The presence of these powers from the second century BCE to the third century CE may be regarded as a period of transition from the Mauryan Empire to the Gupta Empire. At times, the coexistence of a few powers resulted in regular contestations. Otherwise, it was the dominance of a single power. Thus, this region witnessed changing suzerainties that shifted amongst North India, Afghanistan and Iran.

The presence of multiple rulers, naturally, led to rivalry and contestation, leading the rulers to seek validation of their rule. An ambience of political nervousness could have permeated in the region. Striking coins and use of significant images, which echo power and pedigree of the rulers, were a means of seeking legitimation. Thus, visuals became a tool for the representation of power. Images are, at times, much more persistent than written words. In this essay, the power of image and the image of power would be studied through the numismatic lens, as of all the tangible means by which a ruler could communicate with his subjects, coins were ideal. Coins provided the perfect means through which the portrayal of a ruler was possible. They were the principal medium of royal propaganda. The message that the ruler wanted to give his subjects could be best conveyed through a tiny coin. Here, we may cite the case of the diadem. This headband that was worn by all Hellenistic rulers after Alexander was first associated with the status of ruler by Dionysus after his conquest of portions of India. Whenever a king portrayed himself wearing it, he alluded to its legendary origin and its wearer's great Asian conquest, and thus identified himself as heir to that glory and power, which emanated from established kingship. Such was the power of the image of a king with a diadem, which determined the royal lineage by the presence or absence of a diadem in the representation of a portrait.[3]

The discussions will focus on the Bactrian Greeks and the Indo-Greeks, but as a prelude, it is imperative that we try to understand the nature of political interaction or control in this zone prior to the Bactrian Greeks and the Indo-Greeks. After Alexander's death in 323 BCE, it was natural that there would be a scramble for power amongst his generals for control of the empire. The most successful of all his generals was Seleucus I. After a gap of some ten years, the satrapies of Central Asia reappeared in the history of Hellenistic kingdoms through their inclusion in the empire of Seleucus I. He captured Babylonia in 312 BCE and founded the Seleucid kingdom. After consolidating his power over Mesopotamia and northern Syria in 307 BCE, he went on to establish his authority over the satrapies of the Iranian Plateau and Central Asia. Thus, the empire was, like the empire of Alexander, a continuation of the empires before. He expanded his power base to Bactria. Seleucus I and his son Antiochus I were far more interested in the East. The Seleucids, perhaps, deliberately presented themselves as successors of the early empire and intended to use the old structures. Frank Holt has shown that the early Seleucid Empire should not be dismissed as a fragile and fragmentary state.[4] The Seleucid monarchy presented itself in accordance with local expectations when dealing with individual cities or populations, for example by making offerings to local deities or using the local language, while at the same time upholding an umbrella ideology of empire in an overall Greco-Macedonian form. This is apparent, for instance, from the Greek symbolism and text on coins, the principal medium of royal propaganda, and the profound Hellenism of Seleucid court culture. The Seleucid family claimed descent from the saviour god Apollo. For the sake of non-Greek subjects, Apollo and his twin sister Artemis were equated with the various local sun and moon gods worshipped in the multi-polytheistic empire.[5] They continued Alexander's innovation of establishing a standardised coinage throughout the empire. The unification of the empire by Seleucus I from the Levant to the Hindu Kush was the incentive for setting up the first mint in Bactra in Central Asia.[6] The very first coins that were struck were not earlier than 305 BCE. However, Seleucid control over Bactria and Sogdia did not last long and the Greek governor of Bactria, Diodotus I (250 BCE–230 BCE), revolted. According to Justin's history (said to be of the second century CE), adopted from *Pompeius Trogus* (41.4.4–9), during the struggle for power between Antiochus II's sons, Seleucus II and Antiochus Hierux, Diodotus 'broke away and took the title of the king. All the people of the East followed his example'[7]. He was the Seleucid Satrap of Bactria. Thus was born the Graeco-Bactrian kingdom with its capital at Bactra (Balkh, modern Majr-i-Shariff in Afghanistan). The ideal geographical location of Bactria connecting West Asia and Central Asia on one hand, and with South Asia, on the other, held the clue to the rise of the Graeco-Bactrian kingdom.

To begin with the Hellenistic Bactrian kings, their characteristic qualities were, in essence, heroic: courage, bellicosity, grandeur, divine fortune, a certain measure of strategic intelligence and the ability to claim victory in any situation. The royal coinage was carefully designed by the Greeks to enhance the image of a courageous king, giving the public a chance to see the king's portrait, to identify the gods or heroes whose powers the king shared and wielded. These coins were dynastic issues and acted as markers of the sovereign authority of the ruler. For the first time, the region to the south of the Hindu Kush experienced die-struck coinage, portraiture and legend. The devices were carefully drawn to represent the power of the respective rulers. We find that the deities chosen by the Greek kings for representation on coins tended to be those who could be used as symbols of power, such as Zeus, Heracles and Athena. The Asian empires of Alexander and the Seleucids functioned along the lines of Macedonian militarism and pragmatic imperialism, and myth provided a culturally Hellenic image of the naturally endowed king as master and provider.

Zeus, Apollo, Athena, Dionysus, Heracles and the Dioscuri were popular choices for the reverse devices of the coins of the Bactrian Greeks and the Indo-Greeks, though other deities, such as Poseidon, Nike, Hermes, Dionysus, Tyche, Helios and Artemis, were also less frequently represented.[8] These gods were not merely monetary emblems. They represented the chosen beneficent deity.[9] We shall focus here only on the representation of popular deities.

Zeus, striding to the left, bearing the aegis on his outstretched left arm and holding in his right hand the thunderbolt, with the eagle at his feet, became a very popular motif to be used first by Diodotus I (see Image 1.1). The choice of Zeus suits the name of Diodotus—'the gift of Zeus'. On breaking away from the Seleucids, Diodotus called on the greatest of the gods to help him. The figure of Zeus wielding the thunderbolt may have been intended to intimidate Diodotus' enemies. Apollo, the deity represented in the Seleucid coins, was replaced by Zeus thereby bidding adieu to the Seleucid rule.[10] Zeus is one of the most frequently represented gods and is seen occasionally holding goddess Nike with the kings using the title Nikephoros. This, obviously, signifies some kind of conflict between the rival groups. Zeus's son Apollo is also represented either in person or through his symbol, the tripod on the coins of the Bactrian and the Indo-Greek kings.[11] He is important to the Greeks in Bactria and India because he was the patron deity of the Seleucids from whom the Greeks had wrested power in the region. It was thus a political statement along with other cultural importance of Apollo.

**Image 1.1: Zeus with the thunderbolt, c. 250 BCE–230 BCE**

*Credit*: Osmund Bopearachchi

The next important deity to find its way to the Bactrian Greek and the Indo-Greek coinages was Heracles (see Image 1.2). Euthydemus I replaced Zeus with Heracles, and later Heracles was used by Demetrius and Euthydemus II and shown in a variety of poses, but always with his club and lion skin. There are three significant reasons for this choice. Firstly, the king was originally from Magnesia on the Maeander in Ionia, where Heracles enjoyed much popularity. Secondly, he wished to identify himself with Alexander, who was none other than a new Heracles, the mortal who was raised to the pantheon of Olympian gods for his bravery and courage. Thirdly, if we go by Polybius' account, we find that Euthydemus I seized the Bactrian throne by annihilating the descendants of the reigning Diotid family, whose principal reverse device was Zeus.[12] On the coins of Euthydemus I,

Heracles was seated on a rock, and on the coins of Demetrius and Euthydemus II, Heracles was shown standing, holding his club in his left hand and crowning himself with a laurel wreath with his right. The types of coins of Demetrius and Euthydemus II may indicate that the old Heracles, who was seated as if after his labours on the coins of Euthydemus I, stands up with fresh vigour to conquer new lands. Alexander's soldiers had earlier attributed some importance to Heracles as their legendary precursor in Asia. Not only coins but also the archaeological remains of Ai Khanum suggest that a cult of Heracles was also in existence in the sanctuary of the indented temple. The most interesting image of Heracles is a bronze statuette found at Ai Khanum, where Heracles is posed in exactly the same manner as on Demetrius's coins.[13] On the wall of a gymnasium at Ai Khanum, the centre of a traditional Greek establishment for physical and intellectual education, dedication to Hermes and Heracles as protectors of the gymnasium was discovered. Thus, following the precedents in mainland Greece, Heracles was worshipped here as an Olympian deity as well as the patron deity of the gymnasium. The reverse type of Euthydemus II's silver coins is quite similar to that of Demetrius I, except for the fact that Heracles is shown already crowned and holding another wreath in his outstretched right hand. Holding of a wreath by Heracles meant that he was proclaiming Euthydemus II a king, which, in other words, implied that Euthydemus II owed his kingship to Heracles. This particular pose for Heracles was popular throughout the Hellenistic world in the second century BCE. The Heracles statue is an indicator of the extraordinary favour shown to the cult of heroes in Greek Central Asia. Representation of a boar's head in an issue of Menander might link it with the fourth labour of Heracles, the capture of the gigantic boar of Mount Erymanthus and the palm branch on the reverse might signify victory.[14] The symbolism of the obverse portrait with the elephant scalp and Heracles crowning himself on the reverse was so powerful that Lysias, a later Indo-Greek king, adopted the same iconographic design. Apart from images on coins or sculptural motifs, an inscription also records a dedication to Greek goddess Hestia, one of the three chief goddesses, the other two being Athena and Artemis, who would protect Euthydemus and his son Demetrius. This comes from the site of Kuliab, north of the Oxus in modern Tajikistan. This dedication is by a man named Heliodotus, in honour of the local Greek king Euthydemus and his son Demetrius 'in the grove of Zeus'. Euthydemus is declared 'the greatest of all the kings'. Furthermore, it refers to his son Demetrios Kallinikos as 'the glorious conqueror'.[15] Paul Bernard is probably correct in assuming that the glorious victories to which the inscription refer took place during the siege of Bactra by Antiochus III. In Polybius's account (11.39), one should also note that at the time of the siege, it was Demetrius, the son of Euthydemus I, who was appointed to finalise the agreement that brought about a reconciliation between his father and Antiochos III. This Heliodotus must have been a royal officer who publicly sought protection for the royal family from goddess Hestia. The most significant event of Euthydemus' reign—and the occasion for his appearance in Polybius' *Histories*—was his conflict with the Seleucid King Antiochus III Megas.

**Image 1.2: Seated Heracles with club and lion skin, c. 230 BCE–200 BCE**

*Credit*: Osmund Bopearachchi

Close contemporaries of Euthydemus II were Agathocles (185 BCE–170 BCE) and Pantaleon (185 BCE–180 BCE), though Agathocles seems to have ruled for a longer period. His coins are much more diverse than Pantaleon's. Their coinages are considered to be the oldest of all bilingual coins on the basis of minting techniques, iconography and metrology.[16] When the Greek rulers extended their authority to the south of the Hindu Kush, they introduced legends in Prākṛt language, written in Kharoṣṭhī script, on the reverse side of their coins. Thus, legends on the obverse of their coins were in Greek while the reverses were in Prākṛt. Conquest over Indian territories necessitated the issue of bilingual and biscriptual coins. On a few exceptional pieces, we have legends written in Brāhmī script. To cite an example, we have a coin type of Agathocles where, on the obverse, we have a legend in Prākṛt written in Brāhmī, 'Rajine Agathuklayesa', and on the reverse in Greek language and script, 'Basileus Agathokleous'. The obverse depicted a female deity in Oriental costume holding a flower in her right hand and making a movement towards the left; the reverse has the depiction of a lion standing to the right.[17] Agathocles introduced Brahmanical deities on his coins. The silver coins of Agathocles depict the Brahmanical deities Saṁkarṣaṇa-Balarāma and Vāsudeva-Kṛṣṇa, the earliest depictions of these two gods ever attested in India (see Image 1.3). Saṁkarṣaṇa-Balarāma is shown holding a *musala* (pestle) and a *hala* (plough) while Vāsudeva-Kṛṣṇa holds a *cakra* (wheel) and a *śaṅkha* (conch shell). Saṁkarṣaṇa is depicted on the obverse with the legend in Greek while Vāsudeva is represented on the reverse with the legend in Brāhmī. This suggests a period when Saṁkarṣaṇa was at the head of the cult of the five Vṛṣṇi heroes (Pañcavīra) of the Bhāgavata religion. The iconographic features of their coins are indeed indigenous. In this way, they were able to communicate with the indigenous population. The technique followed was similar to the ones followed for the coins of Taxila.

**Image 1.3: Saṁkarṣaṇa-Balarāma and Vāsudeva-Kṛṣṇa, c. 185 BCE–170 BCE**

*Credit*: Osmund Bopearachchi

We know that Menander I expanded his power base and inaugurated new mints to strike his innumerable coinages with new monetary types and systems. He truly became the monarch of the whole Indo-Greek kingdom, integrating several areas of the north-west under a single rule. His dominant reverse type was Athena standing to the left, holding a shield and hurling a thunderbolt (see Image 1.4). Athena as the goddess of war and appropriating her father Zeus' thunderbolt was an appropriate design for Menander. Tarn suggests that as Athena has been a principal deity of the Greek pantheon and was also widely represented on Alexander's coinage. Menander adopted this device in order to emphasise that in spite of the predominantly Indian character of his kingdom, he was still a Greek king.[18] The war-like posture of Athena is accentuated by the fact that her shield is decorated by another of her attributes, the aegis, a monstrous goat skin, decorated with the head of the gorgon Medusa.[19] According to Greek mythology, Perseus killed the gorgon Medusa. She had snakes for hair.[20] The coiled form of the snake has been used as a design for Menander's helmet. The gorgon's head seems to have had an independent existence as a magical symbol to ward off evil. Interestingly, the portrait of Menander on the obverse of the coin shows the aegis appearing on his shoulder and he brandishes his javelin in the same manner as Athena hurled her thunderbolt. By choosing precisely the image of Athena, Menander wanted to make a direct reference both to Alexander as the king of Macedonia and also to the Greek homeland. The point to be noted, here, is that the representation of Athena on the coin is the same as the one that appears on the Macedonian coins of King Antigonus Gonatas and on the Alexander portrait coins of Ptolemy.

**Image 1.4: Athena with shield and thunderbolt, c. 155 BCE**

*Credit*: Osmund Bopearachchi

With Eucratides I (171 BCE–145 BCE), we enter another phase of Bactrian and Indo-Greek political history. He was one of the few Bactrian Greek rulers to have been extensively referred to in Greek and Latin literary sources. Klaus Karttunen has given a succinct account of his place in literary sources.[21] According to him, Eucratides of Bactria was a rather well-known figure in Hellenistic history. Some passages explicitly speak of King Eucratides I Megas, whereas the other kings of the Eucratid dynasty (Heliocles and Plato) are never mentioned in this literature. The texts do not give us any information on the parentage of Eucratides I. Thus, the most important passage on Eucratides is found in the *Epitome of the Lost Historiae Philippicae of Pompeius Trogus* (first century BCE), written by Justin in the third century CE. Justin says that a certain Demetrius was overthrown by the usurper Eucratides, who then invaded Bactria and became a powerful king. The fact that he is referred to as a usurper is evident from his coins, where his father Heliocles is depicted as a commoner and his mother, Laodice, is shown wearing the royal diadem.[22] The date of Eucratides is quite certain as he ascended the throne at the same time as the Parthian ruler Mithridates I, who commenced his reign in 171 BCE. We learn that Eucratides waged many wars. Described as the king of a thousand cities, he made campaigns against Sogdia, Arachosia, Drangania and Aria. However, two satrapies of Bactria, Aspionus and Turiva, were lost to Mithridates I. These were located to the west of Merv and Herat. A few words about the involvement of the Arsacid rulers in the politics of the Indo-Iranian borderlands are in order. Like the Achaemenids, the Arsacids also had political interests in the region around the Lower Indus. Parthian advance to the Indus seems to be indicated by a statement of Paulus Orosius (born in 375 CE) in his *Historiarum Adversum Paganos Libri VII* (*Seven Books of History Against the Pagans*). According to the text, as shown by B.N. Mukherjee, we find a reference to the fact that Mithridates I extended his rule to a certain region immediately to the west of the Indus.

Therefore, there was a Parthian conquest of the Lower Indus, which resulted in the withering away of Greek rule in the Indus Delta.[23] There is ample evidence to show that the Parthians felt themselves to be the heirs of the Achaemenids. Thus, for example, they adopted the Achaemenid title 'King of Kings' on their coinage. The figure of the seated archer that appears very early on the reverse of their coins also derives from the Achaemenids, for whom the bow, as depicted on coins, seals and reliefs, symbolised royalty. The coins of the Arsacids were also used for projecting power. The obverse always shows the head of the king wearing either the Hellenistic diadem or an Iranian royal tiara, in some instances with details of the obvious nomadic origin (e.g. a string of deer on the crest of the crown of Phraates II). The reverses of the drachms bear the stereotyped figure of the dynasty's founder, Arsaces I, enthroned to the right, copied from the seated Apollo on the reverses of Seleucid coins—at first like Apollo sitting on the omphalos (Mithradates I), later like Zeus on the throne (Mithradates II onward). The tetradrachms show the enthroned king holding a bow or a Nike, sometimes Tyche blessing the king, and rarely the king mounted, probably in connection with his investiture.[24]

The Dioscuri, Castor and Pollux, on Eucratides' coins shown charging on horseback and holding spears provide the epitome for a motif running throughout the history of Bactrian kingship and warfare (see Image 1.5). Cavalry forces were a consistent part of Bactrian warfare, whether seen in the backlash Alexander received for seizing horses in Eucratides' cavalry helmet portrait, or in the cataphract horse armour found at Ai Khanum's arsenal.[25] Hellenistic kings were the leaders of armies and their kingship depended on military strength, which in Bactria was cavalry, so for Eucratides, a king who experienced continued warfare, the Dioscuri represent his power base and, if all went well for him, his reason for success. It was a well-known Seleucid-type meaning in a very special sense—a saviour. According to Tarn, Eucratides' use of this type meant he had come to the East as Soter, 'a saviour'.[26] The Dioscuri were part of wider Hellenistic Bactrian culture. This is evidenced by a 150 BCE temple at Dilberdjin, where they are featured in two wall paintings. The image of a king riding a prancing horse is another motif that runs across the coins of the Bactrian and the Indo-Greeks.

**Image 1.5: The Dioscuri, Castor and Pollux, c. 171 BCE–145 BCE**

*Credit*: Osmund Bopearachchi

Though the Iranian gods are not singularly represented on the coins of the Bactrian and the Indo-Greeks, yet they find a place in the pantheon through assimilation. The representative example is the Iranian god Mithra. He has been assimilated with Zeus and also with Apollo.[27] The coin of the Greek king Hermaeus shows Zeus wearing Mithraic cap with a rayed crown. Apollo appeared in the guise of the sun god. Originally, the Greek sun god Helios had a separate identity but, later, he was assimilated in the representation of Apollo shown with a rayed head driving a chariot. Even on the issues where he is shown holding bow and arrow, rays emanating from his head could be seen. Here, Helios-Mithra perhaps converged, forming a single identity of a sun god. Plato introduced in his coinage an unprecedented and unique reverse type in the Graeco-Bactrian coinage, Helios or as Mithra radiate, standing in a quadriga. There is no doubt that the standing deity with a scepter and radiating halo is certainly Mithra, indicating favour towards the cult of Mithra, prevalent in the region.[28] Plato had a very short reign, of perhaps five years (145 BCE–140 BCE), and his territory in southern Bactria would not have been large. The use of sun god as a reverse device and the title 'Epiphanes', which, in turn, was used by Antiochus, are attempts to legitimise his rule among the subjects.

The successors of the Greeks in the east continued the Greek tradition of portraying gods on coins and also appropriated the iconography of Greek deities for their own gods. In addition, their coins reflect a desire on the part of the rulers to incorporate the local deity within the pantheon. Composite images were also created, which symbolised power and the adoption of the local. Thus, Maues (75 BCE–65 BCE) uses the combined attributes of Zeus (thunderbolt) and Poseidon (a trident) to represent a Śiva-like deity. Acknowledging the presence of the local goddess Lakṣmī, Azilises (50 BCE) issued coins where Lakṣmī is represented standing on a lotus pedestal, holding a cup near her breasts, with two lotuses arising on either side of the pedestal. Two elephants stand on these two lotuses and pour water on the goddess. This is known as the *abhiṣiñcan* of Lakṣmī, which signifies her royal and sovereign aspect.[29] Prior to Azilises, some coins bearing the name of Azes have on the obverse the city deity of Pushkalavati and on the reverse a bull. Mukherjee identifies the deity with Amba, who borrowed the turreted crown of Tyche, the city goddess.[30] Tyche is also seen bestowing good fortune and royalty in a silver tetradrachm of Zeionises (10 CE–30 CE), a Scythian Satrap in Gandhāra. On the reverse, we find the Satrap with the Greek city goddess on the right and goddess of good fortune Tyche standing to the left. Tyche holds a diadem/wreath as if ready to crown the Satrap and also has a cornucopia. The offering of the wreath suggests this Satrap received his power from Tyche.

It appears from the foregoing that the gods chosen by the Bactrian and the Indo-Greek rulers were those who represented symbols of royal power. For consolidation of their power, these successors of Alexander used certain sets of deities who symbolised strength and power among the Olympian deities. Another criterion for the choice was their association with Alexander or the Seleucids. These were closely associated with the intention of making the rulers acceptable to the subject population, a sizeable amount of which were Hellenists. Rulers like Agathocles and Pantaleon thought of the Indian population too. Moreover, one must remember that Heracles is also accepted by the Indians, as he is often identified with Kṛṣṇa and sometimes with Śiva. It is also clear from the depiction of the gods and goddesses that the deity supported the right of the king to rule; most rulers had one or two patron deities. However, they did not have any royal cult like the Seleucids nor did they build dynastic sanctuaries like the Seleucids or the Kuṣāṇas. The royal coinage was carefully designed to enhance the image of a courageous king, giving the public a chance to see the king's portrait and to identify the gods or heroes whose powers the king shared and wielded. The Hellenistic identity through the portrayal of the deities was very actively claimed and cherished. Here, perhaps, one can compare these rulers to the Seleucids. The Seleucids ruled a multinational empire as foreign rulers. While conscious of their Macedonian ancestry and shared participation in Greek civilisation, they also acknowledged their role as eastern monarchs. Through a thorough study of an inscription of the Seleucid ruler Antiochus I, commemorating his rebuilding of Ezida, the temple of the god Nabu in the city of Borsippa located some 20 km south-west of Babylon, Paul-Alain Beaulieu has shown that in spite of the Seleucid conquest of Babylon and apparent interest and participation in

Babylonian tradition, Antiochus remained essentially a Greek ruler, one who prayed to Apollo/Apal rather than Nabu.[31] Thus, the validation was through Hellenistic cultural type.

## Endnotes

1 The title of this essay is inspired from Kumkum Roy's book, *The Power of Gender and The Gender of Power* (New Delhi: Oxford University Press, 2010).

2 Suchandra Ghosh, 'Movements and Migrations Around the Porous Indo-Iranian Borderlands: The View from Archaeology and Texts (c. third century BCE–third century CE),' in *Narratives, Routes And Intersections in Pre-Modern Asia*, ed. Radhika Seshan (London and New York: Routledge, 2017), 64–75.

3 Here we may refer to the Heliocles-Laodice coin type of Eucratides I. Heliocles was not from a royal family. Therefore, he was portrayed on the coin without a diadem.

4 Frank L. Holt, 'Thundering Zeus: The Making of Hellenistic Bactria,' *Hellenistic Culture and Society* 32 (1999): 21–29.

5 Roof Strootman, 'Seleucid Empire,' *Encyclopædia Iranica*, online edition, www.iranicaonline.org/articles/seleucid-empire (accessed 5 November 2018).

6 Osmund Bopearachchi, 'The Seleucid Coins of Central Asia and the Bactra Mint,' in *From Bactria to Taprobane, Volume I* (Manohar: New Delhi, 2015), 18.

7 Justin, 'Epitoma Historiarum Philippicarum Pompei Trogi: Accedunt prologi', in *Pompeium Trogum*, eds Franz Ruhl and Otto Seel (Leipzig: In Aedibus B.G. Teubneri, 1972).

8 The study of the Bactrian and the Indo-Greek coins are based on Osmund Bopearachchi's *Monnaies greco-bactriennes et indo-grecques: Catalogue raisonné* (Paris: Bibliotheque Nationale, 1991) and *Sylloge Nummorum Graecorum, The Collection of the American Numismatic Society*, Part 9, Graeco-Bactrian and Indo-Greek Coins (New York: The American Numismatic Society, 1998).

9 For a detailed study on this, see Suchandra Ghosh, 'From the Oxus to the Indus: Religion and Politics of the Bactrian and Indo-Greek Rulers,' in *The Complex Heritage of Early India, Essays in Memory of R.S. Sharma*, ed. D.N. Jha (New Delhi: Manohar, 2014), 373–389.

10 A.K. Narain, *The Indo-Greeks* (New Delhi: Oxford University Press, 1980), 19.

11 This representation suggests his role as a communicator of the will of the gods to mankind through his shrine at Delphi.

12 Osmund Bopearachchi, 'The Emergence of the Greco-Baktrian and Indo-Greek Kingdoms,' in *Coins from Asia Minor and the East, Selections from the Colin E. Pitchfork Collection*, ed. Nicholas L. Wright (Adelaide: Numismatic Association of Australia, 2011), 47.

13 Osmund Bopearachchi, 'Decouvertes recentes des sculptures hellenistiques en Asie central,' in *Art et Archeologie des monasteres Greco-bouddhiques du Nord-Ouest del'Inde et de l'Asie centrale* (Paris: De Boccard, 2005), 51–65.

14 Elizabeth Errington, *From Persepolis to the Punjab: Exploring Ancient Iran, Afghanistan and Pakistan* (London: The British Museum Press), 111.

15 Paul Bernard et al., 'Deux Nouvelles Inscriptions Grecques De L'Asie Centrale,' *Journal des Savants* (2004): 227–356.

16 Bopearachchi, *Sylloge Nummorum Graecorum*, see the section on Agathocles and Pantaleon.

17 Ibid., 42–57.

18 W.W. Tarn, *The Greeks in Bactria and India*, 1st Indian edition (New Delhi: Munshiram Manoharlal, 1980), 261.

19 Elizabeth Errington and Joe Cribb, eds, *The Crossroads of Asia, Transformation in Image and Symbol* (Cambridge: The Ancient India and Iran Trust, 1992), 83.

20 John Pinsent, *Greek Mythology* (London: The Hamlyn Publishing Group, 1988), 86–87.

21 Klaus Karttunen, 'King Eucratides in Literary Sources,' in *Silk Road Art and Archaeology 6: Papers in Honour of Francine Tissot*, eds Elizabeth Errington and Osmund Bopearachchi (Kamakura: Journal of the Institute of Silk Road Studies, 2000): 115–117.

22 Bopearachchi, *Sylloge Nummorum Graecorum*, 526–529.

23 B.N. Mukherjee, *An Agrippan Source: A Study in Indo-Parthian History* (Calcutta: Pilgrim Publishers, 1969), 61–155.

24 M. Alram, 'ARSACIDS iii. Arsacid Coinage,' *Encyclopaedia Iranica*, II/5, 536–540, www.iranicaonline.org/articles/arsacids-iii (accessed 5 November 2018).

25 F. Grenet, J.C. Ligeret, R.D. deValence, 'L'Arsenal,' *BEFEO* (Paris: 1980), 1–3.

26 Tarn, *The Greeks in Bactria and India*, 204.

27 Laurianne Martinez-Sève, 'Pouvoir et religion dans la Bactriane hellénistique. Recherches sur la politique religieuse des rois séleucides et gréco-bactriens,' *Chiron* 40 (2010): 8–9.

28 A.D.H. Bivar, *The Personalities of Mithra in Archaeology and Literature* (New York: Bibliotheca Persica Press, 1998), 41.

29 In the Kuṣāṇa period, Lakṣmī assimilated features of the Greek Tyche and the Iranian Ardoxšo, both being goddesses of fortune as well. One image shows the goddess with cornucopia. It is labelled by an accompanying Kharoṣṭhī

inscription as *śiriye paḍima* (image of shri). Ardoxšo's cornucopia was used here as an attribute of the Brahmanical goddess Śrī.

30 B.N. Mukherjee, *Nana on Lion, A Study in Kushana Numismatic Art* (Calcutta: The Asiatic Society), 14–15.

31 Paul-Alain Beaulieu, 'Nabû and Apollo: The Two Faces of Seleucid Religious Policy,' in *Orient und Okzident in hellenistischer Zeit*, eds Friedhelm Hoffmann and Karin Stella Schmidt (Würzburg 10–13, April 2008): 28–30.

2

# The Ābhīraka Coin: Search for a New Identity

Dev Kumar Jhanjh

A coin is basically a metallic medium of exchange of definite weight made of both precious and base metals. A particular significance of a coin is its connection with long-distance commerce. The intrinsic value of a coin plays a vital role in this context for which the issuer mentions his political profile that also symbolises his political sovereignty. However, the earliest coins of the Indian subcontinent date back to c. 600 BCE, which was found in hoards in Taxila, Bhirmound and Chaman-i-Hazuri without the name of the issuer. The earliest coins belong to different *janapadas* and had 1–4 symbols, followed by the imperial punch-marked coins with 5 symbols on one side and with *kārṣāpaṇa* weight standard (3.04 g) of the Magadha-Maurya series.[1] These uninscribed silver punch-marked coins inform about the absence of sovereignty in this phase. The Indo-Greek rulers (c. second century BCE to first century BCE) introduced the portrait with inscriptions on coins that actually worked as the marker of sovereignty.[2] The Śakas, the Kuṣāṇas, the Sātavāhanas and the Guptas also maintained this tradition. However, inscribed coins were also issued by the so-called 'tribes'[3], which are known as non-dynastic issues, unlike the mentioned monarchical issues. In the deep South, the coins of the Cōḻas, Cēras and the Pāṇṭiyas made of copper signal the transitional phase from chiefdom to kingdom.

The study of numismatics is ultimately connected with the transaction in burgeoning trade. The profusion of Roman coins found in the post-Mauryan phase establishes the vibrant trade with the Roman empire.[4]

A major historiographical debate on early medieval India for the establishment of feudalism theory has been stated by R.S. Sharma[5] and K.M. Shrimali on the basis of the absence of coins that pointed out the decline of trade. However, according to B.N. Mukherjee, B.D. Chattopadhyaya and others[6], the absence of coins does not necessarily indicate a decline of trade, as other media of exchange may have been in use.

Though primarily they are the most valuable records for understanding monetary history, the coins also throw ample light on other historical aspects as well. The realm of cultural and religious history can be cited in this context. The depiction of various deities on the coins can be seen even before the emergence of iconographic texts[7], and this also reveals the relation between religion and polity. For example, the deities chosen by the Indo-Greek kings for representation on coins tended to be those that could be used as symbols of power.[8] Furthermore, the appearance of dates, names, dynastic affiliations, epithets used by the issuer along with certain symbols provides important information for political history. This highlights the difference between the sculptural and the numismatic art. The depictions on coins were done in official mints, possibly by the court artists, with a high degree of attention paid to details. Here, I am particularly looking at the Ābhīraka coin, which is named on the basis of the legend that appears on it. Attempts will be taken to re-examine the Ābhīraka coin with a purpose to offer an alternative identity that will be different from the prevailing ones. It will also throw light on the history of the non-monarchical Ābhīra polity, examining as both political and cultural symbols.

Prevailing scholarship attributes the Ābhīraka çoin to the Satrap ruler Ābhīraka on the basis of the Kharoṣṭhī[9] legend '*khaharatasa khatrapasa Abhirakasa jayatasa/jayatasa Abhirakasa*'[10] (the legend is also found in Brāhmī as *Kṣaharatasa Kṣatrapasa Ā(ghu or bhe) dakasa Iyanasa*, earlier reading)[11], which appeared on one side of this coin. Moreover, the similarities of motifs with the coins of another Satrap ruler, Bhūmaka, led them to place this Ābhīraka at the top of the Kṣaharāta line from where the branch started, succeeded by Bhūmaka and Nahapāna subsequently. The exponents of this theory are Robert C. Senior, Amiteshwar Jha and others, who explained it based on numismatic evidence. I approach the Ābhīraka coin with a set of questions pertaining particularly to other contemporary numismatic evidence. Other sources, especially epigraphic documents, will also be taken into consideration.

**Image 2.1: Ābhīraka coin, c. first century CE**

*Credit*: IIRNS, Nasik Photo Archives

The Ābhīraka coin shows a lion or horse (?) facing the front of a wheel (*cakra*?) on a pedestal along with a Kharoṣṭhī legend and sometimes with a Brāhmī legend on one side (see Image 2.1). The other side depicts a winged Nike standing to the right holding a palm and wreath and a circular Greek legend, which goes as CATAPATOY CATPAΠOY AYBIPAKOY, as interpreted by Senior[12] and Jha.[13] The coins of Ābhīraka are of copper only, struck in several sizes, and have been found in Kutch in Gujarat, Afghanistan, and Mleiha in the United Arab Emirates (UAE).[14]

The Ābhīraka, according to previous readings, was deciphered as Aghudaka,[15] Aubhiraka,[16] Aghudaka Iyana,[17] Arta[18] and Ata[19]. Finally, it ended in Ābhīraka.[20] This Ābhīraka is considered to be the first Satrap ruler heading the Kṣaharāta branch and was succeeded by Bhūmaka (120 CE).[21] Bhūmaka is believed to have imitated the coin device of Ābhīraka depicting lion and wheel, though he replaced the winged Nike device with arrow and thunderbolt. Moreover, unlike the Greek legend of Ābhīraka's coin, he introduced Brāhmī letters.[22] The above-mentioned similarities connect Ābhīraka and Bhūmaka. Certainly, they were linked in some ways, but that is not enough to place them in immediate succession.[23] Moreover, the appearance of the term '*khaharatasa khatrapasa*' cannot necessarily work as proof of them belonging to the same family of the Kṣaharāta branch of the Satraps. The term *Satrap* or *Mahāsatrap* denoted subordinate status and were used not only by the Kṣaharāta family, but also by other rulers.[24] Before going into the Ābhīraka controversy, we should discuss the legends and motifs appearing on this device in detail, and compare them with contemporary evidence. Attribution can then be attempted by situating them within the proper context.

The Ābhīraka coin presents a winged Nike holding wreath and palm. Furthermore, the Greek legend on it certainly indicates its Indo-Greek connection. Secondly, the Kharoṣṭhī legend (on the side showing lion or horse (?) facing a wheel on a pedestal) is proof of their north-western orientation, as it was a Kharoṣṭhī-speaking region since the third century BCE.[25] The same motif has also been found from Kutch in Gujarat with Brāhmī letters, which supplanted the Kharoṣṭhī legend.

There is no debate regarding the north-western or Indo-Greek connection of this issue, but identifying Ābhīraka as a Kṣaharāta ruler seems problematic. Let's have a look at the Kharoṣṭhī legend once again: '*khaharatasa khatrapasa Abhirakasa jayatasa/jayatasa Abhirakasa*'. On the basis of the term '*khaharatasa khatrapasa Abhirakasa*', these coins have been attributed to the ruler Ābhīraka of Kṣaharāta origin. This piece certainly belongs to Ābhīraka but that does not necessarily substantiate his Kṣaharāta origin. This Ābhīraka might have belonged to the Ābhīra community.

Now, the question arises who were the Ābhīras and how is Ābhīraka connected to them? Before throwing light on the Ābhīras, it is imperative to explain the term '*Ābhīrakasa*'. It can collectively represent the Ābhīra group[26] or can be used for the chief who, on behalf of the Ābhīras, represented the whole group. The title *khatrapasa*, as we have already discussed, can be used by any ruler who was in charge of a satrapy or province and symbolises subordinate status. In the case of Ābhīraka, it possibly indicates his/their subordinate status, but who continued the erstwhile tradition of using Greek legend on their coins. Furthermore, a winged Nike with wreath and palm can be seen on the coins of the Indo-Greeks found in Kandahar, Taxila and so on. Interestingly, Nike has been personified as the goddess of victory[27] and the wreath and palm in her hand perhaps indicated the victory of the Ābhīraka over another polity. The appearance of the term '*jayatasa*' is striking, and that literally denotes victory.

The next question that immediately comes to mind is, how do we explain this victory? Put differently, to whom can this reverse be dedicated? The answer lies within the remaining portion of the legend—'*Kṣaharātasa*'. It symbolises the political clash between the Ābhīras and the Kṣaharātas and the victory of the former. This needs to be explained further. These coins with Greek-Kharoṣṭhī legend have been found extensively in Afghanistan and the UAE, and with Greek-Brāhmī legend in Kutch, wherefrom the coins of Bhūmaka have also been found.

To explain the Kṣaharata-Ābhīraka rivalry and to trace the movement of their coin device from Afghanistan to Gujarat, we have to look into the history of the Ābhīras. The Ābhīra occupation in Afghanistan is attested by the presence of people of the Ābhīra community. Major Rawlinson places them along the south of the Hindu Kush mountains, from the Bolan Pass to the Arabian Sea. He further argues that the Sacae, or Scythians, came down from Seistan and conquered them, extending their frontier to Pattalene or Sinde; hence, the Indo-Scythia of Ptolemy and Arrian.[28] D.C. Sircar found their earliest traces in Ābhīravan, an area between Herat and Kandahar.[29] The provenance of the Ābhīraka coin also supports this possibility of Ābhīra occupation in Afghanistan from the second/first century BCE to the first century CE.

Next, they shared space in the valleys of Punjab along with powers like the Indo–Greeks, the Śakas and the Kuṣāṇas during the first century BCE to the third century CE. Furthermore, their repeated mention of *mleccha* identity in the Epic-Puranic sources undoubtedly verifies their aboriginal identity.[30] The import of the term *mleccha* underwent radical changes through ages.[31] Literary sources are replete with their references. The *Mahābhārata* calls the Ābhīras as *mlecchas* in several passages such as this: '*Bahabo mleccharājānaḥ pṛthibāyaṁ manudādhipa, mṛṣānuśāsinaḥ pāpāmṛṣābāda parayenāḥ, āndhrāḥ śakām pulindāśca yavanāśca narādhipāḥ, kāmbojā bāhlikāḥ śūrāstam ābhīrā narottama.*'[32] In the succeeding centuries, the different *Purāṇas* often mentioned them, along with other groups, and put them within the larger category of *mleccha*. Thus, in the *Matsya Purāṇa* (which mentions a list of future kings in the *Kali Yuga*), the Ābhīras along with other political powers like the Andhras, the Śakas, the Pulindas, etc. have been mentioned as *mlecchas* (*'Kṣatrāḥ pārśavāḥ śūdrās tathā'nye bahiścarāḥ andhrāḥ śakāḥ pulindāśca cūlikā yavanā sahā, kaivarttābhīra śabarā ye cānye mlecchasaṁbabāḥ'*).[33] Similarly, The *Vāyupurāṇa* also mentions a list of future kings (in the *Kali Yuga*) where the Ābhīras have been mentioned with other powers like the Andhras, the Śakas, the Pulindas etc. as *mlecchas* (*'Andhraḥ śakaḥ pulinda ca tulika yavanaiḥ saha, kaivartābhīra śabara ye cānye mlecchajātayaḥ')*.[34] What is interesting in these four *ślokas* is they all mention the association of the Ābhīras with the Yavanas (Greek)[35] and the Śakas, and so on. A close examination of these powers clearly locates their habitation in the north-western and western parts of India. Pañcanada, the land of the five rivers, is described as the stronghold of the Ābhīras. When Arjuna, after the catastrophe at Dvārakā, is conducting wives, children and old men from there to Indraprastha, the Ābhīras attack him when he arrives in Pañcanada and robs most of the women ('...*Abhīrāḥ mantrayāmāsuḥ sametyā* śuvadarśanāḥ; *ayamekorjjuno dhanvī vṛddhabālam hateśvaram*; *nayatyasmānatikramyayo dhāścheme hatoujaṣaḥ*').[36] All these references indicate the eastern part of the Punjab between the Sutlej and Yamuna as the stronghold of the Ābhīras.

Above Patalene, Ptolemy places Ābīriā or the land of the Ābhīras.[37] Patañjali locates them in the Sindhudeśa, which, according to W.W. Tarn, is 'the country of the Indus'.[38] Sircar, on the basis of *Periplus*, states 'that part of it (the kingdom of Nāmbārus) lying inland and adjoining Skythiā (Śakasthāna in the lower valley of the Indus) is called Ābīriā (Ābhīra country).'[39] It shows further that Ābīriā or the country of the Ābhīras spread up to the Indus Valley region. Debala Mitra states that the Ābhīras extended their territory from the deltaic region of the Sindhu river till Kathiawar.[40]

That they were closely associated with the Śakas is corroborated by epigraphic documents. Their relation with the Śakas can be discerned from the Gundā stone inscription of the time of Rudrasiṁha I [Śaka] year 103 (181 CE), where we first come across an Ābhīra general (*senāpati*), Bāpaka, and his son, general Rudrabhūti, under the Śaka administration.[41] It records the digging of a tank in the village of

Rasopadra for the well-being of all men by Rudrabhūti, son of general Bāpaka or Bāhaka, during the reign of the Śaka king Rudrasiṁha. Another inscription of 258 CE from Nasik portrays Īśvarasena[42], son of Ābhīra Śivadatta and Mādhāri, as a king (*rājan*). The inscription informs us that Viṣṇudatta (Śakanī), daughter of Agnivarman and mother of the Gaṇapaka Viśvavarmā, wife of the Gaṇapaka Rebhilā, made a perpetual endowment to provide medicines for the sick of the *saṁgha* dwelling in the monastery on Mount Triraśmi. For this endowment, an amount of *kārṣāpaṇas* were invested through the four guilds, evidently of Govardhana (Nashik). Though the exact Śaka-Ābhīra relationship cannot be determined from this record, it definitely indicates some connection between these two powers.

Moreover, two inscriptions from Kanheri and Thane district of Maharashtra present one Śakasena, who was *Mādhāriputra*[43] (son of *Mādhāri*).[44] This Śakasena has been identified with Śaka-Sātakarṇī, whose coins have been found from Andhra Pradesh, and is taken to be a Sātavāhana king and the successor of Yajñaśrī.[45] The view of K. Gopalachari[46] and H.S. Thosar,[47] however, places this Śakasena in the Ābhīra family, which seems to be more logical. In that case, Śakasena might have been a brother of Īśvarasena. What is interesting here is the name Śakasena, which again indicates the Śaka association with the Ābhīras. In another epigraph (283 CE) of *Rājan mahāsatrap* Bhartṛdaman of Kārdamaka branch, we find the mention of an Ābhīra once more, namely Vāsudeva, who appears as the son of a certain Kadaṁba, the grandson of Harihivakaṁda and the daughter's son of a person whose name has been read as Gulaka.[48]

Like the Indo-Greeks and the Śakas, the Ābhīras also came in close contact with the Śudras. Two passages from the *Mahābhārata* can be cited in this context, which clearly bear their association with the Śudras. The Ābhīras lived in the north-west of India with the Śūdras and with those who lived on the bank of the Sarasvatī river, fishermen and mountaineers: '*Śūdrābhīra gaṇāścaiva ye cāśritya sarasvatim; varttayanti ca ye matsyairye ca parvvtavāsinaḥ.*'[49] In another passage, the epic states that the *tīrthavināśana*[50] lay in the country of the Ābhīras as the sacred river Sarasvatī disappeared because of the hatred of the Śūdras and the Ābhīras living there ('*Tato vinaśanam rājana! jagāmātha halāyudhaḥ; śūdrābhīrān prati dveṣād yatra naṣṭā sarasvatī*').[51]

Both the literary and inscriptional evidence tells us that in course of time, they migrated from one place to another, most probably in different branches. The movement of the Ābhīraka device with Brāhmī legend by replacing Kharoṣṭhī perhaps indicates the migration of a branch of the Ābhīras who, during the course of their movement, brought this tradition with them. Their adoption of the Brāhmī script might be explained in terms of their association with the place where it served as the medium of communication. Their migratory nature is also attested by later sources.[52]

Attention may now turn to the coin device once again, which shows the wheel and the lion/ horse to understand its Ābhīra identity. The presence of the wheel connects them with the Indo-Greeks as we shall see later. Although the lion and wheel may signal their association with Buddhism, the wheel (*cakra*) can also demonstrate their affiliation to Vaiṣṇavism. A unique piece of the Indo-Greek king Agathocles (c. 180 BCE—170 BCE) found in the ancient Greek city of Ai Khanum in northern Afghanistan shows Balarāma-Saṁkarṣaṇa and Vāsudeva-Krṣṇa holding a *cakra*;[53] the extension of each spoke of this wheel presents another dotted shape, which can also be seen in the wheel symbol of the Ābhīraka coin, thus linking them.[54] The question that immediately comes to our mind is why did the Ābhīras like Agathocles use this symbol on their coin? It appears, the Ābhīras, like Agathocles, were also connected to Vaiṣṇavism, which possibly led them to depict this symbol on their coins.[55] Their devotion towards Kṛṣṇa is well established and they have been often portrayed as a cowherd community.

Before going into details of the Vaiṣṇavite affiliation of the Ābhīras, I would like to cite another coin, which also presents the *cakra*. It belongs to the Vṛṣṇis,[56] a group where the legendary Kṛṣṇa belonged.[57] The Vṛṣṇi coin portrays the *cakra* along with a circular Kharoṣṭhī legend on one side; another side depicts a joint figure of half-lion and half-elephant on a pedestal surrounded with Brāhmī legend. In the opinion of R.G. Bhandarkar,[58] the Ābhīras were a foreign nomadic tribe who came to India in the early centuries of the Christian era, and brought with them Christian legends of a pastoral god whose identification with Vāsudeva-Kṛṣṇa led to the engrafting of Christian myths, such as the birth of Christ in a stable, the massacre of the innocents, etc., on the latter. The theory of the Christian origin of these stories has been rightly questioned by H.C. Raychaudhuri[59] and is now abandoned altogether on chronological grounds. According to him, the pastoral legends of Kṛṣṇa developed under the influence of groups like the Ābhīras. In the opinion of Suvira Jaiswal,[60] the connection of the Ābhīras with worshipping of Kṛṣṇa as a youthful boy-god is indisputable. She draws our attention to the *Padma Purāṇa*, where Viṣṇu is made to say that he would be born amongst the Ābhīras (*gopas*) in his eighth incarnation.[61]

The term 'Ābhīra' originally did not mean cowherd, but later on, as most of them followed the pursuit of tending cows, it became synonymous with the term *gopa*. From the *Viṣṇu Purāṇa*, we come to know that Kṛṣṇa mentions the nomadic nature of his clans. He states that they neither cultivate nor do they engage themselves in trade. They live in forests. Hence, to them, cows are their gods ('*Na vayaṁ kṛṣikarttārovaṇijyajīvinona ca; gābohasmaddaivataṁ tātavayaṁ vanacarāyataḥ*').[62] Another passage of the same *Purāṇa* elucidates that Vāsudeva, (Kṛṣṇa's father), soon after his release from prison went near the 'vehicle of Nanda' and was very pleased to see the newborn baby. ('*Vimukto vasudevohasya nandasya sakataṁ gataḥ; prahṛṣṭaṃ dṛṣṭavān nandaṁ putrojātomametivai*').[63] This indicates Nanda (Kṛṣṇa's foster father) leaving the land in a vehicle. It is to be remembered that the Ābhīras were also nomadic people. Bhandarkar suggested that the foster parents of Kṛṣṇa belonged to the Ābhīras, who occupied the country from Madhuvana near Mathura to Anūpa and Ānarta—the regions around Dvārakā.[64] Here we may draw attention to a Deoghar relief, which depicts Nanda and Yaśodā, the foster parents of Kṛṣṇa, wearing, in the words of J.N. Banerjea, 'characteristically foreign' garments with a slight touch of the late Gandhāra element in it, and further records that cowherds of Mathura and its environs belonged to the Ābhīra stock.[65] This may indicate that the Gupta artists considered the herdsmen associated with Kṛṣṇa's childhood as foreigners and they may be the Ābhīras. Probably, the Ābhīras and the clans of Kṛṣṇa shared some common cultural complex, which led the Ābhīras to make Kṛṣṇa their god. Furthermore, the Nagarjunikonda inscription of Ābhīra Vasuṣeṇa, regnal year 30 (278 CE),[66] informs of an eight-armed image (*aṣṭabhujasvāmin*) of Viṣṇu made of wood at Setāgiri. The ruler's attempt to re-establish this image, perhaps, again indicates the faith of the Ābhīras towards Vaiṣṇavism. Besides, the Mevasa inscription of Bhartṛdaman (283 CE) mentions Ābhīra Vāsudeva, perhaps, indicating their association with Vaiṣṇavism.[67]

From the foregoing discussion, it seems plausible that the identity of Ābhīraka should be credited to the Ābhīras, rather than attributing them to the Kṣaharāta house. The Ābhīraka coin, as we have discussed, perhaps signalled the victory of the Ābhīra group over the Kṣaharātas. Another possibility could be explained through the joint victory/alliance between the Ābhīras and Kṣaharātas. But it cannot be conclusively established until further evidence comes up.

## Endnotes

1 P.L. Gupta and T.R. Hardekar, *Punchmarked Coinage of the Indian Subcontinent: Magadha-Mauryan Series* (Nashik: IIRNS, 2014).

2 W.W. Turn, *The Greeks in Bactria & India* (Cambridge: Cambridge University Press, 1966 [reprint]); A.K. Narain, *The Coin Types of the Indo-Greek Kings* (Chicago: Arogonaut, 1955); A.K. Narain, *The Indo-Greeks,* (Oxford: Clarendon press, 1957); Suchandra Ghosh, *From the Oxus to the Indus: A Political and Cultural Study c. 300 BCE–c. 100 BCE* (New Delhi: Primus Books, 2017).

3 K.K. Dasgupta, *Tribal History of Ancient India: A Numismatics Approach* (Calcutta: Nababharat Publishers, 1974).

4 D.W. MacDowall, 'Indian Imports of Roman Silver Coins,' in *Coinage, Trade and Economy*, ed. A.K. Jha (Nashik: IIRNS, 1996), 145–163.

5 R.S. Sharma, *Urban Decay in India c. 300–c. 1000* (New Delhi: Munshiram Manoharlal, 1987); K.M. Shrimali, *Numismatic Society Address*, 2014.

6 B.N. Mukherjee, 'Commerce and Money in the Western and Central Sectors of Eastern *India* (c AD. 750–1200)', *Indian Museum Bulletin* XVII *(1982)*, 68–86; B.D. Chattopadhyaya, *Coins and Currency System in South India* (New Delhi: Munshiram Manoharlal, 1977); Susmita Basu Majumdar, 'Monetary History of Bengal: Issues and Non Issues,' in *The Complex Heritage of Early India: Essays in Memory of R.S. Sharma*, ed. D.N. Jha (New Delhi: Manohar, 2014) 585–606.

7 J.N. Banerjea, *Development of Hindu Iconography* (Calcutta: University of Calcutta, 1956); B.N. Mukherjee, *Nana on Lion-A Study in Kushāṇa*

*Numismatic Art* (Calcutta: The Asiatic Society, 1969). Also see B.N. Mukherjee, *Numismatic Art of India*, Vols I and II (New Delhi: Munshiram Monoharlal, 2007).

8 Ghosh, *From the Oxus to the Indus: A Political and Cultural Study*, 135.

9 Instead of conventional 'Kharoṣṭhī', the term 'Kharoṣṭī' is available in various Buddhist and Jaina texts, such as in *Lalitavistara, Mahāvastu* and so on. For details, see B.N. Mukherjee, 'A Note on the Name Kharoshṭhī,' *Journal of the Asiatic Society* 23 (1981), 13–15.

10 R.C. Senior, *Indo-Scythian Coins and History: The Illustrated Catalogue of Indo-Scythian and Indo-Parthian Coins, Vol. II* (Classical Numismatic Group, 2001),193.

11 Amiteshwar Jha and Dilip Rajgor, *Studies in the Coinage of the Western Kṣatrapas* (Nashik: IIRNS, 1994), 79.

12 Senior, *Indo-Scythian Coins and History.*

13 Amiteshwar Jha, *Bharatiya Sikke: Ek Aitihasik Parichay* (in Hindi) (Nashik: IIRNS, 2013), 62.

14 Senior, *Indo-Scythian Coins and History*, 193.

15 Jha and Rajgor, *Studies in the Coinage of the Western Kṣatrapas*, 79.

16 Bob Senior, 'Kshaharata Questions,' *The Oriental Numismatic Society* (July 1949): 1–4.

17 Michael Mitchiner, *Indo-Greek and Indo-Scythian Coinage, Vol. 7–9* (Sanderstead: Hawkins Publications, 1976), 823. Also see, Ajay Mitra Shastri, *The Sātavāhanas and the Western Kshatrapas: A Historical Framework* (Nagpur: Dattsons, 1998), 144.

18 H.V. Trivedi, 'Notes on Some Western Kshatrapa Coins', *The Journal of the Numismatic Society of India* 17, no. 2 (1955): 89–90.

19 Ibid. See the Brāhmī legend *Atasa.*

20 Senior, *Indo-Scythian Coins and History.*

21 Jha, *Bharatiya Sikke*, 62.

22 Mitchiner, *Indo-Greek and Indo-Scythian Coinage*, 823; Osmund Bopearachchi and Wilfried Pieper, *Ancient Indian Coins* (Turnhout, Belgium: Brepols, 1998), 139.

23 Nahapāna continued the tradition of Bhūmaka on his coin by depicting thunderbolt and arrow, and replaced the lion and *cakra* motif with the bust of the ruler, possibly taken from the Indo-Greeks.

24 A copper coin from Taxila (first century CE) bears the Kharoṣṭhī legend *kshatrapa ... Rajuvala*, which indicates Rājuvala, the issuer of the coin, was a Satrap. See, B.N. Mukherjee, *An Agrippan Source: A Study in Indo-Parthian History* (Calcutta: Pilgrim Publishers, 1969), 169–170. Mukherjee thinks that

Rājuvala might have been a subordinate ruler under Azilises or Azes II. But in Mathura Lion Capital inscription, he has been mentioned as *mahākṣatrapa*. See D.C. Sircar (ed.), *Select Inscriptions Bearing on Indian History and Civilization, Vol. 1* (Calcutta: University of Calcutta, 1942), 112–117. Furthermore, the coin of his son Śoḍāsa presents him (Rājuvala) as the *mahākṣatrapa*. For details, see J. Allan, *A Catalogue of the Indian Coins in the British Museum: Coins of Ancient India* (Bihar: Eastern Book House, 1989), 185–191. Moreover, the Mathura votive tablet of the Year 72 (14–15 CE) presents Śoḍāsa also as *mahākṣatrapa*. See Sircar, *Select Inscriptions, Vol. 1*, 118–119. Also see B.N. Mukherjee, *Mathurā and its Society: The Śaka-Pahlava Phase* (Calcutta: Firma KLM, 1981), 1–11. *Kṣatra* denoting 'realm' was actually used by the Achaemenids, which was later changed to Satrap, Chhatrapa or Satrap. For detailed discussions, see Shastri, *The Sātavāhanas and the Western Kshatrapas*, 135.

25 B.N. Mukherjee, *Origin of Brāhmī and Kharoshṭī Scripts* (Calcutta: Progressive Publishers, 2005).

26 Monier Williams, *A Sanskrit-English Dictionary* (Oxford: Clarendon Press, 1964), 145. We also find names ending with 'Ka' belonging to the Ābhīra clan, such as Bāpaka, Bāhaka, or Gulaka, in later sources.

27 This is taken from *Encyclopaedia Britannica*, www.britannica.com/topic/Nike-Greek-goddess (accessed 8 November 2018).

28 Major Rawlinson, 'Comparative Geography of Afghanistan,' *Journal of the Royal Geographical Society* 12 (London, 1842): 112–114.

29 D.C. Sircar, 'The Deccan after the Sātavāhanas,' in *The Age of Imperial Unity* (Bombay: Bharatiya Vidya Bhavan Series, 1968), 221–223.

30 Haridas Siddhantabagish, ed., *Mahābhāratam* (in Bengali), *Bāṇaparvva*, Vol. 9, 159.34–35 (Calcutta: Visvabani Prakashani, 2nd edition, 1384 Bangabda), 1596–1597.

31 The antiquity of the term *mlеccha* can be traced back to the Śatapatha *Brāhmaṇa*, where it has been referred to as a language that was unintelligible to the Vedic Aryans. See A. Weber, ed., Śatapatha *Brāhmaṇa*, 3.2.1 (Varanasi: Chowkhamba Sanskrit Series, 1964), 23–24. Patañjali also mentions this in the sense of a language of the non-Aryans. See K.C. Chatterji, ed. and trans., *Patañjali's Mahābhāṣya* (Calcutta, 1957), 10. For a detailed discussion on *mleccha*, see Aloka Parasher, *Mlecchas in Early India: A Study in Attitudes towards Outsiders Upto AD 600* (New Delhi: Munshiram Manoharlal, 1991). Romila Thapar believes in the cultural entity of the term rather than its linguistic aspect. It has been suggested that *mlecchas* may have been derived from Me-luh-ha, the Sumerian name for an eastern land with which the Sumerians had trading relations, possibly the people of the Indus civilisations. See Romila Thapar, *Ancient Indian*

*Social History: Some Interpretations* (New Delhi: Orient Longman, 2003), 138. With the passage of time, the term was applied to demarcate the territorial land that reflects in the *Deśavibhāga* section of Manu, where except Āryā*varta* (the pure land) all else was regarded as *mlecchadeśa* or where the *mlecchas* inhabit. See Panchanan Tarkaratna, ed., *Manusaṁhitā* (in Bengali), 2.17–23 (Calcutta: Sanskrit Pustak Bhandar, 1993), 22.

32 Siddhantabagish, *Mahābhāratam, Bāṇaparvva,* 1596–1597.

33 Panchanan Tarkaratna, ed., *Matsyapurāṇam* (in Bengali), 50.75–76 (Calcutta: Bangabasi Electronic Press, 1316 Bangabda), 181.

34 Panchanan Tarkaratna, ed., *Vāyupurāṇam* (in Bengali) (Calcutta: Bangabasi Electronic Press, 1317 Bangabda), 637.

35 Cited in the Evolution section of the term *Yavana* in Early India, in Ghosh, *From Oxus to Indus: A Political and Cultural Studies*, 104.

36 Haridas Siddhantabagish, ed., *Mahāhāratam, Mausalaparva* (in Bengali), Vol. 43, 7.46–49 (Calcutta: Visvabani Prakashani, 2nd edition, 1400 Bangabda), 54–55.

37 V.V. Mirashi, ed., *Corpus Inscriptionum Indicarum,* Vol. IV, Part I (Octacamund, 1955), xxxi.

38 Sudhakar Chattopadhyay, *The Periplus of the Erythrean Sea & Ptolemy on Ancient Geography of India* (Calcutta: Prajna, 1980), 68.

39 Ibid., 75.

40 Details of their movements can be found in Debala Mitra, 'The Ābhīras and their contribution to Indian culture,' *Proceedings of the Indian History Congress* (Jaipur, 1951), 91–92.

41 Sircar, *Select Inscriptions,*Vol. 1, 176–177.

42 E. Senart, 'Nāsik Inscriptions (No.15),' *EI* 8, 198188–198189.

43 Using of metronymics can be seen as a shared tradition between the Ābhīras and the Sātavāhanas.

44 V.V. Mirashi, *The History and Inscriptions*, Inscription No. 52. Cited in H.K. Thosar, 'The Abhiras in Indian History,' *Proceedings of the Indian History Congress*, 51st Session (Calcutta, 1990), 60.

45 Ibid.

46 Henry Beveridge, *Comprehensive History of India*, Vol. II (Calcutta, 1957), 3240.

47 Thosar, 'The Abhiras in Indian History,' 56–65.

48 P.R. Srinivasan, 'Mevasa Inscription of Bhartṛdaman, Year 205,' *EI* 37, Part 1–8 (1968), 144–146.

49 Haridas Siddhantabagish, ed., *Mahābhāratam, Sabhāparva* (in Bengali), Vol. 5, 31.9 (Calcutta: Visvabani Prakashani, 2nd edition, 1384 Bangabda), 274.

50 The region of *Vināśana* may be identified with the present Hissar in Haryana. See, Sudhakar Chattopadhyaya, *Some Early Dynasties of South India* (Delhi: Motilal Banarsidass, 1974), 82, 127.

51 Haridas Siddhantabagish, ed., *Mahābhāratam,* Śalyaparva, Vol. 29, 35.1 (Calcutta: Visvabani Prakashani, 2nd edition, 1395 Bangabda), 393.

52 The Ābhīras were spread across the whole country extending from the Punjab in the north to Maharashtra in the south and as far as Bengal in the east and Gujarat to the west. The *Mārkāṇḍeyapurāṇa* in one passage locates the Ābhīras in the north-west, but in another passage, they were placed in the south together with the inhabitants of Mahārāṣṭra, Vidarbha, Asmaka, Kuntala and others. In a third passage, the *Mārkāṇḍeyapurāṇa* groups the Ābhīras with the people of Bhṛgukachchha, Koṅkaṇa, Mahārāṣṭra, Karnāṭa, the country on the banks of the Veni, Nāsikya and others. See F. Eden Pargiter, *The Mārkāṇḍeya Purāṇa* (Calcutta: The Asiatic Society, 1904), 312–314, 334, 362. The composition of the *Purāṇas* possibly indicates their later migration. For the date of composition of the *Purāṇas*, see R.C. Hazra, *Studies in The Puranic Records on Hindu Rites and Customs* (Delhi: Motilal Banarsidass, 1989).

53 While one side of the coin presents Balarāma-Saṁkarṣaṇa with Greek legend ΒΑΣΙΛΕΩΣ ΑΓΑΘΟΚΛΕΟΥΣ, another side depicts Vāsudeva-Kṛṣṇa with Brāhmī legend *Rajane Agathukleyesa.* See R. Audouin and P. Bernard, 'Trésor de monnaiesindiennes et indo-grecques d'Aï Khanoum (Afghanistan). [II. Les monnaiesindo-grecques]', *Revue Numismatique,*(Année 1974), 16, 6–41. Also see Osmund Bopearachchi, 'Emergence of Viṣṇu and Śiva Images in India: Numismatic and Sculptural Evidence,' paper presented at From Alexander the Great to Kaniṣka: Numismatic Evidence in Constructing Early Central Asian and Indian History, Education Studious, Asian Art Museum, San Francisco, 2016.

54 Similar ovoid shapes appearing around Nike's wreath on most of Ābhīraka's coins are found elsewhere only on the coins of Gondophares I, whom R.C. Senior regards as a contemporary of Ābhīraka and whose coins the latter imitated for his obverse. See http://www.orientalnumismaticsociety.org/yahoo_site_admin/assets/docs/RC_Senior_Kshaharata_Questions_Jul_1999.27570724.pdf.

55 That the Indo-Greek rulers came into contact and showed their faith in Vaiṣṇavism is also attested by the Besnagar pillar inscription of Heliodorus, an Indo-Greek king. It was erected in the honour of Vāsudeva. For details, see Sircar, *Select Inscriptions,* Vol. I, 90–91. Also see the appendix of Richard Salomon, *Indian Epigraphy* (New York: Oxford University Press, 1998), 265–267. Moreover, in the coin or medal we have a representation of the Hellenic deity Herakles, bearded and naked and shown as holding or turning a wheel and not his club. The general appearance of the wheel held by Herakles is favourably

comparable with that held by Kṛṣṇa-Vāsudeva on Agathocles' coins. Thus, here we have a new deity Herakles-Kṛṣṇa, holding Kṛṣṇa's wheel, thereby alluding to a fusion of Hellenic and Brahmanical concepts. See B.N. Mukherjee, 'A note on a gold coin or medal found at Tillya Tepe (Afghanistan),' *Mudra* (1989), 37–39. Thanks to Suchandra Ghosh for bringing my attention to this coin.

56 Alexander Cunningham, *Coins of Ancient India: From the Earliest Times Down to the Seventh Century* (Piccadilly, London: B. Quaritch, 1891), 70. For elaborate discussions on *cakra* motifs on coins and its relation to Vaishnavism, see Wilfried Pieper, 'Earliest Garuḍa and Vaiṣṇava deities on ancient Indian coins,' in *Numismatics Digest* 38 (2014): 36–59.

57 'According to Brahmanic, Bauddha and Jain traditions Krishna-Vasudeva was the chief of a warrior tribe, the Yadavas (Vrishnis and Andhrakas) who were Brahmanist Kshatriyas and in the epic period represented the Rigvedic Yadus. But at Mathura and Dvaraka the Vrishnis and the Andhraks lived amidst the Abhiras and Saurashtras who were said to have been outside the Brahmnaic pale (un-Vedic Pancharatra tradition). The un-Vedic or un-brahmanic Pancharatra evidently grew out of the primitive worship of Saṁkarṣaṇa, Vasudeva and other Vrishni chiefs such as Vasudeva's son Pradyumna and his grandson Aniruddha as hero gods by the barbarian Abhiras and Saurashtras.' Cited in Ramaprasad Chanda, 'Archaeology and Vaishnava Tradition,' in *Memoirs of the Archaeological Survey of India*, no. 5 (New Delhi: Archaeological Survey of India, 1998): 165–166. Thanks to Susmita Basu Majumdar for drawing my attention towards this issue.

58 R.G. Bhandarkar, *Vaiṣṇavism* Śaivism and Minor *Religious Systems* (Varanasi: Indological Book House, 1965), 37.

59 H.C. Raychaudhuri, *Materials for the Study of the Early History of the Vaishnava Sect* (Calcutta: University of Calcutta, 1936), 149–151.

60 Suvira Jaiswal, *The Origin and Development of Vaiṣṇavism* (New Delhi: Munshiram Manoharlal, 1981), 83–85.

61 Panchanan Tarkaratna, ed., *Padmapurāṇam, Sṛṣṭikhaṇḍam* (in Bengali), 17.11–20 (Calcutta: Bangabasi Electronic Press, 1326 Bangabda), 189–191.

62 Panchanan Tarkaratna, ed., *Viṣṇupurāṇam* (in Bengali), 5.5.1 (Calcutta: Nababharat Publishers, 1390 Bangabda), 347.

63 Ibid., 5.10.26, 367.

64 Bhandarkar, *Vaiṣṇavism Śaivism and Minor Religious Systems*, 37.

65 J.N. Banerjea, *The Development of Hindu Iconography* (New Delhi: Munshiram Manoharlal, 1974), 422.

66 D.C. Sircar, 'Nagarjunikoṇḍā Inscription of Ābhīra Vasuṣena,' *EI* 34 (1987): 197–203.

67 Srinivasan, 'Mevasa Inscription of Bhartṛdaman, Year 205'.

3

# Emblems of Faith, Monuments of Authority: Brahmanical Iconography in the Temples of the Cālukyas of Badami

Niharika K. Sankrityayan

The western Deccan in the early medieval period witnessed significant transformations in economic, social and political spheres leading to the emergence and establishment of powers like the Cālukyas of Badami. Patronage to temples became an integral part of the expansion and it appears there were different kinds of patronage, where functioning depended on the interplay between the dynasty and the landscape. In the Cālukya period, both royal and non-royal patronage played a significant role in the expansion of religious ideas. It is also important to note that it was through the iconography of cave and structural temples that symbols were often used or chosen to draw parallels between the deity and the king. Scholars have frequently associated the image of dancing Śiva from the Ravana-Phadi Cave at Aihole as a symbolic image parallel to the Cālukya king Maṅgaleśa.[1]

K.V. Ramesh has particularly studied the iconography of the dancing Śiva at the Ravana-Phadi Cave and relates the Saptamātṛkās along with the dancing Śiva to the reference in Cālukyan eulogies—'*sapta-loka-mātṛbhihsaptamātṛbhihparirakṣita*'. It means that the Śiva carved in the cave is a deified image of a Cālukyan ruler, perhaps Maṅgaleśa, since Śiva is accompanied by seven mothers who were guardian deities of the Cālukyan rulers.[2] Ramesh reads the label inscription carved on the rock altar beneath the image of Śiva as 'Raṇavikrā' and claims it as Raṇavikrāntan, the second name of Maṅgaleśa. He suggests that Ravana-Phadi is a corruption of

Rājakula Pratimāgṛha and was made by Maṅgaleśa as a royal portrait gallery where he got himself portrayed as the dancing Śiva with the Saptamātṛkā images.[3] This image of Śiva emphasises the image of a heroic king that draws upon the image of a heroic deity in the eulogy.

It has been pointed out that the placement of *liṅga* in the *garbhagṛha* and Śiva dancing with Saptamātṛkās in the inner antechamber at the Ravana-Phadi cave projects Śiva as the supreme deity watched over by adoring gods carved on the ceiling. Other deities like Harihara and Varāha are carved on the other side of the cave, reflecting their subservient status to Śiva.[4] Certainly, the projection of Śiva as the supreme deity and the merger of Śiva-Harihara as a syncretic image is a sound surmise. The portrayal of Varāha and Mahiṣāsuramardinī as subservient to Śiva is problematic as both Varāha and Mahiṣāsuramardinī imagery symbolise the victory of good over evil. The selection of these two particular imageries can be seen as a conscious effort by Maṅgaleśa to depict victory over his enemy along with the depiction of dancing Śiva.

Apart from the royal images, temples of the early medieval rulers from peninsular India have been interpreted by scholars as statements of royal power and commemorative monuments. Studies on the Kailāsanātha temple at Kanchi, the Virūpākṣa and Mallikārjuna temples at Pattadakal and the Rājarājeśvaram at Tanjavur are some remarkable examples.[5] It is interesting to note that the process of royal image-making in the early medieval period, perhaps, started in western Deccan with the construction of monumental temples at Pattadakal, Aihole and Badami. The Jambūliṅga temple at Badami with a triple shrine structure can be seen as drawing a symbolic parallel between the divine sovereignty over the three realms and the royal control over a vast territory. Here, the ruler's power is associated with Brahmā's creative, Viṣṇu's protective and Śiva's destructive acts.

According to Vidya Dehejia, the kind of patronage of temples where the stress is on gaining *puṇya* or religious merit, which would ultimately incur divine favour on political matters of the state and ensure favourable conditions to future birth, puts patronage in India in a category diverse and unique from patronage in the Western world.[6] Apart from *puṇya*, the royal patron, through the construction of monuments, was adding to his pride as a great builder of monuments.[7] There are several examples where the king builds temples that acted as a testimony to his personal glory.[8] Temples also served as monuments of authority. It can be seen as a declaration of the sovereign's power. Numerous temples built during the time of the Cō̱las, in the 11th and 12th centuries CE, testify this. Rājarāja, after extending and consolidating his empire overseas, built a temple in his capital that was five times bigger than any other temple of his times. The emperor arranged lavish endowments of land and money for its maintenance, and appointed treasurers, accountants and sub-accountants to manage the endowments.[9] James Heitzman points out that the Cō̱la kings were the foremost donors for religious purposes. They claimed to be the protectors and propagators of *dharma*. They won battles, donated lands to *brāhmaṇas* and were leaders of a *dharmic* kingdom.[10] Another significant aspect of the Cō̱la kings was the policy of political integration through temple donations, which would thus enhance agricultural expansion in irrigable zones of Cō̱lamaṇḍalam.[11] According to Heitzman, there was a remarkable presence of rural features in the economy leading to 'temple urbanism'.[12] However, the temples built by the Cālukyas cannot be compared with the size and grandeur of the Cō̱la temples. The period in which the Cālukyas of Badami established their rule marks the beginning of a fresh era in Indian history when certain economic factors played a key role in paving the way for a new social and political structure based essentially on the land system.[13]

The migration of *brāhmaṇas* and acculturation of tribal areas are striking in various regions in the early medieval period. B.D. Chattopadhyaya explains this process in the context of the formation of regional and subregional kingdoms and the methods adopted by them for legitimisation.[14] He argues that the emergence of temple centres is closely linked with gifts of lands (*brahmadeya*) to *brāhmaṇas* and tax-free settlements in particular cases (*agrahāras*).[15] Throughout the exercise of such grants, the king sought not just economic resources vital for the maintenance of his authority and continued popular legitimacy as being efficient redistributors of surplus, but also religious merit. The acquisition of such merit for himself and his ancestors was necessary to invoke his right to be the giver of rewards of land in the material world. He acquired such merit first and foremost by directly appropriating land as a result of conquests. Additionally, through the land grant mechanism, he could acquire religious merit for himself and his ancestors. There are many examples from Cālukya inscriptions that speak of a desire to gain and transfer religious merit to the king and his ancestors.[16]

The early medieval period in the context of South India can be seen as a marker of socio-economic transition. K.M. Shrimali's analysis of Vākāṭaka inscriptions refers to more than 100 settlements that emerged during this time. Grants were made by the Vākāṭakas for donations to temples and local cults, but the major share was given to *brāhmaṇas*. According to Shrimali, these land grants were used to Sanskritise outlying regions and groups living in the periphery who were involved in political activities.[17] He argues that 'the Vākāṭaka ruled for two centuries with non-monetary, small-scale villages and declining urban economy had feudal beginnings'.[18]

By analysing the inscriptions of the Cālukyas, it appears that there was a burgeoning of a new social group comprised of *brāhmaṇas*, who were the chief beneficiaries of the grants. It appears there was no set pattern of land grants; many were given by lesser chiefs who were part of the state structure. There is also a possibility that villages mentioned in the grants were wastelands and therefore granted in order to extend cultivation.[19] However, this is not very clear in these early inscriptions. By looking at the inscriptions of the latter half of the Cālukya rule, temples can not only be viewed as legitimisers of political power but also instruments of peasant subordination and surplus accumulation.[20]

The inscriptional analysis of the Cālukyas of Badami also suggests varied factors behind the spread of temples in western Deccan. Perhaps the focus during the time of the Cālukyas was more on the establishment of Brahmanical traditions through rich temple iconography, and parallels were drawn between the king and Āgamic deities.[21] With the religious developments that were taking place in western Deccan, significant changes were also noticed in the temple architecture and iconography. This served the purpose of spreading Brahmanical tradition, which evolved continuously, growing and changing in new social-religious contexts. Around the same time, epigraphic evidence suggests a strong association of Cālukya kings with the Āgamic deities. The Añjaneri charter of Bhogaśakti of Hariścandravaṃśa describes the king as a devout follower of Viṣṇu. He is compared to Arjuna who followed Janārdana's *jñānopadēśa*.[22] The inscription mentions that Bhogaśakti made an endowment of eight villages together with their revenue to god Nārāyaṇa. The income from this was to be used for buying perfumes and flowers, for the temple's repair and maintenance, and to perform ablutions as well as dance and music in the temple. There is also a reference to the *yātrā* festival in honour of Viṣṇu during a fortnight of the month of Mārgaśīrṣa, which implies *rathotsava* (chariot festival). Merchants were responsible for organising the festival.[23] Another possibility is that such movements encouraged patronage and helped in spreading religious sects.

The Cālukyas of Badami were involved in the construction of temples and they also pursued renovation and maintenance of these monuments.[24] For example, Vikramāditya II, in particular, employed Tamil architects to build temples at Pattadakal, subtly underscoring his victory in the Tamil region.[25]As a result, the temples not only increased in size but also evolved structurally. The new structures, which were to accommodate new cults and rituals, transformed the temples with grace and provided maturity. Percy Brown points out that in this phase of expansion the most important example can be seen at Aihole in the fifth and sixth centuries CE.[26] The entire temple structure in the early medieval period had an expanded architecture.[27] The *śikhara* with its *āmalaka* was to distinguish the temple from other architecture. The pillared *sabhāmaṇḍapa* was meant for the devotees to gather and pray. However, the ambulatory and assembly hall were broadened in later times, as seen during the Cōḻa period, to accommodate more devotees and visitors. Similarly, with the growing needs of temple-related activities, *pradakṣiṇa* was transformed from being a functional feature for facilitating the circumambulation ritual to an architectural device for the projection of Puranic narratives to viewers. The cave temples of the Cālukyas clearly do not have *pradakṣiṇa patha*, while structural temples at Aihole, Pattadakal and Badami show fully evolved *pradakṣiṇa patha* enabling the viewing of narrative and iconic panels on the walls. The Durga temple at Aihole throws an interesting light on glorifying the Puranic narratives, with Puranic religion gaining a stronghold in western Deccan. The Durga temple, for example, has two *pradakṣiṇas*—one inside the shrine, and the other in the form of a colonnaded cloister outside the shrine. The inner *pradakṣiṇa patha* serves perhaps as a ritual feature. The outer *pradakṣiṇa patha* has niches in which sculptures of Puranic deities are fitted, thus serving both as a ritual architectural feature and as a gallery for displaying the Puranic legends of Śiva, Viṣṇu and the goddess. It is interesting to note that no distinct sectarian affiliation is evident in the choice of the theme. As the Cālukya kings were involved with the renovation and maintenance of monuments, some of the structures at Aihole underwent restoration during the eras of Vinayāditya and Vikramāditya II. It is possible that the outer *pradakṣiṇa patha* was added sometime later and the images were carved on loose slabs and fitted in the niches when a need was felt to popularise and glorify Puranic narratives as Puranic religion gained a stronghold.

This, however, is not the case at Pattadakal, which can be seen as the most significant royal centre of the Cālukyas. In most of the temples—Virūpākṣa, Mallikārjuna, Saṅgameśvara or Pāpanātha, a well-marked *pradakṣiṇa patha* with a sculpted gallery is not constructed inside. Instead, the outer walls of the temples are profusely carved with Puranic narratives. It can be argued that the various themes, including scenes from the *Rāmāyaṇa* and *Mahābhārata*, depicted on the temple walls and pillars at Pattadakal, were an attempt by the rulers to enhance the 'sacredness' of Pattadakal as a commemorative site along with a strong political message. These representations certainly suit powerful emblems of divine kingship.

## Tools of Legitimisation

The main task of the Cālukya rulers was to reflect the existing social order and recreate a parallel world of authority in the realm of religion that would help them legitimise the polity established in that period. During the time of the Pallavas, the *bhakti* movement played a significant role in achieving the acceptance of caste and its ideology, which expressed the nature of differentiation, by all sections of the society.[28] The changing religious milieu of the early medieval period is expressed by the central concept of *bhakti* in the emotionally powerful hymns of *āḻvār* and *nāyaṉār* (sixth to ninth centuries CE), a remarkably rich corpus of religious literature, with the temple as its innovative focus.[29] However, the *bhakti* poetry of the Tamil saints had no counterparts in the Deccan; in order to understand the dynamics between the Cālukya kings and the temple as an institution, it is important to analyse the sociopolitical and religious configurations in western Deccan. It is equally significant to note that these temples were richly carved with divine imagery and, often, parallels between the divine images and the kings were drawn.[30]

## Vaiṣṇavism and Śaivism: Affinities, Differences and Manifestations in Western Deccan

Viṣṇu and Śiva were, in many ways, opposed to each other. Viṣṇu is prima facie a solar god, whereas Śiva is a lunar god.[31] Despite their dissimilarities, both Viṣṇu and Śiva have fertility associations; Viṣṇu because he is a solar god, Śiva because he is a chthonic god.[32] Sukumari Bhattacharji argues that 'fertility associations were integral for gods who were worshipped in agrarian communities as they enhanced the sectarian gods' cultic appeal and power'.[33] The importance of fertility in society can be seen in the Balagamve inscription, where a duty was imposed by king Vinayāditya on couples when the husband died without begetting a son (*aputraka-dhana*).[34] It seems the king felt the need to impose such a tax on the general population—from whom he required a constant supply of soldiers—if they were childless, especially sonless.[35] During Vinayāditya's reign, there was a special form of worship of Aditī, the fertility or mother goddess, and rituals of worship were performed at specially designed temples.[36] The worship of Viṣṇu by the Cālukya rulers is further suggested by inscriptions. From the epithets[37] of the first four kings, their Vaiṣṇava affiliation is clear, and the later five were Śaivas. Before 660 CE, there were temples dedicated to Śiva, Viṣṇu and Jina. While Vaiṣṇava kings of the early phase tolerated all sects and religions, Vikramāditya's conversion to Śaivism apparently ended the patronage to Śakti, Vaiṣṇava, Jaina and Buddhist temples. This king underwent the ritual of *Śivamaṇḍala-dīkṣā* and became a *parama-māheśvara*.[38] The obvious background of this conversion was a strong wave of Pāśupata Śaivism of a distinct form that swarmed the Andhra-Karnataka region.

## Cālukya Temples: Brahmānical Deities and Their Iconographic Characters

S.V. Padigar in an article on Vaiṣṇavism in Karnataka has dealt with inscriptional, textual and iconographic sources to unravel the different facets of Vaiṣṇavism in Karnataka.[39] On the section dealing with the Cālukyas of Badami, despite underlining fascinating references to Vaiṣṇava iconography in the temples, he fails to explain the obvious motives for the rich tradition of iconography, which developed in the Cālukya period and was further used by the Pallavas and, later, the Cōḻas.

In the Mudhol plate inscription, Pugavarma, who is identified by some scholars with Kīrttivarman I, renewed a land grant at Maḷakhēṭaka or Mūḷkhēṭaka to the god Varāhadēvasvāmin or Varāha.[40] This can be seen as the earliest-known dedication to god Varāha in Karnataka. The Nerur charter of Maṅgaleśa mentions that the Bhāgavatas observed the twelfth day of the Kārtika month as an important religious day.[41] The Añjaneri charter of Bhogaśakti of Hariścandravaṃśa (710–711 CE) describes the king as extremely devoted to the worship of Viṣṇu.[42]

Viṣṇu, in all his ten *avatāras*, is highly revered. The idea of *avatāras* or incarnations was primarily created to rehabilitate the world.[43] This has to do with the basic nature of Viṣṇu as a benevolent god, essentially interested in the welfare and prosperity of man and the world.[44] The *avatāras* invoke the quality of the interstitial period of *pralaya* (destruction) and recreation through the use of cosmological language describing Viṣṇu's appearance and the events surrounding it.[45] The concept of the *avatāra* associated with Viṣṇu from early times led to the evolution of several incarnations of the deity, of which ten came to be standardised by the seventh or eighth centuries.[46] The concept of *avatāras* also enabled the incorporation of folk and tribal deities and their cult practices into the Vaiṣṇava religion. Thus, we have Varāha or Boar incarnation, Narasiṁmha or Man-Lion incarnation and other human forms like Rāma and Kṛṣṇa among the *avatāras* of Viṣṇu. References to the *avatāras* of Viṣṇu appear in texts like *Śatapatha Brāhmaṇa*, where it is stated that Prajāpati Brahmā took the form of a tortoise.[47] *Taittirīya Āraṇyaka* mentions that the earth was raised from the waters by a black boar with a hundred hands.[48] Almost all the *avatāras* are talked about in the *Rāmāyaṇa*, *Mahābhārata*, *Bhāgavata Purāṇa* and *Viṣṇu Purāṇa*. Among the primary *avatāras*, the forms of Varāha, Narasiṁha and Kūrma were the foremost.[49]

Kings often look for parallel epithets to that of Viṣṇu. Since texts lay emphasis on Viṣṇu's protective activities and his intimate relationship with kingship,[50] there is an exceptional pursuit by kings to follow Viṣṇu and his idea to defend *dharma*, punish the wicked and protect the people.[51] Viṣṇu, the supreme ruler and protector of the universe, is often represented as seated on a royal throne. Several Cālukya temples share a noticeable characteristic where the opening of the raised platform ceiling are or were decorated with large relief panels of Viṣṇu in his *avatāras*. For example, the left end of the veranda in Cave 3 at Badami is occupied by a majestic Vaikuṇṭha Nārāyaṇa relief. Viṣṇu is seated in royal ease on the coils of the cosmic serpent, Ananta, whose hood of five cobra heads protects him. A Nāginī stands on either side, while Garuḍa is seated at his right along with goddess Śrī-Lakṣmī. Viṣṇu's royal nature is significantly associated with Śrī. By the early medieval period, Viṣṇu was considered the divine king par excellence. He is often described as dwelling in a heavenly court, Vaikuṇṭha, and depicted iconographically as a mighty king. His primary role as a king is to institute and maintain dharmic order. Viṣṇu is present wherever righteous kings rule and maintain order.[52] In the representation of Śrī as Viṣṇu's consort, she is to be shown standing or sitting to his right, with her left hand holding a lotus and the right hand in the boon-giving posture or *varada-mudrā*.[53] She follows him when he becomes part of his human agents, which is the righteous king, and she bestows on them her royal power, prosperity and fertility. This, perhaps, could be the reason for the portrayal of Śrī-Lakṣmī with Viṣṇu in the Cālukya temples. This was a way through which the Cālukya kings tried to reiterate their authority and power, and particularly the depictions of Viṣṇu are linked to the sovereign's portrayal as the saviour or protector of his people.

## Vāmana/Trivikrama

Trivikrama is an important *avatāra* of Viṣṇu and underlines the theme of closeness of earth with Viṣṇu. It is an established fact that the Vāmana myth was born in the three steps of Viṣṇu referred to in the *Ṛg Veda*.[54] Unlike other *avatāras*, Vāmana is not a separate entity later synthesised with Viṣṇu, but represents the essential and original aspect of the god.[55] The iconographic representation of Viṣṇu in this *avatāra* is mainly done in two ways. He is either sculpted as Vāmana or a dwarf depicting the earlier part of the story or as Trivikrama—that is, the dwarf who has grown into a gigantic stature measuring the three worlds with three strides. Vāmana is Viṣṇu's fifth *avatāra*, and grew out in stages of the Āditya Viṣṇu's attribute and epithet of Trivikrama.[56]

At Badami, Caves 2 and 3 are of Vaiṣṇava affiliation. The west wall of the veranda of Cave 2 is carved with one of the most unusual depictions of the myth of Trivikrama to the right of the entrance (see Image 3.1). His left leg is kicked high above waist level, with the son of Bali attempting to restrain the right leg of the god, and a small representation of Vāmana holding a parasol standing before the sage Śukarācārya with Bali and his queen depicted at the bottom of the panel. In his eight arms, Trivikrama holds, on the left, a conch, shield and a bow, with one finger pointing towards the moon, and on the right, he holds a club, arrow, *cakra* and a sword.

**Image 3.1: Trivikrama, Cave 2, Bādāmi, c. 560–570 CE**

*Credit*: Author

The eight-armed figure of Trivikrama in Cave 3 holds various weapons, including a *cakra*, *raṇḍaka*, sword, *gadā*, arrow, conch, bow, shield and the remaining hand points to the face of the planet Rāhu. The diminutive son of Bali clutches the god's right thigh, while to the bottom right is a group consisting of Vāmana (uncarved or destroyed) in front of Bali and his wife, preceded by Śukrācārya. The use of a Buddha-like figure has been suggested by scholars as a deliberate attempt to symbolise the victory of Brahmanism over Buddhism.[57]

Pattadakal's Virūpākṣa temple is perhaps the largest of all the Cālukya temples. The narrative of Vāmana-Trivikrama is depicted on the east wall of its *mahāmaṇḍapa*. Vāmana is shown taking water from Bali in the bottom left corner and Trivikrama fills the whole niche in the centre. Garuḍa overpowering Bali is depicted in the bottom right corner and Jāmbavān sounding the victory of the gods is on the top left corner.

The legend of Vāmana emphasises the association of earth with Viṣṇu by depicting him as its lord. It has been suggested by scholars that the Trivikrama image reinforces the Vedic image of Viṣṇu as a solar deity who traverses the universe in three strides.[58] However, it also focuses on the conception of Nārayaṇa as the god of sacrifice, who receives all oblations. In all the Vāmana narratives in various *Purāṇas*, this feature is stated by Bali. It is interesting to note that there is an emblematic meaning to the whole episode. 'Bali' means oblation, and in the legend, he offers himself to the god.

It is interesting to note that through the depiction of Trivikrama, a ruler's potential to conquer and run an unrestrained space is highlighted. The depiction of Trivikrama raising his leg up to the knee signifies the conquest of the earth; up to the navel signifies the conquest of the skies, and up to the forehead signifies the conquest of the heavens.[59] Perhaps this was why the image of Trivikrama was used in the Cālukya monuments throughout their rule, whether during consolidation or in the latter half of their rule, to convey the idea of a powerful conqueror. Viṣṇu, in the form of a dwarf, can enlarge himself in a miraculous way and encompass the whole universe.[60] This quality also equates Viṣṇu as coextensive with all existence and draws a strong parallel between Viṣṇu and the Cālukya kings.

## Narasiṁha

Narasiṁha was always represented as a hybrid form, normally with a lion's head and a human body.[61] The two parts of the name, *nara* and *siṁha*, mark his dual nature—as *nara* he is the Puruṣa Viṣṇu while *siṁha* stands for his terrible Rudraic aspect. T.A. Gopinatha Rao talks about three images of Narasiṁha.[62] One is *Girija* or *Kevala* Narasiṁha; his iconography comprises two or four arms and he is seated on a *padmāsana*, his forelegs bound with a *yoga paṭṭa* belt.[63] The second image is *Stauna* Narasiṁha, seated on a *simhāsana* with his left leg folded, has twelve or sixteen arms, and with two of his hands holding a garland consisting of the entrails of Hiraṇyakaśipu, who is stretched to his left thigh.[64] A third type, in which Narasiṁha is seated on Garuḍa or upon Ādiśēṣa, has not been discovered in any sculptural example.[65]

There are two sculptural reliefs—one on a rock behind the Bhūtanātha temple at Badami and the other on the exterior panel of the Narasiṁha-Kṛṣṇa temple—which were probably created in the early seventh century CE. In the sculpture on the large rock, Narasiṁha has four arms and the figure in the Narasiṁha-Kṛṣṇa temple has eight arms, suppressing *asura* warriors with four. The relief at the Virūpākṣa temple on the exterior west wall of the south porch follows the Badami type (see Image 3.2). The figure is nearly identical in pose to that on the rock behind the Bhūtanātha temple, but it has six arms instead of four. The body of Hiraṇyakaśipu is supported on Narasiṁha's left thigh, but is stretched full length so that his head and shoulders are on the right leg. No auxiliary warriors appear in this version, but an interesting addition is a six-armed figure of Śiva holding his *triśūla*, flying on clouds overhead. This could be a reference to the incident of Śiva's participation in the myth as Śarabha.[66]

At Badami, to the right of Cave 3, is a four-armed *dvibhaṅga* Narasiṁha, with Garuḍa and Prahlāda below, and flying couples above (see Image 3.3). He is represented in his *śānta* (benevolent) rather than his *ugra* (aggressive) form. His lower right hand holds a lotus; his lower left arm leans on a broken club and is crowned with a lotus flower. The Cālukya kings identified themselves with the strength of a lion. This is evident from their coronation names—Jayasiṁha (victorious lion) and Pulakeśin (hairy lion).

**Image 3.2: Narasiṁha, Cave 3, Bādāmi, c. 578 CE**

*Credit*: Author

A significant aspect of Narasiṁha is his non-involvement with the Vedic concept of the solar-universal deity traversing the universe like Trivikrama and Varāha. It appears to have incorporated the folk traditions of a custodian deity of the forest and rural areas into Puranic Vaiṣṇavism. Deborah Soifer points out that 'the *avatāra* continues an alliance with Indra that began as early as Vedic literature, which often united the two gods in battle against demons, portraying Indra as *kṣatriya* par excellence, possessor of physical strength, and Viṣṇu as his aid, his subordinate, who nevertheless possessed a higher, superior power'.[67]

It is interesting to look at two different myths of Viṣṇu as Narasiṁha and Vāmana presenting two outstanding visualisations of one deity. Narasiṁha, on one hand, is direct in his approach. In order to defeat his enemy, he creates a form and employs a weapon, which would not affect the pact. On the other hand, Vāmana is astute and misleading, conceals his original size and begs for a boon from his adversary. As dissimilar as these figures appear, at the same time, we sense something similar about them and their myths. Both descend to confront similar crisis—a demon threatening the welfare and stability of the world. And interestingly enough, both images were categorically used by the Cālukya rulers to profess their different natures as conquerors, protectors or controllers of the universe.

## Śiva

There is epigraphic evidence during the Cālukya rule that hints towards dedication made in honour of Lord Śiva. The Yekkeri Rock inscription mentions grants of lands in Dhūtipura, Āgariyapura and Kṛṣṇapura to Mahādēva.[68] This can be seen as the first reference to a Śiva temple in the Cālukya period. The two Śiva temples, Mahākūṭeśvara and Mallikārjuna, located on the sides of Viṣṇu-*tīrtha* tank, were among the earliest royal temples, perhaps sponsored by Pulakeśsin I and Kīirttivarman I, respectively, during the reign of the Cālukyas. The Dharmasthala plates of Vinayāditya refer to the installation of a golden *caturmukha-liṅga* in a temple in Kirumundame village in Edenāḍu *viṣaya* and the grant of land to a number of *brāhmaṇas* were made.[69] In the Nirpan Plates of Naravardhana, the grant of the village Balegrama in Goparāṣṭra *viṣaya* was made for the purpose of *guggula-pūjā* of god Kapālēśvara and for the enjoyment of the Mahāvratins living in the temple.[70] Padigar points out that Mahāvratins are identified by scholars with the Kāpālikas.[71] He mentions that in Karnataka among the Viraśaivas, the *guggula-pūjā* is a ritual associated with the worship of Vīrabhadra. Perhaps, when the cult of Bhairava declined in this region, the ritual of *guggula-pūjā* was transferred to Vīrabhadra, which apparently rose to prominence. *Guggula-pūjā* as a ritual is also mentioned in the Añjaneri charter with god Bhogeśvaradeva.[72]

In response to the glorification of Viṣṇu in his *avatāras*, the Śaivite sects in South India created two iconographic forms that placed Viṣṇu on a hierarchically lower level than Śiva. These were the Liṅgodbhavamūrti with Varāha and swan, and the Śarabhamūrti. Liṅgodbhavamūrti is one of the common icons portrayed in the niche of the temples in peninsular India. In the *Purāṇas*, Śiva appears as a column of fire before which Brahmā and Viṣṇu must surrender their supremacy, as Śiva has extensively been recognised with Agni—fire.[73] The iconographic portrayal of this form is with Viṣṇu as Varāha furrowing downwards and Brahmā as swan soaring upwards, unable to find the ends of the Śiva *liṅga*. The emphasis here is on downplaying the strength of Varāha and placing Śiva on a higher level than both Brahmā and Viṣṇu.

Śiva's protection is sought because he is the boon-giving god, the omnipresent soul and creator of the universe, the embodiment of its three divisions and because he is the great *deva* of frightful aspects and a conqueror of demonic powers.[74] Śiva in both his benign and terrible aspects provided a variety of metaphors and his sculptures in the temples of the Cālukyas can be viewed as diverse manifestations of the sovereign. Gerard Foekema in his work points at two different links between temple building and rulers.[75] Firstly, the king and his relatives can be the sponsors of a temple. Secondly, a steady rule of a region produces wealth and thus enables other people to construct lavish temples, which may have given fillip to temple-building activities. In this context, the imagery on the temples ought to reflect the patrons' choice.[76] Nowhere does he mention the factors behind the selection of a kind of imagery, or the significance attached to the depiction of Śiva in a particular form.

## Tripurāntaka

The legend of the three cities, the *tripura*, built by the *asuras* on earth, in the sky and in heaven, and respectively, of copper, silver and gold, is as old as the *Śatapatha Brāhmaṇa*.[77] The myth of Śiva Tripurāntaka begins with the penances of the *asura* Maya, who was endowed with extraordinary powers.[78] At first, the *asuras* thrived in their splendid cities, enjoying all earthly pleasures, worshipping Śiva. But then the evils of poverty, jealousy, greed and disunion entered, and after Maya had a sinister dream, they abandoned the path of truth and led a corrupt life. Soon, the whole universe was devastated by their actions and the worried *devas* went to Brahmā for advice. He declared that Śiva alone could destroy Tripura with a single arrow.

The depiction of Tripurāntaka perhaps started in the Cālukya period; it was further used by the Pallavas and gradually fully evolved during the time of the Cōḻas. Gopinatha Rao discusses eight descriptions of the subject of Tripurāntakamūrti as mentioned in the *Kāśyapaśilpam*, *Aṁśumadbhedāgama* and *Uttarakāmikāgama*, of which only the eighth represents Śiva in a chariot.[79] The two explicit images of Śiva as Tripurāntaka in the Cālukya period appear in the Kāśi Viśveśvara and Pāpanātha temples at Pattadakal.

At the Kāśi Viśveśvara, the representation of Tripurāntakamūrti is on a loose slab inside the temple, and was probably originally a part of the enclosure wall. The figure of Śiva stands in a chariot, his body and head facing the front. He is shown drawing a bow. The weapons that Śiva holds are the trident, a sword, shield, serpent and bow. According to C. Sivaramamurti, the *śūla* and the snake are 'distinguishing characteristics of Śiva in northern sculpture and Cālukyan areas of the Deccan'.[80] This *śūla* is of the type he shows for Badami. The *jaṭa* in this example is also of the Badami type, similar to the northern or Gupta type and different from the more canonical southern type.[81] The Aihole *praśasti* of Pulakeśin II refers to the king as Purabhit Prabhe, that is, radiant like the demolisher of *pura*, or Śiva, which replicates the allegory of the Ravana-Phadi Cave.[82]

**Image 3.3: Tripurāntakamūrti, Kaśi Viśveśvara temple, Pattadakal, Karnataka, c. 745–755 CE**

*Credit:* Author

At the Pāpanātha temple, this example is on a pillar of the east porch. It shows Śiva standing in a chariot, facing forward, his left foot raised high and bow held aloft. The bull, representing Viṣṇu, steadying the chariot, is seen below Brahmā, who is shown in profile. The manner of representation and the composition of this work are different from that of the Kāśi Viśveśvara example. Śiva is responsive and in action in the Pāpanātha relief, whereas he is strong and powerful in the Kāśi Viśveśvara panel.

The Tripurāntaka icon can be seen as a strong reflection of symbolic union between the ruler and the divine. It can also be seen as a Śaivite parallel of the Trivikrama narrative. It represents the sovereign's control over a vast territory. Significantly, the images of Tripurāntaka appear in the temples at Pattadakal, which emerged as the last royal centre of the Cālukyas. R. Champakalakshmi points out that the Tripurāntaka form of Śiva was of considerable significance in Tanjavur, repeated in two postures in all the *devakoṣṭhas* (niches) of the upper portion of the *vimāna* wall. She argues that as the Tanjavur temple was a symbol of royal power, the Tripurāntaka image is related to the ideology of the Cōḻa state under Rājarāja I, who played a crucial role in ascertaining the dominance and acceptance of Śaivism as the state religion. She relates it with the rediscovery of *Tēvāram* hymns by Rājarāja I, and points out that the Tripurāntaka episode was one of the dominant myths often referred to by the hymnists. Perhaps the images were intentionally carved on the *devakoṣṭhas* as a symbol of royal power and played a crucial role in asserting Śaivism as favoured by the kings.[83] Champakalakshmi further suggests that the Tripurāntaka form, which was significant in establishing its superiority over *śramaṇic* traditions, was hitherto not chosen for representation and, therefore, its usage seems to be a conscious act to symbolise the ruler as a warrior. The Tripurāntaka legend demonstrates the qualities of courage and determination of a ruler and victory of divine power over evil.[84] Similarly, the Tripurāntaka images of Kanchi and Ellora also reflect the Pallava and Rāṣṭrakūṭa political and territorial expansion.

The selection of the Tripurāntaka form as a conscious effort by Rājarāja I in the Tanjavur temple was however rejected by K.R. Srinivasan. He points out that due to the upper levels not being clearly visible and while lower level niches depicting different forms, there cannot be a satisfactory explanation of such a recurrence as a conscious effort.[85] However, he related the Tripurāntaka form in comparison to Buddha and Viṣṇu as representing the concept of *cakravartin* by earlier rulers and argues that Rājarāja I adopted Tripurāntaka as his favourite choice as the Śaiva counterpart of the *cakravartin* ideal.[86] It can be understood as the image of royalty as the Universal Emperor.[87] Kesavan Veluthat concurs that the ideal of *carkravartin* or *sārvabhouma* was indeed emulated by the monarch in early medieval south India.[88]

## Gaṅgādhara

Gaṅgādharamūrti was a fairly accepted form in the Deccan and South India. In Deccan representations, Śiva is shown holding a strand of his lock to receive Gaṅgā, which falls within the framework of the Puranic narrative of Śiva.

In the Deccan, one of the most significant images of Gaṅgādhara is from Aihole. It is carved on a slab in one of the niches of the outer *pradakṣiṇā* of the Durga temple. Śiva is shown with eight arms holding various weapons and illustrating different mudras. He is leaning on Nandi in a *tribaṅga* pose, and holding out a lock from his hair to receive Gaṅgā.

Another image of Gaṅgādhara from Aihole appears in the Ravana-Phadi Cave. This particular Gaṅgādhara panel is an outstanding piece of art—it shows Śiva holding his locks on both sides with his arms and Bhagīratha performing penance. Standing next to him is perhaps Pārvatī. Three female figures are shown descending from his *jaṭa*, probably representing Gaṅgā with her attendants. It is remarkable to note that such depiction was not imitated anywhere else in the Cālukya monuments or in the Pallavas ones. It could have been an experiment conducted by patron and artist.

Another significant aspect of the Gaṅgādhāramūrti panels from Aihole may be understood in terms of the ruler's control over the Malaprabha valley, as there is also parallelism drawn between Gaṅgā and Kaveri. Michael Lockwood compares Śiva's control of the flow of Gaṅgā and Mahendra's control of the Kaveri valley, which is effectively depicted through a river portrayed as a woman, who can be seen as a symbolic personification of territory. It could be that the Cālukya rulers may have endorsed such a parallel.[89] Aihole, with its fertile agrarian tracts and located on the banks of Malaprabha river, would have served best for the projection of the Gaṅgādhāramūrti image.

## Conclusion

With the Cālukyas of Badami, we come across interesting material in the form of inscriptions, sculpture and monuments. Extensive iconographic survey of the major sites suggests an integrative socio religious process that led to the emergence of such images. A close analysis of their inscriptions suggests that the main reason for patronage was attainment of religious merit as this served the patron's purpose of consolidating his position as a sovereign. This is in juxtaposition with evidence in the form of cave temples and structural temples at Badami, Mahakuta, Aihole and Pattadakal, which are carved with larger-than-life images of Śiva and Viṣṇu, portraying the emergence and prominence of Brahmanical faith in the period. The use of both Śaiva and Vaiṣṇava sectarian traditions for furthering ideological claims of rulers resonates with notions of power, benevolence and protection, which coincide with the attributes meant to be possessed by the ideal king. By looking at the rich Brahmanical iconography of the Cālukyas, it appears that kingship was bolstered through the patronage of temples dedicated to Śiva and Viṣṇu, and images of these sectarian deities were deliberately used to convey the temporal power of the Cālukyas of Badami.

## Endnotes

1 K.V. Ramesh, *Chalukyas of Vātāpi* (New Delhi: Agam Kala Prakashan, 1984), 11–74.

2 Ibid., 71–72.

3 Ibid.

4 Archana Verma, *Temple Imagery from Early Medieval Peninsular India* (Surrey: Ashgate Publishing Limited, 2012), 252.

5 R. Nagaswamy, 'Innovative Emperor and His Personal Chapel,' in *Royal Patrons and Great Temple Art*, ed. Vidya Dehejia (Bombay: Marg Publications, 1988), 37; Carol R. Bolon, 'Two Chalukya Queens and Their Commemorative Temples,'

in *Royal Patrons and Great Temple Art*, ed. Vidya Dehejia (Bombay: Marg Publications, 1988), 61; R. Chamapakalakshmi, 'Iconographic Programme and Political Imagery in Early Medieval Tamilakam: the Rajasimhesvara and the Rajarajesvara,' in *Indian Art: Forms, Concerns and Development in Historical Perspective*, ed. B.N. Goswamy (D.P. Chattopadhyaya, General Editor, History of Science, Philosophy and Culture in Indian Civilisation), Vol. VI, part 3 (2000): 15, New Delhi: Munshiram Manoharlal.

6 Vidya Dehejia, 'Patron, Artist and Temple,' in *Royal Patrons and Great Temple Art*, ed. Vidya Dehejia (Bombay: Marg Publications, 1988), 4.

7 Ibid., 4.

8 There are temples named after the great patron king, such as the Rājasiṁheśvara temple at Kanchipuram and the Rājarājeśvara temple at Tanjore.

9 James Heitzman, *Gifts of Power: Lordship in an Early Indian State* (New Delhi: Oxford University Press, 1997), 882–920.

10 Ibid., 217.

11 Ibid., 218.

12 Ibid., 220.

13 R.S. Sharma, *Indian Feudalism: c. 300–1200* (Calcutta: University of Calcutta, 1965); R.S. Sharma, *Light on Early Indian Society and Economy* (Bombay: Manaktalas, 1966); D.D. Kosambi, *The Culture and Civilisation of Ancient India* (New Delhi: Vikas Publications, 1966; Reprint 1972); Romila Thapar, *A History of India* (Penguin Books, 1966); K.M. Shrimali, *Agrarian Structure in Central India and the Northern Deccan: A Study of Vakataka Inscriptions* (New Delhi: Munshiram Manoharlal, 1987); B.D. Chattopadhyaya, 'Transition of the Deccan in Early Historical Phase,' in *Archaeology and History*, eds B.M. Pande and B.D. Chattopadhyaya (New Delhi: Agam Kala Prakashan, 1987); R.N. Nandi, *State Formation, Agrarian Growth and Social Change in Feudal South India c. AD 600–1200* (New Delhi: Manohar, 1969).

14 B.D. Chattopadhyaya, 'Historiography, History and Religious Centres,' in *Gods, Guardians and Lovers*, eds. Visakha N. Desai and Darielle Mason (Ahmedabad: The Asiatic Society Galleries in association with Mappin, New York, 1993), 42.

15 Ibid., 42.

16 *Indian Antiquary (IA)*, Vol. IX, 1880, 125; *IA*, Vol. XIX, 1889, 19.

17 K.M. Shrimali, *Agrarian Structure in Central India and the Northern Deccan* (New Delhi: Munshiram Manoharlal, 1987), 26–29.

18 Shrimali, *Agrarian Structure in Central India*, 26–29.

19 Niharika K. Sankrityayan, 'Structures of Patronage, Social Transactions, and Sacred Landscape: Brahmanical Iconography in the Western Deccan, c. 550–750 CE' (Unpublished PhD dissertation, Jawaharlal Nehru University, 2014), 44.

20 Nandi, *State Formation, Agrarian Growth and Social Change*, 68.

21 R. Champakalakshmi, 'Urbanisation in South India: The Role of Ideology and Polity,' *Social Scientist* 29, nos 3–4 (March–April 2001): 67–117.

22 N.P. Chakravarti, ed., 'Añjaneri Plates of Bhogasakti', *Epigraphia Indica* (EI), Vol. XXV (1939–1940): 225–236.

23 Ibid., 225–236.

24 R.N. Nandi, *Religious Institutions and Cults in the Deccan* (New Delhi: 1973), 3; D.C. Sircar, 'The Manor Plates of Vinayāditya Mangalarāsa (written by Bhatta Rudranaga)', *EI*, Vol. XXVIII (1945–1946): 17–22. The grant states that some villages and domestic sites were offered to the temple of Sun-god at Manapura for supply of perfumes, flowers, incense, lamps, music and offerings to the god and for repairs to the temple.

25 *IA*, Vol. X, 1881, 170.

26 Percy Brown, *Indian Architecture: Buddhist and Hindu Period* (Bombay: D.B. Taraporevala Sons & Co., 1959), 67–70.

27 Ibid.

28 Kesavan Veluthat, *The Early Medieval in South India* (New Delhi: Oxford University Press, 2009), 68.

29 R. Champakalakshmi, 'The Making of a Religious Tradition,' in *Religion and Society in Peninsular India (6th–16th Centuries CE)*, ed. N. Chandramaouli (New Delhi: Aryan Books International, 2016), 8–26.

30 Kesavan Veluthat, 'Religious Symbols in Political Legitimation: The Case of Early Medieval South India,' *Social Scientist* 21, nos 1–2 (1993): 23–33.

31 Sukumari Bhattacharji, *The Indian Theogony—A Comparative Study of Indian Mythology from the Vedas to the Purāṇas* (Cambridge: Cambridge University Press, 1970), 15.

32 Ibid., 16.

33 Ibid.

34 *IA*, Vol. XI, 1882, 144.

35 Carol R. Bolon, *Early Chalukya Sculpture* (Unpublished PhD dissertation, New York University, 1981), 10.

36 Bolon, *Early Chalukya Sculpture*, 10.

37 The epithet in the case of Vaiṣṇava affiliation of kings was Parama Bhāgavata and in the case of Śaiva, it was Parameśvara.

38 'Amudalapadu Plates of Vikramaditya I', S.V. Padigar, ed., *Inscriptions of the Calukyas of Badami*, Bangalore: ICHR, Southern Region, 2010), No. 42.

39 S.V. Padigar, 'Vicissitudes of Vaishnavism in Karnataka,' in *Religion and Society in Peninsular India (6th–16th Centuries CE)*, ed. N. Chandramaouli (New Delhi: Aryan Books International, 2016), 48–63.

40 *EI*, Vol. XXXII, 293–298.
41 *IA*, Vol. VII, 1878, 161–162.
42 *EI*, Vol. XXV, 225–236.
43 Jan Gonda, *Visnuism and Saivism—A Comparison* (New Delhi: Munshiram Manoharlal, 1976), 13.
44 Ibid.
45 Jan Gonda, *Aspects of Early Visnuism* (New Delhi: Motilal Banarsidass: 1954), 124–163.
46 R. Champakalakshmi, *The Hindu Temple* (New Delhi: Roli, First Edition, 2001), 109.
47 T.A. Gopinatha Rao, *Elements of Hindu Iconography,* Vol. I, Part I (Madras: Motilal Banarsidass, 1914; Reprinted 1985, 1993 and 1997), 124.
48 Ibid.
49 Jan Gonda, *Aspects of Early Viṣṇuism*, 124; Kalpana Desai, *Iconography of Vishnu* (New Delhi: Abhinav Publications, 1973), 1–24.
50 Gonda, *Aspects of Early Viṣṇuism*, 164–167.
51 P.V. Kane, *History of Dharmasastra Vol. II* (Poona: Munshiram Manoharlal, 1941), index 1313.
52 Gonda, *Aspects of Early Viṣṇuism*, 164–167.
53 R. Mahalakshmi, *The Book of Lakshmi* (New Delhi: Penguin, 2010), 100.
54 A.A. Macdonell, *Vedic Mythology* (Varanasi: Indological Book House, 1963), 39.
55 Desai, *Iconography of Vishnu*, 98.
56 J.N. Banerjea, *The Development of Hindu Iconography* (New Delhi: Munshiram Manoharlal, 1956), 417.
57 Ashwin Lippe, *Indian Medieval Sculpture* (New York: North Holland Publishing Company, 1978).
58 R. Champakalakshmi, *Vaisnava Iconography in Tamil Country* (New Delhi: Longman, 1981), 21.
59 Verma, *Temple Imagery*, 93.
60 Gonda, *Aspects of Early Viṣṇuism*, 146.
61 H. Daniel Smith, *A Sourcebook of Vaisnava Iconography According to Pancaratragama Texts* (Madras: Pancaratra Parisodhana Parisad, 1969), 138.
62 Rao, *Elements of Hindu Iconography*, 149–153.
63 Ibid.
64 Ibid.
65 Ibid.
66 To understand the myth of Śarabha, see T.A. Gopinatha Rao, *Elements of Hindu Iconography*, Vol. II, Part I (New Delhi: Motilal Banarasidass, 1997), 171–175.

67 Deborah Seifer, *The Myths of Narasiṁha and Vamana: Two Avatars in Cosmological Perspective* (New Delhi: Sri Satguru Publication, 1992), 8.

68 *IA*, Vol. V, 1876, 6–9.

69 *Journal of Epigraphic Society of India,* Vol. XXI, 1995, 28–31.

70 *IA*, Vol. IX, 1880, 123–125.

71 Padigar, *Inscriptions*, xvi.

72 *EI*, Vol. XXV, 1939–1940, 225–136.

73 Rao, *Elements of Hindu Iconography,* Vol. II, Part I, 105–111.

74 Gonda, *Visnuism and Saivism*, 12.

75 Gerard Foekema, *Fifteen Golden Examples Indian Temple Architecture in Karnataka* (Bangalore: Simova, 2005), 9–10.

76 Ibid.

77 Friedrich Max Müller, ed., 'The Satapatha Brahmana,' in *Sacred Books of the East* Vol. XXVI, trans. Julius Eggeling (Delhi: Oxford University Press, 1963), 105; Rao, *Elements of Hindu Iconography*, Vol. II, Part I, 164–171.

78 Rao, *Elements of Hindu Iconography,* Vol. II, Part I, 164.

79 Ibid., 166–170.

80 C. Sivaramamurti, 'Geographical and Chronological Factors in Indian Iconography,' *Ancient India* VI (1950): 21–63.

81 Sivaramamurti, 'Geographical,' 55.

82 *EI*, Vol. VI, 1900–1901, 1–12.

83 R. Champakalakshmi, 'Urbanisation from Below,' in *Trade, Ideology and Urbanisation* (New Delhi: Oxford University Press, 1999): 424–440.

84 C. Sivaramamurti, *The Chola Temples* (New Delhi: ASI, 1960), 18. Dealing with the Rājarājeśvara fresco, Sivaramamurti opines that 'Tripurantaka form of Śiva can be seen as the ideal warrior'.

85 K.R. Srinivasan, 'An Interesting Sculpture in Tanjavur,' mentioned by Gary J. Schwindler in 'Speculations on the theme of Śiva as Tripurantaka as it appears during the reign of Rajaraja I in the Tanjore area, c. AD 1000,' in *Ars Orientalis* 17 (1987), 163–178.

86 Schwindler, 'Speculations,' 163–178.

87 Kesavan Veluthat, *The Political Structure of Early Medieval South India* (New Delhi: Orient Blackman, 2012), 66–67.

88 Veluthat, *The Political Structure*, 67.

89 A detailed discussion of this aspect has been undertaken in the essay by R. Mahalakshmi in this volume.

4

# Controlling the Waters: Divine Imagery and Royal Enterprise in Early Medieval Tamil Nadu

R. Mahalakshmi

This essay seeks to revisit the debate on the Asiatic mode of production (hereafter, AMP), particularly its reorientation in the theory of the hydraulic society and oriental despotism. One of the major problems with the whole debate is the manner in which the question of irrigation is tended to be viewed, with suspicion on the one side, while on the other the emphasis has largely been on description rather than analysis. I focus here on some of the important writings on the subject, in the first and second parts of the essay, to argue that royal control over irrigation need not be summarily dismissed or skirted. The third section looks at mythic, iconographic and inscriptional evidence that underscores the importance of water, and the implications of association and management of water resources for kingship and state power, with special reference to the Pallava and Cōḻa states (sixth–thirteenth centuries CE). It is obvious from various sources that control of overflowing waters, literally and figuratively, signified power and authority. In many early Indian sources, it is the river Gaṅgā that is venerated, and in different regional contexts, the local rivers are seen as forms of her. The Tamil context is no different, and I offer a few examples of the significance of the symbolism of this river through a reading of the Śaiva icon of Gaṅgādhara, and some inscriptional references.

# I

Karl A. Wittfogel propagated the idea of a 'hydraulic (Oriental) society', which was based on his study of the 'large-scale and government-directed waterworks' in the premodern Chinese context.[1] He applied 'the term "hydraulic agriculture" ... to a system of farming which depends on large-scale and government-directed water control ... to agrarian societies in which agro-hydraulic works and other large hydraulic and non-hydraulic constructions that tend to develop with them are managed by an inordinately strong government.'[2] For Wittfogel, these states could be designated by the term 'Oriental despotism', whose 'constructional achievements ... include the creation and maintenance of large waterworks for productive and protective purposes (irrigation and flood control) and, under certain conditions, the creation of navigation canals and extended aqueducts for conveying drinking water. Among the non-hydraulic installations that tend to grow with the growth of the various hydraulic installations we find monumental defense works (long walls and fortresses), far-flung roads, "big houses" (palaces, temples), and colossal tombs (pyramids etc.).'[3] Designating Buddhist India as a 'peacefully interrelated territorial state', Wittfogel believed there was a transition from the simple to a semi-complex hydraulic society with the growth of merchant and artisanal classes outside of state control in these societies.

In the Indian context, many scholars have critiqued this concept, as well as the (re)interpretation of Karl Marx's theory of oriental despotism as developed by Wittfogel. Some like D.D. Kosambi focused on the characterisation of Chinese civilisation in particular, and the denunciation of the communist regime, as it was seen as merely a different form of the despotic state, as reactionary and motivated.[4] On the question of the unchangeableness of Asian societies, it is argued that since it was predicated on the idea of self-sufficiency of villages, it was flawed at the onset. In the Indian subcontinent, two essential commodities—salt and metal—were not available everywhere, hence, exchange was an important part of the historical development, leaving no room for insularity of village life.[5] Further, technological changes, such as the invention of the plough, meant that the productive process was being accelerated and transformed. Others like Irfan Habib and Bipan Chandra placed Marx's ideas on oriental despotism in historical perspective before demolishing Wittfogel's arguments. For Habib, 'the emergence of peasantry is apparently also that of the emergence of a differentiated society.... Full-fledged agriculture meant creation of surplus enough to feed a certain number of food producers. In the arid zone in which agriculture had to spread first, dykes and embankments to hold and divert flood waters were a prerequisite; and these demand a certain amount of social and administrative organisation—the bedrock of Marx's Oriental Despotism.'[6]

Chandra refers to the hypertrophied character of the state as presented by Marx with regard to India, who attributed this to the climatic conditions here, resulting in a functional relationship between Asiatic despotism and irrigation.[7] Marx further argues that the despotic government sought legitimacy by creating conditions for the unhampered pursuit of productive activities by the common people.[8] Chandra stressed, through research on the precolonial period, that agriculture was not dependent on, nor dominated by large-scale irrigation works, nor has the state played an important role in this. For Chandra, Marx's analysis rested on the assumption that British rule was ultimately positive in ways that it would break the stagnation of the precolonial economy and result in capitalist development in India. Refuting this line of thought, Chandra points out that colonialism cannot be understood as a historical stage in the development of humanity, or as a mode of production that evolves from the disintegration of the old one.[9]

R.S. Sharma posits that the 'pedigree of oriental despotism in Europe can be traced back to Plato and Aristotle. But it was only when the mercantilist and first-generation industrial powers had acquired colonies in India and other parts of Asia that the idea was popularised. Amongst others it is found in the writings of Adam Smith, Montesquieu, Richard Jones and Hegel, and was propagated by James Mill. They talked not only of oriental despotism but also of the unchanging east.'[10] While Marx and Freidrich Engels accepted the idea of oriental despotism, according to Sharma, they attempted to explain it through a class analysis, as factors advanced by Montesquieu were not acceptable on the grounds that India is a subcontinent with no single ecology. The requirement for irrigation in these arid societies as leading to oriental despotism, as expounded by Marx, is rejected by Sharma because no single factor is seen to give rise to the kinds of states that emerged in the subcontinent.[11]

Romila Thapar, while criticising the proponents of the AMP and oriental despotism model, points out that bureaucratic control over the economy, as enunciated by Marx, was derived from the revenue extraction mechanisms in place. Hydraulic control by the state was not common, and it appears in many contexts that the actual control over the numerous wells and tanks built for the purpose of irrigation was at the local level. She states: 'The more relevant question is not that of the state ownership of the hydraulic machinery, but the variation in irrigation technology and the degree to which irrigation facilities gave an individual or an institution a political edge over others.'[12]

Shireen Moosvi has argued that the decline of the apparently stable states in Europe with the emergence of absolute monarchies, subsequently the growth of constitutional orders and, finally, the revolutionary movements, was contrasted by travellers like the Frenchman Francois Bernier (1620–1685) with the situation in the Orient, leading him and others to critique the despotic oriental state.[13] Marx's AMP, which rested on the two pillars of the despotic king and the village community, was seen as deriving from this already prevailing understanding, although Marx emphasised the mutual benefits the system provided. The ruler received revenues and had absolute military control. The village communities were provided protection and irrigation facilities to fulfill their agrarian requirements.[14] While largely this theory was laid to rest, it resurfaced in the work of Wittfogel in the context of the Cold War of the 1950s, which cannot be seen as accidental or innocent, according to Moosvi.[15]

Despite such incisive critiques, these theories in their different avatars keep coming back, as for instance Kathleen Gough's insistence on the AMP in a modified version as being relevant in South India.[16] She argues: 'Contrary to the views of many, but not all, modern Marxist writers, there was an Asiatic Mode of Production (AMP) in the Hindu Kingdoms of most of Southern India prior to conquest by the Mughals and/or the British. The various kingdoms which more or less conformed to Marx's model of the AMP had their heartlands at different periods in the major river valleys with their associated irrigation works. In Tanjavur, site of the irrigated delta of the river Kaveri, the AMP flourished from at least the first to the fourteenth century, and with modifications until about 1770. Some features of it remained until the 1890s and traces are visible today. Although conforming to Marx's model in fundamental respects, the AMP in Tanjavur permitted greater social change, social stratification, development of the productive forces, urbanisation, and commodity production....'[17] She sees the huge semi-arid region requiring large-scale irrigation projects that were organised by the *brāhmaṇas* among others through the aegis of the temple as nothing more than 'arms of the state'.[18]

Hans-Georg Bohle, borrowing from the regional development model of John Friedmann, has coined the phrase 'hydraulic integration and spatial system' to refer to the Cōḻa period in South India.[19] Largely, this work is a complete rip-off of Burton Stein's segmentary state thesis, although the packaging appears to be new.[20] He identifies the evolution of five 'hydraulic systems' along the major river valleys of the Coromandel plains—Palar, Ponnaiyar, Kaveri, Vaigai and Tamraparani. The technical dimensions of this system were visible through 'the construction of large dams, weirs and sluices, raising of river dams and digging of large new tanks and irrigation channels'.[21] The institutional dimensions included the development of a central authority in the person of the king. He also sees the local producing communities as enjoying considerable autonomy. The *brāhmaṇas* acted as intermediaries between the ruler and the communities and effected an institutional integration that served to stabilise the hydraulic society. Spatially, a four-tier hierarchy of territorial units comprised of the Cōḻa empire as a whole, various subregional units or *maṇḍalams*, numerous peasant localities called *nāṭus* and finally, the many villages.[22]

What is very interesting about Gough's and Bohle's analysis is the incredibly huge time frame they use, and the complete lack of reference to any primary sources. In that sense, Stein's work appears to at least be rooted in historical methodology, although quite flawed in interpretation.

The debate on hydraulic systems seems to be predicated on the understanding of an authoritarian state and insular society, both being static, with colonialism actually bringing about major transformation in the political economy of agriculture. Scholars, such as Dharma Kumar and Haruka Yanagisawa, in the context of South India, on the other hand, appear to be anxious to not pin the growth of landless labour and distress in the agricultural sector in the 19th or the 20th centuries on colonial agrarian policies, which leads them to acknowledge some degree of change in the premodern context.[23]

In our understanding, irrigation is an important element in the development of agrarian societies, and the expansion and intensification of agriculture depended on the construction and maintenance of irrigation facilities. Furthermore, royal initiatives to promote irrigation in premodern societies were neither new nor exclusive to the Indian subcontinent. While the notion of hydraulic society and its extension as a hydraulic civilisation is quite problematic, as presented by Wittfogel, the significance of hydraulic machinery in the expansion and intensification of agricultural processes cannot be underestimated. In the next section, we look at a few works that have highlighted the importance of irrigation in the context of early medieval Tamil Nadu.

## II

Noboru Karashima actively engaged with the debates around the AMP and hydraulic society, starting from the premise that the view of an unchanging village community was completely erroneous and must be refuted at the onset.[24] His study of two villages in the Cōḻa heartland amply demonstrates this. Taking the analysis of Gough head-on, Karashima shows the flaws in her arguments. Gough uses Darcy Ribeiro's understanding of the theocratic irrigation state applied in the South American context to classify the Cōḻa state (ninth–thirteenth centuries CE), taking her analysis up until the eighteenth century. Here, communal landholding, peasant slavery and state control of irrigation and other means of production were stressed.[25] With the appearance of big temples and landed intermediaries in the Vijayanagara period, a despotic salvationist empire emerged, according to her. As Karashima argues, given the narrow micro-regional analysis, Gough misses, for instance, the integration of other regions, such as Jayamkoṇṭacōḻamaṇṭalam with Cōḻamaṇṭalam in the Cōḻa period.[26]

Karashima was not averse to sample studies, as long as they demonstrated a larger pattern. In a microstudy, using three inscriptions from the great temple in Tanjavur and one from Kaṅkaikoṇṭacōḻapuram, a total of 47 villages are identified. Various aspects related to the settlement, including temples, cemeteries, pasturage, cultivable land, etc. are disaggregated. On the question of irrigation, Karashima demonstrates that only in 29 villages do we have references to ponds or water tanks, indicating the extent and control as well as management of water resources. Further, some of these were apparently not meant for irrigation but for domestic purposes. Water channels appear only in 18 villages, indicating, according to him, the cooperation among villages to share irrigation water for agricultural purposes.[27]

Brian Murton, in his study of Salem and Baramahal region, peripheral regions in the political geography of the early medieval times, demonstrates the evolution of a close relationship between the *nāṭus* and irrigation systems.[28] Inscriptional records, particularly of the 12th or the 13th centuries, indicate the introduction of wetland cultivation and the presence of numerous non-agrarian craft and artisanal communities, who were obviously subsisting on agrarian surpluses. R.A.L.H. Gunawardana points out that even in the megalithic context, sites have been identified beside small reservoirs and artificial water bodies that indicate local level enterprise.[29] The early historic period in Sri Lanka saw the evolution of reservoirs, such as the third-century Lake Minneri, so much so that by the fifth century, there were 66 irrigation works including 11 more artificial lakes.[30] Possibly a century earlier, the cistern sluice was invented; we hear of sluices as well as waste weirs in later texts. In the South Indian context, Gunawardana identifies six reservoirs that were excavated by Pallava kings in early medieval Tamil Nadu—Mahendrataṭāka (Mahendravadi), Parameśvarataṭāka (Kuram), Tīraiyaṇēri (near Kanchi), Vayiramēkataṭāka (Uttaramerur), at Kāvēripākkam (near Walajapet) and Māmaṇḍūr (near Kanchi).[31] Gunawardana suggests, given the chronology of the appearance of the hydraulic systems, the nature of the technology and the geopolitical proximity of the two regions, that the technology moved from Sri Lanka to South India.[32]

In my own work on goddess traditions in the early medieval Tamil region, I have identified various goddesses who were considered beneficent deities because of their association with fertility and water, and were obviously locality deities. This explains why many of the names, such as Ēri Naṅkai, Ūruṭaiya Cuṉaimēn Naṅkai or Malai Naṅkai, suggest that she overlooked the settlement from her abode near the water bodies and on top of hills. The reference to Kōnēri Naṅkai—the benevolent goddess of the tank/lake—with the *ko* prefix, hints at a royal connection with the water source. The term *cuṉai* is conventionally understood as referring to a mountain pool or spring, a tank, reservoir or a pasture ground with tanks and shady trees.[33] This name Cuṉaimēn Naṅkai thus appears to refer to a benevolent goddess propitiated for water and agriculture. Ethnographic evidence indicates that groups of seven goddesses referred to as 'Saptakaṇṇikais' or Ākāśakaṇṇikais were the tutelary deities of tanks. Often, rows of sculptures were placed on temple bunds, and in North Arcot district, it is said that these seven were so quarrelsome that the stamping of their feet resulted in breaches emerging in the tanks.[34] In Maharashtra, Anne Feldhaus has referred to a group of river goddesses, again represented along reservoirs and river banks.[35] Apparently, the community was as concerned about harnessing water as the state.

What is interesting in these accounts is that without belabouring the point about the significance of irrigation in a predominantly agrarian society, there is an attempt to locate the contexts in which the technologies develop, and the implications for the political economy of agriculture. The diversity of technologies, the differential spread of irrigation methods, and royal, as well as non-royal, enterprise in irrigational systems is well-documented. While local efforts at the upkeep of these systems cannot be underestimated, what is striking is the concerted efforts by rulers in the early medieval period in Tamil Nadu to promote irrigation. While the welfare of the common people was the ideational principle behind such efforts, the major reason was obviously the generation of surpluses for the purpose of revenue extraction. It is in this sense that the state's role in promoting hydraulic technologies needs to be understood.

## III

In this section, I would like to draw attention to the figure of Gaṅgādhara in epic-Puranic mythology, and the meanings that can be read into this conceptualisation of the sectarian deity Śiva. Further, in the early medieval Tamil context, given the close parallels with gods in the evocation of the royal personality, the king appears to have substituted Śiva as the controller of waters. A few literary, inscriptional and iconographic examples will be used to demonstrate how effectively rulers during this period invoked such an image. Given our discussion on the importance of water resources in agrarian contexts, such an invocation cannot be seen as arbitrary, neither can its significance in asserting political authority be underplayed.

The icon of Gaṅgādhara depicts Śiva as the benefactor of Bhagīratha, the ruler of Ayodhya belonging to the legendary Sūryavaṁśa dynasty.[36] The king took to austerities to redeem his ancestors, the 60,000 sons of Sāgara, who were reduced to ashes by sage Kapila, by performing purificatory rituals in the holy waters of river Gaṅgā. However, since the cascade of heavenly waters would result in the destruction of the earth, lord Śiva is prevailed upon to control the river by receiving her on his head. Because he agrees to mediate between heaven and earth in this cosmogonic act, he is known thereafter as Gaṅgādhara.[37] The most evocative representation of this myth is found on a large, open-air rock relief carved on two monoliths in Mamallapuram in Tamil Nadu, about 15 metres high and 30 metres wide, where Bhagīratha's penance and Śiva's benefaction are clearly depicted (see Image 4.1a).

**Image 4.1a: Descent of Gaṅgā, Mamallapuram, c. early seventh century CE**

*Credit*: Sabya Sachi Ghosh

The scene depicts the 'descent of Gaṅgā', vividly describing the forest and riverscape, flora and fauna, and ascetics and semi-divine beings. The fissure between the two rocks is masterfully utilised to depict the flow of the river Gaṅgā, and just above the centre to the right of the stream is a bearded ascetic, with his right foot above the ground and bent at the knee and balancing on his left foot with folded palms held above his head (see Image 4.1b). To his right, towering above him, is the trident-wielding four-armed figure of Śiva. There is a tank on top of the large rock face where this has been carved, and it is believed that on special occasions water was released to symbolise the gushing of the waters. There are a number of other features of this scene that deserve comment, particularly the sages offering worship in numerous ways, the herd of elephants, including their calves, on the banks of the river and the interesting depiction of deer and lion as well as cat and mice in close proximity to one another.[38] All of these tell the story of the new cultural landscape being envisaged in the Tamil region with *brāhmaṇas* and the Brahmanical forms of worship, which was concomitant with the emergent state structure of that time. It is in this context that the images of the deer and lion shown together, or the other animals mentioned above, gain significance. They exhibit kingship, authority and protection, just as the release of the water clearly points towards control.[39]

**Image 4.1b: Descent of Gaṅgā (partial view), Mamallapuram, c. early seventh century CE**

*Credit*: Sabya Sachi Ghosh

In the *Bālakāṇḍa* of the *Rāmāyaṇa*, there is an allusion to river Gaṅgā being sought by the gods to purify the worlds, moving freely along three paths to finally join with the ocean.[40] Her father Himālaya offers her to the gods when they approach him with this request, as it was meant for the welfare of the world. In the following *sargas* of the text, the story of the river continues, and we find the tale of Bhagīratha's penance, along with his redemption through Śiva's intervention, also being recounted. The tale of *Gaṅgāvataraṇa* is predicated on the ability of Śiva alone to hold her, for the earth would not be able to withstand her fall from the heavens directly.[41] She took an extremely powerful form before plunging onto his head, where she was rendered into confusion due to the thick coils of his *jaṭa*. She remained trapped there, swirling endlessly in his locks, unable to find a way out.[42] The popular visualisation of the icon in the Tamil region, as we shall see later, is of Śiva extending his lock of hair to capture and tame the flow of the celestial river.

The *bhakti* tradition, marked by the composition of hymns by *nāyaṉārs* and *āḻvārs* to the sectarian deities Śiva and Viṣṇu respectively, can be understood as transforming the cultural landscape of the Tamil region, at a time when the process of state formation was underway. Motifs from the epics and the *Purāṇas* were utilised to locate iconic forms of these deities in specific sites. More importantly, mythologies of these deities were elaborated with a view to familiarising the local populace with the heroic feats of these deities. Among the many themes referred to by the Śaiva hymnists, the story of Gaṅgādhara was quite popular; however, what is interesting is the manner of portrayal of this icon. Kāraikkāl Ammaiyār, the only woman composer of hymns who lived in the fifth century CE, jokingly paints a scenario wherein the goddess who occupied the left half of Śiva's body became cognisant of Gaṅgā's presence on his head.[43] Appar (seventh century) at Tiruvilimilalai also refers to both these goddesses together: while Śiva tried to attract Umā on the one hand, with his austere, mendicant-like appearance, he let Gaṅgā swirl in his matted locks.[44] In the Tirukkōṭi Kuḻakar *patikam*, the seventh-century saint Cuntarar speaks of Kanyakumari being the home of the denizen of the forests, Kāṭukiḻāḷ.[45] This is also the place where Śiva is said to have escaped to, unable to bear the burden of the two women who shared his body—his consort and the celestial river Gaṅgā.[46]

These allusions are reminiscent of Kālidāsa, who, in the *Meghadūta*, refers to the jealousy of Gaurī because of Gaṅgā's presence in Śiva's *jaṭa*.[47] In the *Bālakāṇḍa*, the possible roots of this jealousy are laid out. Thwarted by the gods from bearing the seed of Śiva, his consort and the younger daughter of Himavan and Menā is furious and curses them to also be childless. However, Śiva had already released his semen, which was too fiery for anyone but Agni to hold it.[48] Agni, in turn, showered the semen over the river Gaṅgā who assumed a divine form.[49]

Haimavatī, the daughter of Himālaya, was apparently confused and burnt by the seed she was carrying. Was this confusion an indication of Gaṅgā's guilt at carrying the seed of her sister's husband? Also, the fact that the only force capable of countering and quelling her agony was again her sister's husband is further justifiable cause for Gaurī's jealousy, given the symbolic patriarchal allusion to the male as the dominant figure as far as a married couple was concerned. Given the frequent allusions to the polygamous family, Gaurī was perhaps indicating her affront at her sister's association with her husband, and the latter being given a superior position at the head of Śiva. Clearly, the Tamil hymns used this motif to their own advantage, serving to humanise Śiva at the psychological level and establish his power and control at the transcendent level.

The earliest image from early medieval Tamil Nadu is found at Tiruchirappalli in the rock-cut cave temple Lalitāṅkura Pallaveśvaragṛham, named after a title of Mahendravarman I (600–630 CE), where it is mentioned as a royal enterprise in a Sanskrit inscription found on the beam of the inner row of pillars here.[50] There is a huge panel on the left wall of the *maṇḍapa* opposite the cell that is carved out on the right wall; the back wall remains empty. This depicts a four-armed Gaṅgādhara Śiva, with his left leg straight and the right bent at the knee with the thigh parallel to the floor, as in the *ūrdhvajānu* pose (see Image 4.2).[51] The upper right arm holds a strand of his tresses and the upper left holds an *akṣamālā*, while the lower right holds a snake and the lower left is in *kaṭi*. To the left of his head is the minuscule figure of Gaṅgā with folded hands, visible above the hips from behind a cloud, and she appears to be descending into Śiva's outstretched lock. It is striking that Gaṅgā, the powerful river in the literary narratives, is insignificant in the representation of this myth, even though she provides Śiva with his iconic identity. But what is equally striking is the overpowering figure of Śiva, and our argument regarding the correspondence being sought between the deity and the ruler makes apparent the reason for this.

**Image 4.2: Gaṅgādhara, Tiruchirappalli, c. early seventh century CE**

*Credit*: Sabya Sachi Ghosh

In early Cōḻa iconography, there are about ten representations of this kind, and four images that include Pārvatī in the frame, although she is shown looking away from Śiva.[52] This is reminiscent of the *bhakti* hymnists' comment on Śiva angering Pārvatī by sharing his body with Gaṅgā, as discussed earlier. At the 11th-century magnum opus of the great king Rājarāja (985–1014 CE), the Rājarājeśvaram at Tanjavur, the first of the massive 'cathedral' temples of the Cōḻa period, the Tiruchirapalli imagery resurfaces, where it is Śiva in all his glory who occupies the frame, sans spouse. Gaṅgādhara is portrayed in a gentle *dvibhaṅga*, with Śiva's right hand bent at the elbow, palm facing the sky and fingers pointing to the head, holding the lock of hair carrying Gaṅgā.[53] But it is at Kaṅkāikoṇṭacōḻapuram, in the temple built by

Rājarāja's son Rājēndra (1012–1144 CE) and also called Rājarājeśvaram, that we have the most evocative Gaṅgādhāra Āliṅgaṇamūrti, with Pārvatī turned away to her left and Śiva cajolling her with one hand, as another is extended upwards to hold the lock of hair on which Gaṅgā rests (see Image 4.3). Both these rulers are credited with the expansion of the Cōḻa dominions, pushing the agrarian frontiers, structuring the administrative edifice and integrating the empire they were creating through conquest and consolidation. The iconographic plan of their temples was meant to reflect their imperial image, and icons like Gaṅgādhāra appeared to be appropriate choices to reinforce connections between sacred and temporal power.

**Image 4.3: Gaṅgādhara, Rājarājeśvaram temple, Gangaikonda Cholapuram, c. 11th–12th centuries CE**

*Credit*: Sabya Sachi Ghosh

Two early seventh-century Sanskrit inscriptions in Grantha script from the Lalitāṅkura Pallaveśvaragṛham at Tiruchirappalli are very important because, in addition to the Gaṅgā, they refer to the Kāvīrī river, which was the heartline of the Cō<u>l</u>a country.[54]

In the first verse of the first record, it is said:

> 'Being afraid (*sāśankā*) that the god who is fond of rivers (*nadīpriya*) having perceived the Kāvīrī, whose waters please the eye (*nayanābhirāma salilām*), who wears a garland of gardens (*ārāma mālādharām*), and who possesses lovely qualities (*priya guṇām*), might fall in love (with her), the daughter of the mountain (*girikanyakā*) has, I think, left her father's family and resides permanently on this mountain, calling this river the beloved of the Pallavas.' (Verse 1)[55]

In another verse, we are told that 'this mountain resembles the diadem of the Cō<u>l</u>a province (*viṣaya*), this temple of Hara its chief jewel (*mahāmaṇi*), and Śankara its splendour (*jyotih*).'[56]

The second inscription also refers to the ruler, called by two of his titles—Guṇabhara and Śatrumalla—as performing the benevolent act of construction of the temple on top of the mountain:

> 'King Śatrumalla built on this temple of Giriśa, the husband of the daughter of the king of mountains (*girindrakanyāpate*) ... after Hara had graciously asked him: "How could I, standing in a temple on earth, view the great power of the Cō<u>l</u>as or the river Kāvīrī?" King Guṇabhara, who resembled Manu in his manner of ruling, assigned to him this mountain temple.' (Verses 2–3)[57]

Stietencron interprets this icon and inscriptional reference in the context of Mahendravarman I's conflict with Durvinīta of the Western Gaṅgas, who had allied with Pulakeśin II, the Cālukya ruler of Badami.[58] The defeat of the enemies at Pu<u>ḷḷ</u>alūr provides meaning to the invocation of this icon. Just as river Gaṅgā had arrogantly challenged Śiva, the Gaṅgas had provoked Mahendravarman I. Similarly, the stoic posture of Śiva and his ability to easily quell the river was also the stance of the Pallava king in the face of his enemies. Thus, 'no image of any other form of Śiva, and no other myth could have served to translate this actual historical situation more effectively into a work of religious art.'[59]

There appears to be a problem in this direct interpretation of the development of the iconography, as the icon remained popular even during Cō<u>l</u>a times. Instead, it would be more fruitful to see this icon as an assertion of the supremacy of Śiva, at a time when sectarian concerns permeated the religious landscape. Śiva's performance of a feat—taming the celestial river in his locks of hair—was beyond the capacity of the other gods. Secondly, there is certainly a political association we can read in this icon. It was the standard format in inscriptions across the subcontinent to refer to the ruler as a conqueror, who had the goddess of victory, the earth goddess and the goddess of wealth as his consorts/supplicants. The transposition of the deity with the king through the employment of certain terminological and ritualistic devices allowed for the ruler's claim to supremacy as well.[60] It is in this sense that the iconography marking the exploits of great Puranic deities need to be read, which would also explain their prevalence across time and in different forms. The way god Śiva had tamed the river, the king also was staking a claim to do so. This was particularly relevant in the newly emerging state dependent on agricultural surplus.

The third important aspect is the significance of Gaṅgā as a cultural marker, which is known not only from inscriptions in India but also Sri Lanka. The emulation of Bhagīratha's actions permeates mythic lore, whether it is the case of the legendary Ceṅkuṭṭuvan, or the historical Rājendra Cōḻa. Perhaps, this is why the image of Śiva as the bearer of Gaṅgā appears in settings where the image of divine power is related to the temporal through the ideal of kingship. She not only waters the plains and ensures fertility of the soil, which is so crucial in an agrarian setting, her waters are also considered purificatory. Ritually, after cremation in the Brahmanical tradition, the scattering of the ashes in the river Gaṅgā is understood as providing *mokṣa*. The exposition in the *Bālakāṇḍa* of the *Rāmāyaṇa* on the course of the river Gaṅgā was meant to highlight this purifying aspect. The ruler as a benefactor as well as a conqueror is thus projected through association.

Most significant for our purposes in the context of our discussion in the previous sections is that harnessing the flowing river signifies the use of her waters. Hydraulic machinery was certainly an important component in a predominantly agrarian setting, and the king's act of controlling the waters indicates his act of benevolence as far as his toiling subjects were concerned. Śiva's act of grace is emulated here. It is certainly no accident that the inscriptions from Tiruchirappalli identify the river Kāvīrī with Gaṅgā, by alluding to the jealousy of the goddess Pārvatī. Further, by referring to the Kāvīrī as part of the Cōḻa country, there's subtle indication of Pallava control over a region outside their traditional domain. Many Cōḻa inscriptions also allude to the importance of both these rivers. For instance, in the Sanskrit *praśasti* of the Tiruvalangadu copper plate (1028 CE), the great-grandson of the eponymous Cōḻavarman is said to have brought the river of the gods, Gaṅgā, in the form of Kāverakanyakā to his own dominions, just as Bhagīratha brought the former down to the earth.[61] His descendant, Kalikālan, constructed embankments on either side of the river Kāvīrī.[62] While praising the exploits of Rājendra Cōḻa (Madhurāntaka/Uttama Cōḻa), we are told that he sent his commander to conquer the rulers of kingdoms along the banks of the Gaṅgā. The purpose behind this was to bring the waters of Gaṅgā into his own realm through the power of his arms, rather than through austerities like Bhagīratha.[63] His commander brought the most sacred (*pāvanam param*) waters back, which were received by Rājendra.[64] He is then said to have constructed a tank, Cōḻa-Gaṅgam, in his own *maṇḍala* containing the Gaṅgā *jalam*. Further, this tank itself was a *jayastambham* or pillar of victory.[65]

To conclude, I would like to reiterate that the coinage 'hydraulic apparatus' has gained a pejorative colour, thanks to the writings of Wittfogel and others, since it appears to bring back the clearly untenable notion of the AMP. It is my contention that we need to retrieve such terminology and locate these apparatuses within contexts to identify modes of their creation, maintenance and expansion. In the Tamil (and presumably other) contexts, there is no single term to refer to various devices and technology for the purpose of water harnessing. T.M. Srinivasan refers to the *Caṅkam* (Sangam) texts and early Tamil records that mention devices for water-lifting like the *picotah* (ēttapuḻam, in common usage *ēṟṟam*/*ēttam*); *tev* and *edā* were palm leaf baskets, while *piḻa* was a metal basket.[66] The *ēttapādam* were the *jala yantra* or water levers found in Sanskrit texts.[67] Clearly, the local enterprise was behind these technologies providing 'intermittent' water supply. It is from the Pallava and Pāṇṭiya periods that we find references to the reservoirs—*ēri*, *taṭāka*/*kuḷam* and *kāl*/*vāykkāl*/*aṟṟukkāl*, as well as to sluices, *madagu*/*tūmbu*.[68] This is also the period of consolidation of state power, predicated on resource appropriation by the ruling elites. It is in this context that state interest in creating and maintaining irrigation works needs to be situated. It is also in this context that the significance of the icon of Gaṅgādhara Śiva can be read, as it was introduced at this point and became a regular feature of early medieval temple art.

## Endnotes

1 Karl A. Wittfogel, 'Development Aspects of Hydraulic Societies,' 15, www.columbia.edu/itc/anthropology/v3922/pdfs/wittfogel.pdf.
2 Ibid., 17.
3 Ibid., 17–18.
4 D.D. Kosambi, 'The Basis of Despotism,' *The Economic Weekly,* 2 November 1957, 1417–1419, https://www.epw.in/system/files/pdf/1957_9/44/the_basis_of_despotism.pdf.
5 R.S. Sharma and D.N. Jha, 'The Economic History of India up to AD 1200: Trends and Prospects,' *Journal of the Economic and Social History of the Orient* 17, no. 1 (1974): 48–80.
6 Irfan Habib, 'The Peasant in Indian History,' General President's Address, *Proceedings of the Indian History Congress*, 43rd Session (1982): 7.
7 Bipan Chandra, 'Karl Marx, His Theories of Asian Societies, and Colonial Rule,' *Review* 5, no. 1 (Summer 1981): 19–20.
8 Ibid., 21.
9 Ibid., 84.
10 R.S. Sharma, *Aspects of Political Ideas and Institutions in Ancient India* (Delhi: Motilal Banarsidass, 1996, 1959), 77.
11 Ibid., 78–79.
12 Romila Thapar, 'Ideology and Interpretation of Early Indian History,' *Review* 5, no. 3 (Winter 1982): 403.
13 Shireen Moosvi, 'The Pre-Colonial State,' *Social Scientist*, 33, no. 3/4 (March–April 2005): 42.
14 Ibid., 42.
15 Ibid.
16 Kathleen Gough, 'Modes of Production in Southern India,' *Economic and Political Weekly* 15, no. 5–7 (16 February 1980): 337.
17 Ibid., 337.
18 Ibid., 345.
19 Hans-Georg Bohle, 'From Centre to Periphery: Changing Spatial Structures in Rural South India, 985–1985,' *GeoJournal* 10, no. 1, South Asian Affairs II (January 1985): 7.

20 Much has been said on Burton Stein's analysis, including by me, and these will not be repeated here. See R. Mahalakshmi, 'Re-visiting the Political Economy of Pre-Modern Tamil Nadu,' in *The Complex Heritage of Early India: Essays in Memory of R.S. Sharma*, ed. D.N. Jha (New Delhi: Manohar, 2014), 555–584.

21 Bohle, 'From Centre to Periphery,' 7–8.

22 Ibid., 8.

23 See Dharma Kumar, 'South India,' in *Cambridge Economic History of India*, eds Dharma Kumar and Tapan Raychaudhuri, Vol. 2 (Cambridge: Cambridge University Press, [1983] 1989), 208–211; Haruka Yanagisawa, *A Century of Change: Caste and Irrigated Lands in Tamilnadu, 1860s–1970s* (New Delhi: Manohar, 1996).

24 Noboru Karashima, 'The Past as Known from Tamil Inscriptions: Village Community and Challenge to the Caste System,' 5, https://f.hypotheses.org/wp-content/blogs.dir/439/files/2012/05/Karashima_paper_toronto_2012.pdf.

25 Noboru Karashima, *History and Society in South India* (New Delhi: Oxford University Press, 2001), xxiv, xxviii–xxix.

26 Ibid., xxix.

27 Ibid., 10.

28 B. Murton, 'The Emergence of Sedentary Agriculture in Interior Tamil Nadu in the Thirteenth Century,' in *Structure and Society in Early South India: Essays in Honour of Noboru Karashima*, ed. Kenneth R. Hall (New Delhi: Oxford University Press, 2001), 173.

29 R.A.L.H Gunawardana, 'Intersocietal Transfer of Hydraulic Technology in Precolonial South Asia: Some Reflections Based on a Preliminary Investigation,' *Southeast Asian Studies* 22, no. 2 (September 1984): 115–116.

30 Ibid., 118.

31 Ibid., 119–121.

32 Ibid., 122–124.

33 Thomas Burrow and Murray B. Emeneau, *Dravidian Etymological Dictionary* (New Delhi: Oxford University Press, 1961), 2717. See also, *Madras Tamil Lexicon*, Vol. 3 (Madras: University of Madras, 1924–1936), 1, 554; *cuṉai* (3): mountain pool or spring, tank, reservoir, pasture ground with shady trees.

34 Rev. Henry Whitehead, *Village Gods of South India* (Oxford: Oxford University Press, 1916), 26. Also, cited in Yoshinori Onishi, *Feminine Multiplicity: A Study of Groups of Multiple Goddesses in India* (New Delhi: Srī Satguru, 1997), 43.

35 Anne Feldhaus, *Water and Womanhood: Religious Meanings of Rivers in Maharashtra* (New York: Oxford University Press, 1995).

36 See Steven G. Darian, *The Ganges in Myth and History* (New Delhi: Motilal Banarsidass, [1978] 2001), 18–19.

37 Heinrich von Stietencron, *Hindu Myth, Hindu History: Religion, Art, and Politics* (Delhi: Permanent Black, 2005), 10.

38 C. Sivaramamurti, *Mahābalipuram* (New Delhi: Archaeological Survey of India, 2004 [1952]), 22–23.

39 A different interpretation of the image is that it depicts the penance of Arjuna as narrated in the Mahābhārata to obtain the Pāśupata weapon from Śiva, a story that was embellished in Bhāravi's retelling in the sixth century poem *Kirātārjunīyam*. See, C. Sivaramamurti, *Mahābalipuram*, 24. A third interpretation sees both these interpretations as valid and as deliberately used by the artists and patron, Narasiṁhavarman, also known as Māmalla (the great wrestler), to reflect the persona of the king in multiple ways. The bringing down of Gaṅgā river is one motif, while the other plays on the story of Arjuna encountering Śiva in the form of a hunter (Kirāta), and not recognising him, engaging in a wrestling match with him. This has been compared to the literary device *sleśa*, rendering double meanings through one allusion. Yigal Bronner, *Extreme Poetry: The South Asian Movement of Simultaneous Narration* (New York: Columbia University Press, 2010), 92–97.

40 *The Rāmāyaṇa of Vālmīki An Epic of Ancient India, Vol. 1, Bālakāṇḍa*, Introduction and translation by Robert P. Goldman (Princeton: Princeton University Press), *Sarga* 35, Verses 10–17, 190.

41 Ibid., *Sarga* 41, Verse 22–23, 205.

42 Ibid., *Bālakāṇḍa*, *Sarga* 42, 206.

43 *Tiruviraṭṭai Maṇimālai*, Verse 5, in *Kāraikkāl Ammaiyār Tirumuṟai*, ed. Vi Kalyanasundaranar (Chennai: Balan Patippuk Kalakam, 1947), 14.

44 T.V. Gopala Iyer and Francois Gros, eds., *Tēvāram Hymnes Śivaites Du Pays Tamoul*, Vols 1–3 (Pondicherry: Institut Francais D'Indologie, 1984, 1985, 1991) Vol. 2, Patikam 266, Verse 10, Line 1, p. 303.

45 *Tēvāram*, Vol. 2, Patikam 32, Verse 5, Line 3, p. 401.

46 The story of Gaṅgā is well known in the epic-Puranic tradition. Bhagīratha, born in the lineage of a great king called Sāgara, performed severe austerities to bring the celestial river down on earth to purify the ashes of his ancestors. Because the torrent of the river would have wreaked destruction on earth, Bhagīratha prayed to lord Śiva to hold her in his hair, so that the torrent could be stemmed, and the river could thereafter flow gently on earth. See Steven G. Darian, *The Ganges in Myth and History* (New Delhi: Motilal Banarsidass, 2001 [1978]), 17–19.

47 'The Cloud-Messenger', in *Kalidasa Translations of Shakuntala, and Other Works,* Arthur W. Ryder (London: J.M. Dent and Sons, 1914), 194, https://www.sacred-texts.com/hin/sha/sha17.htm.

48 *The Rāmāyaṇa of Vālmīki An Epic of Ancient India, Vol. 1, Bālakāṇḍa, Sarga* 35, 190–193.

49 Ibid., *Sarga* 36, Verses 7–14, 194.

50 T.V. Mahalingam, ed., *Inscriptions of the Pallavas,* No. 35 (New Delhi: Indian Council of Historical Research, 1988), 133.

51 For a description of the *ūrdhvajānu,* see Adya Rangacharya, *The Nāṭyaśāstra English Translation with Critical Notes* (New Delhi: Munshiram Manoharlal, 1996), 93.

52 See R. Mahalakshmi, *The Making of the Goddess: Ko<u>r</u><u>r</u>avai-Durgā in the Tamil Religious Traditions* (New Delhi: Penguin, 2011), 278.

53 Ibid., 281.

54 Mahalingam, *Inscriptions of the Pallavas,* nos 32 and 33, 124–127.

55 Ibid., 124; E. Hultzch, ed., *South Indian Inscriptions* 1, no. 33 (Madras: Government Press, 1890): 29.

56 E. Hultzch, *South Indian Inscriptions,* 30.

57 Ibid., 30.

58 Steitencron, *Hindu Myth,* 11.

59 Ibid.

60 See Kesavan Veluthat, *The Political Structure of Early Medieval South India* (Delhi: Orient Longman, 1993), 60.

61 H. Krishna Sastri, ed., 'Tiruvalangadu Copper-Plates,' in *South Indian Inscriptions* 3, Part 3, Plate IIIa, Verse 35 (Madras: Government Press, 1929), 395.

62 Ibid., Verse 42.

63 Ibid., Verses 109–110.

64 Ibid., Verses 115–118.

65 Ibid., Verse 124.

66 T.M. Srinivasan, 'Water-Lifting Devices in Ancient India: Their Origin and Mechanisms (From the Earliest Times to Circa AD 1000),' *Indian Journal of the History of Science* 5, no. 2 (1970): 381.

67 Ibid., 382.

68 Noboru Karashima, 'Agrarian Development', in *A Concise History of South India: Issues and Perspectives,* ed. Noburu Karashima (New Delhi: Oxford University Press, 2014), 93–96.

# II

# Conceptualising the Divine Feminine: Forms, Meanings and Symbols

# 5

# Giving *Ākāra* to the Goddess: Kālī in Textual and Visual Traditions

Sneha Ganguly

One of the key questions to have been raised by various scholars is the antiquity of image worship in India.[1] In *Introduction to Indian Art*, Ananda Kentish Coomaraswamy argues that the worship of the personified powers of nature in anthropomorphic form was a marker of early Vedic religion, but there is no evidence, and little probability, that what was described in the texts materialised in the form of sculptures or paintings.[2] At the same time, he draws our attention to the autochthonous (Dravidian) cults (of the phallus, mother goddesses, *Nāgas*, *Yakṣas*, etc.),[3] and suggests the possibility of images being made of wood and bricks by the non-Aryan communities.[4] He also suggests the possibility of the Dravidian elements playing an important role in the development of popular image worship.

T.A. Gopinatha Rao, another pioneer in the field of art history, posits that the worship of the image in India appears to be extremely old and can be dated back to the ancient period and probably even the Vedic times.[5] He disagrees with the argument that image worship was a result of the followers of Buddha worshipping him after his death, maintaining that it was prevalent long before the time of Buddha, and draws a connection between yoga and image worship.[6] After looking at various sources, he states that 'development of image worship amongst the Hindus was contemporaneous with, if not older than, the development of yoga, which is older than Buddha as he was declared to have been initiated into its practice....'[7]

One might wonder about the need felt for worshipping images. Rao argues that according to the *Śāstras*, image worship was prescribed for those who couldn't attain the height of realisation and were weak and unevolved in nature.[8] The images were, thus, the representations of various conceptions of the divine, constructed for the ignorant to facilitate the realisation of the supreme Brahman within oneself.[9]

Scholars working on images of the Indian subcontinent recognised the need for contextualising them in a specific culture, and reading and understanding the images as they might have been understood at the time of their production. One of the ways in which this kind of study could be undertaken was by examining the relationship between the textual tradition and visual tradition, and also by placing them within the larger context of the temple. This essay aims to study how Kālī is represented in the textual and visual traditions, and understand the various aspects she symbolises that contribute to her conceptualisation. Though the effort will be to foreground the visuals, an attempt will be made to look at the Puranic corpus to study the context in which she appears in these texts.

## Visualising Kālī in Myths

Kālī is a feminine adjectival form meaning the dark, blue-black one, but it has undertones of the masculine noun *kāla*, which means 'time or the fullness of time',[10] and is also associated with Śiva. In the *Liṅga Purāṇa*, while saluting the forms of Śiva, it is stated, 'O Vāmadeva, salutation to you, the eldest being, the bestower of boons, salutation to Rudra and Kāla, the controller of time.'[11] In another reference in the same text, Śiva is explicitly described as the producer of time.[12]

Due to the nature of the visual sources being examined, such as stone sculptures and bronzes, one cannot say for sure what the colour of the goddess is, but there are many references in textual traditions that indicate that the goddess was considered blue-black (the colour of collyrium) in complexion.[13]

The first time we meet goddess Kālī is in the *Devī Māhātmya*, the oldest-known treatise on Devī as the supreme truth and creator of the universe, composed in the sixth century CE. This is in the context of the battle between the goddess and the demons, Caṇḍa and Muṇḍa: 'Ambikā then uttered a great wrathful cry against them and her face became *black as ink* [emphasis mine] in anger and from the knitted brows of her forehead's surface immediately came forth Kālī.'[14] In *Agni Purāṇa* (ninth century CE), she is mentioned as the 'controller of all beings,'[15] and the 'goddess or energy regulating the order of eternal time....'[16]

In the *Liṅga Purāṇa* (sixth to tenth centuries CE), an interesting myth is told. A *rākṣasa* named Dāruka was creating havoc and nobody could stop him. The gods and sages went to Śiva, who then requested Pārvatī to kill the demon. On listening to Śiva, she entered his body and turned herself into the colour of the poison lodged in the throat of Śiva, who then from his third eye produced Kālī with a blue throat. Along with Kālī, Vijayaśrī (the goddess of victory) also appeared.[17] 'With the emerging of Kālī with *the blue throat and issuing fire flames from her mouth*, all the humans, gods and *siddhas*, including Brahmā, Viṣṇu and Indra fled in fright. She had *an additional eye in the forehead; a crescent moon lodged over her head, the terrific poison in the throat and held a horrible trident in her hand*. She was adorned with *all suitable ornaments* over all the limbs of her body' (emphasis mine).[18]

In another reference from the same text, in the context of the destruction of the city of Tripura, Kālī is mentioned. She is described as holding a skull cup in her hand. She was clad only in elephant hide, holding a trident in her hands and drinking the blood of *asuras*.[19] It is to be noted that while in other references she is clad in tiger skin, here she is said to be wearing elephant hide. This probably indicates her association with Śiva who is known to have vanquished the *asura* who took the form of an elephant to disturb meditating devotees. One of Śiva's famous forms in iconography is that of *Gajasaṁhāramūrti*.[20]

In the *Upapurāṇa* text from eastern India, the *Kālikā Purāṇa* (tenth or eleventh century CE), which is the first major *Śākta* exposition, there are again many references to her complexion. In one of the references, she is described as being 'black in complexion, seated on a lion ... a blue lotus and a sword in her hands while the other two hands are in the *varada* and *abhaya* pose. She has red eyes, open hair....'[21] In another mention, at the time of feeding rice for the very first time, Himavat calls his daughter Kālī as her complexion resembled the petals of the blue lotus.[22] Her complexion is again alluded to during a conversation between Śiva and Kālī, where Śiva tells her: 'O Kālī, you are as black as the spreading collyrium; you must however, true to your womanly conduct, have a mutual dialogue with Ūrvaśī and host of other nymphs....'[23]

E.B. Havell, D.R. Rajeshwari and Sarbeshwar Sathpathy, among others, have tried to figure out why the goddess is depicted in blue-black colour, but their arguments are primarily based on the tantric tradition. Havell[24] argues that Kālī's association with Śiva (he believes that Kālī is Śiva's *śakti*) in the form of Mahākāla or time resulted in the goddess dissolving the world at the end of the cosmic cycle. She even destroyed her own husband and reduced nature and the *devas* to their formless, unconditioned state. This understanding of Havell is based on his reading of the *tantras* from where he quotes the symbolism of the colour black.[25]

Rajeshwari argues that the colour black denotes the *tāmasic* tendency, as the goddess embodies *tamasaguṇa*. Black isn't actually a colour but the negation of colours, as all colours get absorbed in it. Kālī is black as she denotes the ultimate power where all distinctions disappear. She is *nirguṇa* and helps devotees transform themselves into *nirguṇa* so as to merge with the supreme.[26] 'In the power of time, all colour dissolves into darkness and all shapes return to shapelessness in the all-pervading darkness of the eternal night.'[27] One point that needs to be kept in mind is that Rajeshwari's discussion of goddess Kālī is in the context of the *Daśa Mahāvidyā*.

Thomas B. Coburn sees Kālī as the destroyer, bringing things to an end.[28] In the *Koṭirudra Saṃhitā* of the *Śiva Purāṇa*, an important text within the text, dated to ninth or tenth century CE, it is stated: 'Restrictions of time are for others and not for Rudra. He is Mahākāla himself associated with Mahākālī. The *brāhmaṇas* claim Rudra and Kālī to be the cause of all....'[29] All the Puranic references to Kālī are unambiguous about her *raudra rūpa* or terrifying form, marked by her dark and fiery appearance. Further, they suggest a transcending of the blood and gore she is connected with by linking her to *kāla* or time. In the *Liṅga Purāṇa* and *Śiva Purāṇa*, the association with Śiva is obvious; in the *Agni Purāṇa*, a *Vaiṣṇava* context for the appearance of the goddess is found. In the chapter dealing with the 'manifestation of Viṣṇu as Kṛṣṇa', it is stated that when Kaṁsa went to kill the girl child of Devakī, she threatened him with impending death and vanished. 'Having told so, she disappeared. And she having killed Śumbha and other demons and being praised by Indra (was differently known as) the Āryā, Durgā, Ambikā and as Bhadrakālī (the beneficent Kālī)...'[30]

The Puranic corpus is replete with references to Kālī's association with death and destruction, and the emission of flames at the time of dissolution, all of which point to her *ugra* nature. In *Śiva Purāṇa*'s *Sṛṣṭi Khaṇḍa* of *Rudra Saṁhitā*, it is stated that Kālī's form should be linked with the Rudra form of Śiva, and that she should engage (along with Rudra) in the dissolution of the world.[31]

In the retelling of the myth of Dakṣa's sacrifice, it is stated: 'Then Rudra, the destroyer of the universe, plucked a lock of hair from his head and threw it over the mountain.... Vīrabhadra was born. He looked like the flames of the fire of the time of dissolution.... From the other part of the matted lock of hair, Mahākālī was born. O dear one, she was terrible to look at, and was surrounded by crores of goblins.'[32] In another reference, Kālī is engaged in a battle with Śaṁkhacūḍa, where she throws fire during the time of dissolution at the demon.[33] Further, she is said to shine like the flame of fire at the end of the *kalpa* that burns the universe.[34] The *Liṅga Purāṇa* shows an interesting imagery of Śiva as the child who pacifies Kālī after the anger of the goddess' fire grips the universe in terror.[35] The myth seems to highlight her benevolent nature once pacified by Śiva, when otherwise she is seen as a terrifying goddess.

## Kālī in Prescriptive Texts

Prescriptive literature, like the *Purāṇas*, have stray references to Kālī and she is not directly mentioned, though, through the symbolism of the colour black and association of *tamasa* with destruction, we can argue they all indicate to Kālī being *tāmasic* in character. In the *Viṣṇudharmottara Purāṇa*, composed around the fifth or sixth century CE in and around modern-day Kashmir, there isn't a single reference to Kālī. Did the artists not make images of Kālī before she was mentioned in the textual tradition? Unless we find more visual evidence, it would not be possible to provide any definitive answer to this question. What we do find in this text is a reference to the symbolism of the colour black. Chapter 47, which deals with rules of image-making, says: 'The universe is regarded as transformation of the supreme being. All transformation consists of *kṛṣṇa* (black) colour, and through that is the sustenance of the worldly life....'[36] Stella Kramrisch adds a note to the translation, stating 'there is a pun on the word *kṛṣṇa*, suggesting at the same time an identification of Brahmā and Viṣṇu or Kṛṣṇa, and making the black colour, i.e. the strain responsible for the manifestation of the world, contrasted with pure existence that becomes no stain and no colour.'[37] There is also reference to the association of the *raudra* form with *tamas* and destruction. In Chapter 44, while Mārkaṇḍeya tells Vajra how to make images, especially that of Viṣṇu and his three forms (since it is primarily a Vaiṣṇava text), it is stated that 'the *raudra* (form) is *tamas*—predominating, causing destruction'.[38]

In the *Mayamatam*, an important *Śilpa* text of South Indian provenance of the ninth to twelfth centuries CE, the part where the text discusses the installation of the mothers (*mātṛkās*) provides a description of Cāmuṇḍī, and the identities of the latter and Kālī are collapsed. Even in the *Devī Māhātmya*, the identities of these two goddesses are interchanged, especially glaring in the myth of *Raktabīja*.[39]

In *Mayamatam* it is stated: 'Cāmuṇḍī holds the skull and the trident and makes the gestures of bestowing and absence of fear. (Otherwise) she is represented with eight arms; she holds, in addition to the trident and the skull, the mace, the bow, the sword, the shield, the noose, the arrow, on the left (?). Such are (the attributes) (held) in her eight hands. When she has 10 arms, however, the *ḍamaru* and the trident (?) are to be added to what has already been given. She has red eyes; she is seated aslant (?) and has cobra in place of a breast band; she wears a garland of heads as sacrificial thread (*yajñopavīta*) and her mount is a corpse. She has thin stomach and she has three eyes. She is clothed in a tiger skin and has hair arrangements of bristling snakes. She grants wishes. Kālī's limbs are emaciated and she is black and her back to a banyan. Her face is marked by terrifying fangs; Cāmuṇḍī's emblem is a vulture.'[40]

*Mānasāra* (ninth to twelfth centuries CE), a comprehensive treatise on iconography and architecture, doesn't have references to the iconography of Kālī, though the text does allude to her in the chapter, 'The One Storied Building'. While discussing the images that are to be carved on the doors and pavilions of the temple, it states: 'The image of *Vyāna Dakṣinā* (Kālī with projecting tongue pressed between the teeth) should be carved on the middle compartment to the right of the (main) temple. Above that, on the compartment, in the neck part, should be the image of Vīrabhadra in a singing posture.'[41] Mention is also made of her temple being outside the village towards the northern direction.[42] Interestingly, Durgā is the one who is always associated with the northern direction, which has been interpreted as related to the protection of settlements, since the north, as per Āgamic and other traditions, is associated with danger.[43]

Even when she is not mentioned directly, as in the *Śilparatnakośa*, a *Śilpa* text from Odisha, dated to the 17th century CE, the discussion on the types of images placed on the temple walls indicate that Kālī (in the mythological description and visuals) would fall both in the *ugra* and *bhayaṁkara* category. The text says, 'Three types of images are best: *lāsya, ugra, bhayaṁkara* (gentle, powerful, terrifying), corresponding to the three *guṇas, sattva, rajas* and *tamas* respectively. Peaceful face, gentle hands, absence of muscles, always endowed with youthfulness, these are the features of a gentle image (*lāsya vigraha*). The characteristics of a powerful image (*ugra*) are beautiful limbs and a fierce face. A terrifying (*bhayaṁkara*) image has scattered limbs and a dreadful face.'[44] As will be seen in the subsequent discussion, the analysis of iconography and mythologies of Kālī will categorise her in both *ugra* and *bhayaṁkara* kinds of images.

## Kālī in Early Medieval Indian Iconography

Images of Kālī have been extremely difficult to locate.[45] In this essay, I will be focusing on six stone and one bronze sculptures, all from South India, from the early medieval period (ninth to twelfth centuries CE). These will be taken up for discussion in terms of their iconographical specificities, common symbols and their correspondence with textual traditions, both symbolically and in terms of physical attributes. The provenance of two of the images discussed here is the same: the west wall of the *garbhagṛha* of the Lakṣmaṇeśvara temple at Avani in the Kolar district of Karnataka, dated approximately between the eighth and fourteenth centuries CE. There is one image, identified as Niśumbhasūdinī/Kālī, found in the Ugramahākālī temple at Tanjavur, dated to c. 851–875 CE. Two images of Kālī used here are from the National Museum, Delhi, although originally their provenance is believed to have been from around Chennai; one dates back to the ninth century and the other to the twelfth century. The bronze image used here is of a dancing Kālī found in the Śrī Vaṭāraṇyeśvarar temple at Tiruvalangadu, belonging to the late Cōḻa period.

According to Rao, images are classified in various ways; one way is to categorise based on their terrific (*raudra* or *ugra*) or pacific (*śānta or saumya*) nature. The *raudra* or *ugra* images are generally classified by sharp, long tusks and nails and many hands carrying *āyudhas* or weapons. These images also have 'wide circular eyes, flames of fire round their heads, and are in some cases adorned with human skulls and bones. The *raudra* forms of images are worshipped for the attainment of objects requiring the use of violence.'[46] The association of evil and violence with deities also suggests discordant notes in the process of assimilation.[47]

**Image 5.1: Niśumbhasūdinī /Kālī, Ugramahākālī temple, Tanjavur, c. 851–875 CE**

*Credit*: American Institute of Indian Studies

The iconographic representation of goddess Kālī points to her *raudra* nature in at least four images in consonance with the mythological descriptions. Even when she has a *saumya* expression, her *āyudhas*, which will be discussed later, indicate her association with death and destruction. The hair of the goddess in Images 5.1, 5.4, 5.5 and 5.6 is in the *jvālākeśa/ jvalitaśikhā* form, literally meaning 'flamed hair'. This can be seen as a substitute for the flames of fire around the head that signifies destruction[48] as seen in the case of the famous bronze image of dancing Kālī from the Śrī Vaṭāraṇyeśvarar Temple at Tiruvalangadu.

**Image 5.2: Caption: Kālī, west wall (*garbhagṛha*), Lakṣmaṇeśvara temple, Avani, c. 8th–14th centuries CE**

*Credit*: American Institute of Indian Studies

Coburn highlights that the myths of Kālī emitting fire eventually came to symbolise Kālī as an agent of burning of the world (possibly also suggesting rejuvenation after destruction).[49] Therefore, it seems that the *jvālākeśa* denotes characteristics of destruction and dissolution, which was largely associated with Śiva. Coomaraswamy uses the dance of Śiva and its association with the burning ground to understand the symbolism of fire—'a visual connect between the earth and sky, the perceived and the intuitive, and the tangible and the intangible'—represented in the circle of fire or the *tiruvāci* that encompassed the Naṭarāja form of Śiva,[50] which later came to be associated with Kālī. In the rest of the images, the hair of the goddess is in the *jaṭāmaṇḍala* style (most noticeable in Image 5.2), unbound and dishevelled and appearing as if snakes are coming out of her head, which is reminiscent of the imagery of Medusa in the Greek context.[51] This way of wearing the hair too signifies the fearsome and destructive aspect of the wearer.[52] Seema Mohanty connects Kālī's hair to her representing the wild untamed aspects of the forest, which is the place where sex and violence is unrestricted, primarily governed by the quest for survival; the hair is a metaphor for sexuality (of women especially) and in the Brahmanical tradition, the widow's hair is shaved off to de-sexualise her while the 'young virgin's hair' is always tied.[53] In the case of Ko<u>r</u>ravai as highlighted by R. Mahalakshmi, her 'dangerous power that comes from her beauty underlines the emphasis on her innate violence and aggression. It appears that the power of the goddess derives in part from her sexuality. It also underscores the equation of women's sexuality with danger.'[54]

Image 5.3 depicts Kālī standing on what seems like a corpse, accompanied by a jackal. It is a very significant image, as the jackal and corpse together seem to indicate that the setting is that of a cremation ground. In the *Pārvatī Khaṇḍa* of *Rudra Saṁhitā*, Menā, seeing Śiva and his *gaṇas*, started cursing everyone and told her daughter, 'stopping the serving of the lion, you served a jackal...'[55] This statement clearly associates jackals with Śiva as he is said to reside in the cremation ground. In the *Liṅga Purāṇa*, after killing Dāruka, Kālī was still so angry that the entire universe was gripped by terror from the 'anger of the fire of the goddess Kālī'. Śiva, on seeing this, took the form of a child and lodged himself on the cremation ground to pacify the goddess.[56]

**Image 5.3: Kālī, west wall (*garbhagṛha*), Lakṣmaṇeśvara temple, Avani, c. 8th–14th centuries CE**

*Credit:* American Institute of Indian Studies

In *Devī Māhātmya*, during the battle of the goddess with Śumbha-Niśumbha, the *śakti* of Caṇḍikā, gruesome and yelping like a hundred jackals, threatened the *asuras* that if they don't do the needful, her jackals will satiate themselves on their flesh.[57] Though it is not clear who this *śakti* is, but going by her nature and the association with jackals, one can argue that she is none other than Kālī, though she is called Śivadūtī, since she sends Śiva as her messenger but is later identified with Kālī.[58] In *Kālikā Purāṇa* also, Śivadūtī is said to be surrounded by jackals. Interestingly, the iconographical description of Śivadūtī in *Kālikā Purāṇa* has some similarities with Image 5.3. It is stated that 'Śivadūtī is with four arms, a huge body, which shines like the vermillion, with red teeth, she wears a wreath of human hands, along with matted hair, provided with the crescent moon, she is splendid with her snake earrings and snake necklace, she shines brightly, with her (long) nails, wears a tiger skin as the garment, holds a trident and a sword in her two right hands, a noose, a shield of hide in her two left upper and lower hands respectively, her face is rough, lips are thick, and she is tall in stature, and looks dreaded, she stands by putting the right foot on the corpse and while her left foot on the back of a jackal, and surrounded by hundred of jackals.'[59] This particular image could possibly depict the goddess Śivadūtī, who is strongly associated with Kālī in the textual tradition.

One of the most interesting iconographic features that has intrigued scholars is the *muṇḍamālā* or the garland of skulls that the goddess wears, depicted in all except one sculpture (Image 5.4). Kālī isn't the only goddess who wears the *mālā*; even Cāmuṇḍā wears it, which is one of the reasons scholars have identified one as the other many a time. This collapsing of iconographic identities is also in keeping with the description in the *Mayamatam*. In textual traditions, mention is made of Kālī's 'skull-topped staff' and sometimes she is said to be carrying a *kapāla* or a skull. The first is visible in only one image (Image 5.2), while the latter is found in two images. Scholars have understood the association of the skull with Kālī in different ways, including reading it against the backdrop of Tantric philosophy,[60] and from a psychoanalytical perspective.[61]

**Image 5.4: Kālī, National Museum, most probably from Madras, c. 12th CE**

*Credit:* American Institute of Indian Studies

Jeffery J. Kripal and C.D. Daly have tried to study Kālī (in the Tantric literary tradition) from the psychoanalytical perspective but ended up using European materials to decode many of the iconographical features of the goddess. Daly argues that the garland of skulls, the skirt of arms (a later iconographic development) and the lolling tongue take on phallic meanings. For Daly, Kālī is the 'castrating mother' who produces anxiety in the son and dominates the father, and, in a way, delays the son's anxiety about his own feared castration by directing her rage to the father. This explanation is based on the reading of 'Hindu mythology as a product of an elaborate process of psychological splitting (between the two contradictory mother figures), in which the different features and attributes of the son's early object-libido are projected onto the screen of religious belief'.[62]

According to Rajeshwari, Kālī is the supporter of both the dead and the living, and the *muṇḍamālā* actually highlights this attribute of the goddess. Just as day and night are inseparable, similarly life and death are inseparable too, and the common support for both life and death is Kālī. 'All life rests on her and whatever remains after life also depends upon her. The dead leave traces behind, which also rests upon her. Hence, she is represented as wearing a garland of skulls. The skulls once carried life and are left behind as the reminder of death.' As per esoteric explanations, this garland is made up of the heads of the demons the goddess has conquered, as a power of righteousness.[63] In *Devī Māhātmya*, it is Kālī who cuts off the head of the demons Caṇḍa–Muṇḍa. 'Kālī…mounting her great lion, the goddess ran at Caṇḍa and Muṇḍa, having seized him [Caṇḍa] by the hair, she cut off his head with her sword.'[64] The skull indicates her association with death, as do some other iconographic features. Psychoanalysts have traditionally read decapitation as a symbolic form of castration. In Tantric symbolism, it is the head that is the storehouse of semen and 'the ascetic is literally "he whose semen is turned up" (*urdhvaretas*). In *Kuṇḍalinī*, energy rises up from the genital region to the top of the skull where it bursts into a kind of mystical orgasm.'[65]

David Kinsley argues that Kālī wasn't part of the Brahmanical pantheon,[66] but assimilated through religious processes that were underway. The images show the goddess wearing the *muṇḍamālā* as a *yajñopavīta*, the sacrificial thread worn by *brāhmaṇas*. It seems to indicate that the goddess was now part of the Brahmanical pantheon; however, clearly there were contestations and the goddess retained some of her 'wild' attributes. Anncharlott Eschmann argues that the first and sometimes the only step to facilitate the transformation of the tribal goddess, whose depiction is invariably anthropomorphic to the goddess of the Brahmanical pantheon, is by providing her with the head and drawing her eyes. She argues that the anthropomorphisation of symbols into a head or figure where the head is the most prominent feature corresponds to or has originated from a particular popular iconography of Devī, which is associated with the idea of sacrifice.[67] Such a reading, when applied to understand the iconographic feature of *muṇḍamālā*, clearly highlights Kālī's association with the non-Brahmanical tradition. Further, it could be that the *muṇḍamālā* and *kapāla* became the iconographic feature of Kālī so as to associate her with Śiva; the latter in the Dakṣa myth wasn't given a share in the sacrifice because he was a *kapālin*,[68]and he assumed his Rudra or Mahākāla form, which further strengthened not only Kālī's nature as the destroyer but also as a deity who was outside the Brahmanical order.

Interestingly, in all the visuals, the goddess is bare-breasted and in some of them, she wears the snake above her breasts, as mentioned in *Mayamatam*. Mahalakshmi, in her study of the South Indian images of goddesses, highlights that those who were considered spouse goddess didn't wear a *kucca-bandha*.[69]

The snake strengthens Kālī's association with Śiva, as do her other attributes like the blue throat and the three eyes. In the textual tradition, it is Śiva who is identified as the *Śitikaṇṭha/Nīlakaṇṭha*.[70] The description in *Mayamatam* might confuse readers as to whether the text is alluding to Kālī or Cāmuṇḍā, but what is undoubtedly clear is the strong association with Śiva. In the myths, it is clearly Śiva who wears the tiger skin and snakes.[71] In the Tamil traditions, Murukaṉ is said to be the son of the deity who sits under the banyan tree in atonement and we know clearly from the Puranic pool of myths that Śiva is considered the father of Kārttikeya, who is later associated with the Tamil Murukaṉ.[72] Furthermore, it is Śiva who is said to be the carrier of the flag with the insignia of a vulture, probably associating him with the dead.[73]

There are many references in the *Śiva Purāṇa* that demonstrate that Śiva was considered the spouse of the goddess. In the *Pārvatī Khaṇḍa* of

*Rudra Saṁhitā*, mention is made of Śiva and Kālī going around the sacred fire altar.[74] While eulogising Śiva, the gods refer to him as the husband of Kālī.[75] In *Kālikā Purāṇa*, after being eulogised by Brahmā to marry Śiva, Yoganidrā as Kālī states, 'O creator in every age of creation, after dissolution of the world, I in the shape of a woman, shall continue to follow Hara with great earnestness'.[76] This not only indicates the identification of Śiva with the dissolution of the world but also that the goddess, probably Kālī, takes part in it with her husband.

Generally, divinity is marked by multiple arms and heads. In the case of Kālī too, in all the images used here, she is shown with multiple arms, and in the textual traditions, she is said to have as many as eighteen arms. Scholars have argued that the Tantric ideas in Hinduism (primarily Brahmanical tradition) and Buddhism led to the degeneration of art and the divine came to be depicted with many heads and hands, which was regarded as 'unnatural and clumsy'.[77] Coomaraswamy discusses how similar questions regarding degeneration and unnatural elements in Indian imagery had been raised primarily by his contemporaries and even earlier. He argues that one must understand each work of art 'upon its own merit' and the artist is primarily looking at the canon to make the images. He says, 'Whatever in a work of art is ostensibly representative must be judged according to the logic of the world it represents—even if that would be no other than the ideal world of the *sādhana* and *dhyāna* mantras.' Furthermore, he posits that one should not concentrate on the peculiarities of the art to appreciate it but instead try and take for granted whatever the artist has taken for granted, as there are no motifs and symbols that appear peculiar to those who have been doing the same task for generations and are, thus, familiar with it.[78]

Havell too is of the opinion that artistic convention is justified as it is used to express the ideas the artist wishes to convey, and one must read these symbols in 'light of Indian [in this case Brahmanical] religion and philosophy, which inspired both the artists and the people to whom the art was addressed'.[79] Like Coomaraswamy, he argues for the location of the art in its local environment as well, and the thought that was responsible for such creations.

P.K. Agrawala reasons that iconographical 'peculiarities' evolved against the backdrop of extremely complex mythology and diverse symbolical formulations. Such features are not limited to Indian images, but what is striking in the Indian context is the 'natural presence and the balanced composition of their additional limbs, which generally appear as presenting nothing against the norm. The additive principles employed in the iconoplastic fashioning of extra arms and heads are indeed well experimented and standardised in their rhythmic geometry by generations of artists.'[80] One might still wonder why it is that divinity is mostly depicted in the anthropomorphic form with many hands and faces. Various scholars have given reasons for 'such peculiar attributes'. According to A.A. Macdonell, the innovation of many arms was required for a practical purpose—the means of displaying the symbols without which the gods and goddesses couldn't be identified when they were represented by themselves.[81] Furthermore, 'it was when there are four hands it is the natural ones that are employed in any action or pose, while the added ones then hold the distinctive symbols of the deity.' But S.V. Venkateswara highlights how there are images with just two hands that can be identified even when there are no *vāhanas* nearby. He argues that many arms and heads don't necessarily mark a distinction as much as they symbolise the superhuman strength of divine powers.[82]

Rajeshwari opines that the entire universe is a reflection of the supreme reality but it's 'the human form which is the highest manifestation of god in this nature'. However, sometimes the human form is not perfect in its expression of the supernatural abilities of the divine, due to which 'the artist has taken help of more limbs, *mudras* and other attributes'. Thus, the gestures, posture, attributes, *vāhana* and every part of the image is a symbolic representation of the divine.[83] This leads us to question the objects the divinities hold in their hands, which are numerous, ranging from weapons to musical instruments and animals and birds.[84]

In the textual tradition, Kālī holds many such objects. In her description in the *Devī Māhātmya,* she is described carrying her dreadful sword and noose. 'She also carried a strange skull-topped staff, and wore a garland of human skulls; she was shrouded in tiger skin and looked utterly gruesome with her emaciated skin…'[85] In the visuals, the *āyudhas* that she is seen holding are *aṅkuśa* (elephant goad), *pāśa* (noose), *kheṭaka* (shield), *khaḍga* (sword), *ḍamaru* (drum), *pātra* (bowl), *triśūla* (trident), *vajra* (thunderbolt), *sarpa* (snake) and *ghaṇṭā* (bell). Her lower right hand is generally in the *abhaya* mudra (removing fear gesture) and the left hand in the *varada mudra* (bestowing boon gesture). In the religious schema, the *āyudhas* symbolise various elements. What is interesting is that the *āyudhas* that Kālī holds are associated with Śiva, clearly highlighted by Rao's discussion on the symbolism of these weapons.[86] Furthermore, in the myth of Mahiṣa in *Devī Māhātmya*, various gods give various weapons to the goddess; Śiva gives her a *triśūla* and Kāla gives her a *khaḍga* and the *kheṭaka*.[87] According to the *Śaivāgamas* that Rao refers to, the *triśūla* symbolises the three *guṇas* of *prakṛti*, namely *sattva, rajas and tamas*.[88] The *khaḍga* represents Śiva's valour and in the *Viṣṇu Purāṇa* it symbolises *vidyā* (spiritual wisdom), while the scabbard in which it is kept represents *avidyā* (ignorance). The *pāśa*, which is a threefold cord or rope, indicates the threefold bondage of incarnated life consisting of *karma*, *māyā* and *mala*, that is, work, delusion and impurity. The *vajra* is equated with vigour and is said to drive away evil spirits. In the context of Tantrism, *vajra* symbolises the creative principle of the *liṅga*.[89]

The *ghaṇṭā* symbolises sound, looked upon as the original cause of creation and indicative of the mystic sound-form (*nāda*) of Śiva.[90] It could also be that the bell, unlike the *ḍamaru*, is used for alerting and warning,[91] which seems to indicate the fierce nature of the goddess. In *Devī Māhātmya*, during the battle with Śumbha-Niśumbha, the goddess is said to fill all 'directions with the sound of her own bell, which destroyed the radiance of all the demon armies'.[92] In another reference in the same text, when the gods are praising the goddess, they allude to 'that bell that destroys demonic splendours, having filled the world with its sound, may that bell, O Goddess, protect us from evils as if we were children'.[93] James G. Lochtefeld suggests that the roaring voice of Kālī is associated with a tolling bell and is one of the reasons she holds it in her hand.[94] If one goes by that suggestion and further draws from the Puranic myths, it's almost always after killing the *asuras* that the goddess screams and roars,[95] and it seems that the bell also associates the goddess with death and dissolution.

The *ḍamaru*, especially in the dance contest, is the cause of sound as well, thus creation.[96] The *kapāla* (human skull) is used by Śiva as a receptacle for food and drink. Later, the word came to mean the cut half of an earthen pot, and then a basin or a bowl.[97] There are instances in the *Purāṇas* where while on the battlefield, Kālī drinks wine/blood, after which she starts dancing.[98] During the battle with the demon Śaṁkhacūḍa itself, there are many instances where Kālī is described as devouring demons and drinking their blood.[99] In sculptures, the *kapāla* occurs as a common spherical or oval bowl—the *pātra*.

**Image 5.5: Kālī, National Museum, most probably from Madras, c. 9th CE**

*Credit*: American Institute of Indian Studies

In Image 5.5 from Tamil Nadu, it looks like the goddess is touching the pudendum, which is generally associated with the *yakṣi* cult and symbolises fertility.[100] Could it be that this particular iconographic feature was a result of regional development where local cults were often assimilated into a Puranic goddess cult, resulting in non-conventional iconographic features?

Something that might strike the observer is that the tongue, which is such an integral part of the iconographic feature of goddess Kālī in treatises and later specimens, is missing from the visuals. There are numerous instances where Kālī's protruding or lolling tongue is mentioned in the Puranic corpus along with her fangs; the latter is visible in the iconography of the goddess.[101] In *Devī Māhātmya,* during the battle between the goddess and the demons, Kālī's lolling tongue is mentioned. We have already stated that in the *Mānasāra,* goddess Vyāna Dakṣiṇā (Kālī with projecting tongue pressed between the teeth) is mentioned. Interestingly, in Upaniṣadic philosophy, *vyāna* means the vital air that circulates in the body and is associated with *dakṣiṇā* or fire (in the navel), also called southern fire.[102] It is important to note that the very first appearance of Kālī is with fire—she appears in the *Muṇḍaka Upaniṣad* as one of the seven quivering tongues *(lelāyamānasaptajihvāḥ)* of Agni along with Karālī, Manojavā, Sulohitā, Sudhūmravarṇā, Sphuliṅginī and Viśvarūpī.[103] The connections and associations need to be probed further.

The image of Kālī standing on Śiva with her tongue extended has been especially reinterpreted in the Odishan context, where it's no longer seen as 'Tantric rituals of sexual hierarchy reversal', but reflecting the ideals of women's modesty and shame as approved by society. 'The "shame" the culture feels for its own Goddess is thus displaced and projected onto the Goddess herself in an interpretation that finds little, if any, support in the historical texts.'[104] Jeffery Kripal, in his article 'Kālī's Tongue and Ramakrishna: "Biting the Tongue" of the Tantric Tradition,' demonstrates that the biting tongue has Tantric overturns (though he reads the tongue in the psychoanalytical tradition).[105] Due to lack of any other reference, nothing concrete can be said about the symbolism of biting of the tongue in the *Mānasāra*.

**Image 5.6: Dancing Kālī, Śrī Vaṭāraṇyeśvarar temple, Tiruvalangadu, Late Cōḻa period**

*Credit*: Lotus Sculpture, https://www.lotussculpture.com/Bronze-Dancing-Kali-Statue.html

Kālī is shown to be dancing in Image 5.6. The dance motif is an interesting one and has been studied by various scholars but the seminal work of Coomaraswamy, and more recently, the analysis of Mahalakshmi, provide important insights for understanding the symbolism of dance,[106] and to situate the motif in the larger context of the Puranic process of acculturation, respectively.[107] It is evident that the image is similar to the Naṭarāja image of Śiva in symbolism, though they have somewhat different iconographic features. Kālī doesn't raise her leg and doesn't participate in the movements within the cosmos, which the upright leg of the *Ūrdhvatāṇḍava Mūrti* represents. Yet, in a way, she does join in the cosmogonic process, which is symbolised by the *tiruvāci* and shown through the *ghaṇṭā* and *ḍamaru*. She too helps in releasing countless human souls from the snare of illusion represented not only by the *pāśa*, but also by her association with fire.

## Conclusion

The *Purāṇas* reflected the diverse religious strands and beliefs encountered by the Brahmanical ideologues that were assimilated and incorporated, conceptually woven together with *bhakti* or devotion. It is in this context that it becomes necessary to situate the study of Kālī's iconography, where she not only gets an *ākāra,* but also a place within the physical space of the temple complex, which became the locus of the Brahmanical forms of worship. The diversity in the Brahmanical texts and traditions resulted in an elaboration of forms of various deities and the mythologies connected to them and connecting them, as is evident from the common iconographic features that Śiva and Kālī share and the myths woven around them. The question of 'spousification' of this originally independent deity as a result of her assimilation into the Saivite pantheon is a persistent one. Probably, Kālī already had a similar nature to Śiva when she was an 'independent' deity, which made it easier for her to be associated with Śiva, though not without some contestation.

The study of the iconography of goddess Kālī also reveals her *tāmasic* character, visible in the textual traditions, and is indicated through her association with time and colour, and also with fire, which symbolises the destruction and dissolution of the cosmos. Her association with death is emphasised by the imagery of the cremation ground, the garland of skulls and her *āyudhas*. At the same time, birth and regeneration follow death and dissolution, and according to scholars, this aspect is highlighted (and explained) in the Tantric traditions.[108] Kālī instills fear: she kills demons, dances in the battlefield, drinks wine and blood; yet, she also removes fear and bestows boons. The reference in the *Liṅga Purāṇa* throws some light on the aspect of the goddess as a 'mother'. Finally, the visual representations of Kālī appear to tease out the symbolisms and associations presented in the textual traditions, thus providing an *ākāra* to the goddess. They also bring to the forefront the ways in which her depictions conformed to the text, thereby highlighting that the image-makers were aware of the texts, as well as diverged from them, possibly due to the local/regional contexts. The visual representations discussed in this essay hail from early medieval South India, which has a rich tapestry of local and Puranic goddess traditions as discussed by several scholars. The representations of Kālī are a testimony to the manner in which a regional tradition gives space to the goddess in her varied forms, as described in prescriptive and narrative accounts, revealing incorporation and assimilation while retaining distinctiveness.

## Endnotes

1 The debate on image-making and worship needs to be situated in the backdrop of colonial institutionalisation of art and architectural studies on the one hand and archaeological endeavours on the other. Many early writings on the theme traced the beginning of art and image-making to Europe, primarily Greece and Rome. See A.K. Coomaraswamy, 'The Origin of the Buddha Image,' *The Art Bulletin* 9, no. 4 (June 1927): 287–329.

2 A.K. Coomaraswamy, *Introduction to Indian Art* (New Delhi: Munshiram Manoharlal, 1969), 1–2.

3 A.K. Coomaraswamy, *History of Indian and Indonesian Art* (New York: Dover Publications, 1965), 5.

4 Coomaraswamy, *Introduction to Indian Art*, 3.

5 T.A. Gopinatha Rao, *Elements of Hindu Iconography*, Vol. I, Part I (New Delhi: Motilal Banarsidass, 1914), 5.

6 'The employment of an external object to concentrate the mind upon in the act of meditation in carrying on the practice of Yoga is in India quite as old as Yoga itself.' Rao, *Elements*, Vol. I, Part I, 1.

7 Rao, *Elements*, Vol. I, Part I, 5.

8 This has some resonance to the kind of reasoning given for writing the *Purāṇas* for people of the Kali age; for example, *Liṅga Purāṇa,* ed. and trans. Shanti Lal Nagar, Ch. 1, Verse 10 (New Delhi: Primal Publications, 2007), 1.

9 Rao, *Elements*, Vol. I, Part I, 26.

10 Thomas B. Coburn, *Devī-Māhātmya: The Crystallization of the Goddess Tradition* (New Delhi: Motilal Banarsidass, 1988), 108.

11 *Liṅga Purāṇa*, ed. and trans. Nagar, Ch. 16, Verse 11, 53.

12 Ibid., Ch. 28, Verse 14, 110.

13 If we are to go by textual prescriptions, the goddess was meant to be depicted in blue-black colour, and it appears that when the images decorated the stone temple walls, they were painted. I have given some references in the subsequent discussion.

14 Thomas Coburn, ed. and trans., *Encountering the Goddess: A Translation of the Devī Māhātmya and A Study of Its Interpretation* Ch. 87, Verse 7.4–7.7 (New York: SUNY Press, 1991), 61.

15 J.L. Shastri, trans., *Agni Purāṇa*, Ch. 137, Verse 1 (New Delhi: Motilal Banarsidass, 1998), 401.

16 Ibid., Ch. 146, Verse 10, 420.

17 J.L. Shastri, ed. and trans., *Liṅga Purāṇa*, Ch. 106 (New Delhi: Motilal Banarsidass, 1951), 544–546.

18 Ibid., Ch. 106, Verses16–17, 545.

19 Ibid., Ch.72, Verses 66–67, 336.

20 T.A. Gopinatha Rao, *Elements of Hindu Iconography*, Vol. II, Part 1 (New Delhi: Motilal Banarsidass), 150.

21 Biswanarayan Shastri, ed. and trans., *Kālikā Purāṇa*, Ch. 8, Verse 9 (New Delhi: Indira Gandhi National Centre for Arts and Motilal Banarsidass, 1994), 38.

22 Ibid., Ch. 41, Verse 47, 271.

23 Ibid., Ch. 45, Verse 53, 307.

24 E.B. Havell, *Ideals of Indian Art* (New York: University of California, 1911), 58–59.

25 Ibid., 89–93.

26 D.R. Rajeshwari, *Sakti Iconography* (New Delhi: Intellectual Publishing House, 1989), 64.

27 Ibid., *Sakti Iconography*, 64.

28 Coburn, *Devī-Māhātmya*, 108.

29 Shanti Lal Nagar, ed. and trans., *Śiva Mahāpurāṇa* (New Delhi: Primal Publications, 2007); J.L. Shastri, ed. and trans., *Koṭirudra Saṁhitā*, Ch. 42, Verses 24, 26 (New Delhi: Motilal Banarsidass,1950), 684.

30 Shastri, *Agni Purāṇa*, Ch.12, Verses12–13, 26.
31 Nagar, *Śiva Mahāpurāṇa*, *Rudra Saṁhitā—Sṛṣṭikhaṇḍa*, Ch. 9, Verses 51–52, 205.
32 Ibid., *Rudra Saṁhitā—Satī Khaṇḍa*, Ch. 32, Verses 22–23, 25, 398.
33 Ibid., *Rudra Saṁhitā—Yuddha Khaṇḍa*, Ch. 38, Verses 6, 8, 234.
34 Ibid., *Vāyavīya Saṁhitā*, Ch. 21, Verses 10–11, 389.
35 Nagar, *Liṅga Purāṇa*, Ch. 106, Verses 19–24, 545–46.
36 Stella Kramrisch, ed. and trans., *Viṣṇudharmottara Part III: A Treatise on Indian Painting and Image-Making* (Calcutta: Calcutta University Press, 1928), 69.
37 Ibid., 69.
38 Ibid., 65.
39 Coburn, *Encountering the Goddess*, Ch. 88, Verse 8.49–8.60, 66–7.
40 Bruno Dagens, ed. and trans., *Mayamatam-Treatise of Housing, Architecture and Iconography*, Ch. 36, Verses 229–234a (New Delhi: Indira Gandhi National Centre for Arts and Motilal Banarsidass, 2007), 877.
41 P.K. Acharya, ed. and trans., *Architecture of Mānasāra*, Vol. IV, Ch. 19 Verses 222–223 (New Delhi: Munshiram Manoharlal, 1980), 235.
42 Ibid., Ch. 9, Verses 286–288.
43 R. Mahalakshmi, *The Making of the Goddess: Koṟṟavai-Durgā in the Tamil Traditions* (New Delhi: Penguin Books, 2011), 236.
44 Bettina Baumer and Rajendra Prasad Das, ed. and trans., *Śilparatnākośa*, Verses 18–21 (New Delhi: IGNCA, 1994).
45 In a lot of instances across libraries and archives, images have been incorrectly labelled as Kālī.
46 Rao, *Elements*, Vol. I, Part I, 19.
47 Ibid., 381.
48 A.K. Coomaraswamy, *The Dance of Shiva* (New Delhi: Rupa, 2013), 56.
49 Coburn, *Devī-Māhātmya*, 108.
50 Coomaraswamy, *The Dance of Shiva*, 55.
51 Miriam Robbins Dexter, 'The Ferocious and the Erotic: "Beautiful" Medusa and the Neolithic Bird and Snake,' *Journal of Feminist Studies in Religion* 26, no. 1 (Spring 2010): 31.
52 Margaret Stutley, *The Illustrated Dictionary of Hindu Iconography* (London: Routledge and Kegan Paul, 1985), 59.
53 Seema Mohanty, *The Book of Kālī* (New Delhi: Penguin, 2004), 11–12.
54 Mahalakshmi, *The Making*, 59.
55 Nagar, *Śiva Mahāpurāṇa*, *Rudra Saṁhitā—Pārvatī Khaṇḍa*, Ch. 44, Verse 13, 611.
56 Nagar, *Liṅga Purāṇa*, Ch. 106, Verses 21–22, 544–545.

57 Coburn, *Encountering the Goddess*, Ch. 88, Verses 8.22, 8.26, 64–65.

58 Ibid., Ch. 88 Verse 8.27–8.31, 65.

59 Shastri, *Kālikā Puṛāṇa*, Ch. 61, Verses 104–108, 451.

60 Sarbeshwar Sathpathy, *Śakti Iconography in Tantric Mahāvidyās* (Calcutta: Punthi Pustak, 2008), 119.

61 Jeffery Kripal, 'Why the Tāntrika Is a Hero: Kālī in the Psychoanalytic Tradition,' in *Encountering Kālī: In the Margins, at the Center, in the West*, eds. Rachel Fell McDermott and Jeffery J. Kripal (California: University of California Press, 2003).

62 Ibid.

63 Satpathy, *Śakti Iconography*, 119.

64 Coburn, *Encountering the Goddess*, Ch. 87, Verse 7.18–7.19, 62.

65 Kripal, 'Why the Tāntrika Is a Hero.'

66 David Kinsley, *The Sword and the Flute: Kālī & Kṛṣṇa: Dark Visions of the Terrible & Sublime in Hindu Mythology* (California: University of California Press, 2000).

67 Anncharlotte Eschmann, 'Hinduization of Tribal Deities in Orissa: The Śākta and Śaiva Typology,' in *The Cult of Jagannātha and the Regional Tradition of Orissa*, eds. A. Eschmann, Hermann Kulke and G.C. Tripathi (New Delhi: Manohar, 2014), 148.

68 Shastri, *Kālikā Purāṇa*, Ch. 16, Verse 29, 85.

69 Mahalakshmi, *The Making*, 303–305.

70 Nagar, *Liṅga Purāṇa*, Ch. 21, Verses 54–55, 79; Ch. 32, Verse 4, 126.

71 Ibid., Ch. 18, Verse 33b, 65.

72 Mahalakshmi, *The Making*, 63.

73 Shastri, *Kālikā Purāṇa*, Ch.18, Verse 16a, 95.

74 Nagar, *Śiva Mahāpurāṇa, Rudra Saṁhitā—Pārvatī Khaṇḍa*, Ch. 49, Verse 3, 633.

75 Ibid., Ch. 51, Verse 37, 644.

76 Shastri, *Kālikā Purāṇa*, Ch. 6, Verse 7, 28.

77 Rao, *Elements*, Vol. I, Part I, 30.

78 A.K. Coomaraswamy, 'Indian Images with Many Arms,' in *The Dance of Shiva*, 63–93.

79 Havell, *Ideals of Indian Art*, 57.

80 P.K. Agrawala, 'Iconoplastic Beginnings of Multi-Headed and Multi-Armed Images at Mathura,' in *Studies in Indian Iconography* (Jaipur: Publication Scheme, 1994).

81 A.A. Macdonell, 'The Development of Early Hindu Iconography,' *The Journal of the Royal Asiatic Society of Great Britain and Ireland* (July 1917): 592–602; except when they were shown with their *vāhana*.

82 S.V. Venkateswara, 'The Development of Early Hindu Iconography,' *The Journal of the Royal Asiatic Society of Great Britain and Ireland*, (July1917), 587–592.

83 Rajeshwari, 'Introduction,' *Sakti Iconography*.

84 Rao, *Elements*, Vol. I, Part I, 294.

85 Coburn, *Encountering the Goddess*, Ch. 87, Verse 7.4–7.7, 61.

86 Ibid., Ch. 87,Verse 7.4–7.7, 61.

87 Ibid., Ch. 82, Verses 2.19, 2.23, 41.

88 See Tracy Pintchman, *The Rise of the Goddess in The Hindu Tradition* (New York: SUNY, 1994); also, Kunal Chakrabarti, *Religious Processes: The Purāṇas and The Making of a Regional Tradition* (New Delhi: Oxford University Press, 2001).

89 Stutley, *The Illustrated Dictionary*, 151.

90 Rao, *Elements*, Vol. I, Part I, 294.

91 I am grateful to R. Mahalakshmi for bringing this to my attention.

92 Coburn, *Encountering the Goddess*, Ch. 89, Verse 9.18, 69.

93 Ibid., Ch. 89, Verse 11.26, 76.

94 James G. Lochtefeld, *The Illustrated Dictionary of Hinduism A–M* (New York: The Rosen Publishing Group, 2002), 246.

95 Coburn, *Encountering the Goddess*, Verse 7.18, 62: 'Kālī, her ugly teeth gleaming, within her dreadful mouth, angrily cackled with terrible sounds.'

96 Coomaraswamy, *The Dance of Shiva*, 56.

97 H.K. Sastri, *South Indian Images of Gods and Goddesses* (New Delhi: Asian Educational Services, 1995), 151–56.

98 Coburn, *Encountering the Goddess*, Verse 8.52–8.56, 67; Nagar, *Śiva Mahāpurāṇa, Rudra Saṁhitā—Yuddha Khaṇḍa*, Ch. 38, Verses1–3; 19–33, 233–235.

99 Nagar, *Śiva Mahāpurāṇa, Rudra Saṁhitā—Yuddha Khaṇḍa*, Ch. 37, Verses 7–8, 230.

100 T. Richard Blurton, *Hindu Art* (Cambridge: Harvard University Press, 1993), 163.

101 There are references in the *Purāṇas* where Kālī is described with protruding fangs; Nagar, *Śiva Mahāpurāṇa, Rudra Saṁhitā—Yuddha Khaṇḍa*, Ch. 38, Verse 3, 233.

102 Friedrich Max Müller, ed., *The Sacred Books of the East*, Vol. 14 (Oxford: Ohio State University, 1884), 280; Müller, *The Sacred Books*, Vol. 15, Part 2, 278.

103 Coburn, *Devī-Māhātmya*, 111.

104 Mohanty, *The Book of Kālī*, 10–11.

105 Jeffery Kripal, 'Kālī's Tongue and Ramakrishna: "Biting the Tongue" of the Tantric Tradition,' *History of Religions* 34, no. 2 (November 1994): 152–189.

106 See Coomaraswamy, *The Dance of Shiva.*

107 See R. Mahalakshmi, 'Dance as a Metaphor,' in *The Making*, 2011.

108 David Kinsley, 'Freedom from Death in the Worship of Kālī,' *Numen* 22, Fasc. 3 (December 1975): 204.

6

# Prajñāpāramitā: The Making of the First Buddhist Goddess

Megha Yadav

*Prajñāpāramitā* has been translated as 'the Perfection of (Transcendent) Wisdom'[1] and can be seen as the doctrine of emptiness and selflessness. The pursuit of *Prajñāpāramitā* is elucidated in the genre of texts known as the *Prajñāpāramitā Sūtras*; some scholars believe that the earliest *Mahāyāna Sūtras* were of the *Prajñāpāramitā* type.[2] The concept of *Prajñāpāramitā* flourished in these texts over many centuries, before the influence of Tantric elements—which became very popular in the Indian subcontinent after the fifth or sixth century CE—became a part of it. Many scholars believe that these are the oldest texts to mention a Buddhist goddess.[3] Hence, the feminine principle makes its first appearance in Buddhism as the goddess who personified the 'Perfection of Wisdom' (*Prajñāpāramitā*).[4] This goddess is regarded as the 'mother' of all beings who attain enlightenment, for it is her wisdom that engenders liberation.[5] This essay is an enquiry into the process of the making of the first Buddhist goddess and her transition from a philosophical concept into a deity. To do so, we first have to look at the concept itself, after which we can understand the process through which *Prajñāpāramitā* acquired the form of a deity. To comprehend this transition, the study of the representation of the goddess becomes very important. This essay tries to look at the ways in which Prajñāpāramitā has been discussed in the texts, primarily focusing on how her physical form has been described. It also attempts to look at the iconographic representations of the goddess and make an analytical study between the way in which the goddess has been described in the texts and how she has been visually represented.

## *Prajñāpāramitā* as a Concept

> '*Prajñāpāramitā* cannot be expounded, or learned, or distinguished, or considered, or stated, or reflected upon by means of the sense organs, mental faculties, or sense objects... Where there is no perception, appellation, conception, or conventional expression, there one speaks of "*Prajñāpāramitā*".'[6]

The term *Prajñāpāramitā* carries a multitude of philosophical meanings depending on the location of the receiver. Edward Conze notes: 'The Sanskrit word, *Prajñāpāramitā*, literally means "wisdom gone beyond", or "transcendental wisdom".'[7] Linnart Mäll, on the other hand, argues against the use of the etymological meaning of the term. He says *Prajñāpāramitā* is a completely independent term whose semantic field does not coincide at all or partly coincides with the meaning of its elements *prajñā* and *pāramitā*.[8] On the basis of the study of *Aṣṭasāhasrikā Prajñāpāramitā*, he further argues that the term essentially refers to two things:[9]

1. Inner speech, oral speech or written text is manifested as *Prajñāpāramitā*, the purpose of which is to create the ultimate state of the human mind. It is generated by following special rules.
2. *Prajñāpāramitā* is one of the names of the ultimate state of mind reflecting the ability of a person to fully understand the *Prajñāpāramitā* text and create new texts of the same type.

In *Aṣṭasāhasrikā Prajñāpāramitā*, the term also denotes the ultimate state of mind in the list of 'six *Pāramitās* (perfections)'.[10] These *Pāramitās* are considered to be perfections of cardinal virtues, which entitle one to Buddhahood.[11] They are deified in human form with colour and weapons:

1. *Dānapāramitā* (perfection of giving): Consists of giving material things, *dharma* instruction, one's body and one's own life and the merit accrued thereby for the benefit of other beings.[12]

2. *Śīlapāramitā* (perfection of morality): Consists of following the 10 wholesome ways of acting, or the five precepts.[13]
3. *Kṣāntipāramitā* (perfection of patience): Non-anger and non-agitation with regard to pain, hardship, abuse, and in regard to difficult and uncongenial doctrines.[14]
4. *Vīryapāramitā* (perfection of vigour): Derived from the word for a hero (*vīrya*) and implying heroic endeavour to benefit other living beings as well as unremitting effort in overcoming one's own faults and cultivating virtue.[15]
5. *Dhyānapāramitā* (perfection of concentration): A narrowing of the attention that results in quiet calm. It is also seen as the first step of taking *samādhi.*[16]
6. *Prajñāpāramitā* (perfection of wisdom).

The canonical list of six *pāramitās* is a part of many Mahāyāna *Sūtras*, but in some Mahāyāna texts and Pāli works, we find a list of 10 or 12 *Pāramitās.*[17] Guenther argues that *Prajñāpāramitā* is the last member not only in the formal list of six *Pāramitās* but also in Buddhist practice: *Pāramitās* are attained in a time sequence starting from *Dānapāramitā* and ending with *Prajñāpāramitā.* In the *Prajñāpāramitā Sūtras, Prajñāpāramitā* is the primary and predominant member among the six *Pāramitās.* The other *Pāramitās* alone cannot bring merit to the Bodhisattva; they have to be accompanied by *Prajñāpāramitā.* It's the presence of *Prajñāpāramitā* that brings greater merit.[18] The other *Pāramitās* only exist as elements of the *Ṣaṭpāramitā* list.

In the broader scheme of knowledge in Buddhism, it is believed that the common sense of things around us is based on false appearances. The ultimate facts of reality, technically known as *dharmas*, are different. Normally, they are covered from sight by ignorance. In order to penetrate them, one must generate in oneself a special virtue or force known as 'wisdom'(*prajñā*), which alone is able to attain the knowledge of what the *dharmas* themselves are of their 'own being'.[19]

*Prajñāpāramitā* is the knowledge of the things as they are without any external intervention. It is the capability to see and understand things in terms of their existence and non-existence. It is non-dual knowledge, meaning the abolition of all viewpoints that restrict and distort reality.

*Prajñā* as a non-dual knowledge is attained by the negation of synthesis of particular points of view. Therefore, absolutism is established by the negation of duality as an illusion. *Prajñāpāramitā* as non-conceptual knowledge removes ignorance, which conceptualises things.[20]

This non-duality of knowledge also implies that if one follows this, he or she would be able to see that there is equality between all the things and that they are essentially the same. This non-differentiation also means that one would not mind the impact of anything on himself or herself and instead, everything would be outside of them. To emphasise this point, Conze[21] has argued that to become perfectly even-minded, one will have to overlook the difference between *nirvāṇa* and this world. This would help one grow in fearlessness. Disgust with this world and fear of life seem to be signs of lack of courage and low spiritedness, which are permissible on the lower but not on the highest stages of the path. Far from trying to get out of conditioned existence as soon as they can, the followers of *Prajñāpāramitā*, armed with strong courage and unlimited compassion, voluntarily take upon themselves the calamities of further existence. Approaching *nirvāṇa* even in this life, the saved ones do not isolate themselves from the world but become its saviours.

This early conception of *Prajñāpāramitā* philosophy also paved the way for the Bodhisattva philosophy in the future. The basic idea, as Conze has suggested, is to not dissociate yourself from the world but become its saviour, and that's precisely what Bodhisattva philosophy says and does. So, in this way, *Prajñāpāramitā* can be seen as the mother philosophy of one of the most important aspects of Tantric Buddhism.

In the end, the primary focus of the concept of *Prajñāpāramitā* seems that one should become Bodhisattva, that is, one should gain all knowledge not only for himself/herself but for the sake of all human beings. At the same time, if we apply the concept of non-duality (which makes up the core of all knowledge and discussion within this literature), that would imply there is no such thing as a Bodhisattva or all knowledge. It seems that the perfection of wisdom lies in the understanding and acceptance of these two contradictory facts; to understand both these sides at the same time implies the attainment of perfect knowledge, that is, *Prajñāpāramitā*.

## Feminisation of the Philosophical Principle

According to Buddhist tradition, Buddha had entrusted the *Book of Transcendental Knowledge*, that is, *Prajñāpāramitā*, to the care of the Nāgas in the nether regions, as in his time people were not sufficiently intelligent to grasp the true meaning of the doctrines it contained. It was later restored by Nāgārjuna in the second century CE.[22] As all the respect that should be paid to Buddhas was transferred to *Prajñāpāramitā*, hence the worship of the text exceeds the worship of all other objects. The superiority of text worship can be seen in the fact that it includes the worship of Buddhas and, at times, even overshadows it. According to *Aṣṭasāhasrikā Prajñāpāramitā*, the worship of *Prajñāpāramitā* is even greater than the worship of Buddha or any of the relics.[23] As Miranda Shaw says, 'To worship a Buddha, the relics of a Buddha, or a stupa is to honour what she (*Prajñāpāramitā*) has brought into being; to revere her is directly to worship the source.'[24] This literature exalts *Prajñāpāramitā* as the highest object of worship. The 8,000-line perfect wisdom scripture weighs the relative merits of objects of reverence and proclaims worship of *Prajñāpāramitā* to be superior in every case. It claims that veneration of *Prajñāpāramitā* supersedes that of the Buddhas because she is the 'real eminent cause and condition' of the Buddhas' omniscience. Therefore, if one honours *Prajñāpāramitā*, one has worshipped all the Buddhas of the past, present and future throughout the universe.[25] To see the world as it is—a dynamic, fluid, open horizon of meaning—is to gaze upon her divine body and holy face.[26]

As mentioned earlier, the element of the worship of *Prajñāpāramitā* was present even in the early *Mahāyāna Prajñāpāramitā* literature. The *Aṣṭasāhasrikā Prajñāpāramitā* uses many epithets to place emphasis on the importance of the worship of *Prajñāpāramitā*.[27] Mäll attributes the need for the worship of *Prajñāpāramitā* to the new processes that took place within the Buddhist community in the first century BCE: the schism and appearance of many new schools, the emergence of written texts, etc. He further argues that the authors of the *Aṣṭasāhasrikā Prajñāpāramitā* thought that the main goal of the worship of *Prajñāpāramitā* was to prepare the reader or the listener for the process of subjectivising the text.

Although Prajñāpāramitā, like her namesake wisdom, is supposed to transcend all categories and be beyond form, she has traits of gender and femaleness as central to her character. She hypostasises the wisdom most often designated in this literature by the feminine noun *Prajñā*. But Shaw argues that 'her femaleness has an internal logic that goes beyond mere linguistic coincidence. There are deep metaphorical resonances between motherhood and the matrix of wisdom and reality she represents. If gender is to be assigned to a generative principle, the feminine gender is a logical choice, for the womb is the most tangible source of generation in human experience. Just as male bodies derive biologically from female ones, it stands to follow in the religious sphere that male Buddhas would have a female source. Thus, the femaleness of Prajñāpāramitā carries the force of logic and observation.'[28] To Shaw, the choice to represent wisdom in a female form seems natural and logical; wisdom naturally acquires the female gender.

As wisdom makes the attainment of Buddhahood possible, Prajñāpāramitā is an enduring reality, whereas her children, the Buddhas and the Bodhisattvas, are ephemeral and illusory: 'Prajñāpāramitā, Mother of the Buddhas, is the...sole reality. The emanation bodies of Buddhas and Bodhisattvas appear and disappear, whereas the wisdom light of Mother Prajñāpāramitā is always shining.'[29]

*Aṣṭasāhasrikā Prajñāpāramitā Sūtra* emphasises the theme that Buddhas cannot bring themselves into being but 'owe their existence' to her.[30] The text develops the metaphor of motherhood at length. She nurtures her progeny by providing the knowledge they require to fulfill their highest destiny, namely to understand the nature of reality, and dedicate themselves to the welfare and liberation of all beings.[31] She is the 'inexhaustible storehouse' of truth that is given voice by all Buddhas of the past, present and future.[32] When Buddhas teach, *Prajñāpāramitā* is the source and content of their teachings. As the fount of all truth, it is she who sets in motion the wheel of *dharma*.[33] Thus, a Buddha may teach for the duration of one lifetime, or even in myriad worlds and aeons, but the teachings of the mother, Prajñāpāramitā, flow for all eternity.

On the question of the transformation of the *Prajñāpāramitā* concept into a deity, Shaw argues that Prajñāpāramitā was personified before she was cast into iconographic form. The literature characterises her as a female being and describes her as a mother, teacher and guide to seekers of spiritual awakening. There is, however, no attempt to envision her as a deity with specific bodily attributes. Shaw argues that the primary reason for this initial lack of iconographic presentation may be that *Prajñāpāramitā* by nature transcends symbolic representation. She is identical to the highest wisdom and represents a vision of reality that lies beyond all conceptual, linguistic and symbolic constructs. *Aṣṭasāhasrikā Prajñāpāramitā Sūtra* emphasises that the non-dual wisdom she personifies is inconceivable and indescribable. Hence, there is no philosophical impetus within the philosophy to cloak the wisdom mother in a figural form, which might disavow her transcendence.[34]

Furthermore, supplementing this philosophical reason with a historical one, the literature in which Prajñāpāramitā makes her debut predates the worship of votive images as a major *Mahāyāna* practice. Moreover, the 'Perfection of Wisdom' literature promotes manuscripts, rather than effigies of the goddess as objects of ritual devotion, giving rise to the term 'cult of the book'.[35] Hence, Shaw argues that on both theological and historical grounds, it is unsurprising Prajñāpāramitā is not vested with bodily attributes in this literature.

On the basis of *Aṣṭasāhasrikā Prajñāpāramitā Sūtra*, the concept of *Prajñāpāramitā* was conceived as an all-encompassing concept from which all other philosophies will emanate, that is, in the role of a mother. When looked at from this perspective with these details in mind, it seems when the need to provide a body to the concept arose, it was the female body that was chosen.

## Iconography of Wisdom/Mother/Philosophy

The Chinese pilgrim Fa-Hsien, in his travelogue, records that he witnessed the veneration of a deity known as Prajñāpāramitā.[36] This mention establishes that by this time, the worship of Prajñāpāramitā had already been established; but no evidence in favour of the presence of a sculptural representation of the deity has been found from this time period.[37] The earliest-surviving visual representation of the goddess comes from the seventh or eighth century CE,[38] but the earliest available literary documents mentioning the goddess are found in Chinese. The oldest is the *Dhāraṇīsamuccaya*, which was translated before 625 CE.[39] In this work, in the discussion about Bodhisattva, we find a description of the goddess as well. Here, the figure of the goddess, her *mudrās*, *mantras*, *maṇḍalas* and ritual are provided.[40] We have our first literary description of the two-armed Prajñāpāramitā in this work.[41] Our second document explaining the goddess is a commentary on a Japanese text, 'Rules on the Place of Worship and the Chanting of the Liturgies of the *Ninnō*,' which has been lost but its translation in Chinese, from around 750 CE, is available.[42] This text gives a full description of the goddess—she is supposed to be sitting cross-legged on a white lotus, her body is golden-yellow, grave and majestic, with a precious necklace and a crown, from which silken bands hang down on both sides. Her left hand, near her heart, carries a book. Her right hand, near her breast, makes the gesture of argumentation.[43]

Among the texts composed in the Indian subcontinent, she is found in the *Manjuśrīmūlakalpa* (fifth–eight centuries CE). In this text, we find at least two *maṇḍalas* in which Prajñāpāramitā occurs, but as a subordinate figure.[44] The cult of Prajñāpāramitā experienced resounding success under the Pāla dynasty, which ruled Magadha and Bengal between 750 and 1200 CE, and patronised Buddhism in the form of a mixture of Prajñāpāramitā and Tantra. Dharmapāla (770 CE–815 CE) reputedly founded a total of 50 religious schools, out of which 35 were devoted to the exposition of the *Prajñāpāramitā*.[45] The work of interpretation increased in momentum under the Pāla dynasty. The teachers of this period regarded *Prajñāpāramitā* as Buddha's 'second turning of the wheel of Dharma', the *Hīnayāna* being the first and *Yogācāra* being the third. Another Tantric text, *Prajñāpāramitā Sādhanā*, which can be seen as part of the *Sādhanamālā* (earlier than 1100 CE), gives nine *sādhanas* of Prajñāpāramitā. It explains the procedure for conjuring the Prajñāpāramitā, but with no special significance attached to her, treating her in the same manner as other deities. But a clear difference can be seen in the subject matter of earlier types of *Prajñāpāramitā* literature and Tantric *Prajñāpāramitā* literature. After 1200 CE, the development of *Prajñāpāramitā* literature stopped in India.

## Visualising Prajñāpāramitā

The visual portrayal of any deity provides a very interesting and unique insight into not only the nature of the goddess but also of her worshipers. A close inspection of the visual representation of any deity, or for that matter any figure, can help us to understand the characteristics of the personality represented. For example, the representation of Vajrayoginī, the supreme goddess of the Tantric Buddhist pantheon, who is depicted as fully enlightened, makes her character very clear to any close observer. Her body is bright red, which symbolises the heat of her yogic power. In her right hand, she carries a curved knife, which is used by her to sever all illusions and duality from the root itself. The crook of her left arm supports a staff, a phallic symbol signifying that she has integrated eroticism into her spiritual path.[46]

**Image 6.1: Prajñāpāramitā, Cave 10, Ellora, Maharashtra, c. seventh century CE**

*Credit*: Sneha Ganguly

The earliest known image of Prajñāpāramitā dates from the seventh century CE and is found at the cave site of Ellora (Image 6.1).[47] She is portrayed in a standing posture, with one hand displaying the boon-granting gesture (*varada mudrā*) and the other grasping a lotus supporting a manuscript.[48]

The next few centuries saw a series of visual representations of the wisdom goddess. Tantric texts describe various epiphanies of the goddess along with the *mantras* that invoke her presence.

For the purposes of identification, mainly three kinds of sources of information have been used:

1. Inscriptions on the images themselves.
2. The literary descriptions of the deities in the *Sādhanamālā* (late eleventh or early twelfth century CE).
3. The context in which the images are found.

But there are many problems with the use of all of these sources. For instance, inscribed images are comparatively rare. Many works of art that are studied in museums, etc., have been removed from their original context. The *sādhanas* that have come down to us are not by any means complete, nor do we really know much about their affiliation to the various schools of Tantric traditions. Despite the limitations, the study and analysis of visual representations as well as the literary iconographical descriptions can help us greatly in understanding the making of the first Buddhist goddess.

A great variety can be seen in different forms of the goddess on the basis of features, such as the number of arms she has, the colour of the body, attributes she is carrying or the *mudrās* she is exhibiting. However, despite these differences, some common features can be found amongst all the forms. Our primary literary source for the study of Prajñāpāramitā is *Sādhanamālā* (composed before 1100 CE).[49] It is a collection of *sādhanas* to various deities. In this text, we find nine *sādhanas* and one *stuti* devoted to Prajñāpāramitā. These *sādhanas* describe various attributes, gestures and colours of the goddess. The following is a discussion of all the attributes and gestures associated with Prajñāpāramitā, either found in literary descriptions or in visual representations.

## Attributes of Prajñāpāramitā

In terms of attributes the goddess carries, there are similarities between the descriptions found in the *Sādhanamālā* and the visual depictions.

Primarily, she is supposed to carry a *padma* (lotus), a *pustaka* (book), the *akṣamālā* and the *vajra* (sword). In *Sādhanamālā*, we find a description of two forms of the goddess: Kanaka Prajñāpāramitā and Pīta Prajñāpāramitā. Both are supposed to carry a combination of two attributes, that is, *padma* and *pustaka*, with the *pustaka* placed on the *padma*.[50]

All the attributes of the goddess carry a specific meaning in the context of Buddhist philosophy, specifically *Prajñāpāramitā* philosophy. The *Padma* chiefly signifies purity but can also represent different ideas depending on the context. *Pustaka* has been recognised to be *Prajñāpāramitā Sūtra* itself. In *Prajñāpāramitā* philosophy, a rosary has threefold use:[51]

1. In meditation, a rosary ensures none of the repetitions are omitted.
2. The *Sūtra* contains a chapter on '*dharani*-doors' in which, on the principle of A for apple, C for cat, etc., 42 letters of a mystical alphabet—the *Arapacana*—sums up the doctrine in all its aspects. For example, the letter B is the door to the insight that the bonds have departed from all *dharmas*.
3. Later, 400 CE onwards, teaching was summed up in a number of short *mantras* that had to be repeated as often as possible. A rosary was used to count the number of repetitions.

*Vajra* is supposed to cut through the darkness of ignorance. It was a symbol of wisdom in Buddhism even prior to the cult of Prajñāpāramitā. The *vajra* is also seen as a symbol of the emptiness that constitutes the core of the doctrine of perfect wisdom.[52]

## Gestures of the Goddess

Prajñāpāramitā is primarily found in three *mudrās*:[53]

1. The *Dharmacakramudrā* or *Vyākhyāna mudrā*: This is one of the most commonly found *mudrās*. It denotes preaching by setting the wheel of law into motion,[54] and it can be seen as a reference to the teaching of *Prajñāpāramitā* philosophy this deity is supposed to personify.

2. The *Vitarka mudrā:* This can be seen as the *mudrā* of argument, preaching, theological disputation or discussion. In this *mudrā,* the hand is raised, and the index finger touches the tip of the thumb.[55]
3. The *Abhaya mudrā*: This *mudrā* is found among various religious sects of South Asia. Its meaning varies from sect to sect.[56] Within Tantric Buddhism, it denotes the action of pacification. This action can mean two situations, the transmission of protection against harm, and granting of the condition of being without fear, the imparting of calm or reassurance.[57] In this *mudrā*, the arm is raised and the palm is turned outward.
4. This gesture can symbolise two aspects of Prajñāpāramitā. It refers to her being the supreme source of protection and at the same time, the absence of all fear is often stated to be the sign that perfect wisdom has been attained.[58]

## Various Forms of Prajñāpāramitā

Both in literary descriptions as well as in visual representations, various forms of the goddess can be seen. Mostly, scholars have created a classification of artistic representations of Prajñāpāramitā according to the number of arms the deity possesses. Apart from this, the colour of the goddess is also a defining feature. In different forms, different attributes and gestures become decisive for recognising the goddess. Not many images of all the forms have survived. On the basis of the number of arms, six forms of the goddess have been identified so far, out of which we have maximum information about three: two-armed, four-armed and six-armed goddesses.

| Number of Arms | Āsana (Posture) | Attributes | Mudrā | Colour | Number of Heads |
|---|---|---|---|---|---|
| Two | *Vajrapar-yaṇkāsana, Sattvapar-yaṇkāsana* | *Prajñāpāramitā Pustaka, Padma* | *Vitarka, Dharmacakra* | Golden Yellow, White, Blue | One |
| Four | *Vajrāsana* | *Prajñāpāramitā Pustaka, Padma* | *Dharmacakra, Abhaya Mudrā* | White, Yellow | One |
| Six | | *Prajñāpāramitā Pustaka* | *Dharmacakra Mudrā* | | One |

| Ten | Standing posture | *Prajñāpāramitā Pustaka* | Other features are not recognisable | | Four, five |
|---|---|---|---|---|---|
| Twelve | | *Prajñāpāramitā Pustaka* | *Dharmacakra* | | |
| Twenty-One | Standing, seated | | | | Eleven |

## Two-Armed Images

One of the earliest literary descriptions of this Prajñāpāramitā image is found in a commentary to *Prajñāpāramitā Sūtra of a Benevolent King*, which was translated into Chinese around 750 CE. A detailed account of this form is found in *Sādhanamālā*, which has nine *sādhanas* to elucidate the procedure of her worship. Out of them, eight *sādhanas* (151–155, 157–159) describe the two-armed Prajñāpāramitā. Apart from *Sādhanamālā*, *Ekallavīra Caṇḍamahāroṣaṇa Tantra* also provides us with the description of two-armed Prajñāpāramitā.

*Pustaka* and *padma* are the decisive attributes of this form and she is mainly found in two colours: white (*śukla* or *sita*), and yellow or golden (*pīta*, *kanaka* or *suvarṇa*).[59] A description of blue (*nīla*) has also been found, but only in *Ekallavīra Caṇḍamahāroṣaṇa Tantra.*

The arrangement of *pustaka* and *padma* vary greatly. The figure is either sitting or standing. As stated previously, she is said to sit cross-legged on a white lotus. The body is golden-yellow, grave and majestic, with a precious necklace and a crown from which silken bands hang down on both sides. Her left hand, near her heart, carries the book. Her right hand, near her breasts, makes the *Vitarka mudrā*.

*Sādhanamālā* gives three *sādhanas* (151, 154, 155) with the description of the two-armed white form of Prajñāpāramitā. She has one face, sits in the *Vajraparyaṅka* attitude on a white lotus, and carries the red lotus in the right hand and the *Prajñāpāramitā* book in the left. She is decked up in all sorts of ornaments, has beautiful features and a pleasant expression. She originates from the knowledge of the letter '*aṁ*' and releases immense delight.

There are five *sādhanas* in the *Sādhanamālā* that describe the yellow form of Prajñāpāramitā (Pīta Prajñāpāramitā)—152, 153, 157, 158 and 159. All yellow forms have the hands in the *dharmacakra mudrā*. Sometimes, there is one *padma*, with a *pustaka* on top of it, on the left side of the seated figure. In other cases, two lotuses rise on right and left, the stalks twisted around the arms, with a book on top of each lotus. The lotuses are not always blue, as the *sādhanas* (152, 159) demand; in some cases, two red lotuses are shown.[60]

**Image 6.2: Sanskrit *Aṣṭasāhasrikā Prajñāpāramitā Sūtra* manuscript; *dvibhuja Kanaka* Prajñāpāramitā, Nālanda, c. seventh–eleventh centuries CE**

*Credit*: https://commons.wikimedia.org/wiki/File:Astasahasrika_Prajnaparamita_Image_of_Prajnaparamita.jpeg, accessed on 2:41 PM, 29 May 2019, New Delhi

The golden form of Prajñāpāramitā, also known as Kanaka Prajñāpāramitā, is identical in all respects with one of the forms described previously. The difference lies in the fact that although she exhibits the *dharmacakra mudrā* with two hands, there are two books on two lotuses rising from under her armpits.[61]

The only example of the blue form of Prajñāpāramitā is found in *Ekallavīra Caṇḍamahāroṣaṇa Tantra*. It describes the goddess as:

> 'The goddess sits in the *sattvaparyaṅkāsana*, and who is sixteen years in age. She is blue in colour, full of good fortune, and is stamped with (the figure of Akṣobhya). Her right and left hands hold respectively a red and a blue lotus on each of which rests a book on *Kāmaśāstra*. She has youthful and elevated breasts, large eyes, and pleasant speech.'[62]

We have already seen that Prajñāpāramitā is almost invariably associated with a *Prajñāpustaka* or a *Prajñāpāramitāpustaka*. But in this description, their replacement by the *Kāmaśāstra* is no doubt interesting. If we look closely, we can see that the change in the book changes the very concept of the goddess. As D.C. Bhattacharyya writes, it transforms her character, from the philosophical or rather the metaphysical domain to the realm of *kāma* (desire or worldliness), around which Tantric mysticism seems to have flourished.[63]

Apart from all these representations, a few more images have been found in various places, with some dissimilarities either in the colour of the lotus or the placement of the book, sword, lotus or image of the Buddha.

1. In Cambodia, we often find a standing Prajñāpāramitā, who holds a book in the right hand and a lotus bud in the left. The deity is bare to the waist. The sarong is held by an ornate belt and falls to the ankles. A crown is worn on the head. In some cases, a Buddha in meditation is found in the crown. Two *sādhanas* (151 and 153) place the Buddha Akṣobhya in the crown of Prajñāpāramitā. Sometimes, the figure holds a lotus in each hand.
2. A graceful bronze from Sumatra shows the two-armed form in the gesture of teaching, but without lotus or book.[64]

## Four-Armed Goddess

Descriptions of the four-armed Prajñāpāramitā in the texts only mentions two colours: white and yellow. With her principal set of hands, she shows *dharmacakra mudrā,* while her other right and left hands hold a rosary and *pustaka* respectively. Prajñāpāramitā with four arms is described in the *Sādhanamālā* as follows:

> 'She bears a head-dress of twisted hair; she has four arms and one face. With two of her hands she makes the gesture of expounding the dharma and she is adorned with various jewelled ornaments. She blazes like the colour of gold and in her (second) left hand she holds a blue lotus with the *Prajñāpāramitā* book upon it. She wears various garments both below and above and with her (second) right hand she makes the gesture of fearlessness.'[65]

This form is apparently not found among the images that have survived.

The only example of her white form with four arms is found in *Dharmakoṣa Saṁgraha*, dated 1826, which is more or less consistent with the description given in *Sādhanamālā*. But it is the only text that describes Prajñāpāramitā possessing four hands, which is a very common representation in the art form. The earliest representation known so far is found in *Aṣṭasāhasrikā Prajñāpāramitā*, Ms. dated 1028 CE.[66] In this text, she has been described in multiple verses. In one it is said that:

> Prajñāpāramitā has one face, four hands and white colour. She shows the *Dharmacakramudrā* with two principal hands. Her (remaining) right hand holds the rosary, and the left a book or a *caitya*. She possesses six auspicious marks. She has knowledge of everything.'[67]

In another verse, she has been described as:

> 'The goddess has one face and is golden-hued. She possesses ornaments like the aureole (*cakra*), earring (*kuṇḍala*), torque (*kaṇṭhī*), bracelet (*rucaka*), girdle (*mekhalā*) and anklet (*nūpura*). She has four hands, of which a pair of right and left hands are disposed in the *Dharmacakra mudrā*, and the other two hands hold the rosary and the book. Her breasts are elevated. She sits in the *vajrāsana* on a lotus.'[68]

In *Dharmadhātuvāgīśvara-maṇḍala* of the *Niṣpannayogāvalī*, the description of four-armed Prajñāpāramitā as a part of 12 *pāramitās* has been given. In it, she is of golden colour. With her principal hands, she displays *dharmacakra mudrā*, while her other hand holds a lotus supporting the *Prajñāpāramitā* book. Her other right hand probably holds the *cintāmaṇi* banner, which is a usual right-hand attribute of the 12 *pāramitā* goddesses.[69]

**Image 6.3: Caturbhujā Prajñāpāramitā, Northeast India, 12th century CE, Pāla Period, Bronze exhibit currently in the Fitchburg Art Museum, Fitchburg, Massachusetts, USA**

*Credit*: https://commons.wikimedia.org/wiki/File:Prajnaparamita,_northeast_India,_12th_century_AD,_Pala_Period,_bronze_-_Fitchburg_Art_Museum_-_DSC08844.JPG, accessed on 2:44 PM, 29 May 2019, New Delhi

Other representations available to us are either from manuscripts or paintings and statues from Nepal and Tibet. In them, usually in the four-armed images, two hands are in the gesture of teaching, while the second right hand holds a rosary, and the second left hand a *pustaka*. Where colour has been shown, it is golden-yellow or a reddish-brown. A few four-armed forms in Nepal and the Lamaist world, all of them very late, show a different pattern (Image 6.4).

**Image 6.4: Thangka with Caturbhujā Prajñāpāramitā, Nepal, c. 17th or 18th century CE**

*Credit*: https://commons.wikimedia.org/wiki/File:Nepal_Thangka_with_Prajnaparamita.jpg **Accessed on 2:31 PM, 29th May 2019, New Delhi**

## Six-Armed Prajñāpāramitā

A six-armed form is preserved only in the *Shingon* sect in Japan. It came to Japan from China, and to China from India through Śubhākarasiṃha, a monk from Nālandā, who arrived in 716 CE at Ch'ang-an and translated the *Mahāvairocana Sūtra* in 724 CE. A description of a magical circle of outstanding importance, the *garbha dhātu maṇḍala*, has been found in this text. In the magical circle, Prajñāpāramitā sits in the centre of the 'light-bearing assembly'. Her six hands are said to represent the six perfections (*pāramitā*).[70]

Apart from these two-, four- and six-armed representations, a ten-armed depiction with four or five heads has been found in Cambodia. The figure is standing, but the attributes cannot be distinctly made out. Another 12-armed form is preserved in a statue from Nālandā. Two of the hands are in the gesture of teaching, while the others hold various attributes. It is not very clear from the iconography of these two figures that they are Prajñāpāramitā, but they are generally regarded as such. Again, from Cambodia, we have recovered a form of Prajñāpāramitā with 11 heads and 22 arms. She is either standing or seated. The identification seems assured by the inscription on the pedestal of one of the statues, which reads: *Vrah Rüpa Vrah Prajñāpāramitā* (Holy Image of the Holy Perfection of Wisdom). Two of the images have a figure of a meditating Buddha in the crown.[71]

## Conclusion

The making of the first truly Buddhist goddess, *Prajñāpāramitā*, signalled a radical change in the mythological sphere of Buddhist deities. She is different from her female predecessors with regard to their origins. As mentioned earlier, all the female deities prior to *Prajñāpāramitā* were 'borrowed' from other cultural practices.

The creation of Prajñāpāramitā gives us a combination of mind/wisdom with femininity, contrary to the contemporary idea of women being associated with nature and men with mind/wisdom. It is almost impossible to pinpoint any one particular reason for this kind of development. But what the innumerable texts bound into the corpus of *Prajñāpāramitā Sūtra* reveal is the non-linear process through which the goddess eschatology evolved. What we can be certain of are the consequences of this development. It certainly paved the way for feminine divinities to arise in the future.

The cult of Prajñāpāramitā and its success became the pedestal upon which the great tales of future female deities and female Buddhas would stand.

As we have seen in the earlier category of texts, *Prajñāpāramitā* was a concept, a philosophy on which 'spiritual elites'[72] were supposed to spend their lives focusing. In the later texts, *Prajñāpāramitā* was transformed from an idea into a goddess. She is a goddess who was there for everybody, and the change in the audience might explain the change in the nature of the conceptualisation of *Prajñāpāramitā*. Earlier, it was for monks or other such people who are not supposed to have much materialistic desires; later, it came to cater to the needs of common people. Hence, it was addressing day-to-day issues like success in work, success over the enemy, etc. It was this context in which *Prajñāpāramitā* lost its philosophical content and came to be represented in a form that anybody could approach and worship, personified as a goddess.

## Endnotes

1 Edward Conze, *Materials for A Dictionary of the Prajñāpāramitā Literature* (Tokyo: Suzuki Research Foundation, 1973), 269.

2 Edward Conze, 'The Ontology of the Prajñāpāramitā,' *Philosophy East and West* 3, no. 2 (1953): 117.

3 Although we find mention of female deities such as Hāritī and Uṣā, these goddesses existed in other contemporary religious traditions as well. On the basis of the historicity of these cults, it seems that Buddhism 'borrowed' these goddesses into its own mythology. On the other hand, *Prajñāpāramitā* seems to be the first goddess to be 'invented' by the Buddhists.

4 Stephen Beyer, *The Cult of Tārā: Magic and Ritual in Tibet* (Berkeley: University of California Press, 1973).

5 Miranda Shaw, *Buddhist Goddesses of India* (New Delhi: Munshiram Manoharlal, 2007), 166.

6 *Aṣṭasāhasrikā Prajñāpāramitā,* trans. Edward Conze (California: Four Seasons Foundation, 1975), 138.

7 Edward Conze, *Buddhism* (USA: Oneworld Publication, 1993), 124.

8 Linnart Mäll, *Studies in Aṣṭasāhasrika Prajñāpāramitā and Other Essays* (New Delhi: Motilal Banarsidass, 2003), 65.

9 Mäll, *Studies in Aṣṭasāhasrika Prajñāpāramitā*, 66.

10 Ibid., 78.

11 Benoytosh Bhattacharya, *The Indian Buddhist Iconography: Mainly Based on the Sādhanamālā and Cognate Tantric Texts of Rituals* (Calcutta: Firma K.L. Mukhopadhyay, 1968), 323.

12 Conze, *Aṣṭasāhasrikā Prajñāpāramitā*, 316.

13 Ibid., 319.

14 Ibid., 320.

15 Ibid., 324.

16 Ibid., 313.

17 Mäll, *Studies in Aṣṭasāhasrika Prajñāpāramitā*, 78.

18 Conze, *Aṣṭasāhasrikā Prajñāpāramitā*, 111.

19 Conze, 'Ontology,' 117–129.

20 Thupten Tenzing, 'An Introduction to the Perfection of Wisdom,' *Digital Himalaya: Bulletin of Tibetology*, Vol. 33 (Gangtok: Namgyal Institute of Tibetology, 1997), 29.

21 Conze, 'Ontology,' 129.

22 Bhattacharya, *The Indian Buddhist Iconography*, 197.

23 Shaw, *Buddhist Goddesses*, 169.

24 Ibid., 166.

25 Conze, *Aṣṭasāhasrikā Prajñāpāramitā*, 108, 111, 267.

26 Shaw, *Buddhist Goddesses*, 171.

27 Conze, *Aṣṭasāhasrikā Prajñāpāramitā*, 30.

28 Shaw, *Buddhist Goddesses*, 167.

29 Lex Hixon, *Mother of the Buddhas: Meditations on the Prajnaparamita Sutra* (Chennai: Quest Books, 1993), 76.

30 Conze, *Aṣṭasāhasrikā Prajñāpāramitā*, 172.

31 Shaw, *Buddhist Goddesses*, 168.

32 Conze, *Aṣṭasāhasrikā Prajñāpāramitā*, 268.

33 Ibid., 135.

34 Shaw, *Buddhist Goddesses*, 171–172.

35 Ibid., 172.

36 A Chinese traveller who came to India in the late fourth or early fifth century CE.

37 Shaw, *Buddhist Goddesses*, 474; Edward Conze, *Thirty Years of Buddhist Studies: Selected Essays* (Oxford: Bruno Cassirer, 1967), 244.

38 Conze, *Thirty Years*, 244; Geri Hockfield Malandra, *Unfolding a Maṇḍala: The Buddhist Cave Temples at Ellora* (SUNY Press, 1993), 58.

39 Edward Conze, *The Prajñāpāramitā Literature* (New Delhi: Munshiram Manoharlal, 2008), 14.

40 Ibid., 14.

41 Ibid.

42 Ibid.

43 Ibid.

44 Ibid., 15.

45 Ibid., 16.

46 Miranda Shaw, 'Is Vajrayogini a Feminist? A Tantric Buddhist Case Study,' in *Is the Goddess a Feminist? The Politics of South Asian Goddesses*, eds Alf Hiltebeitl and Kathleen Erndl (Sheffield: Sheffield Academic Press, 2000), 166.

47 Malandra, *Unfolding a Maṇḍala*, 58.

48 Ibid.

49 Conze, *Thirty Years*, 246.

50 Bhattacharya, *The Indian Buddhist Iconography*, 197–198.

51 Conze, *Thirty Years*, 245.

52 Ibid.

53 Pushpa Niyogi, *Buddhist Deities* (New Delhi: Munshiram Manoharlal, 2001), 114.

54 Fredrick W. Bunce, *Mudrās in Buddhist and Hindu Practices: An Iconographic Consideration* (New Delhi: D.K. Printworld, 2005), 58.

55 Bunce, *Mudrās*, 278.

56 For other meanings, see Ibid., 2–4.

57 Bunce, *Mudrās*, 2.

58 Conze, *Thirty Years*, 244.

59 Ibid., 246–248.

60 Thomas Eugene Donaldson, *Iconography of the Buddhist Sculpture of Orissa* (New Delhi: Abhinav Publication, 2001), 277.

61 Bhattacharya, *The Indian Buddhist Iconography*, 199.

62 Donaldson, *Iconography*, 278.

63 Dipak Chandra Bhattacharyya, *Tantric Buddhist Iconographic Sources* (New Delhi: Munshiram Manoharlal, 1974), 44.

64 Bhattacharyya, *Tantric Buddhist*, 44.

65 Conze, *Thirty Years*, 248.

66 Bhattacharyya, *Tantric Buddhist*, 66.

67 Ibid., 33–34.

68 Ibid.

69 Donaldson, *Iconography*, 278–79.

70 Conze, *Thirty Years*, 249.

71 Ibid., 250.

72 I am using the term 'spiritual elites' for people who had renounced the world and devoted their whole lives for religious works, such as monks and nuns in Buddhist and Jain traditions. Also, they were the group that had more reason to be engaged in religious and spiritual activities—according to social hierarchies—such as the *brāhmaṇas* in Brahmanical religion.

# 7

# Representation of Sixteen Mahāvidyā in the Dilwara Jaina Temple

Virendra Singh Bithoo

When an idea takes shape—engages in debates and discussions and moves to a broader canvas—it gets transformed into a philosophical school. When this philosophical school interacts with symbolism, and symbols become more important than the philosophy, the context for the emergence of icons is created. These symbols are dictated by texts but it is not necessary that they are followed as per textual prescriptions. They are modified with the ideas of the practitioners. In other words, religion is a complex phenomenon that cannot be understood only through scripture or philosophy; the social context of the origins and development becomes important.

The basis of Jaina philosophy is its three gems: *samyakdarśana* (right faith), *samyakcaritra* (right action) and *samyakjñāna* (right knowledge).[1] According to Jainism, right knowledge cannot be gained without right conduct; hence, it is very important that a person follows all these three things in life. This idea is visible in early medieval temple architecture where the Tīrthaṅkara is depicted in certain postures in the sanctum, and the Mahāvidyā are depicted before the *gūḍhamaṇḍapa* (the vestibule) in the *raṅgamaṇḍapa* (performance hall), which might be a representation of this philosophical idea.[2] I have chosen the Dilwara Jaina Temple to elaborate on the concept of the 16 Mahāvidyā, and attempted to look at the philosophical and sociopolitical dimensions with regard to the iconography of these deities.

**Figure 7.1: Diagram of the entrance of the Ṛṣabhnātha temple, Ranakpur, c. 14th–15th centuries CE**

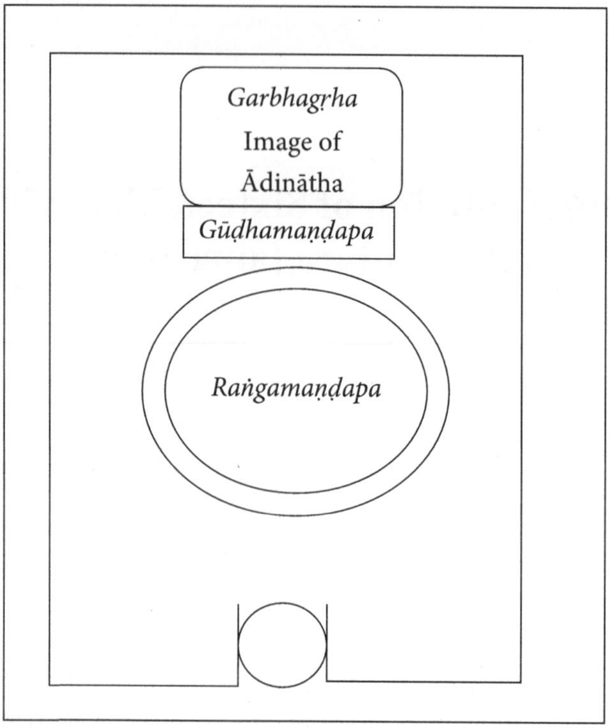


*Source*: Author

Entering the temple, a conch is depicted at the doorstep on both sides, symbolising birth or new life, enjoining right action.[3] On the ceiling, just after the first step, are four Śruta Devī—the symbol of knowledge preached by teachers due to the belief of *śabda-pramāṇa* in Jainism.[4] Immediately after that, we enter the *raṅgamaṇḍapa*, where the 16 Mahāvidyā are depicted on the ceiling, which are the symbols of *samyakjñāna*. Following this, in the *garbhagṛha*, the image of the Tīrthaṅkara depicts the right faith, in addition to the previous two virtues. This is one way of looking at art through the lens of Jaina philosophy, but it cannot be said that this is the only way of interpreting it. I have looked at literary texts and also depictions in architecture to trace the development of the Mahāvidyā in Jaina temple architecture.

## Textual Analysis

B.C. Bhattacharya points out that the Vidyādevīs in conception were placed after the Yakṣiṇīs, on the ground of priority of the Yakṣiṇīs in mythology and ritual with the Tīrthaṅkara in Jainism.[5] According to the Jaina text *Pratiṣṭhāsāroddhāra*, through the worship of the Mahāvidyā, the devotee achieves knowledge, character, religion, effort and mental qualities of many kinds.[6] In Jaina literature, there is a line drawn between *mantra* and *vidyā*.[7] These 16 are considered Mahāvidyā among the 48,000 *vidyās* that are enumerated, and existing texts talk about their iconography, as for example the *Rūpamaṇḍana*. But these texts do not talk about the rites or *sādhanās* of the goddesses. *Vidyānupravādapūrva* was one of the 14 *pūrva* texts dealing with a number of powerful *vidyā* and their *sādhanās*, which is now lost.[8] In *Mahāniśītha Sūtra*, the *Śrutadevatā Vidyā* and *Varddhamāna Vidyā* are mentioned. The *Sūtrakṛtāṅga Sūtra* also discusses many *vidyās*, which are termed *pāpaśrutas*, among them Gaurī and Gāndhārī, which are also two of the 16 Mahāvidyā.[9] The earliest Jaina account of the origin and worship of the Vidyādevīs and the Vidyādharas on the basis of availability is the *Vasudevahiṇḍī* of Saṅghadāsa (500 CE).[10] These 16 Mahāvidyā are associated with the narrative of Nāmi–Vināmi of Hemacandra in *Triṣaṣṭīśalākāpuruṣacaritam* of the eleventh or twelfth century CE. According to this text, 'Once upon a time when the first Jina Ṛṣabhanātha was practicing austerities, Nāmi and Vināmi went to him and began worshipping him with the desire of obtaining worldly prosperity from the Lord. But the great sage was in meditation and remained unconcerned. Thereupon, Dharaṇa, the king of the Nāgakumāras, came to the spot and in order that the worship of the Lord may not be spoken of as fruitless, granted to Nāmi and Vināmi lordship over the Vidyādharas. Both the devotees were asked to found two groups of cities on the northern and southern slopes of the Vaitāḍhya mountain and were given forty-eight thousand *vidyās*, Gaurī and Prajñapti being the chief amongst them. Nāmi founded fifty cities on the Vaitāḍhya mountain in a southern row while Vināmi made sixty in a northern one. There were sixteen clans of Vidyādharas named after the class of *vidyās* they possessed.'[11] Hemacandra comes out with a long list: From the *vidyā* called Gaurīs came the Gaureya clans, from the *vidyā* called Manu came the Manupūrvaka clan, the Gāndhāra clan from Gāndhārī, the Mānava clan from Mānavī, the Kaiśikī-pūrvaka clan from Kaiśikī, the Bhūmituṇḍaka clan from Bhūmituṇḍa, the Mūlavīryaka clan from Mūlavīrya, the Śaṅkukā clan from Śaṅkuka, the Pāṇḍuka clan from Pāṇḍukī, the Kālikeya clan from Kālī, the Śvapāka clan from Śvapākī, the Mātaṅgas from Mātaṅgī, the Pārvata clan from Pārvatī, the Vaṃśālaya clan from Vaṃśālayās, the Pāṃśumūlaka clan from Pāṃśumūla and the Vṛkṣamūlaka clan from Vṛkṣamūla.[12] The account of Nāmi and Vināmi is also found in *Harivaṃśa* written by Jinasena I.[13] In this text, we learn about the Vidyādharas; eight of them were associated with the Āryas, the Ādityas or the Gandharvas, while the other eight belonged to the Daityas, the Pannagas or the Mātaṅgas.[14] So, in the two accounts, one is dealing with geographical location and the other is dealing with the Ārya and the Daitya concepts. Both show that these goddesses were associated with Tantric practices and these goddesses are depicted in an inferior position to the Tīrthaṅkara. So, the concept of these Vidyādevīs numbering 16 is present in these texts. But this is not the standard form that exists in temple architecture.

The account of Nāmi and Vināmi is suggested in earlier texts like *Āvaśyaka Niryukti*, but it neither mentions any of the chief *vidyās* nor does it refer to the 16 classes of the Vidyādharas and Vidyādevīs.[15] *Paumacariyam* composed by Vimalasūri from the third to fifth centuries CE contains an account of Nāmi and Vināmi, but not of the 16 Mahāvidyā.[16] In *Āvaśyaka Cūrṇi* composed by Jinadāsa, we come to know that only Gaurī, Gāndhārī, Rohiṇī and Prajñapti were considered the chief amongst them.

The author of the *Harivaṁśa* gives a list of Mahāvidyā, the chief position among all *vidyās*: Prajñapti, Rohiṇī, Aṅgāriṇī, Mahā-Gaurī, Gaurī, Mahāśvetā, Māyūrī, Ārya-Kūṣmāṇḍa-Devī, Acyutā, Āryavati, Gāndhārī, Nirvṛtti, Bhadra-Kālī, Mahā-Kālī, Kālī and Kālamukhī. This is one of the earliest complete lists of the 16 *vidyās* available to us; it differs largely from the somewhat later lists supplied by writers of both the sects. In later texts like *Abhidhāna Cintāmaṇi*, *Pratiṣṭhāsāroddhāra*, *Rūpamaṇḍana*, etc., the 16 Mahāvidyā are: Rohiṇī, Prajñapti, Vajraṣṛṅkhalā, Vajrāṅkuśā, Cakreśvarī (Śve)/Jāmbūnadā (Dig), Naradattā or Puruṣadattā, Kālī, Mahā-Kālī, Gaurī, Gāndhārī, Sarvāstra Mahājvālā (Śve)/Jvālāmālinī (Dig), Mānavī, Vairoṭyā

(Śve)/Vairoṭī (Dig), Acchuptā (Śve)/Acyutā (Dig), Mānasī and Mahā-Mānasī.[17]

Thus, we come to know that after the eighth century CE, the 16 Mahāvidyā become popular in Jaina literature. Texts like *Tijayapahutta Stotra*, *Caupannamahāpuruṣa Cariyam* of the ninth century CE, and Bappabhaṭṭī Sūri and Śobhana Muni praised the 16 Mahāvidyā with the Tīrthaṅkaras instead of the Yakṣiṇīs.

## Architectural Analysis

The very first depiction of 16 Mahāvidyā is found in an Osian temple. The main goddess was converted into a Jaina goddess known as Sacciyā Mātā; in the *raṅgamaṇḍapa* of this temple are depicted the 16 Mahāvidyā. In this temple, before its conversion into a Jaina temple, blood sacrifice and Tantric rituals were performed. We can also see a depiction of Mahāvidyā in the Kumbharia Jaina temple. In the Dilwara Jaina temple complex, constructed between the eleventh and fourteenth centuries CE, there are three temples, and only in two—Vimala Vasāhi and Lūṇa Vasāhi—the 16 Mahāvidyā are depicted.

This is one of the rare traditions to have so many goddesses of knowledge, and along with these 16 Mahāvidyā, we also have one Śruta Devī depicted. The latter is a Jaina form of the Brahmanical goddess Sarasvatī, and on the occasion of Vasanta Pañcamī, this goddess is worshipped. In Digambara texts, she is shown with a peacock as her vehicle. According to the Śvetāmabara tradition, she wears a white cloth and is of white colour. She rides a swan and has four hands. In her left hands, she holds the *vīṇā* and a white lotus, and in her right hands, a book and a rosary.[18]

In the *raṅgamaṇḍapa* of the Vimala Vasāhi Jaina Temple, there is a representation of a four-armed Śruta Devī in *lalitāsana* (with right leg hanging and left being tucked up), and on either side are shown two bearded men with folded hands. In this image, she has a lotus, a book, the *varadākṣa* and a pitcher and she is shown with her *vāhana*, the swan. On a corridor ceiling in Lūṇa Vasāhi, Śruta Devī is shown with six arms—on the right side she has lotus, a cymbal and the *varadākṣa* and on the left is a *vīṇā*, a cymbal and a book—with the swan mount. In the same corridor, on the ceiling, there is another image of a 16-armed Śruta Devī sitting in *lalitāsana*. In her right hand, she holds a lotus, a conch, a *daṇḍa*, a *vīṇā* (*varada* mudrā, *abhaya* mudrā) and a noose; on the left side, she is holding a book, pitcher, lotus, *vīṇā*, *aṅkuśa* and fruit.[19] We also see with this an image of a six-armed drummer on one side and a dancer on the other.

**Image 7.1: 16-armed Śruta Devī in corridor ceiling in Lūṇa Vasāhi, Mount Abu, c. 11th–14th centuries CE**

*Credit*: Author

On the upper part of this panel, the *aṣṭamātṛkās* are also depicted, and on both sides of the drummer may be seen a depiction of Bhairava. These images indicate the Tantric influences and practices assimilated within Jainism.

## Sixteen Mahāvidyā and their Depiction

On the main dome of the *raṅgamaṇḍapa* in the Lūṇa Vasāhi temple, all the 16 Vidyādevīs have been represented. They may be identified as Rohiṇī, Prajñapti, Vajraśṛṅkhalā, Vajrāṁkuśā, Apraticakrā or Jāmbūnadā, Naradattā, Kālī, Mahā-Kālī, Gaurī, Gāndhārī, Mahājvālā or Jvālāmālinī, Mānavī, Mānasī, Vairoṭyā, Acchuptā and Mahāmānasī on the basis of literary sources, with specific iconographic representations.

**Image 7.2: Image of 16 Mahāvidyā in *Raṅgamaṇḍapa* of Lūṇa Vasāhi temple, Mount Abu, c. 11th–14th centuries CE**

*Credit*: Author

### Rohiṇī

According to the Śvetāmbara sect, she rides a cow and holds in her hands a conch, a rosary, a bow and an arrow, while according to the Digambara tradition, she holds an urn, a conch, a lotus and a fruit. As mentioned, strict observation of the canon was not seen in making the sculptures.[20]

In the Vimala Vasāhi temple, the goddess is shown with 16 arms in a sitting position, while in the *lalitāsana*, she carries a noose, a sword, a *triśūla*, a *vajra*, an arrow, a *vyākhyānamudrā*, a fruit and *varadamudrā* in the right hands, and *daṇḍa*, shield, *aṅkuśa*, *vyākhyānamudrā*, a bow, a mace, a pitcher and *abhayamudrā* in the left.

## Prajñapti

According to the Śvetāmbara text *Ācāradinakara*, she rides a peacock and holds a lotus and *śakti*, and according to *Nirvāṇakalikā*, she depicts *varada*, holds a *śakti*, citrus and *śakti* again. According to Digambara tradition, she holds a sword and a disc.[21] In Image 7.4 (upper right one among the four), she is seated on a peacock. She has four hands and holds a *śakti* and a peacock, and her other two hands are in *varadamudrā* and *abhayamudrā*.

## Vajraśṛṅkhalā

According to *Ācāradinakara*, she is seated on a lotus and carries a chain and a club, and according to *Nirvāṇakalikā*, she is again seated on a lotus but has four hands, with one hand in *varadamudrā*, and others holding a chain, lotus, and again a chain. According to Digambara texts, she only holds a chain.[22] She has four arms and is seated on a lotus (see Image 7.3, lower right). She has four hands: one is in *varadamudrā* and instead of a lotus, she has *gadā* in the other and she is holding a chain with her other two hands.

## Vajrāṅkuśī

According to *Ācāradinakara*, she rides an elephant and as weapons, she bears a sword, *vajra*, a shield and a spear. According to *Nirvāṇakalikā*, she is riding an elephant, in *varadamudrā*, with a *vajra*, a citrus and a goad in her three hands. In Digambara tradition, she is represented in a *puṣpa-yāna* and holding a goad and a lute in her hands.[23] In Image 7.3, she (lower left) has four arms. She is holding a *vajra*, an *aṅkuśa*, a *kamaṇḍalu* and one of her hands is in *varada mudrā*. She is seated on her *vāhana*, an elephant.

**Image 7.3: Images of four-armed *lalitāsana* Vajrāṅkuśī, Cakreśvarī, Prajñapti and Vajraśṛṅkhalā, Vimala Vasāhi temple, Mount Abu, c. 11th–14th centuries CE**

*Credit*: Author

## Apraticakrā or Jāmbūnadā

She rides a *garuḍa* and each of her arms carries a disc. She is called Jāmbūnadā by the Digambaras, who represent her as riding a peacock and bearing a sword and a spear.[24]

## Naradattā or Puruṣadattā

According to *Ācāradinakara*, she holds a sword and shield, and according to *Nirvāṇakalikā*, she rides a buffalo and her four hands are in *varadamudrā*, holding a a sword, a citrus and a shield, respectively. As per Digambara tradition, she rides a peacock and holds a *vajra* and a lotus as symbols.[25]

## Kālī

According to *Ācāradinakara*, she is seated on a lotus and holds in two hands a club and a *varada*; according to *Nirvāṇakalikā*, in four hands she has a rosary, a club, a *vajra* and one of her hands is in *abhayamudrā*. As per *Digambara* tradition, she rides a deer and has a staff and a sword.[26]

### Mahā-Kālī

According to *Ācāradinakara*, she stands on a man and holds a rosary, a fruit and a bell, and one hand is in *varadamudrā*. According to *Nirvāṇakalikā*, she stands on a man but holds a rosary, a *vajra*, a bell and one hand is in *abhayamudrā*. According to Digambara tradition, she is standing on a corpse, bearing in her hands a bow, a sword, a fruit and a weapon.

### Gaurī

According to Śvetāmbara tradition, she rides an alligator and her four hands are equipped with a *varada*, a club, a rosary and a water lily. According to the Digambara tradition, she has an alligator as her vehicle and holds a lotus as her symbol.

### Gāndhārī

According to Śvetāmbara tradition, she is seated on a lotus and holding a staff and a *vajra* or a *varada*, and one hand is in *abhayamudrā*. According to Digambara tradition, she rides a tortoise and holds a disc and a sword.

### Mahājvālā or Jvālāmālinī

According to *Ācāradinakara*, she rides a cat, but according to *Nirvāṇakalikā*, she rides a boar and holds many weapons, but the description of the weapons is not available. According to Digambara tradition, she rides a buffalo and holds weapons, such as a bow, a shield, a sword and a disc.[27]

### Mānavī

According to *Ācāradinakara*, she sits on a blue lotus and a twig and according to *Nirvāṇakalikā*, she sits on a lotus and has four hands with a *varada*, a rosary and holding the bough of a tree. According to Digambara tradition, she rides a boar and is described as blue in colour and bears a trident.[28] She is depicted with a trident, a *śakti*, a *kamaṇḍalu* and one hand is in *varadamudrā*.

## Vairoṭī

According to the Śvetāmbara tradition, she rides a snake and she is carrying in her hands a sword, a shield and a snake.[29] According to Digambara tradition, she rides a lion and has a snake as her symbol. In Image 7.4, we see that she has a snake as her *vāhana* but has 16 arms instead of four. She is seated in *lalitāsana*. She carries in her right arms a snake, a *cakra*, a trident, a noose, a sword, and her two hands are in *vajraghaṇṭā* and *varadamudrā*. In her left hands, she has a snake, a shield, a *daṇḍa*, a lotus, a *vajra* and a *kamaṇḍalu*. Her two arms are on the heads of two snakes.

**Image 7.4: Goddess Vairoṭī on a corridor ceiling in Vimala Vasāhi temple, Mount Abu, c.11th–14th centuries CE**

*Credit*: Author

## Acyuptā

According to the Śvetāmbara tradition, she rides a horse and is holding a bow, a sword, a shield and an arrow. According to Digambara tradition, she rides a horse and holds the symbol of a sword.[30] In Image 7.5, goddess Acyuptā is seated in *lalitāsana* on her horse. She is depicted with 16 arms. In her right hands she carries a *cakra*, a goad, a noose, an arrow, a *paraśu*, a chain, a conch and one of her hands is in *vyākhyānamudrā*. In her left hand, she carries a chain, a trumpet, a *daṇḍa*, a bow, a *vajra*, a pitcher, a club and one of her hands is in *abhayamudrā*. On either side are *caurī* bearers performing *abhiṣeka* to the goddess.

**Image 7.5: Image of Goddess Acyuptā on a corridor ceiling in Vimala Vasāhi temple, Mount Abu, c.11th–14th centuries CE**

*Credit*: Author

## Mānasī

According to *Ācāradinakara*, she rides a swan and bears attributes of a *varada* and a *vajra*, while according to *Nirvāṇakalikā*, she sits on a lion and has four hands. One hand is in *varadamudrā*, and the other hands carrying a *vajra*, a rosary and again a *vajra*. According to Digambara tradition, she sits on a snake.[31]

### Mahāmānasī

According to Śvetāmbara tradition, she rides a lion and bears in her four hands the symbol of a *varada*, a sword, a *kamaṇḍalu* and a lance. According to Digambara tradition, she sits on a swan and holds a rosary, a goad a garland and the other hand is in *varadamudrā*.[32] She is depicted with 20 arms on the corridor ceiling in the Vimala Vasāhi temple. It appears that in the Vimala Vasāhī temple, all the Vidyādevīs on the corridor ceiling are represented with more than four arms.[33]

## Purpose of the Mahāvidyā

The earliest representation of Mahāvidyā as a temple decoration are found at the Mahāvīra temple at Osian (Rajasthan) built by Pratihāra Vatsarāja at the close of the eighth century CE. These Mahāvidyā figures almost fully correspond to the iconographic forms enjoined by the *Caturviṁśatikā* of Bappabhaṭṭi Sūri (743 CE–838 CE), which is the earliest known iconographic text dealing with the individual iconography of the Jaina Mahāvidyā. In the Śāntinātha temple (1077 CE) at Kumbharia (north Gujarat), the ceiling contains the figures of the 16 Mahāvidyā. Thus, we come to know that by the eleventh to thirteenth centuries CE, representations of the group of 16 Mahāvidyā had become common.[34]

Now the question that arises is why are these goddesses depicted mostly in Jaina temples, although these have a close relation with—and many of them are—prominent Brahmanical goddesses? R.N. Nandi has pointed out that with the spread of Jainism, these Brahmanical deities, who were worshipped mostly in Tantric rituals, were incorporated.[35] According to *Bhairava Padmāvat Kalpa*, Jvālāmālinī is related with the crematorium, crossroads, or the shadow of a tree. In *Samarāiccha Kahā*, it is mentioned that beautiful women should be used to obtain magical powers. *Bhāratī Kalpa* of Mallisena of the late eleventh century CE and the *Sarasvatī Kalpa* of Arhaddāsa are devoted to Tantric *sādhanā* of Sarasvatī. We come to know that *vidyās* are described as occult power, but by the time period of *Vāsudevahiṇḍi* (500 CE–700 CE), they are described as goddesses. Hemacandra, as discussed earlier, narrates how Nāmi and Vināmi worshipped Ṛṣabhanath to obtain worldly prosperity, but as he was meditating he paid no heed to them, so Dharaṇendra, to keep the worship of Ṛṣabha, gave them lordship over the Vidyādharas.[36] Through this, we come to know that it was primarily as a magical power that the Śvetāmbara tradition enumerated the first four Mahāvidyā between the fifth and ninth centuries CE. They eventually adopted 16 as the standard number, and its best example is seen in the Dilwara temple. We learn about different *vidyās* associated with Rāma and Rāvaṇa in *Paumacariyam*.[37] Among these, there is a mention of the Mahāvidyā too.[38]

When we look at religions in India, our first tendency is to look at themes like religious practices in Jainism, Buddhism, Hinduism, etc., which leads us in the wrong direction. The perspective of colonial writing forces us to think in this way, and we divide traditions completely, as if they inhabit in different planets. We forget that Jainism and Buddhism developed at a time when *varṇāśrama* and polytheism were well known, and the philosophical goal of all these sects was to know the ultimate truth and reach enlightenment. Social practices of that time looked at philosophers or saints with high regard and considered them full of mystic power, and most literature associated with them also testifies this.[39] The beliefs and mention of different *vidyās* in texts are mostly associated with the social circumstances of that time. We hear of *Jāṅgoli-vijjā*, which is associated with the removal of poison after a snake bite, as elaborated in *Sthānāṅga Sūtra*, and a myth about removing the poison after a snake bite of a king's son is known from Osian.

Most known sects like Buddhists, Jainas, Śaivas, Vaiṣṇavas and Śāktas disagree about the formation of the world. Jaina and Buddhist traditions are silent on the creator of the world, but other sects attribute the creation of the world to their respective gods and goddesses. In temple architecture, these gods and goddesses become the main presiding deities. All of them support the idea of mysticism. However, in all the aforementioned sects, we find the role of Indra is to maintain divine order, and also acceptance of popular beliefs in *tithi* and *śakuna*. An ordinary worshipper has expectations from the deity that all problems will be solved, and that the deity will make the person prosperous and healthy and realise all ambitions. We find many stories of how a god or goddess helped the believer during difficult times;

the idea of many forms of gods and goddesses emerged to assimilate and incorporate local gods and goddesses within these sects. In the case of Jainism, the *Jina* does not give any boon himself, and in the art form also he is always depicted either in *dhyānamudrā* or in *kāyotsarga* form. It is in this context that the need to incorporate existing local gods and goddesses who could grant boons to worshippers was felt.

Local goddesses were absorbed as Yakṣiṇīs, as is the case of Padmāvatī. She was the *kuladevī* of many ruling families in the Deccan, such as the Śilāhāras, the Raṭṭas and the Sāntaras; it is mentioned in their *praśastis* that they were devotees of Padmāvatī. In the case of Saccikā or Sacciyā, the *kuladevī* of the Osvāl community of Rajasthan, she became a Jaina goddess. Saccikā in iconography is Mahiṣāsuramardinī Durgā.[40] Hemacandra mentions that the main reason for the worship of Jaina goddesses is to get worldly prosperity. Furthermore, it would be easier to expand any religion in specific local and regional contexts when local elements are appropriated and assimilated.

Increasing the number of arms and weapons in the iconography of the Jaina Vidyādevīs, which is originally a philosophical exposition, also suggests such assimilations. It may be that the adaptation of Vidyādevīs became more important because they came to be associated with caste. According to *Ādipurāṇa*, *vidyās* are acquired in two ways: through *kula* (family and caste) or through personal efforts.[41] The Vidyādevīs were, therefore, also a means to popularise Jainism within the family and caste groups. The popularity of these goddesses and their associations and symbolism were used to spread Jainism; for instance, Jvālinī was supposed to help overpower the antagonist in religious disputes. Hence, development in the iconography of these goddesses clearly indicates Tantric influence and through accepting these goddesses, it became easier for Jainism to spread in such areas where belief in these goddesses was more popular.

We find a struggle with regard to superiority of knowledge among two *varṇas* the *brāhmaṇa* and the *kṣatriya*, in Jainism.[42] The association of the Tīrthaṅkara with the *kṣatriya kula* helped the tradition to flourish in early medieval times. In Rajasthan, we find many inscriptions that clearly show that Jainism was greatly patronised by the ruling class, and many temples were constructed, and various festivals associated with Jainism were celebrated on different *tithi*. Many royal orders were passed prohibiting the killing of animals to support the idea of non-violence in Jainism.[43] With the emergence of different *gachcha* or lineages, the popularity of Jainism increased in this region.[44] We come to know that with the help of mystic practices, these *gachcha* succeeded in spreading the idea of non-violence and also converted whole villages and communities to vegetarianism. In Rajasthan, there was a continuous transformation of goddesses within the Jaina realm, as for example Sarasvatī at Pallu, Sacciyā Mātā at Osian, and Kevāya Mātā at Kinasariya, which are clear examples of the association of Puranic goddesses with Jainism. But above and beyond them, the superiority of Jaina Tīrthaṅkara is clearly shown, and conspicuously found, in conceptual terms and in iconographic representations.[45]

## Endnotes

1 Kailash Chand Jain, *Lord Mahāvīra and His Times* (New Delhi: Motilal Banarsidass, 1991); Paul Dundas, *The Jainas* (London and New York: Routledge, 2002). Also see Jeffrey D. Long, 'Glossary,' in *Jainism: An Introduction* (London: I.B. Tauris, 2013).

2 Those who attain the highest position are called tīrthaṅkara in Jainism. These are 24 in number and Mahāvīra is a historical figure among them.

3 Sehdev Kumar, *Jaina Temples of Rajasthan* (New Delhi: Abhinav Publications, 2001).

4 Ibid.

5 B.C. Bhattacharya, *Jaina Iconography* (New Delhi: Motilal Banarsidass, 1974), 123–124.

6 Ibid.

7 U.P. Shah, 'Iconography of the Sixteen Jaina Mahāvidyās,' *Journal of Indian Society of Oriental Art* 15 (1947): 114–177. He has made this point on the basis of texts like *Piṇḍaniryukti*, *Pañcāśaka* of Haribhadra. Both mantra and *vidyā* possess magic powers, but whereas mantras constituted letters like *Om*, *Hrim*, *Svāhā*, etc., presided over by male deities and mastered by repetition, *vidyās* are combinations of words invoking female divinities and mastered only by the prescribed rite.

8 Shah, 'Iconography,' 171.

9 *Pāpaśrutavidyā* is considered a sinful science and among different *vidyās*, Gaurī is attached to sinful science. She is also one of the Brahmanical goddesses associated

with Śiva. *Mahāniśītha Sūtra* was re-edited by Haribhadrasūrī (707 CE–770 CE) and *Sūtrakṛtānga Sūtra* is the second Jaina canonical text. Shah, 'Iconography,' 115.

10 Shah, 'Iconography,' 115.

11 Ibid., 116.

12 Ibid.

13 Ibid. This is a Digambara narrative and it was composed in 783 CE–784 CE.

14 Manu, Mānavā, Kauśikā, Gaurikā, Gāndhārā, Bhūmituṇḍakā, Mūlavīryā and Śaṅkukā belonged to the Āryas, Ādityas or Gandharvas, while the other eight, namely the Mātaṅga, Pāṇḍuka, Kāla, Śvapāka, Pārvata, Vaṃśālaya, Pāṇḍumūla and Vṛkṣamūla, belonged to the Daityas, Pannagas or Mātaṅgas.

15 The *Āvaśyakaniryukti* is a sort of commentary on the *Āvaśyaka Sūtra* composed after the manner of the Brahmanical *Sūtras* and sometimes giving only suggestive words; it was composed by Bhadrabāhu II in fourth or fifth century CE.

16 Shah, 'Iconography,' 117.

17 Bhattacharya, *Jaina Iconography*, 122–132. Also see, Kumar, *Jaina Temples*; Harihar Singh, *Jaina Temples of Western India* (Varanasi: Parshvanath Vidyashram Research Institute, 1982).

18 Bhattacharya, *Jaina Iconography*, 123.

19 Kumar, *Jaina Temples*, 119.

20 Bhattacharya, *Jaina Iconography*, 124.

21 Ibid.

22 Ibid.

23 Ibid.

24 Ibid., 125.

25 Ibid., 126.

26 Ibid., 128.

27 Ibid., 129.

28 Ibid., 130.

29 '*Vairoṭīmśyāmavarṇāmajagaravāhanāmcaturbhujāmkhaḍagorgālaṅgakṛta-dakṣiṇakarāmkheṭakāhiyutvāmkarām.*' *Nirvāṇakalikā*; Bhattacharya, *Jaina Iconography*, 130.

30 Bhattacharya, *Jaina Iconography*, 131.

31 Ibid.

32 Ibid., 132.

33 Kumar, *Jaina Temples*, 87.

34 U.P. Shah and M.A. Dhaky, eds., *Aspects of Jaina Art and Architecture* (Ahmedabad: Gujarat State Committee for the Celebration of 2500th Anniversary of Bhagavan Mahavir Nirvana, 1975).

35 R.N. Nandi, *Religious Cults and Institutions in the Deccan* (New Delhi: Motilal Banarsidass, 1973), 152–155.

36 John Cort, 'Medieval Jaina Goddess Traditions,' *Numen* 34, Fasc. 2 (December, 1987): 239.

37 Shah, 'Iconography,' 117–118.

38 Ibid. In *Paumacariyam*, Rāvaṇa's *sādhanā* of *Bahurūpāvidyā* is mentioned, which is considered as a Mahāvidyā, and other *vidyās* associated with him are Prajñapati, Kaumārī, Aṇimā, Laghimā, Vārāhī, Kauberī, Yogeśvarī, Caṇḍālī Śaṅkarī, etc.

39 Shah, 'Iconography,' 115–117.

40 Cort, 'Medieval Jaina Goddess,' 245.

41 Shah, 'Iconography,' 169

42 According to Jaina scriptures, only those born in *kṣatriyakula* can become a tīrthaṅkara; the story of transfer of an embryo is popular in the textual and art traditions, clearly conveying this idea.

43 See Ram Vallabh Somani, *Jaina Inscription of Rajasthan* (Jaipur: Rajasthan Prakrit Bharati Sansthan, 1982). Also see, Ratanlal Mishra, *Inscriptions of Rajasthan*, Vols 1–4 (New Delhi: Himanshu Publications, 2006).

44 K.C. Jaina, *Jainism in Rajasthan* (Sholapur: Gulabchand Hirachand Doshi Jaina Saṁskṛti Saṁrakshaka Sangha, 1963), 53–109.

45 Virendra Singh Bithoo, 'Goddesses in Early Medieval Rajasthan: Iconography, Mythology and Historical Geography' (MPhil dissertation, Jawaharlal Nehru University, 2014).

Thangka with Caturbhujā Prajñāpāramitā, Nepal, c. 17th or 18th century CE

Sanskrit *Aṣṭasāhasrikā Prajñāpāramitā Sūtra* manuscript; *dvibhuja Kanaka* rajñāpāramitā, Nālanda, c. seventh–eleventh centuries CE

*Vīrakal*, Near Whitefield, Bangalore, Karnataka, 13th–14th century CE

# III

# Religious Traditions, Visual Representations and Regional Contexts

8

# Icons and Patterns of Worship from the Fringes of South India: The Religious Landscape of Northern Tamil Nadu

V. Selvakumar

The patterns of worship and iconography from the fringes of early medieval South India (sixth to tenth century CE), particularly in the northern part of Tamil Nadu, form the focus of this essay. The term 'fringe' refers to the images/shrines (i.e. of Durgā, Ayyaṉār, Jyeṣṭhā, Gaṇeśā, hero stones, rock art sites and natural forms) from isolated contexts of the landscape, that is away from the village settlements and 'major' centres of worship.[1] The complex ritual centres were, in fact, supported and worshipped by all sections of the society, including royal households and the *brāhmaṇas*. The term fringe is used here in a spatial sense, as these shrines occur on the outskirts of the villages, and also in a cultural sense, as they are 'non-formalised' places of worship, that is without full-time priests and with simple modes of worship. In discussions on the *nāyaṉmārs* (Śaiva saints), especially Kaṇṇappa Nāyaṉār and Atipatta Nāyaṉār respectively from the clans of hunters and fisherfolk, 'fringe' refers to social groups other than the dominant sections of the society. The idea of fringe can be traced both from *emic* as well as *etic* perspectives. In the early medieval times, hierarchy developed in society, as well as in the worship of gods, and certain deities were seen as 'smaller' or less powerful, when compared to Śiva or Viṣṇu. The *bhakti* movement was an attempt to build 'greater' traditions of Śiva and Viṣṇu worship, dissuading people from other modes of worship, including Jainism and Buddhism. The *etic* perception of historians, anthropologists and archaeologists, outsiders to the reality, seems to have considered these shrines and deities as marginal, and they do not find due attention in discussions on the early medieval religion.[2]

## The Research Problem

The religion, art, architecture and iconography of the Tamil region have been investigated by several researchers, including S.R. Balasubrahmanyam,[3] K.R. Srinivasan,[4] R. Champakalakshmi,[5] R. Nagaswamy,[6] R. Mahalakshmi[7] and Archana Verma.[8] The so-called 'folk' deities and shrines have been studied by researchers from the colonial period, and anthropologists, historians and folklorists have concentrated on them. Post the 1950s, monuments and icons have been correlated with sociopolitical and cultural contexts, and scholars have highlighted the influence and fusion of local traditions with the Brahmanical traditions in various forms of worship.[9] While many art historians have studied temples, art, architecture and iconography, archaeologists have focussed on the discovery and identification of archaeological sites with sculptures and inscriptions that are located away from the major centres in the countryside.[10]

The high degree of emphasis on civilisation and empires,[11] attractive antiquities, masterpieces of art and architecture, major monuments, and religious texts during the colonial period, perhaps, contributed to the thrust on the ideological, archaeological and socio-economic aspects of Brahmanical temples. The idea that the nature of worship and belief systems varied across the region is highlighted by the concept of *tiṇai* of the *Caṅkam* Tamil texts. However, in order to understand spatial variation, further research, including mapping the patterns of worship archaeologically and ethnographically, is necessary. Himanshu Prabha Ray observes that 'archaeology presents a very different perspective on the study of religious transformation and patronage in early South Asia when compared to conventional historical writings on the subject, which focus on religious architecture and *brāhmaṇas* being agents of political legitimisation and hegemonic control.' She adds that 'both in Vidarbha and in Andhra, Buddhist shrines and temples form a part of the landscape along with the megalithic burials sites and memorials to the deceased.'[12]

A similar religious landscape is encountered in the northern part of Tamil Nadu.

Archaeologists situated their studies on large sites and mounds, like the art historians who focussed on large monuments and masterpieces in the early part of the twentieth century. The theoretical development of settlement pattern studies, Lewis Binford's regional approach,[13] ecological approaches,[14] the concept of Robert Foley's 'off-sites'[15] and recent formulations on landscape archaeology have all begun to stress the need for looking at a landscape holistically to understand the diverse manifestation of archaeological cultures. Archaeological surveys have helped to accumulate empirical data on sculptures, shrines and rock shelters across the landscape of Tamil Nadu. The data available on shrines has not been placed in historical and cultural contexts. By mapping the shrines and icons, we could reconstruct the iconographic landscape, their diversity and contexts, and attempt to explain the factors leading to a variety of worship.

The early medieval period in the region of Tamiḻakam, from around sixth century CE, witnessed diverse political, social and cultural developments.[16] The Pallavas and Pāṇṭiyas controlled the agriculturally potential parts of the Tamil country, while the smaller chieftains occupied the dry, marginal regions. Land grants to the *brāhmaṇas* were a significant development, and the temple as a religious institution and centre of organised worship was gaining importance primarily with royal support. The Brahmanical religions—Śaivism and Vaiṣṇavism, and the *Itihāsa-Purāṇa* ideas of worship—in fact, gained ground from this period; the *bhakti* movement was developing, while Buddhism and Jainism had their presence in certain areas.

## The Icons and Shrines in the Pre-Early Medieval Period[17]

The concept of sacred space in the early pre-agrarian societies centred on natural forces and features, such as hills, forests, trees, rock shelters or caves and termite/snake mounds. Such sacred spaces existed in the *Caṅkam* Age and also continued in the medieval and modern periods.[18] Hills have been always associated with Murukaṉ in the Tamil tradition.[19] An interesting aspect is the association of hills and caves with the shrines/caves of Jainism, as well as the worship of Murukaṉ or Śiva on the hills of Tiruparankunram and Tiruchirappalli. The sites of Jaina caves of the early historic period in Tamil Nadu with Tamil-Brāhmī inscriptions[20] also have evidence of microliths and rock paintings at a few locations.[21] The hills were probably centres of religious activities because of their landscape attributes and the perception of psychological loneliness of humans on the 'slippery landscape'. Such localities gained importance because of the significance of the water resources (springs) and their locational command over surrounding territories. These hills and rocks provided clean, solid and barren locations away from the thickly populated settlements. The megalithic burials/monuments and hero stones were important sacred spaces of this period, and some of these monuments are in the shape of anthropomorphic figures—for example, Modur and Udaiyanattam in the northern part of Tamil Nadu.[22] No clearly identifiable religious structures have been encountered in archaeological excavations of port towns like Arikamedu,[23] Alagankulam,[24] or Pattanam[25] in Kerala, but Buddhist remains were found at Kanchipuram and Kaveripumpattinam[26] excavations. The temple structure excavated at Saluvanakuppam near Mamallapuram by the Archaeological Survey of India is considered to be of the *Caṅkam* age by a few researchers because of the presence of large bricks and tiles; however, it appears to be an early medieval structure.[27]Archaeological evidence of images/icons of the early historic period is scanty. Perhaps, paintings and terracotta/ceramic images and motifs were worshipped. Interestingly, an appliqué ceramic motif from the site of Adichanallur is an important pointer to the nature of worship. A figure of a woman is depicted near a plant (probably rice) on which sits an egret.[28] An antelope and lizards are depicted nearby. This image is identified with mother goddess. The pattern of worship included natural elements, hero stones representing heroes and an early form of rock art, such as in the Edakkal cave of Kerala that has engravings of early forms of Teyyam (devil dance). The concepts of divinities, such as Vēlaṉ, Murukaṉ, Aṇaṅku, Koṟṟavai and cognate forms, may have evolved from the prehistoric to the early historic period, and the iconographic features of these forms might have been modelled on or fused with the ideas that came from the northern part of India in the early medieval period.

## Early Medieval Shrines from the Margins

The archaeology of the early medieval period has been largely ignored in Tamil Nadu, while inscriptions and architectural remains have been studied extensively. The impact of the Tamil nationalist approach, which glorified the *Caṅkam* age and the Indo-Roman trade with focus on the period from the third century BCE to the third century CE, is one factor responsible for this development. The historical developments from the third century CE to the ninth century CE need to be focussed on more carefully using archaeological and textual materials.

The major religious and political centres and settlements of the Pallavas developed in Toṇḍaimaṇḍalam, which is in the north-eastern part of Tamil Nadu. The development of tank irrigation in the eastern part of the Toṇḍaimaṇḍalam region, which receives relatively high rainfall, facilitated the expansion of wet agriculture, which was established during the early historic period. The Pallavas further developed irrigation activities to support more settlements and donated land to the *brāhmaṇas*. The use of stone for the construction of temples gained importance, and rock-cut caves, such as Mamandur, Dalavanur, Mamallapuram and Siyamangalam, as well as the structural temples of Kanchipuram, Mamallapuram, Panamalai and other centres heralded complex religious institutions. The religious landscape of northern Tamil Nadu during the Pallava period was diverse; while the main centres had square/rectangular shrines with settlements in front or all around, at many of the villages, people installed images of deities, such as Durgā, Jyeṣṭhā and Ayyaṉār, in the remote areas.[29] At a few sites of northern Tamil Nadu, evidence of Jainism and Buddhism is found.

Why did the Pallavas create temples? The Siyamangalam inscription of Mahēndravarman I mentions that king Lalitāṅkura created the temple 'in order to obtain merit in future life'.[30] Clearly, religious sects had influenced the king to make him believe that such deeds would bring benefits in his future life. The Pallava temples were concentrated in urban centres, that is Kanchipuram and Mamallapuram, and in the *brahmadēya* settlements of the northern part of Tamil Nadu. There are caves on rocks and hills, for example, the Panamalai temple and the Tiruchirappalli cave *maṇḍapa*; the inscription from the latter site mentions a statue of Satyāsandha on the hill.[31] The Pallavas were creating a cultural landscape, with temples, cities and tanks named after the king.[32] Villages of the early historic period were named after hills, flora and fauna, but from the Pallava period, they were created after the name of the ruler. From the Mahēndravāḍi inscription, it is clear the temple was named Mahēndra Viṣṇugraha, the tank was called Mahēndra Taṭāka, and the name of the town was Mahēndrapura.[33] Temples served as a very powerful medium of asserting the authority of the king on landscapes.

A survey of literature revealed the existence of 88 images of deities, such as Durgā, Jyeṣṭhā and Ayyaṉār panel sculptures in isolated contexts in northern Tamil Nadu, besides their representations in the major temples, such as Kailāsanāthar temple, Kanchipuram. About 100 hero stones of the early medieval period also exist in this region. Their presence across the northern part of Tamil Nadu suggests the popularity of these deities and hero stone worship during the Pallava times.

## Durgā/Koṟṟavai

The earliest representations of Durgā occur in Mamallapuram and Kanchipuram.[34] Durgā images as panel sculptures in isolated contexts dated to the early medieval period have been documented at 51 sites. Durgā is represented in *samabhaṅga* posture with eight hands, with all the attributes, such as conch and wheel, bow and arrow, sword and shield, dagger, *pāśa* (rope), *abhaya mudrā* and *kaṭihasta*, and standing on the head of a buffalo. The *Viṣṇu Purāṇa*, *Suprabhedāgama* and other texts mention her attributes.[35] Inscriptions have references to Piṭāri and Paṭāri,[36] and an inscription from Chengam refers to the donation of land to the family of a person who offered his head to *Paṭāri*.[37] The practice of offering the head to Koṟṟavai/Durgā occurs in *Cilappatikāram* and similar depictions are found in Māmallapuram and other sites. An image from Sikkadu near Villupuram has the inscription 'Śrī Nandivarman', associated with the Pallava king Nandivarman II,[38] and this image has a person sacrificing his head. Another image of Durgā at Ayankunjaram is dated to the seventh year of Paramesvaravarman, made by Sendakodan of Tirukunram. The inscription says the images are meant for the worship of *perumakkaḷ* (seniors) and *iḻamakkaḷ* (juniors).[39] Another image from

Siddhalingamadam has reference to a water sluice; perhaps, it was installed near a water sluice. Lion and antelope are depicted as the vehicles of Durgā here.

## Jyeṣṭhā

Jyeṣṭhā or Cēṭṭai is another important image associated with village shrines. Twenty-one images of this deity have been identified in the northern part of Tamil Nadu. Jyeṣṭhā is equated with Alakṣmī and attributes are found in various texts, including *Baudhāyana Gṛhyasūtra.*[40] Jyeṣṭhā is depicted as a middle-aged woman with a prominent belly and spread-out legs in a seated position. *Māntaṉ*, her son, with the head of a nandi or bull, is depicted along with a crow and a broom. Jyeṣṭhā, who was worshipped extensively, was abandoned at a later period and the images were also perhaps discarded. Images of Jyeṣṭhā are found in several villages, such as Tiruvennainallur, Tiruvatikunnam and Vikkiravandi.

### Śāstā/Ayyaṉār

Ayyaṉār images are found at 12 sites in isolated contexts away from main settlements. Ayyaṉār is found in a seated position in *utkaṭāsana* with *yogapaṭṭa* and *jaṭāmuṭi*. A horse or dogs are sculpted along with the images.

### Hero Stones

Several hero stones from the Pallava period have been reported mainly from the north-western region of Tamil Nadu.[41] For this study, 100 hero stones were examined. These hero stones, many of which show Pallava affiliation, clearly reveal the pastoral nature of the region, where cattle lifting and recovery are frequently mentioned. The hero stones have the depiction of a hero with a bow and/or a sword, a dagger or a shield; in addition, a *kalaśa* with a spout (*keṇḍi*), which sometimes resembles a *stūpa* in design and is identified as a toddy pot, and what appears to be a Śiva *liṅga* are also carved. In a rare instance at Eduttanur, a dog that lost its life is also depicted (see Image 8.1).[42]

**Image 8.1: A hero stone of Pallava period for a hero and a dog, Eduttanur, Tamil Nadu, c. seventh century CE**

*Credit*: Historical Atlas Project of South India

The posture of warriors depicted on the hero stones resembles the image of Mahiṣa depicted in the early seventh century CE Mahiṣāsuramardinī panel in the Mahiṣāsuramardinī *maṇḍapa* at Mamallapuram (see Image 8.2). The representation of the hero on the hero stones is on the left side of the panel, facing the right; on the contrary, in the Mahiṣāsuramardini panel at Māmallapuram, Mahiṣa is on the right, while Durgā is depicted on the left side. Although the impression is that Mahiṣā is on retreat, when compared with the hero stone panels, it is clear he is in an attack mode.

**Image 8.2: Mahiṣa from Mahiṣamardinī Panel, Mamallapuram, c. seventh century CE**

*Credit*: R. Ramesh, Archaeological Survey of India, Chennai

While many hero stones are related to battles and clashes (54) and cattle lifting (32), a few depict heroes, who lost their lives fighting wild animals. These hero stones are found mainly in the region of Villupuram, Tiruvannamalai, Krishnagiri and Dharmapuri districts, while Vellore and Kanchipuram have a limited number of early medieval hero stones (see Table 8.1). Temporally, the hero stones are concentrated in the periods of sixth, seventh and eighth centuries CE suggesting the popularity of the hero stone tradition and political instability witnessed in the region in the context of the establishment of Pallava rule (see Table 8.2).

**Table 8.1: Distribution of Hero stones in different districts of Tamil Nadu**

| Dharma-puri | Krishnagiri | Salem | Thiruvan-namalai | Vellore | Kanchi-puram | Villupuram |
|---|---|---|---|---|---|---|
| 32 | 9 | 2 | 36 | 1 | 1 | 19 |

*Source*: Author

**Table 8.2: Distribution of Hero stones by century CE**

| 4th | 5th | 6th | 7th | 8th | 9th | Total |
|---|---|---|---|---|---|---|
| 1 | 5 | 45 | 24 | 18 | 7 | 100 |

*Source*: Author

The hero stones are worshipped today as temples of Vediyappaṉ in many parts of northern Tamil Nadu.

## Rock Painting Sites

Sites with rock paintings are found at Kilvalai, Settavarai and a few sites near Tiruvannamalai. They could have been centres of worship in the early historic and the medieval times. Kilvalai is located near Tirukkovilur in Villupuram district of Tamil Nadu, 24 km northwest of Villupuram; it's an important rock-art site of Tamil Nadu and has paintings of a human figure seated on a horse.[43] These could be the earliest form of representation of heroes.

## Shrines Under Trees with Polished Stone Axes

There are shrines under trees in Salem, Dharmapuri and Krishnagiri, and other parts of northern Tamil Nadu with polished stone axes or Neolithic celts (see Image 8.3). They are worshipped even today and we do not know how old this practice is.

**Image 8.3: Polished stone axes ('Neolithic Celts'); Left: Mulavi, Right: Nettakalankottai, Salem district**

*Credit*: R. Ramesh, Archaeological Survey of India, Chennai

## Patterns of Distribution of Shrines/Sculptures in Northern Tamil Nadu

The data collected on stone sculptures from northern Tamil Nadu, located in isolated contexts away from temples and settlements and datable from the seventh to the tenth century CE, reveals the predominance of Durgā images, followed by Jyeṣṭhā and Ayyaṉār (see Table 8.3). This distribution may not be representative, as the dataset is not complete. However, it may point to the popularity of Koṟṟavai or Durgā worship. The patterns of distribution of Durgā and hero stones seem to show different trends. The hero stones are found mostly in the district of Tiruvannāmalai and Dharmapuri, Krishnagiri and Villupuram, where the presence of Durgā images is minimal, with the exception of Villupuram (see Image 8.4). The hero stones are dominant in the region that was in the control of the chieftains, while images of Durgā are concentrated in the core areas of the Pallavas in Toṇṭaimaṇṭalam.

**Table 8.3 Distribution of sculptures in the northern part of Tamil Nadu**

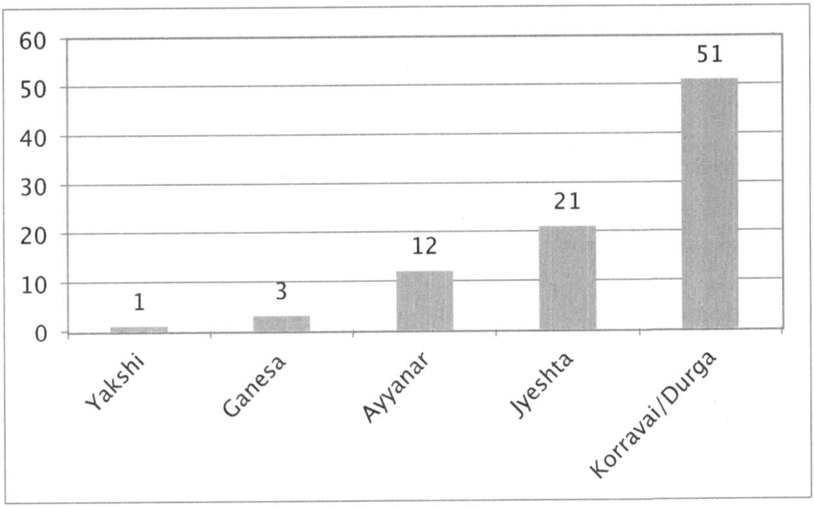


*Credit*: Author

**Image 8.4: Distribution pattern of different types of shrines in the northern part of Tamil Nadu, CL: shrines with Celts; RP: sites with rock paintings; HS: Hero stones; SC: sites with sculptures of deities**

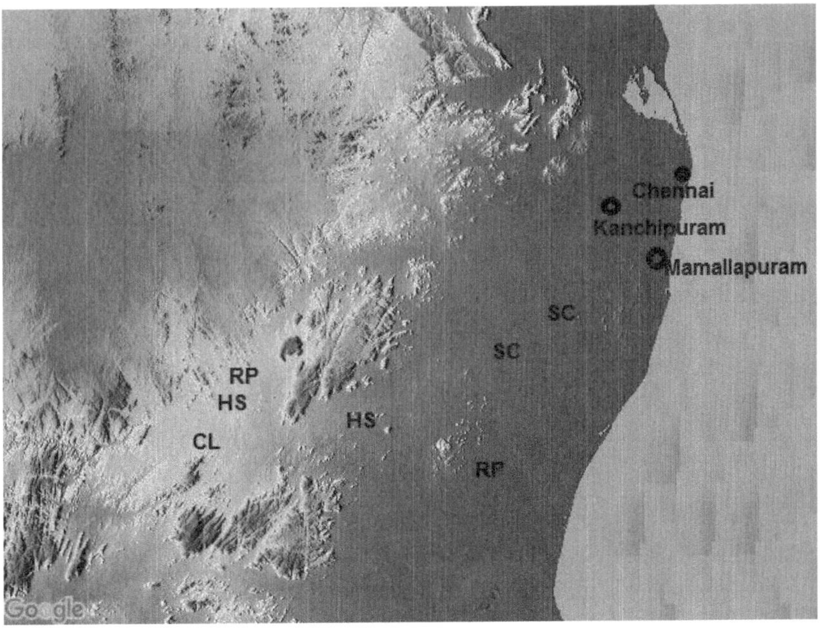


*Source*: Author

### Locational Context

The location of the shrines is very important to understand spatial organisation in villages. The shrines are not generally found in the centre of the villages. Instead, they are located along water tanks and near boundaries. Some of them are also in areas with a dense growth of trees. The location of these shrines is in contrast to the major centres where the *brāhmaṇa* residences are located in the front or all around the temple.

### Guardian Deities

The deities are known as guardian deities, as people believed that they guard the water sources and village boundaries. In the village of Sikkadu, people reported that Durgā saved many people during a cholera attack. We need to look at the micro-ecological systems as well as the health and hygiene conditions (spread of diseases and mosquito menace) of the villages, where a lot of water was stored for agriculture in tanks since the time of the Pallavas. They may have been used as boundary markers for villages.

### Festivals and Rituals

Periodic festivals are associated with these shrines. In some villages, they are linked to the main shrines. The dynamics linking the icons with the belief systems and other ritual centres of the villages are important. At Siddhalingamadam near Villupuram, during a festival, the main deity is taken in a procession to the location of the Durgā image near the boundary of the village.

## Saints from the Fringes

The *bhakti* movement in South India is one of the important religious developments of the early medieval period and it contributed to the development of *Śaiva* and Vaiṣṇava worship across the region.[44] The cult of *nāyaṉmārs* became well-established by the 12th century ce.[45] Here, I take up the case of two saints—Kaṇṇappar Nāyaṉār and Atipatta Nāyaṉār—who belonged to the clans of hunters and fisherfolk respectively.[46]

## Kaṇṇappar

Kaṇṇappar was a devotee and hunter of the Kalahasti region of Andhra who offered his eye to lord Śiva when he saw the *Śivaliṅga* bleeding. According to Dennis Hudson, the earliest representation of Kaṇṇappar occurs in the ninth century CE. From then on, the images of Kaṇṇappar are found frequently in temples. At the Krupānāthasvāmi shrine of Tiruppanangadu in Cheyyar Taluk, there is an inscription mentioning the hunters who claim to belong to the family of Tirukaṇṇappar.[47] Interestingly, the tradition of Kaṇṇappar is prevalent among the communities of Vaḷaiyars, Veṭṭuvars and Paḷiyars from the remote hills of Varushanad, near Madurai, in Tamil Nadu.[48] A life-size image of Kaṇṇappar, made of basalt stone, is found in the Cōḻa temple at Darasuram (see Image 8.5), which has the panel sculptures of the stories of *nāyaṉmārs*.

**Image 8.5: Image of Kaṇṇappar, Darasuram temple**

*Credit*: Vetriselvi, Archaeological Survey of India, Chennai

Kaṇṇappar has been portrayed as a hunter here with a moustache, leather dress, *jaṭāmukuṭa* and *patrakuṇḍala*, with his plucked eye in his right hand. He has bird's feathers on his headdress. He is shown wearing a garland and a *cannavīra* of cowrie shells. In many Cōḻa temples, he is seen plucking his eye with an arrow, while a hand emerging from the *liṅga* seeks to stop him from doing so. In some of the images, he is shown as placing his leg on the *liṅga* when he wanted to remove his second eye. Such representations are considered to belong to the period after the composition of *Periya Purāṇam*. Kaṇṇappar's story was very powerful, and hence was given importance through portrayal at many temples. The story reflects the importance of *bhakti*, and the offering of meat by Kaṇṇappar reflects the different modes of worship that existed in the shrines away from major ritual centres.

## Worship of Atipatta Nāyaṉār

Atipatta Nāyaṉār was another Śiva saint who belonged to the fisherfolk community, and his story is related to the Kāyārohaṇeśvarasvāmi temple at Nagapattinam. The *utsavar* (processional image) of the temple is taken to the fisherfolk settlement on a particular day for the festival associated with Atipatta Nāyaṉār even today. His image is not frequently represented like that of Kaṇṇappar. Tirukkolili or Tirukkuvalai Śiva temple has an inscription of Rājarāja III, dated 1220 CE, which mentions Atipatta Nāyaṉār's image installed by Alan; that he begged for 2,100 *kācu* from his caste people (*cātiyār*) and created an endowment for offering two *nāḻi* of rice to one Damodarapaṭṭaṉ.[49] When we visited the temple in 2014, we could not identify the image that was installed by Alan at this temple; perhaps it was shifted or removed later.

The stories of the *Nāyaṉmār*s suggest the attempt to depict the *bhakti mārga* of persons belonging to various social groups. What is more interesting are the references to the installation of images and offering of worship of these saints by people who claim to belong to their community/caste. Remarkably, the story of Kaṇṇappar is prevalent in the oral traditions of various communities, especially among the hunters of Tamil Nadu. These portrayals reveal the endeavour to build a socially inclusive society by incorporating people from the margins, at least symbolically. Several such attempts to associate communities living in the margins are found in the *sthalapurāṇas* of a few temples (e.g. *Ampar Purāṇam* of Ambāḷ temple in Nagapattinam district).

## Conclusions

The survey of the evidence suggests the existence of diverse patterns of worship, such as natural trees or forests, shelters with paintings, hero stones across the landscapes and sculptural panels in the fringes away from major complex ritual centres, that is temples. This required the construction of large, permanent structures and the creation of a system for regular worship and performance of rituals according to Āgamic principles in early medieval Tamil Nadu. Interestingly, more or less similar patterns of worship have continued to survive to this day, but not without a lot of changes and transformations.

Toṇḍaimaṇḍalam, covering the districts of Kanchipuram, Tiruvallur, Vellore and Villupuram, which had most of the agrarian settlements, formed the core of the Pallava's domain. Most Pallava rock-cut caves and monumental temple structures, supported by the royals and the elite, as well as royal or urban hubs with a large population like Kanchipuram and Mamallapuram, are located in this region. The presence of elites, including the *brāhmaṇas*, merchants and royals in these hubs, required complex ritual centres. Large monumental temples were constructed at these hubs. In the well-irrigated areas of Toṇṭaimaṇṭalam, temples were constructed with *brāhmāṇa* settlements in the front. In urban centres, a square temple led to the construction of streets all around the temple. The construction of large temples required a lot of resources and Pallava kings were directly involved in this process. These temples symbolically represented their authority and control over the landscape.

The villages with farming communities and without the *brāhmaṇa* population had shrines of Durgā, Ayyaṉār and Jyeṣṭhā in the margins. The inscriptions clearly reveal that these images were installed for worship by the people. The creation of such shrines along the boundaries of the villages could be for the protection of their resources from enemies and also from the diseases that emerged with new ways of life and increased agrarian activities, which may have caused changes in the micro-environment.

The construction of large-scale tanks as well as wet-rice agriculture would have contributed to a new microbiological system and the rise of certain infectious diseases.

The requirement of a village, the nature and occupation of the population and their cultural affiliations, and sociopolitical conditions determined the pattern of worship. In northern Tamil Nadu, regions of higher elevation and those with dry pastoral conditions such as Dharmapuri, Krishnagiri and Tiruvannamalai districts have a higher number of hero stones. These regions did not support wet agriculture because of the nature of the terrain and erratic rainfall. There were pastoral groups here—people who were involved in dryland farming—and hunter-gatherers in the periphery of the Pallava domain, therefore frequent battles and clashes occurred for political domination among local chiefs. The hero stone inscriptions indicate that the Pallavas did not have total political and administrative control over these regions, although the chiefs owed their allegiance to the Pallavas nominally. The Pallavas probably used these hunters and chiefs in their army. The requirement of warriors for protecting villages and the cattle and buffalo population created a necessity for the cult of heroes in this region. The warriors who sacrificed their lives for the cause of villages, or the chiefs had to be placed on a sacred pedestal. It appears that in these regions, hero stones were more important than the images of Durgā/Ko<u>r</u><u>r</u>avai; these deities seem to have been worshipped mostly in the region of Toṇṭaimaṇṭalam. Although the hero stone tradition was older, with the new use of stone sculptures and scripts, the hero stone tradition took a fresh form in the emerging political scenario of the early Pallava period.

The worship of Durgā seems to have been promoted for motivating warriors and young men, to prepare them for contingencies in the villages and the Pallava kingdom. The establishment of Durgā or other deities was strong in the early medieval period, as we know that king Vijayālaya Cō<u>l</u>a built a shrine for Niśumbhasūdinī at Tanjavur after his conquest of the region. It is not clear if the images were also installed along the boundaries of the *brāhmaṇa* villages as territorial markers and guardians of the villages.

The linking of the main shrine with other sacred and social spaces of villages is an important part of the dynamics related to belief systems and their social integration. The Brahmanical temples were linked to various groups of the villages through festivals and rituals, perhaps in order to maintain harmonious bonds among the communities as well as within the village and larger territories of *nāṭu*. Some festivals were not just confined to the villages, but drew people from larger territories. At Nagapattinam, the story of Atipatta Nāyaṉār is associated with the main deity and the *utsavamūrti* of Śiva is taken to the settlement of fisherfolk. The temple precincts, especially the circumambulation, became a site for the representation of saints from the margins and stories were carved on the *gopuras* and *makara toraṇa* above the niches.

Noboru Karashima, in the context of the Cōḻa period, argues that the *brahmadēya* settlements 'must have been the local nuclei of the Cōḻa power structure, their function being to integrate and control the surrounding non-*brahmadēya* villages'.[50] This argument could be extended to the conditions of Sanskritisation in the early medieval period. Brahmanical ideology, comprising the Brahmanical religions, temple worship, the settlement of *brāhmaṇas* and the knowledge system, assisted the state in controlling territories through religion. The liberal *brāhmaṇa-veḷḷān* alliance vernacularised Brahmanical ideas through *Tēvāram* compositions and gained the support of major sections of society.[51] Many sections were integrated into Brahmanical ideology through the *bhakti* movement, a major powerful ideological force.[52]

Through the adoption of Brahmanical ideas, agrarian elites too created their own Tamil Śaiva ideology, which in a sense helped the non-*brāhmaṇa* social groups to be integrated into society at least symbolically in the divine realm. The arrangement for singing *Tiruppatiyam* in the temples in Tamil and the rise of *nāyaṉmār* cult are indicators of the Veḷḷāḷa community and other sects gaining a role in temple worship.

As society was transforming, new social groups were gaining importance or seeking social space, and there was a necessity to incorporate all kinds of communities into mainstream society while maintaining a social hierarchy. The *bhakti* movement itself sought to maintain caste distinctions and reinforce social hierarchy.[53] The composition of *Periya Purāṇam* and the popularisation of the stories of *nāyanmārs* through visual media seem to point to attempts to theoretically incorporate people from the fringes into society through iconography and a belief system, at least in certain geographical contexts. Perhaps the *bhakti* movement and this incorporation of marginalised people into temple worship worked as a continuous process throughout the early medieval period. During this time, while there were attempts at selective incorporation of groups or rather their representative saints into temple worship after struggles and excuses, in the later medieval period, social hierarchy became rigid and only the representatives of marginalised communities had a place along the fringes of the temple complex. The *bhakti* movement, in a sense, supported the elite among the non-*brāhmaṇas* in gaining access to temple worship, while fringe groups were symbolically represented. However, the level and degree of temple orthodoxy varied in space, as prevalent even today (e.g. Chidambaram), according to local factors such as the numbers and dominance of the *brāhmaṇas*, *veḷḷāḷas* and other groups, and their degree of influence and persistence. The ideological system would have been flexible in remote contexts (as at Tiruppanangadu and Tirukkuvalai), while they were rigid in the major centres with a large orthodox population; therefore a rigid system could not be proposed for the whole of south India. The stories of *Periya Purāṇam* are part of a poetic, literary landscape and the ideas of a few intellectuals, but in the actual social landscape, the rules were different and unyielding. The *bhakti* movement integrated society and incorporated people from the upper strata of non-*brāhmaṇa* groups, but also helped to maintain caste hierarchy.

## Endnotes

1 There is objection to the use of categories like 'little' and 'greater' to describe folk and religious traditions, respectively. We could label them as 'simple' or 'complex' ritual centres of worship, but one may still find issues with these terms. In fact, the mode of worship at these shrines on the fringes is very simple compared to the complex rituals, architecture, iconography and *Puranic* stories associated with the Brahmanical temples. The construction of architectural edifices and maintenance of regular worship at temples through the performance of *pūjās* is a difficult managerial task that requires a lot of resources. It is precisely because of this reason we could consider the temples as major ritual 'centres'.

The representations of these deities also occur in the Brahmanical temples as panel sculptures or small shrines. In this essay, I have not discussed about the images of these deities found in the Brahmanical temples. Even in many early medieval temples, such images are in the margins, that is, in the niches or *devakoṣṭhas*, while deities such as Śiva, Viṣṇu and Brahmā (as listed in the scheme of Mandagapattu inscription of Mahēndra Pallava) occupy the centre of the temple as *mūlavar* (presiding deity). Some of the Pallava caves have five cells, perhaps meant for deities other than the trio, and the Pāṇṭiya cave at Tiruchirapalli has several deities. We do have Durgā as the presiding deity in the Draupadī *ratha* at Mamallapuram. The monopoly of Śiva and Viṣṇu, perhaps, emerged slightly later. The idea that these deities are 'smaller' compared to the greater deities is reflected in the hymns of the *bhakti* saints, as for instance Toṇṭaraṭipoṭi *āḻvār* who compares between Jyeṣṭhā and Viṣṇu. See T.A. Gopinatha Rao, *Elements of Hindu Iconography*, Vol. I, Part II (New Delhi: Motilal Banarsidass, 1914), 390.

2 Hence, I have used the term fringe here. However, I do not consider that these shrines were on the fringes in terms of importance; for the people in the villages, they might have been their own 'centres', while the Brahmanical temples were on the fringes. Perhaps, from the view of the elite or dominant sections, it was the other way round, which is also reflected in medieval literature. See Note 1.

The 'site' and 'off-site' concepts of archaeology can be compared to antiquarian induced perceptions of monumental architecture or masterpieces and loose sculptures.

3 S.R. Balasubrahmanyam, *Early Chola Art*, Part I (Bombay: Asia Publishing House, 1966); S.R. Balasubrahmanyam, *Middle Chola Temples* (Faridabad: Thomson Press, 1975).

4 K.R. Srinivasan, *Temples of South India* (New Delhi: National Book Trust, 1972).

5 R. Champakalakshmi, *Trade, Ideology and Urbanization: South India 300 BC to AD 1300* (New Delhi: Oxford University Press, 1996).

6 R. Nagaswamy, *Vishnu Temples of Kāñcīpuram*, (New Delhi: D.K. Print World, 2011).

7 R. Mahalakshmi, *The Making of the Goddess: Koṟṟavai-Durgā in the Tamil Traditions* (New Delhi: Penguin Books, 2011).

8 Archana Verma, *Temple Imagery from Early Mediaeval Peninsular India* (Surrey: Ashgate Publishing, 2012).

9 Mahalakshmi, *The Making of the Goddess*, 88.

10 K. Rajan, V.P. Yatheeskumar and S. Selvakumar, *Catalogue of Archaeological Sites in Tamil Nadu*, Vols I and II (Tanjavur: Heritage India Trust, 2009);

C. Veeraraghavan, 'Natunattupaguthiyil Grama Theivacchirpankal,' Kovilur Athinam Endowment Lecture 2014, *Āvaṇam* 26 (2014): 291–303.

11 There was compulsion among certain Indian intellectuals to paint a greater picture of India's past in the light of colonial critiques of India.

12 H.P. Ray, 'The Archaeology of Sacred Spaces in India: From Multi-Religious Sites to Monuments,' Presidential address at the annual meeting of the Indian Archaeology Society 2013, *Purātattva* 44 (2014): 1–15.

13 Sally R. Binford and Lewis Binford, *New Perspectives in Archaeology* (Chicago: Aldine Press, 1968).

14 K. Paddayya, 'Ecological Archaeology and Ecology of Archaeology,' *Bulletin of the Deccan College Research Institute* 42 (1981–1982): 130–151.

15 R.A. Foley, 'Off-Site Archaeology: An Alternative Approach for The Short-Sited,' in *Pattern of the Past: Essays in Honour of David Clarke*, eds I. Hodder, G. Isaac and N. Hammond (Cambridge: Cambridge University Press, 1981).

16 The beginning of social transformation in the medieval period could be traced from the Pulankurichi inscription.

17 While studying the early historic and early medieval periods, in my opinion, independent analysis of archaeological remains, on one level, without the incorporation of literary texts, offers better perspectives.

18 The *kōyilkāṭu* of Tamil Nadu and *kāvu* of Kerala fall under this category.

19 The association of hilltops with power could be seen in the references of the *Caṅkam* texts.

20 Iravatham Mahadevan, *Early Tamil Epigraphy From The Earliest Times to The Sixth Century AD* (Chennai: Cre-A and the Department of Sanskrit and Indian Studies, Harvard University, 2003).

21 V. Selvakumar, 'Settlement Systems in the Upper Gundar Basin' (Post-Doctoral Research, ICHR, Deccan College, 2001).

22 K. Rajan, *Archaeological Gazeteer of Tamilnadu* (Tanjāvur: Manoo Pathippakam, 1997), 319.

23 Vimala Begley et al., *The Ancient Port of Arikamédu: New Excavations and Researches 1989–1992*, Vol. 1 (Paris: L'École Française d'Extrême-Orient, 2004).

24 T.S. Sridhar, ed., *Alagankulam: An Ancient Roman Port City of Tamil Nadu* (Chennai: Department of Archaeology, 2005).

25 P.J. Cherian, M. Nambirajan, K.P. Shajan, V. Selvakumar and K. Rajan, *Pattanam Excavations: Interim Reports 2011* (Trivandrum: KCHR, 2011).

26 K.V. Soundararajan, *Kaveripattinam Excavations 1963–73: A Port City on the Tamil Nadu Coast* (New Delhi: Archaeological Survey of India, 1994), 16.

27 Sathyabhama Badhreenath, 'Māmallapuram, the Port City: New Revelations,' in *Ports of the Ancient Indian Ocean*, eds M.F. Boussac, J.F. Salles and J.B. Yon (New Delhi: Primus, 2016), 275–288.

28 T.S. Subramanian, 'Unearthing A Great Past,' *Frontline* 22, no. 13 (June 18–July 1, 2005).

29 Several publications list the identification of such deities in Tamil Nadu. A description of the images from *Naṭunāṭu* is found in Veeraraghavan, 'Natunattupaguthiyil,' 291–303.

30 *Annual Report on Indian Epigraphy* (1900): 67; T.V. Mahalingam, *Inscriptions of the Pallavas*, no. 29 (New Delhi: Indian Council of Historical Research and Agam Kala Prakashan, 1988).

31 Mahalingam, *Inscriptions*, no. 32, 125.

32 For example, the Dalavanur cave was named Śatrumalleśvarālaya after the name of the king. See *Annual Report on Indian Epigraphy* (1905), 51.

33 *Annual Report on Indian Epigraphy* (1896): 13.

34 Mahalakshmi, *The Making of the Goddess*, 252–254.

35 Rao, *Elements*, 341–357.

36 Mahalakshmi, *The Making of the Goddess*, 160.

37 N. Vanamamalai, 'Naṭukarkaḷum Nampikkaikaḷum,' in *Seminar on Hero-Stones*, ed. R. Nagaswamy (Chennai: Tamil Nadu State Archaeology Department, 1974), 52.

38 Veeraraghavan, 'Naṭunāṭṭupakutiyil,' 293.

39 Ibid., 294.

40 Rao, *Elements*, 390–399.

41 R. Nagaswamy, ed., *Ceṅkam Naṭukarkaḷ* (Chennai: Tamil Nadu State Archaeology Department, 1972); R. Nagaswamy, ed., *Seminar on Hero-Stones* (Chennai: Tamil Nadu State Archaeology Department, 1974); K. Rajan, *Memorial Stones of South India* (Tanjāvur: Heritage India Trust, 2000); S. Krishnamurty, *Naṭukarkaḷ* Chidambaram: Meyappan Pathippakam, 2004); V. Kesavaraj, *Tennintiya Vīrakkarkaḷ* (Chennai: Kavya, 2008); R. Poongunran, *Naṭukal Kalveṭṭukaḷ* (Chennai: Heritage Treasures, 2017).

42 Poongundran, *Naṭukal*, 265.

43 R. Poundurai, *Tamiḻaka Pāṟai Oviyaṅkaḷ* (Chidambaram: Meyyappan Tamil Ayvagam, 2001); D. Dayalan, 'Rock Art in Tamil Nadu and its Archaeological Perspective,' *Purakala* 23 (2013): 5–18.

44 Champakalakshmi, *Trade, Ideology and Urbanization.*

45 D. Dennis Hudson, 'Violent and Fanatical Devotion Among the Nāyanārs: A Study in the Periya Purāṇam of Cēkkilār,' in *Criminals Gods and Demon*

*Devotees: Essays on the Guardians of Popular Hinduism*, ed. A. Hiltebeitel (New York: State University of New York Press, 1989), 373–404.

46 K.R. Hanumanthan, 'Evolution of Untouchability in Tamil Nadu up to AD 1600,' in *Subordinate and Marginal Groups in Early India*, ed. Aloka Parasher-Sen (New Delhi: Oxford University Press, 2004), 125–156; V. Selvakumar, 'Subaltern Archaeology and the History of Marginalized Communities: Perspectives from South India,' in *Recent Developments in Indian Archaeology*, ed. Ravi Korisettar (New Delhi: Primus, Forthcoming).

47 *Annual Report on Indian Epigraphy*, (1906): 247. This inscription dates to the period of Sambuvarāyar.

48 We do not know if the story is based on a real incident. However, it would not be surprising if such an incident had happened, since the belief systems of ancient and medieval periods are sometimes far from the understanding of present times. In this context, an incident from Karnataka, where a devotee offered his eye to god and numerous people offering their body parts or even life to political leaders or for various movements in South India can be cited. These are instances of blind devotion. See V. Selvakumar, 'Hunters and Hunter-gatherers in Historical India,' *The Eastern Anthropologist* 67, nos 3–4 (2014): 257–274.

49 *Annual Report on Indian Epigraphy*, (1950-51): 246; N. Marxia Gandhi and S. Rajagopal, eds, *Nākapaṭṭinam Māvaṭṭak Kalveṭṭukaḷ* (Chennai: Tamil Nadu State Archaeology Department, 2007), 93.

50 Noboru Karashima, *History and Society in South India: The Cholas to Vijayanagar* (New Delhi: Oxford University Press, 2001), 20. Similar ideas have been presented by Burton Stein in *Peasant, State and Society in Medieval South India* (New York: Oxford University Press, 1980), 276–280; and Champakalakshmi, *Trade, Ideology and Urbanization*, 38–39.

51 Sisir Kumar Das, *A History of Indian Literature 500–1399: From Courtly to the Popular* (Sahitya Academi: 2005), 31–35.

52 R. Champakalakshmi, 'From Devotion and Dissent to Dominance: The Bhakti of the Tamil Āḻvārs and Nāyaṉārs,' in *Tradition, Dissent and Ideology: Essays In Honour of Romila Thapar*, eds R. Champakalakshmi and S. Gopal (New Delhi: Oxford University Press, 1996), 135–162.

53 Patton Burchett, 'Bhakti Rhetoric in the Hagiography of "Untouchable" Saints: Discerning Bhakti's Ambivalence on Caste and Brahminhood,' *International Journal of Hindu Studies* 13, no. 2 (2009): 115–141.

9

# From *Virajā Tīrtha* to 'Allegorical' *Nābhi Gayā*: Exploring the Changing Religious Landscape of Jajpur (Sixth to Fourteenth Centuries CE)

Umakanta Mishra

Jajpur, known as *Virajā-kṣetra*, has been one of the most prominent religious *kṣetras* (centres) of Orissa since, at least, the fifth century CE. The *kṣetra* limit expanded and new centres were added to *Virajā-kṣetra* throughout the historical period. The *Mahābhārata* refers to the sacred river Vaitaraṇī and presiding deity Virajā—a form of Mahiṣāsuramardinī Durgā. A recension of the *Brahma Purāṇa* devotes 12 *ślokas* (verses) to *Virajā-kṣetra* and refers to eight Śaiva *tīrthas*, goddess Virajā and Viṣṇu Varāha, and mentions the *kṣetra* as one among the *pitṛ tīrthas*. The *kṣetra* limit of Virajā further expanded in the 13th/14th-century text *Kapila Saṁhitā*, a *sthala māhātmya* on Odisha. Two chapters were devoted to the description of the *Virajā Tīrtha*. It adds numerous other cults within the *kṣetra* as well as the sacred place Nābhi Gayā, where oblation is offered to dead ancestors (Ch.7.16–17). Finally, the *Brahmāṇḍa Purāṇa*, dated to the 14th century CE, incorporated all these earlier versions and developed the *sthalapurāṇa* called *Virajā-kṣetra Māhātmya* within it, comprising 29 chapters. The *kṣetra* limit was enlarged in the *Māhātmya* by including 68 centres within the *Virajā-kṣetras*. More importantly, *Virajā-kṣetra Māhātmya* describes the Nābhi Gayā centre and contextualises it by bringing in the Gayāsura episode of the *Vāyu Purāṇa*, associating Jajpur as the place where the navel portion of Gayāsura fell. Thus, around the 14th century CE, there was a deliberate attempt by Vaiṣṇava religious ideologues to connect Jajpur with the Vaiṣṇavite Gayā and Gayāsura episode. Is the Gayāsura episode an allegory to the domination of Buddhism by Vaiṣṇavism in Odisha, in general, and Jajpur, in particular, as argued by Rajendralala Mitra?[1] There are numerous Buddhist sites in and around Jajpur, such as Ratnagiri, Udayagiri and Solampur, which existed and expanded at the same time as Brahmanical religions appeared and progressed in and around the region. These Buddhist sites declined during the 13th century CE, juxtaposed with or followed by the appearance of the Gayāsura theme in the *Virajā-kṣetra Māhātmya*. This decline was also marked by the emergence of the cult of Jagannātha in Puri as the state cult of Odisha (Utkala). These juxtapositions—the decline of Buddhism on the one hand, and emergence of the Vaiṣṇavite Nābhi Gayā theme in Jajpur and Jagannātha cult as an imperial cult, on the other, during the 13th and 14th centuries CE—raise several questions. This essay explores the evolution and changes in the religious landscape of *Virajā-kṣetra*, the relations between the Buddhist and Brahmanical orders in Jajpur, in particular, and Odisha, in general, from the sixth to thirteenth centuries CE, and the possible context in which the Nābhi Gayā of the *Vāyu Purāṇa* entered the *Virajā-kṣetra Māhātmya* by studying various texts and exploring archaeological and sculptural remains in a 25 km radius of Jajpur town.

## Evolution of *Virajā-Kṣetra*: Jajpur as a Religious and Political Centre, Puranic and Epigraphic References

Jajpur or *Virajā-kṣetra* is located on the northern bank of river Vaitaraṇī. It is considered to be an important *tīrtha* (pilgrimage centre) of Odisha and India. The *Mahābhārata* refers to Vaitaraṇī and *Virajā tīrtha* as a place for offering *piṇḍas* to ancestors. In the *Tīrtha Yātrā* section of *Vana Parvan* of the *Mahābhārata* [3.83.6–7], sage Pulastya speaks of important *tīrthas* in India and refers to *Virajā tirtha* being situated on the banks of Vaitaraṇī. In the course of describing the *tīrtha yātrā* of the Pāṇḍavas, the text mentions this site as *pitṛ tīrtha* (oblation to ancestors). The *Mahābhārata* dedicates only two *ślokas* to the place, stating that Vaitaraṇī is capable of destroying all types of sins, and the 'one who visits *Virajā Tīrtha* shines like moon'. 'In addition to sanctifying his *kula* [family] he cleanses himself of all his sins. One who bathes in *Virajā Tīrtha* reaps the merit of donating thousand cows besides sanctifying his *kula*.'[2] It is important to note here that the *Mahābhārata's* reference to Virajā refers to a place named after goddess Virajā, a form of Durgā on whose name Jajpur is named as *Virajā-kṣetra*. The presiding deity of Jajpur is Virajā, a two-armed Mahiṣāsuramardinī Durgā ascribed to the Gupta period on the basis of iconographic similarities with Mahiṣāsuramardinī Durgā of Bhumrā.[3]

The list of *tīrthas* in *Virajā-kṣetra* is considerably elaborated in the *Brahma Purāṇa*. Many manuscripts of the *Purāṇas* were found in Odisha with varying composition dates. The *Brahma Purāṇa* states the extent of Oḍra *deśa* (coastal Odisha) and mentions *Virajā-maṇḍala* as the northern boundary of the country (the southern part being *Puruṣottama-maṇḍala*).[4] The reference to *Puruṣottama-maṇḍala*, a reference to *Puruṣottama* of Puri, indicates that the insertion of the *Virajā-kṣetra* portion in the *Brahma Purāṇa* came later because the *Puruṣottama-kṣetra* of Puri began to appear in epigraphic records only around the 10th/11th centuries CE.[5] Similarly, the Varāha image in the Viṣṇu Varāha temple of Jajpur can be dated to the 12th/13th century CE in terms of the iconographic style. The Cateśvara inscription from the time of Anaṅgabhīmadeva III (1211–1238 CE) states that new recensions of *Purāṇas* were made during his reign.[6] It is probable that the *Puruṣottama Māhātmya* and *Virajā-kṣetra* of *Brahma Purāṇa* were inserted in the 13th century. In comparison to the *Mahābhārata's* two *ślokas*, the *Brahma Purāṇa* devotes 12 verses to *Virajā-kṣetra* and refers to eight Śaiva *tīrthas*, goddess Virajā and Viṣṇu Varāha in its description of the cults in the *Virajā-kṣetra*.[7] It also refers to the sacred river Vaitaraṇī. It describes Virajā as the *kṣetra*'s presiding deity, and mentions it as one among the *pitṛ tīrthas*. However, there was no allusion to the Gayāsura episode and Nābhi Gayā *tīrtha* of *Virajā-kṣetra* in the *Brahma* and *Vāmana Purāṇa*.

The *kṣetra* limit of *Virajā-kṣetra* further expanded in the 14th century text *Kapila Saṁhitā*, a *sthala māhātmya* of Odisha.[8] Chapters seven and eight deal with the description of *Virajā-kṣetra*. It is described as a *Pārvatī kṣetra*, adding numerous other cults along with the description of its various centres, a sacred place called Nābhi Gayā, where oblation is offered to the dead ancestors. But the *Kapila Saṁhitā*, for the first time, names the place as Nābhi Gayā where *piṇḍas* (oblations) are offered to one's forefathers.[9] It incorporates all *tīrthas* of the *Brahma Purāṇa* and adds three more Śaiva centres—Akhaṇḍaleśvara, Mukteśvara and Trilocaneśvara—all of which exist today. Finally, the *Brahmāṇḍa Purāṇa* incorporated all the earlier versions and developed the *sthala Purāṇa* called *Virajā-kṣetra Māhātmya* within it, comprising 29 chapters. The *kṣetra* limit was enlarged in the *Māhātmya* by including 68 centres in the *Virajā-kṣetra.* More importantly, *Virajā-kṣetra Māhātmya* added the Gayāsura episode of *Vāyu Purāṇa*, associating Jajpur as the place where the navel portion of Gayāsura fell.

Jajpur was also an important political centre of Odisha from the sixth century CE and served as the capital of the Bhaumakaras and Somavaṁśīs from the eighth to twelfth centuries CE. In the 13th century CE, Anaṅgabhīmadeva III shifted the capital to Cuttack. The Parlakimedi copper plates of Śrī Pṛthivī Mahārajā, who ruled parts of the region during the sixth century CE, refers to Virañjānagar, which has been described as a *skandhāvāra* (a military cantonment).[10] Virañjā in the copper plate is identified with Virajā. The Soro copper plates of Mahārājā Bhānudatta (mid-seventh century CE) states that Virajānagar was the capital of an extensive territory. The Badakhemidi plates of Jayavarman of Śvetaka Gaṅgas (second half of the eighth century CE) states that Virajā was the capital of the Bhaumakara king Śivakaradeva.[11] Virajānagar (*Virajāvāstavya*) is also mentioned as a city in the Dhauli cave inscription (829 CE), which refers to a physician and *paṇḍita* of Virajānagar named Nannaṭa, whose son, Bhīmaṭa, dug the cave in the Dhauligiri during Bhaumakara king Śāntikaradeva's reign.[12]

## Phase 1: The Religious Landscape of Jajpur (Fifth to Eighth Centuries CE): Sculptural Evidence

The *Virajā-kṣetra Māhātmya*, while describing the origin of the *kṣetra*, states that Brahmā performed a Vedic *yajña* at Jajpur in order to propitiate Viṣṇu, from which Īśāneśvara and goddess Virajā emerged.[13] The name Jajpur is derived from *Yajñapura*, the place where Brahmā was believed to have performed a Vedic sacrifice. To perform the *yajña*, he required water for which he brought river Vaitaraṇī, who is also described as a form of river Gaṅgā, from the mountain to Jajpur plains. Brahmā brought the sacred river to *yajñasthala* (the *yajña* site) from Gonāsikā mountain through the tribal-dominated Keonjhar district. Vaitaraṇī followed Brahmā. Brahmā, after some distance, could not hear the sound of the river. When he looked back, he could not find her. In meditation, Brahmā realised that Vaitaraṇī, after seeing the nude tribal women, feared to have committed a sin by looking at them, and, therefore, had disappeared. 'If Śiva *liṅgas* were established at regular, Vaitaraṇī could be free from sin. Brahmā, therefore, established a Śiva *liṅga* in each *kośa* (a unit of distance) and brought the river to Jajpur to perform successfully the Vedic sacrifice. From the sacrificial fire, Virajā emerged. So also emerged lord Śiva-Īśāneśvara and Yajña-Varāha, a form of lord Viṣṇu, as a result of the sacrifice of Brahmā and decided to settle in Jajpur.'[14]

The historical process of the origin and growth of the various Brahmanical cults in the sacred centre of Jajpur is partly embedded in this Puranic narrative. The flow of the river through tribal lands, the idea of a *yajña* to propitiate Viṣṇu, the consecration of Śiva *liṅgas* in the tribal-dominated lands (*krośaliṅgas*) and the rise of goddess Virajā—all these motifs refer to the process of Brahmanisation of the land. The allusion to *yajña* refers to the Vedic *Śrauta* tradition, while the association of Śiva-Īśāneśvara and Virajā refer to the close juxtaposition of Śaiva-Śākta traditions. The allusion to Yajña Varāha also indicates the superimposition of Vaiṣṇava tradition in the Śaiva-Śākta *pīṭha* in the 13th and 14th centuries CE. It is important to explore the evolution of these strands at Jajpur following the evidence found in and around the region.

The Gupta period saw the expansion of Brahmanical religious orders in various parts of India, including Odisha. Temples were constructed, land grants were made to *brāhmaṇas* and important *tīrthas* were developed.

**Image 9.1: Ādimūrti-Viṣṇu image from Trilocaneśvara temple complex, Jajpur, c. 6th century CE**

*Credit*: Author

Explorations in Jajpur and the surrounding area confirm the presence of Vaiṣṇavism, Śaivism and Śāktism in the late fifth or in early sixth centuries CE. In the Trilocaneśvara temple complex, two Ādimūrti images of Viṣṇu are found (Image 9.1). The iconographic features closely resemble those of the immediate or late post-Gupta period as found at many sites in Bihar and Bengal.[15] Similarly, ithyphallic Ekamukha Śiva *liṅgas* were found in different areas of Jajpur, dateable to the early sixth century CE on iconographic grounds (Image 9.2). Saivism expanded in Jajpur and coastal Odisha in the post-sixth century CE. The *Brahma Purāṇa*'s reference to many Śaiva centres in Jajpur is substantiated by sculptural representations of different forms of Śiva, which iconographically belong to the seventh/eighth centuries CE. Ekapāda Bhairava forms of Śiva were found in the precincts of the present Virajā temple, in the niches of the pond known as Brahmākuṇḍa near the temple, and Atharnalā bridge, along with Ardhanārīśvara, Lakulīśa and Kārttikeya images.

**Image 9.2: Ekamukha Śiva *Liṅga* from Trilocaneśvara temple, Jajpur, c. 6th century CE**

*Credit*: Author

The *Mahābhārata* refers to Virajā but is silent about her form. Virajā is a two-armed Mahiṣāsuramardinī Durgā whose detailed iconographic study has not been possible. Scholars tend to ascribe a late Gupta period stamp to the image on iconographic grounds.[16]

Brahmanical texts do not mention about the presence of Buddhism in this period, but archaeological evidence points to the existence of Buddhism in Jajpur and surrounding areas earlier than Brahmanical cults—in sites such as Ratnagiri, Udayagiri and Lalitgiri, located within a 30 km radius of Jajpur. According to the 17th-century history of Buddhism in India by Lāmā Tāranātha, King Narasinghagupta constructed the Ratnagiri monastery in the early fifth century CE. The *Pratītyasamutpāda Sūtra* is found on terracotta plaques from the *stūpa* area of Ratnagiri, which was written in Sanskrit-Brāhmī of Gupta character. There are numerous other Buddhist establishments in Jajpur from the early historical period. One of the notable Buddhist sites of Odisha is Udayagiri, which also had early origins. The circular *caitya*, followed by an apsidal *caitya* in front of the *Siṁhaprastha Mahāvihāra* (Monastery 2), attest to its origins around second century BCE. Similarly, the Lalitgiri and Langudi Buddhist complex, which originated in the second century BCE, continued to grow during the Gupta and the post-Gupta periods. The early historic Buddhist monastic complexes of Lalitgiri,[17] Udayagiri,[18] Ratnagiri[19] and Langudi expanded first in the fifth century CE and, thereafter, in the seventh and eighth centuries CE. The latter period saw the emergence of temples and shrine complexes within the monasteries; numerous Buddhas, Bodhisattvas, gods and goddesses emerged in the Vajrayāna period in the Buddhist landscape of Odisha. Votive *stūpas* of Ratnagiri attest to the thronging of pilgrims to sacred Buddhist sites.[20]

One notable feature of the period is the influence of Buddhism on Śaiva sculptures. Many Lakulīśa images of Odisha were strongly influenced by Buddha images. Lakulīśa is seated cross-legged with two soles visible, and displays, like Buddha, *dharmacakrapravartana mudrā*. Moreover, his hair and elongated ears follow the iconographic style of representation of Buddha. His hair is depicted in *suncī keśa* (very short hair) style, formed of tightly coiled snail-shell curls turning from left to right (*dakṣiṇāvartamurdhaja*) and cranial protuberance (*uṣṇīṣa*), as found in Buddha images. It is important to note that Śiva's other forms are also moulded along the lines of Bodhisattva Avalokiteśvara. In the Śiśireśvara temple of Bhubaneswar, there is an image of *sthānaka* (standing) Śiva holding a lotus stem in his left hand. This representation resembles that of Avalokiteśvara Padmapāṇi, who similarly holds a lotus stem.

## Phase 2: Coexistence and Competition: Śaiva-Buddha Equations in the Bhaumakara Period in Jajpur (Eighth to Tenth Centuries CE)

The period between the eighth and tenth centuries saw the permeation of tantric elements in both Brahmanical religions, especially in Śaiva-Śākta orders, and Buddhism. It was also marked by the simultaneous growth and expansion of Śaiva-Śākta centres and Buddhism in Jajpur. Buddhist tantric texts also incorporated many features from the Śaiva-Śākta texts and practices of this period. The iconographic forms of Avalokiteśvara, such as Nīlakaṇṭha Avalokiteśvara, Sugatisandarśana Lokeśvara and Lokeśvara, which were found from Odisha, were influenced and moulded by representations of different forms of Śiva.

The Bhaumakara ruled over coastal, northern and central Odisha during this period (755 CE–955 CE) with their capital at Guhādevapāṭaka, which has been identified with Jajpur. They professed themselves to be devout Buddhists but also gave grants to *brāhmaṇas*, constructed Śaiva-Śākta temples and donated land for them. Unlike the political landscape of the first period, which saw local *rājās* ruling over different small localities of Odisha, the kingdom of Bhaumakaras included Ubhaya Tosalī, covering the coastal tract of present-day Odisha known as Utkaladeśa in their inscriptions. They also succeeded in extending their sphere of influence to northern Odisha—to Khiñjali-*maṇḍala* where the Bhañjas ruled but acknowledged the authority of the Bhaumakaras, and central Odisha in undivided Dhenkanal district, where Tuṅgas and Śulkis also acknowledged the authority of the Bhaumakaras. Therefore, the Bhaumakaras succeeded in creating a subregional kingdom for the first time.

The period of political expansion to the interiors of coastal and central Odisha was also characterised by another trend, that is the spread of various religions from Jajpur to the interior areas of Keonjhar district. During this time, various religious orders—Śaiva, Śākta, Vaiṣṇava and Buddhist—incorporated many autochthonous elements. The presence of Tantric and folk elements can be learned by a study of iconography as well as Buddhist and Śaiva-Śākta texts. The Terasingha copper plates refer to Bhagavatī Stambheśvarī as the tutelary deity of Mahārājā Tuṣṭikāra.[21] The Śulkis, who ruled Kodālaka-*maṇḍala* (Dhenkanal district) as feudatories of the Bhaumakaras, used the epithet *stambha* as their surname suggesting that they wanted to associate themselves with Stambheśvarī. The Gonds, likewise, were worshippers of Stambheśvarī, as were the Tuṅgas who, as feudatories of the Bhaumakaras, ruled Yamagartta-*maṇḍala* in the present Anugul district of undivided Dhenkanal.[22] Although the Khiñjali Bhañjas, who had their capital at Dhrītipura (Boudh-Sonepur), were devout worshippers of Śiva, pillars and posts were worshipped as goddesses and gods. In his Aida copper plate charter dated to his ninth regnal year, which is now in the Odisha State Museum, Raṇabhañja, though a worshipper of Śiva (*paramamāhesvarah*), calls himself *Stambheśvarī lavdha vara prasāda* (gained the boon and grace of goddess Stambheśvarī).[23]

Hermann Kulke argues that royal patronage of autochthonous cults not only gave the royalty legitimation, it also resulted in transformation and elevation of autochthonous cults into 'subregional' or 'regional' Brahmanical cults.[24] It is important to emphasise that the process of incorporation and integration of folk and autochthonous elements was not restricted to Brahmanical religions alone, but was also found in other religions in this period. The Buddhist goddess Parṇaśabarī (leaf-clad Śabarī) is described in the Buddhist texts as *sarvaśabarāṇām bhagavatī* (goddess of all *Śabaras*).[25] Slightly later, in the eighth century CE in Odisha, there seem to have been numerous common cultural motifs appearing both in Brahmanical religions and Buddhism. The presence of Abhiṣeka Lakṣmī, Nāga and Nāgi *stambhas*, and Yakṣa and Yakṣī in the Buddhist sites of Ratnagiri, Udayagiri and Jajpur attest to the incorporation of folk elements into Buddhism. For instance, the Sapta Matṛkā set on the banks of Vaitaraṇī was juxtaposed with Hārītī as a fertile goddess in the Buddhist establishments of Lalitgiri and Ratnagiri. Hārītī, Sapta Mātṛkā, Yakṣa and Yakṣī are deities associated with wealth and fertility.[26] During his visit to India in the first half of the seventh century, Yuan Chwang refers to a *stūpa* dedicated to Hārītī, to which common people seeking children offered prayers.[27] I-tsing says that in the Indian monasteries, the Buddhist goddess Hārītī was offered food after all *arhats* and *bhikṣus* were served.[28] Hārītī and her male counterpart Jambhala are found extensively in the Buddhist sites of Jajpur.[29]

With Guhādevapāṭaka as their capital, the Bhaumakaras patronised Śaiva, Śākta and Buddhist traditions in Jajpur and the areas where they expanded their authority. The *Brahma Purāṇa*[30] refers to eight sacred places within *Virajā-kṣetra*, including many Śaiva centres, such as Kapila, Gograha, Soma, Alavu, Mṛtyuñjaya,[31] Krodha (Varāha),[32] Vāsuka and Siddhakeśvara,[33] in addition to reiterating the sacred nature of river Vaitaraṇī, goddess Virajā and Īśāneśvara.[34] In the Siddheśvara temple, which is one of the eight sacred centres of Jajpur in the *Brahma Purāṇa*, images of Bhairava, Ekapāda Bhairava, Aṣṭika Jaratkaru, Janārdana Viṣṇu and Viṣṇu Lokeśvara are found. While Bhairava, Ekapāda Bhairava and Cāmuṇḍā images belong to the eighth century CE, Viṣṇu Lokeśvara and Janārdana images belong to the ninth century CE. Many detached Śaiva sculptures from this period are also encountered in the Virajā complex and the Brahmā *kuṇḍa* near the Virajā temple. Early images within the compound include Ardhanārīśvara, Cāmuṇḍā, Ekapāda Bhairava, Hara-Pārvatī, Kārttikeya and Lakulīśa.[35]

The reference to the consecration of thousand Śiva *liṅgas* from Gonāśikā mountain to Jajpur's Siddheśvara temple underscores the Śaiva-Śākta mode of acculturation of the tribal areas of Keonjhar. Many Śaiva temples and sculptures of the ninth/tenth century CE are found in the Anandapur and Hatadiha blocks of tribal-dominated district. Mention may be made of the Śaiva remains at Kosaleśvara temple, Bancho and Podasingidi. According to the Haṁseśvara temple inscription of Mādhavīdevī, queen of Śubhākara I of the Bhaumakara dynasty built a Śaiva temple Mādhaveśvara in the eighth century CE in Jajpur to perpetuate her memory. The inscription also states that a Śaiva Pāśupata ascetic was placed in charge of the deity.[36] A *vāpī* (well) was dug in front of the temple and a market was started, the income from which was set apart for the management of temple affairs. A notable feature of the Śaiva-Śākta order in this period is the emergence of Cāmuṇḍā as an important form of Devī, and Bhairava as a form of Śiva. The one-line inscription on the pedestal of Cāmuṇḍā in the Trilocaneśvara temple complex states that the image was installed by a queen Vatsadevī, a Bhaumakara queen.[37] The Śaiva-Śākta alignment is found elsewhere in Jajpur—in the Siddheśvara temple where one finds Cāmuṇḍā and different forms of Śiva, Virajā temple, as well as the Śiśireśvar-Vaitala complex of Bhubaneswar. There are many Śiva temples such as Kusumeśvara, Laliteśvara and Daṇḍīśvara named after Bhauma kings Kusumahāra, Lalitahāra, and Daṇḍīmahādevī.

Buddhism made great strides in Jajpur during this period. New Buddhist establishments, numbering almost 50, came up, and existing ones saw massive expansion. Buddhist sculptural *maṇḍalas*, monasteries and *stūpas* came up in Ratnagiri, Udayagiri, Lalitgiri and Langudi.[38] The Udayagiri *Mahāstūpa*, which was modelled on the *Garbhadhātū-maṇḍala*, came up in the eighth century CE. Monastery 1 near the *Mahāstūpa* area, known as Mādhavapura *Mahāvihāra*, with its seals, was built and expanded during this period while the circular *caitya* area saw the coming up of the Siṁhaprastha *Mahāvihāra*.[39] Ratnagiri became an important centre of Buddhist learning during the eighth to tenth centuries CE. Tibetan and Chinese sources associate Ratnagiri with Buddhist monks, such as Śubhakarasiṁha, Bitobā and Celuka, who played an important role in the growth of Vajrayāna orders in India and outside.[40]

In Jajpur, the Buddhist monastic establishment of Solampur came up in the eighth century CE. It is located on the left bank of river Vaitaraṇī, opposite the Saptamatṛkā temple and the famous Daśāśvamedha *ghat* on the right bank of the river, on the city side. The village is approachable from the embankment road alongside Jajpur city on Vaitaraṇī. One has to cross the second bridge over the river to take a left turn to reach the village. Archaeological explorations in village Solampur have brought to light numerous Brahmanical and Buddhist sculptures as well as the remains of a possible monastery. Solampur is mentioned in the royal grants of Bhaumakaras in the ninth- and twelfth-century Somavaṁśī records. While the remains of the monasteries can be seen in the western section of the village, most of the sculptural ruins are located in the Śānteśvarī Thakurani shed, and in and around the Raghunāth temple. Some Buddhist sculptures found from Solampur include two images of Sita Tārā (four-armed and two-armed), Jambhala, Avalokiteśvara, Vajrasattva, Vajrapāṇi, Mañjuśrī, Buddha images and a three-headed Prajñā.

Solampur is mentioned in two copper plate grants—the Neulpur grant of Śubhākaradeva of the Bhaumakara dynasty, and the Ratnagiri plate of the Somavaṁśī ruler Karṇa belonging to the eighth and twelfth centuries respectively. The Neulpur copper plate charter was issued from the victorious city of Guhādevapātaka (Jajpur) by *Paramaśaugata* (a devout Buddhist) and records the grant of two villages, Komparaka *grāma* and Daṇḍankiyoka, which were merged and renamed Saloṇapura and given to 200 *brahmāṇas* belonging to various *gotras* and *pravaras* of all four *Vedas*.[41] It is important to mention that this land donation gives the names of the individual donee *brāhmaṇas* who got village land as donation at a time when the same village saw the establishment of a Buddhist monastic establishment. Archaeological evidence from the site reveals many sculptures and remains of a monastic establishment. The second epigraph, which refers to Solampur, is the Ratnagiri Copper Plate charter of the Somavaṁśī king Karṇa, who has been described as *paramamāheśvarah*.

The charter was issued in his sixth regnal year (twelfth century CE) from Yayātinagarī (Jajpur) and records the grant of village Kona in favour of Rāṇī Karpūraśrī, daughter of lady *Māhārī* Māhuṇadevī and granddaughter of Udayamati, who hailed from the *Mahāvihāra* of Saloṇapura.[42] An image of Janārdana, dated ninth/tenth century CE, is also affixed on the porch of Raghunāth temple.

The epigraphic and archaeological remains of Solampur are important, for they shed light on the nature of sacred shrines in early medieval Odisha. First, Solampur was not only a Buddhist establishment as is known from sculptural remains, but also a habitation settlement constituted by merging two villages. It was a habitation of 200 Vedic *brāhmaṇas*, who were donated this village by the Buddhist king Śubhākaradeva, who styled himself as *paramaśaugata*. The Buddhist monastery seems to have existed from at least the eighth century CE, when it was founded (if we go by the dates of various sculptures), up to the end of the twelfth century CE, when lands were granted to a Karpūraśrī, who has been described as a Māhārī (temple *devadasi*), clearly indicating that Brahmanical practices had entered the Buddhist monasteries. Buddhism declined around the thirteenth century CE in Solampur, but the site was incorporated in the narrative of the *Virajā-kṣetra Māhātmya* as a gateway to *Virajā-kṣetra*.[43]

The expansion of Śaiva-Śākta and Buddhist orders in this period raises questions about their equations. What is the evidence of their interaction during this period? As mentioned in the previous section, Buddhist influence was discernible in the representation of Lakulīśa and Śiva. What was the nature and effect of such interactions between the orders?

One of the most important characteristics of the period, as Alexis Sanderson states, is the coming of the Śaiva Age.[44] Śaiva-Śākta order dominated the religious landscape of not only Jajpur and Odisha, but India as a whole. According to Sanderson, the simultaneous expansion and existence of Vajrayāna form of Buddhism and Śaivism in the Bhaumakara era were facilitated by the adoption of Śiva's features in the many forms of Avalokiteśvara and other Bodhisattvas, as well as the adoption and integration of the set of rituals that paralleled those of the Śaivas. In Odisha, one finds numerous forms of Avalokiteśvara, such as Halāhala Lokeśvara and Jaṭāmukuṭa Lokeśvara, which were modelled on

Umā-Maheśvara and Śiva respectively. There are other gods and goddesses who developed parallel to the Brahmanical pantheon. For instance, in the *Guhyasamāja Tantra*, Mañjuśrī is described as Kārttikeya.[45] But this is also true of Brahmanical religion, which incorporated the Buddhist goddesses Vajrayoginī and Tārā as Chinnamastā[46] and Tārā, who appear as *daśamahāvidyā* in the *Devībhāgavata Purāṇa*. Similarly, goddess Śītalā in Odisha is worshipped for preventing epidemics, modelled on Parṇaśabarī. However, such functional and iconographic similarities merely underscore fluidity in the religious history of South Asia. The Buddhist goddess Vasudharā appears in Odisha first in the eighth century CE in Lalitgiri. Her description in *Sādhanamālā* reflects her adaptation from Śrī-Lakṣmī. She is also identified with Virajā in Nepalese Buddhist texts. The Vasundharā-Vratotpatti-Avadāna, a Sanskrit Buddhist text copied in Newari Saṁvat 923 (1802), claims that the goddess assumes a three-fold form of Vasudhārā, Mahālakṣmī and Kumārī.[47]

Sanderson argues that Buddhist adoption of the Śaiva system was not restricted to iconography alone but extended to many realms. For instance, Śaiva *ācāryas* were performing rituals for the royalty to avert danger and attain glory. Tāranātha refers to the performance of such rituals for the protection of the state at Vikramaśilā under the direction of Buddhajñāna during the reign of Dharmapāla (775–812) to ensure the longevity of the Pāla dynasty.[48] Similarly, the *Mañjūśrīmūlakalpa* and *Durgatipariśodhana Tantra* refer to the initiation of royalty to *maṇḍala* rituals, which is similar to *maṇḍala* initiation in the Śaiva system.[49] The *Mantrayāna* also followed the example of the Śaivas by devising Tantric ceremonies for patrons in the public domain, the consecration of temple images, and painting of deities on cloths (*paṭṭah*), manuscripts of sacred texts, monasteries, shrines, *caityas*, reservoirs, gardens and the like.

This adoption of Śaiva practices took place when the Buddhist sites of Jajpur saw the organisation of the Buddhist pantheon on the *maṇḍala* theme. The *Mahāvairocana Sūtra*, a Buddhist *Caryā Sūtra* of the seventh century CE, refers to the categorisation of Buddhist divinities on the *maṇḍala* theme in which Buddha Vairocana occupies a central position and the other four Buddhas—Akṣobhya, Amitābha, Amoghasiddhi and Ratnasaṁbhava—occupy the eastern, western, northern and southern directions respectively. Text from the *Mahāvairocana Sūtra* appears on the back slab of the Abhisaṁbodhi Vairocana image from Lalitgiri, which is palaeographically dated to the seventh century CE.[50] From this image and its inscribed text, it can be inferred that the Buddhist pantheon began to be organised on the *maṇḍala* theme of the *Mahāvairocana Sūtra* in Odisha from the seventh century CE, and there is ample evidence of *maṇḍalas* and sculptures from Odisha. The *Mahāvairocana Sūtra* anticipated the incorporation of many practices, including *maṇḍala* rituals from the Śaiva order, arousing suspicion among people that this was not the teaching of the Buddhas but of outsiders.[51] The *Sarvatathāgata Tattva Saṁgraha*, a Buddhist *Yoga Tantra* text of the early eighth century, refers to the Śaiva practice of possession (*āveśa*) during initiation of the Buddhist *yogin*. The *Vajrācārya* puts the initiate into a state of possession, offers a flower on the *maṇḍala*; the section of the *maṇḍala* on which the flower falls determines the *mantra* deity from which he (initiate) will obtain *siddhi*, and then, while he is still in this state, *Vajrācārya* removes his blindfold to reveal the *maṇḍala*. In addition to the *maṇḍala* possession of the initiate, Sanderson cites other evidence of incorporation of Śaiva-Sākta practices in Vajrayāna Buddhism, such as the emergence of *prajñās* of five *tathāgatas* instead of *pañca tathāgatas* in the *maṇḍalas*, and inclusion of sexual intercourse in the activities of worship as a higher form of practice. That Tantric Buddhists incorporated specialised knowledge of Śaiva-Śākta liturgies is proven by the *Guhyasiddhi* of Padmavajra (eighth century), which states that any initiate in the practice of the Buddhist *Tantra* is not only familiar with the Śaiva scripture but also able to enact their rituals by assuming the role of Śaiva guru, implying thereby that 'such initiates were typically converted from the *mantra mārga* with experience both of its texts and practices'.[52] The Śaiva-Śākta influence reached its height when *Yoginī tantras*, such as *Cakrasaṁvara* and *Hevajra Tantra*, visualised Buddhist practices on the model of *Bhairava Tantras*.

Vajrayāna Buddhism developed a pantheon structured largely on Brahmanical religions, assigned deities with instrumental functions, innovated *maṇḍalas* in order to accommodate a diverse array of deities, and constructed temples within the monastic structure for their worship. In short, Vajrayāna tried to make the religion more *laukika* (laity-oriented) in the same manner the Puranic religions did to Vedic religion in the post-Gupta period, centred around Viṣṇu, Śiva, Śakti, Gaṇapati and Sūrya.[53]

This attempt on the part of Vajrayāna Buddhism to adapt and integrate Śaiva order into its religion created some degree of conflict as these innovations aimed to cater to the same social groups as Śaivism. Both emphasised rituals and worship of deities for fulfilling existential needs of laities; both had rituals for *siddhi* and acquiring magical powers; both incorporated fertility cults such as Yakṣa, Nāga-Nāgī and autochthonous elements. Moreover, both had prescribed rituals for the initiation of royalty, including those to attain fame. Furthermore, many forms of the Bodhisattva Avalokiteśvara, or forms of Tārā such as Durgottaraṇī Tārā, Siṁhanāda Tārā and Aṣṭamahābhaya Tārā, are not only iconographic parallels of their Brahmanical counterparts but also performed the same roles.

## Phase 3: Śaiva-Śākta Assertion and Evidence of Animosity Between Brahmanical Religion and Buddhism in the Somavaṁśī Period (Tenth to Twelfth Centuries CE)

The previous section deals with the evidence of mutual borrowing in a cultural ecology best described as poly-religious. The political establishment also patronised all religions, despite their personal affiliations. However, starting with the Somavamśīs, the religious landscape began to change, with increasing evidence of animosity. The Buddhist adaptation of Śaiva-Śākta order—*maṇḍalas*, initiation rituals for kings, protection rituals, incorporation of folk and autochthonous elements—made the religion more *laukika*. *Maṇḍala* sculptures, *dhāraṇīs* and temples dominated the Buddhist landscape of Odisha, but the Śaiva-Śākta order had considerably expanded its support base by the ninth to tenth centuries CE. With its Puranic and Tantric mixture, locii in temples and monasteries, a dedicated ascetic tradition (Pāśupatas and Kāpālikas), and many other innovations outlined by Sanderson, the order became the most important element in Jajpur's landscape, in particular, and Odisha, in general, by the ninth century CE. This is amply attested by existing temples, sculptures and epigraphic references from Odisha dated between the sixth and tenth centuries CE.

The Buddhist adaptation and integration of Śaiva practices provided an opportunity for the Śaivas to make inroads into the Buddhist establishments of Odisha. In Ratnagiri, we find Śiva *liṅgas* and Śaiva-Śākta divinities such as Gaṇeśa and Mahiṣāsuramardinī Durgā. The precise time when Brahmanical elements began to make their presence felt in Jajpur cannot be precisely dated, but iconographically, these deities belong to the ninth century CE. The process may have started earlier. In Lalitgiri, we have early iconographic representation of Viṣṇu, which can be dated to the eighth century CE, and in Udayagiri there's a Mahiṣāsuramardinī Durgā of the late eighth century (Image 9.3).

**Image 9.3: Standing Viṣṇu from the excavation of Lalitgiri, c. 8th century CE**

*Credit*: Author

The expansion of both Śaiva-Śākta religion and Buddhism to the peripheral tribal pockets resulted in increasing animosity between them. The Buddhist *locus classicus*, *Sarvatathāgata Tattvasaṁgraha* [eighth century][54] carries the story of subduing of Maheśvara by Vajrapāṇi, which was repeated later in the *Yoginī Tantra* of *Cakrasaṁvara* (tenth century CE), where Heruka subdues Maheśvara. As Ronald Davidson says, 'Maheśvara occupies the place of Māra of early Buddhism in the Mantrayāna tradition.'[55] In the *Cakrasaṁvara Tantra*,[56] Heruka imitates the system of the opponents in order to destroy them. In this story of imitation and destruction of Maheśvara lies the story of adaptation of Śaiva practices and an attempt by the Buddhists to make their religion more *laukika* and attractive at the expense of the Śaiva-Śākta system. *Cakrasaṁvara*'s story is telling, for it refers to Oḍra as the place of emanation of Maheśvara and Bhairavas. According to it, at the beginning of this *Kali Yuga*, there was mutual slaughter and bloodbath. Out of the blood, clouds developed; from the cloud, rains came, rainwater led to the rise of eight rivers and… then to the south of Sumeru, in the continent of Jambūdvīpa, Maheśvara's emanation occurred. Then came 24 self-originated places, from where 24 ferocious Bhairavas arose. Out of these, one appeared in Oḍra (coastal Odisha) and one in Kaliṅga (southern Odisha). Following the emanation of the 24 Bhairavas and their consorts, Mahādeva climbed the peak of Mount Sumeru, having four heads and 12 arms, naked, black, with his hair tied up in matted locks and smeared with ash. His consort, Umā Devī, was red, with one face and two arms, and they were in sexual union. In conjunction with Maheśvara, his four Umā and eight Matṛkā emanated. As a shrine (*caitya*) for each of these Bhairavas, Maheśvara provided 24 *liṅgas* in the forms of self-produced stones. Once established in Jambūdvīpa, Maheśvara and his minions began to conduct themselves in a most irregular manner. They ate human flesh and drank human blood. They made ornaments of human bones—circlets, earrings, necklaces, bracelets and belts—all smeared with the ashes of human bones. From human hair, they wove their Brahmanical threads and fashioned garlands of human skulls. In order to bring them under control, the 'causal form of Vajradhārā'—the experiential body (*saṁbhogakāyā*) in Akaniṣṭha heaven—manifested 62 varieties of the emanation body (*nirmāṇa-kāyā*) as the 'resultant Vajradhārā'. Heruka and his consort Vajrayoginī emerged in opposition to Maheśvara and Umā Devī. The story then goes on to repeat the subduing of Maheśvara by Heruka.

In this tale lies the story of competition among the Śaiva-Kāpālikas and Mantrayāna Buddhists. Heruka replaced Vajrapāṇi in this *Tantra*. But both in *Tattvasaṁgraha* and *Cakrasaṁvara Tantra*, Maheśvara represented the Śaiva Kāpālikas' antinomian behaviour. While the text refers to the subduing of Maheśvara by Heruka when the Kāpālika Śaivas conducted themselves in an irregular manner, which is an allusion to represent Śaivism in subordinate light, the strategy Buddhists adopted was largely modelled on the Śaiva system as Sanderson has shown. It is to be noted in this connection that Heruka's iconographic representation with skull cups, *khaṭvāṅga*, and dancing on the corpse clearly indicates an attempt to adapt Śaiva idioms even though the text states the need to replace the Kāpālikas for they created disorder in society with their irregular conduct. The victory of Buddhists over the Śaiva order was represented in the iconography of many Buddhist divinities from Odisha, such as Heruka, Vajrahuṅkāra/Trailokyavijaya and Saṁvara, who have been shown trampling Bhairava and Ratī. Jajpur was the capital of Oḍradeśa or Utkaladeśa in the ninth/tenth century CE, and the *Cakrasaṁvara Tantra*'s reference to the emanation of Maheśvara and Bhairavas in Oḍra refers to expansion of Śaivism in Odisha by the eighth century CE. The subduing of Maheśvara and Bhairavas by Cakrasaṁvara is a reference to the Buddhist attempt to compete with expanding Śaivism by making numerous innovations in Mantrayāna Buddhism, which have been outlined in the previous section.

The expansion of the Śaiva-Śākta order and Buddhist attempts to appropriate, adapt and integrate Śaiva-Śākta elements but simultaneously showing Śaiva divinities in an inferior light (as being trampled by Buddhist divinities), resulted in great animosity between Buddhism and Brahmanical religions. It began to show in the late eighth century but gained greater salience from the tenth century when the Somavaṁśī united coastal Odisha with western Odisha by defeating the Bhaumakaras and shifted their capital from Vinītapura (Sonepur) to Jajpur, which was rechristened Yayātinagar after its ruler Yayāti I (922 CE–955 CE). Unlike the Bhaumakaras who patronised all cults, the Somavaṁśīs were strong Śaivites and are credited with the resurgence of Śaivism-Vaiṣṇavism in Jajpur. Yayāti

Keśarī is credited with the famous *yajñas* on the bank of river Vaitaraṇī, to which he invited 10,000 *brāhmaṇas* from Kanauj. He constructed many temples, including an auspicious pillar, which symbolised his victory over Buddhism.

Again, iconography offers a glimpse into this conflict. Sculptures on the ground were active participants in the social life of its communities and reflect the social process.[57] The conflicts between the Buddhists and Śaiva-Śākta order were represented in many sculptures in Odisha. The Buddhist sites from the ninth century CE onwards became home to many fierce deities of *Yoginī Tantras* trampling on Bhairavas and Kālarātrī. Mention may be made of Saṁvara of Ratnagiri, the Vajrahuṅkāra of Acutarajpur hoard in Puri district, and many other images, such as Heruka and Yamāri from Ratnagiri and Udayagiri. Debala Mitra suggests that the image of Vajrahuṅkāra was deliberately designed and made with a specific purpose.[58]

Another sculpture that reflects this animosity was found from Buhalo in the Nischintkoili block of the Chitroptola river valley in Cuttack. It is a Buddha figure in *bhūmisparṣa mudrā* flanked by Maitreya and Avalokiteśvara. He is framed by a trefoil-shaped *haṁsa* (swan), and *toraṇa* (arch) with a miniature *rekha deula* at the apex. The four Brahmanical gods, Indra, Brahmā, Viṣṇu and Śiva, are represented as four *māras* (evil forces) twice on the upper right half, where the principal set of hands display *añjali mudrā*, as prescribed in the *Dharmadhātu-vāgīśvara-maṇḍala* of the *Niṣpannayogāvalī* of Abhayankara Gupta, implying they are paying homage to the victorious Buddha.[59] The front edge to the left of Viśvapadma is marked by a *vajra*. This dramatic sculptural representation shows the degree of subordinate integration of Brahmanical divinities within the Buddhist pantheon. The Brahmanical texts of Odisha also referred to increasing conflict between the Buddhists and Śaivas. The *Ekāmra Purāṇa*, a Śaiva *sthala māhātmya* on Bhubaneswar from the 13th century CE, refers to the dreadful war waged by Śiva against *asuras* on the banks of river Gandhavatī for control of *Ekāmra* (Bhubaneswar). The Gandhavatī corresponds to the modern Gangua river, which flows through Bhubaneswar, before joining the Dayā river. Hiraṇyākṣa, the demon king, advised by his guru Śukrācārya, had tried to stop the *yajña* the gods wanted to perform on the banks of the river, and at first, the *asuras* were successful in defeating them. Śiva's intervention caused the final defeat of Hiranyākṣa.[60] K.C. Panigrahi observed that the *devāsura* conflict at *Ekāmravana* mirrored 'a conflict between the Śaivas and the Buddhists' and the text, as a Śaiva work, liked to term the Buddhists as *asuras* and the followers of Śiva as gods.[61] This process merely reflects the Śaiva attempt to dominate Bhubaneswar at the expense of the Buddhists. Panigrahi alludes to many pieces of evidence of such a process. Bhāskareśvara *liṅga*, according to Panigrahi, is actually an Aśokan pillar, which was converted to a Śiva *liṅga* in the eighth/ninth century CE. The *Dharmapujā-vidhāna*, a 13th-century text, refers to the *sadharmis* and Buddhists of Jajpur who were persecuted by the *brāhmaṇas*. The *Caitanya Bhāgabata*, composed by Īśvara Dāsa towards the end of the 16th century CE, records how Anangabhīmadeva sided with the *brāhmaṇas* and clubbed 32 Buddhists when they failed to satisfy him in a test.[62] The *Madalāpañji* (Jagannātha temple chronicle) records a similar story of persecution of Buddhists by Madana Mahādeva, who is presented in the text as a brother of Anangabhīmadeva.[63] In the *Bhakti Bhāgavata* of Kavi Diṇḍima Jīvadeva (early 16th century CE), it is stated that the famous *brāhmaṇa* Bhāvadeva, who was the family priest of Somavaṁśī king Udyotakeśari, lifted the world when it was submerged in the ocean of *Tantras*.[64] The Somavaṁśī king Yayāti II opposed Buddhism and killed 600 Buddhists and converted Buddhist establishments into Śaiva ones.

The sculptures of the period also reflect the conflict between Śaivas and Buddhists. One instance is the representation of Buddha in the sacrificial *yūpa* outside of the entrance of the Śaiva Kāpālika, the eighth-century Vaitala temple, Bhubaneswar. Outside the temple, in front of the entrance to the *jagamohana* (porch), there is a much worn, reworked Buddhist sculpture serving as the base of the *yūpa*—the socket on top was made to insert another stone on a wooden figure—testifying to the sacrifices offered to the goddess Cāmuṇḍā (Image 9.4). Panigrahi has shown on textual basis that the Cāmuṇḍā of the Vaitala Deul was a shrine of the Kāpālikas, its name derived from the Vetālas or spirits whose assistance helped them to attain their *siddhis*.[65] This sacrificial *yūpa* echoes the sacrifice of Buddha at the hands of Kāpālikas, thus representing the Śaiva-Buddha conflict.

**Image 9.4: Cāmuṇḍā sitting on a corpse. The corpse looks like a Buddha figure, Trilocaneśvara temple, Jajpur, c. 8th–9th century CE**

*Credit:* Author

Many Śiva images in his Bhairava aspect and the goddess in her Cāmuṇḍā aspect have been represented in Odishan sculptures standing/sitting on a corpse. The corpse is peculiarly represented as having elongated ears and curled hair, which is associated with the Buddha figure in Odisha. Is there a connection between the sacrificial *yūpa* with the representation of Buddha and Cāmuṇḍā or Bhairava standing on corpses, whose hair and ears follow the depiction of Buddha? The *Ekāmra Purāṇa* assigns a role to Pārvatī, who, in the *Ekāmravana*, kills the demons Kīrti and Vāsa who wanted to enjoy her person.[66] Pārvatī, in her Cāmuṇḍā aspect, and Śiva, in his Bhairava aspect, merged as the embodiments of the battlefield. The *Agni Purāṇa* provides a number of impressive innovations to address Cāmuṇḍā in order to obtain victory in the battle, and in the *Kālīkā Purāṇa* she is worshipped with bloody rituals during the new moon night of autumn.

The representation of the corpse as a dead warrior, and in certain cases, the short sword in the sheath that he wears on his waist belt is clear. In some cases, as in the late 10th-century stele from Devagrāma in

Mayurbhanj district, the dead man is richly clothed, wearing necklaces and bracelets and identifiable as a native ruler. There are steles from Odisha and Bihar where Bhairava was represented trampling shaven heads or the head of Buddha.[67] Giovanni Verardi interprets these images as evidence of the period of Śaiva assertion during Somavaṁśī rule from mid-tenth century CE, and Śaivite opposition of not only Buddhism but also local Buddhist *rājās* of Odisha, who protested against the Somavaṁśī persecution of Buddhism.[68] The arrival of *brāhmaṇas* as agricultural landowners, as reflected in the Yayāti tradition of 10,000 *brahmāṇas* brought from Kanauj to Jajpur, led to clashes between new *brahmāṇa* settlers and the old elites who were the landowners. The Bhairava and Cāmuṇḍā sculptures represent the quelling of these local *rājās* and Buddhists, who had control over the land in the Bhaumakara period.

## Phase 4: *Nābhi Gayā*, Vaiṣṇava Domination of Jajpur and Emergence of the Jagannātha Cult (Thirteenth/Fourteenth Centuries CE)

As demonstrated, the Somavaṁśī period saw assertion of the Śaiva-Śākta tradition and growing animosity between the Buddhists and Śaiva-Śāktas. Mutual borrowing and adaptation gave way to open display of antagonism in Jajpur. The *Kapila Saṁhitā* and *Ekāmra Purāṇam* also refer to the gradual expansion of Śaiva-Śākta tradition in Jajpur. *Kṣetra-Māhātmaya* refers to the Śaiva centres of Khilāteśvara, Varuṇeśvara and Beleśvara forming the three vertices of the inverted triangle of *Virajā-kṣetra*.[69] Explorations have revealed the 10th/11th-century Umā-Maheśvara images from Beleśvara and Khilāteśvara coming up on previously Buddhist ruins. Images of Heruka and other Buddhist gods are found along the ruins of the Khilāteśvara. In Jajpur, many Śaiva establishments, such as Mukteśvara, Trilocaneśvara and Ākhaṇḍaleśvara temples, also came up during this period. Śaivism expanded to the tribal-dominated Keonjhar area as well. Moreover, the *Kapila Saṁhitā*, for the first time, refers to the Nābhi Gayā tradition. By the fourth century CE at least, the story of the Pāṇḍavas performing *śrāddhas* on the bank of Vaitraraṇī in the *Virajā-kṣetra* points to the early origin of

Jajpur as a centre for performing rituals for the dead. But for the first time, the *Kapila Saṁhitā* brought in the *Vāyu Purāṇa* theme of the Nābhi Gayā. As described in the *Vāyu Purāṇa*, Gayāsura's head touched Kolāhala hill in Gayā, his navel touched *Virajā-kṣetra* and feet the Mahendra mountain in Piṣṭapuram in the south. Gadādhara Viṣṇu tried to keep him still with his mace.[70] In lieu of this great sacrifice, his wish of being remembered was granted by creating these as *pitṛtīrthas*. In this way, the *Trigayā* idea originated. The *Virajā-kṣetra Māhātmya* of the *Brahmaṇḍa Purāṇa* repeats the same story in Chapter 17.[71] 'To the northeast of the Virajā is situated the Nābhi Gayā. Those who offer *piṇḍas* to their ancestors here ... release twenty-one generations of their ancestors from the hell.'[72] The Gadādhara image of Viṣṇu is found affixed to the inner western wall of the Nābhi Gayā. The image is a Janārdana form of Viṣṇu and iconographically dateable to the 10th century CE but it's affixed in the Nābhi Gayā complex and worshipped as Gadādhara. The composition of the *Kapila Saṁhitā* is ascribed to the 13th century CE and the *Virajā-kṣetra-māhātmya* to the fourteenth. At what time did the Vaiṣṇava theme of Nābhi Gayā appear in Jajpur? In our view, starting with Yayāti II in later half of the 10th century CE, Vaiṣṇavism began to gain ground in the region. The antiquity of Viṣṇu worship in Jajpur goes back further in time, but from the 10th century CE, Viṣṇu images expanded here. The theme of Nābhi Gayā entered Jajpur during the 13th/14th century CE, with its religious landscape dotted with an increasing presence of Viṣṇu images, including the massive Garuḍa pillar or as śubha stambha (auspicious pillar). Jajpur as a centre for performing rituals for the dead is older, but what is newer is the tradition of Nābhi Gayā, which copied the more famous counterpart of Gayā, Bihar. We are not limited by historical questions concerning the antiquity of the Bodh Gayā versus Viṣṇupāda Gayā. What is important to understand is the context of the emergence of the Vaiṣṇava theme of Nābhi Gayā in Jajpur. This most likely occurred in the 13th century CE shortly before the composition of *Kapila Saṁhitā,* when Vaiṣṇava order emerged as the most important one, with active patronage of Puri's Jagannātha by the ruling Gaṅgas from the 12th century CE.

The emergence of Jagannātha under Anantavarman Coḍagaṅgadeva in early 12th century CE and subsequent declaration of the Gaṅga kings as the *rāuta* (servant) of the *rāṣṭra devatā* Jagannātha, the real ruler of

Utkaladeśa, marked a decisive shift in its religious landscape. Vaṣṇavism and the Jagannātha cult began to emerge as the most important cults in Odisha. Most likely, it was during this period of Vaiṣṇava assertion that the theme of Nābhi Gayā entered Jajpur. The Vaiṣṇava also made inroads into Ekāmra *kṣetra* by constructing the Ananta Vāsudeva temple in the 13th century CE, thanks to patronage by Gaṅga kings and queens. The *Ekāmra Purāṇa* and *Ekāmra Candrikā* prescribe visiting the Vaiṣṇava shrine of Ananta Vāsudeva first, before paying obeisance to the central shrine of *Ekāmra kṣetra,* Lingarāja.[73]

The emergence of the Nābhi Gayā tradition and expansion of Vaiṣṇava order in Jajpur, the patronage of Vaiṣṇava Jagannātha as state cult under the Gaṅgas and Gajapatis, and construction of the Ananta Vāsudeva Temple by a Gaṅga queen in the last quarter of the 13th century CE (marking the entry of Vaiṣṇavism into Ekāmra) were made clear not only by the decline of Buddhist centres in Odisha but also the identification of Buddha with lord Jagannātha. Many Vaiṣṇava poets of the fifteenth/ sixteenth centuries equated Jagannātha with Buddha. Saralā Dāsa, the *śūdra* poet who composed the Odia Mahābhārata in the 15th century CE, gives a curious account of the origin of the Buddha image. According to the text, Kṛṣṇa's dead body was thrown into the sea near Dvārakā. It came floating to Puri and remained in the custody of the Śavara tribe for some time before mysteriously becoming a tree, out of which a statue was carved in the form of Buddha. This was considered the incarnation of Viṣṇu immediately after Kṛṣṇa. Dāsa, in many verses of the Odia *Mahābhārata,* equates Buddha with Jagannātha.[74] Jagannātha replaced Buddha as the ninth *avatāra* of Viṣṇu in the *daśāvatāra* panel painting inside the *jagamohana* of the Puri Jagannātha temple. G.C. Tripathi argues that both Buddhism and the Jagannātha cult existed beyond the pale of Puranic Hinduism and therefore, it was easy to dislodge the heterodox Buddha by Jagannātha. 'The Buddha incarnation came here handy, as it stood outside the pale of Brahmanism but still loosely connected with it and further, the iconography of the different forms of Buddha was not so well-known to Hindus that they would have hesitated to accept his identity. Besides, this was the incarnation of Viṣṇu, which could have been most easily dislodged for the sake of Jagannātha from the classical scheme of the incarnation since it was not so firmly established in Hinduism.'[75]

There were two trends at work in Odisha during the 13th to 15th centuries CE. The decline of Buddhism was followed by the identification of Jagannātha with Buddha. Secondly, there was evidence of the taking over of Buddhist establishments by Śaiva ones. The pattern is also visible in the Buddhist establishments of Ratnagiri and Udayagiri. In Ratnagiri, a Śaiva temple called Vajra Mahākāla temple was constructed in the 13th century CE. The presiding deity is the Buddhist god Mahākāla, but he is being worshipped as a form of Śiva. *Vajra-mahākāla-vrata* is observed in the locality on the bright fortnight of the Kārtik month, considered a special day for Śiva. Similarly, the Vajra Mahākāla Temple and Śaiva monastic establishment came up in Udayagiri, possibly on the ruins of the Buddhist system. In Jajpur, many Śaiva establishments came up on the ruins of the Buddhist establishments in the 12th century CE. The Buddhist establishment of Solampur was reconfigured in the new Puranic narrative of *Virajā-kṣetra Māhātmya* as the starting point of the pilgrimage of *Virajā-kṣetra*, to begin on the 14th day of the new moon of Vaiśākha or Māgha by taking a dip in the *tīrthadvāra* (gateway) located to the east of the Varāha temple, on the northern bank of river Vaitraraṇī. Verse 21 of Chapter 4 of the *Virajā-kṣetra Māhātmya* elaborates that the pilgrim should go to goddess Santeśvarī, and worship her after taking a dip at *tīrthadvāra*. Santeśvari is still worshipped as the *iṣṭadevī* (presiding goddess) of Solampur. Thus, the village was reconstituted as part of the pilgrimage field of *Virajā-kṣetra*. The process of appropriation of Buddhist sites finally ended in Odisha with a Śaiva and Vaiṣṇava takeover around the 14th century CE, when Vajra Mahākāla temple was constructed at Ratnagiri. In the next century, Buddha was identified as Jagannātha in the regional tradition of Odisha.

## Conclusion

The essay is a preliminary attempt to map the evolution of the sacred geography of Jajpur and its surrounding areas by studying the dynamic nature of its religious landscape from the fifth to fourteenth centuries CE. It argues that Śaiva, Śākta and Viṣṇu images appeared in the post-Gupta period while Buddhism was concentrated in the surrounding areas of Udayagiri, Lalitgiri, Ratnagiri, Langudi, etc. from an earlier period. In the Bhaumakara era, the religious landscape was characterised by the simultaneous expansion of Śaivism, Buddhism and Vaiṣṇavism, resulting in the emergence of poly-religiosity. Śaiva centres named after Pāśupata teachers and Bhauma kings and queens appeared in Jajpur. Buddhist sites like Santa Madhava, Khadipada, Solampur and many others also emerged in and around Jajpur. There is also evidence of mutual borrowing between Brahmanical religions and Buddhism, appropriation of autochthonous elements into Śaiva-Śākta and Buddhist Tantras and pantheon structure. Starting around the late 9th and early 10th centuries CE, Śaiva-Śākta came of age under the Somavaṁśīs. The *kṣetra* limit was expanded, Śaiva-Śākta cults penetrated surrounding tribal pockets of Anandpur plains in Keonjhar and the iconographic and textual evidence indicate growing animosity between Buddhism and Brahmanical religions. Finally, with the emergence of Vaisaṇava Jagannātha cult as state cult under the Gaṅgas and Gajapatis, the *Virajā kṣetra*, known as a Śākta-Śaiva *kṣetra*, saw the incorporation of the *Vāyu Purāṇa* theme of Nābhi Gayā, which may be an allegory of the decline of Buddhism and domination of Vaiṣṇavism. Nābhi Gayā appeared at a time when Jagannātha, regarded as a form of Viṣṇu, replaced Buddha as the ninth *avatāra* and is regarded as a form of Buddha in Dāsa's *Mahābhārata* and emerged as the *rāṣṭra devatā* (regional cult) under the Gaṅgas and Gajapatis in Odisha.

## Endnotes

1 Rajendralala Mitra observes the following in the context of the Gayāsura myth, in Section II of the *Gayā Māhātmya* of the *Vāyu Purāṇa*: 'Gayāsura revels not in crime, he injures none, offends neither the gods nor religion by woes or deed [...] The most serious charge brought against him was that he made salvation too simple and summary. The epithet in his case can, therefore, only mean that he did not profess the faith of the *brāhmaṇas*, nor follows their ways: in short he was a heretic. This character has always been assigned to the chief among the Buddhists. They were pious, they were self-mortifying, they devoted themselves greatly to penance and meditation; but they did away with the sacrifices and ceremonies of the *brāhmaṇas*, and Gaya, therefore,

may safely be taken to be personification of Buddhism [...] The attempts of the gods to put down the head of the monster typifies the attempts of the Hindus to assail Buddhism at its inspiring centre, the headquarters; and the thwack of Viṣṇu's mace indicates the resort which had been made to force when religious preaching had failed to attain the end. The rock of the religion was placed on the head of the infidel, and the force of the gods kept it fixed and immovable. It was the blessings of the gods, too, which sanctified the seat of Buddhism into a principal sanctuary of the Hindu faith.' Rajendralala Mitra, *Buddha Gaya: The Great Buddhist Temple, The Hermitage of Śākya Muni* (New Delhi: Indological Press, 1972), 17–18.

2 *Tato vaitaraṇīṃ gatvā nadīṃ pāpapramocanīm/Virajāṃ tīrtham āsādya virājati yathā śaśī//prabhavec ca kule puṇye sarvapāpaṃ vyapohati/gosahasraphalaṃ labdhvā punāti ca kulaṃ naraḥ*. See 3.83. 6–7 of V.S. Sukthankar, ed., *Mahābhārata* (Poona: Bhandarkar Oriental Research Institute, 1942).

3 K.C. Panigrahi, *History of Orissa* (Cuttack: Kitab Mahal, 1986), 331. Ram Prasad Chanda, who explored Orissa in the 1920s, also had the view that the image of Virajā can be placed in the fourth century CE on iconographic grounds. Ram Prasad Chanda, 'Explorations of Orissa,' *Memoirs of the Archaeological Survey of India* 44–47, no. 44 (1930), 4.

4 H.N. Apte, ed., *Brahma Purāṇa*, ASS 28, Verses 28.I ff; 42.1–12 (Poona: Anandasrama Press, 1895).

5 For the origin and evolution of the *Puruṣottama Kṣetra* of Puri, see H.V. Stietencron,'Evolution of Vaiṣṇavism in Orissa,' in *The Cult of Jagannātha and Regional Tradition of Orissa*, eds. A. Eschmann, H. Kulke and G.C. Tripathi (New Delhi: Manohar, 1978), 2–30.

6 The Cateśvara inscription of Anangabhīmadeva III (1211–1238) states that new recensions of the *Purāṇas* were made in Odisha through the efforts of his efficient minister Viṣṇu Ācārya, incorporating the glory of different sacred places of Odisha in an elaborate manner (*Epigraphia Indica* XXIX, 121–123). There is a difference in opinion among scholars about the date of composition of the *Brahma Purāṇa*, which contains references to the *Puruṣottama Māhātmya* (Puri-Jagannātha) and *Virajā-kṣetra*. Lakṣmīdhara (1100–1150), the author of *Kṛtyakalpataru*, quoted some verses of the *Brahma Purāṇa*, which are not available in published editions. However, Hemādri (1265–1270), in his *Caturvarga Cintāmaṇi*, quoted some verses of the *Brahma Purāṇa*, which are found in the published editions of the text found in Odisha. Narasimha Vājapeyī, a Sanskrit Pandit in the royal court of the Gajapati Mukundadeva (1559–1568), opined that Hemādri's reference to sections of *Brahma Purāṇa*, which contained reference to *Virajā-kṣetra*, *Puruṣottama kṣetra* belongs to

a later period, whereas the *Brahma Purāṇa* quoted by Lakṣmīdhara belongs to an earlier period. Taking these views into consideration, *Brahma Purāṇa*, which refers to various *tirthas* of *Virajā-kṣetra*, can be placed between late 12th and early 13th centuries CE.

7 *Brahma Purāṇa* refers to the following sacred centres of Jajpur: Virajā, Kapila, Gograha, Soma, Alavu, Mṛtyuñjaya, Krodha (Varāha), Vāsuka and Siddheśvara. These are the holy places of bathing in the *Virajā-kṣetra* (*Brahma Purāṇa* 42: 1–12, 253).

8 The *Kapila Saṁhitā* describes the four major cult centres of Odisha, namely Jagannath Puri, Konarka-Surya, Śaiva-Ekāmra *kṣetra* at Bhubaneswar and *Virajā-kṣetra* of Jajpur. See Pramila Mishra, ed., *Kapila Samhitā* (New Delhi: New Bharatiya Book Corporation, 2005).

9 Ibid., 7.16–17.

10 S.N. Rajaguru, ed., *Inscriptions of Orissa*, Vol. I, pl II (Bhubaneswar: Orissa State Museum, 1958).

11 *Epigraphia Indica*, XXIII, 203.

12 Ibid., XIX, 263–264.

13 The *Virajā-kṣetra Māhātmya* of *Brahmāṇḍa Purāṇa* does not state the reason for the performance of Vedic *yajñas* but merely states that during the *yajñas*, Brahmā requested Śiva to stay here with his consort Pārvatī, who emerged from the sacrificial fire in the form of Virajā. Thus, according to *Virajā-kṣetra Māhātmya*, the place was the seat of Viṣṇu, Śiva and Virajā. U.N. Dhal, ed., *The Glory That Was Virajā-kṣetra* (New Delhi: Nag Publishers, 1984).

14 B.C. Dash, *Jajipur-Virajākṣetra Parikramā* (Odia), Sarojini Das (Cuttack, 1983), 6–7.

15 The Viṣṇu image in the Trilocaneśvara temple complex has a squat body and all four arms are lowered, with back resting on *ayūdha-puruṣa*—Gadādevī and Cakrapuruṣa (right). The head is framed by an undecorated halo. He wears truncated mitre-like crown with loose strands of hair splaying symmetrically out on either side down to his shoulders. There is no evidence of *śrīvatsa* or *kaustubha*. He has a beaded *keyūra* and a chain-like girdle. He wears a *yajñopavīta* but no *vanamālā*, but the *yajñopavīta* is framed by wooden flowers and may double as *vanamālā*. For the evolution of *sthānaka* Viṣṇu image in the Gupta and post-Gupta period, see F. M. Asher, *The Art of Eastern India, 300–800* (Minneapolis: University of Minnesota Press, 1980).

16 *Brahma Purāṇa*, Verses 28.I ff; 42.1–12.

17 On the basis of various layers, the apsidal *caityagṛha* complex and *Mahāstūpa*, Lalitgiri, can be chronologically divided into four phases: phase 1 from second century BC to fourth century CE; phase 2 from fourth/fifth century CE to seventh

century CE; phase 3 from seventh/eighth century CE to late tenth/eleventh century CE; and phase 4 from late tenth century CE to twelfth/thirteenth century CE. J. Patnaik, 'Excavations at Lalitagiri,' *Memoirs of the Archaeological Survey of India*, no. 112 (New Delhi: ASI, 2017).

18 Udayagiri's *caityagṛha* belonged to the post-Mauryan period, around the second century BC. The Buddhist site of Udayagiri expanded in the fourth/ fifth centuries BC, blooming between eighth and tenth centuries CE. The site started declining from the eleventh century onwards. P.K. Trivedi, 'Further Excavations at Udayagiri-2, Orissa (2001–2003),' *Memoirs of the Archaeological Survey of India*, no. 104 (New Delhi: ASI, 2011), 15–24.

19 The foundation of Ratnagiri is ascribed to the fifth century CE by Debala Mitra, the excavator of the site, on the basis of the inscriptions of the *Pratitya Samutpāda* of the fifth-century characters from the *stūpa* area. However, Mitra suggests an earlier beginning for Ratnagiri based on finding a structure below the foundation level of the *Mahāstūpa* area. See Debala Mitra, 'Ratnagiri I (1958–1961),' *Memoirs of the Archaeological Survey of India*, no. 80 (New Delhi: ASI, 1981), 27.

20 Regarding the cult preferences of the pilgrim see, U. Mishra, *Vajrayāna Buddhism: Study in Social Iconography*, Chapter 5 (New Delhi: Pratibha Prakashan, 2009).

21 Hermann Kulke cites the patronage of Stambheśvarī, Maṇināgeśvarī and other goddesses as instances of integration of tribal autochthonous elements into Brahmanical religion and culture under the active patronage of Brahmanised *rājās*. Kulke's discussion on the integration of tribal elements and the symbiotic relations between cult integration and royal patronage is discussed in H. Kulke, 'Royal Temple Policy and the Structure of Medieval Hindu Kingdoms,' in *The Cult of Jagannātha and Regional Tradition of Orissa*, eds. A. Eschmann, H. Kulke and G.C. Tripathi (New Delhi: Manohar, 1978), 125–137. For Terasingha Plates, see *Epigraphia Indica* Vol. 30, 271–275.

22 R.D. Banerji, 'Talcher Plate of Gayadatungadeva,' *Journal of Asiatic Society of Bengal* 12 (1916): 291–295.

23 S. Tripathy, Inscriptions of Orissa Vol. 6 (Bhubaneswar: Orissa State Museum, 1974), 65–70.

24 Kulke, 'Royal Temple Policy'.

25 Alice Getty, *History of Northern Buddhism* (Oxford: Clarendon Press, 1978), 134. The Bhadrak (in Bhadrak district, Odisha) inscription of ruler Mahārājā Gana of the third century CE refers to a goddess named Parṇadevatī (leaf-clad goddess). For Bhadrak inscription, see *Epigraphia Indica* Vol. 29 (1951–1952): 169–74. For the interpretation related to the goddess at this site, see

K.C. Pangrahi, 'Bhadrakali Inscription of Gana: Regnal Year 8', *Indian Historical Quarterly* 35 nos 1–4 (1959): 240–246. Today, a village-level goddess, namely Patrāsuṇī, is quite widespread in Odisha.

26 D.D. Kosambi points out that like goddess Hārītī, many regional goddesses in the state of Maharashtra were incorporated into Buddhism. Kosambi is not alone in making this observation. For example, Gail Sutherland talks about the assimilation of many folk legends of local goddesses into the Buddhist mythology of Yakṣiṇīs. See, D.D. Kosambi, *Myth and Reality: Studies in the Formation of Indian Culture* (Bombay: Popular Prakashan, 1983), 82–109. See, G.H. Sutherland, *The Disguises of the Demon* (Albany: State University of New York Press, 1991), 143. For the fertility aspect of Abhiṣeka Lakṣmī, Nāga and Nāgi *stambhas*, and Yakṣa and Yakṣī, see A. Snodgrass, *The Symbolism of the Stūpa* (New Delhi: Motilal Banarsidass, 1986), 292–305.

27 T. Watters, *On Yuan-Chwang's Travels in India* (New Delhi: Munshiram Manoharlal, 1961), 21.

28 I-tsing, *A Record of the Buddhist Religion as Practised in India and Malay Archipelago (AD 671–695)*, trans. J. Takakusu (New Delhi: Munshiram Manoharlal, 1966), 37.

29 Jambhala images have been found in Udayagiri, Ratnagiri, Solampur, Kuansa Mangala, Nathuabara, Erada (Dharmasala block), Kesariapur and Kapila of Jajpur district, while images of Hārītī have been found from Lalitgiri and Ratnagiri.

30 *Brahma Purāṇa*, Ch. 42, 1–12.

31 This Śaiva centre is located in the Virajā temple complex near Nabhī Gayā.

32 The present-day Varāha temple on the opposite side of the river and Saptamtrka Temple was constructed in the 15th century CE upon the ruins of an earlier temple. The iconography of Varāha can be dated to the 10$^{th}$ century CE.

33 Siddheśvara temple contains many images, namely Bhairava and *ekapāda* Bhairava, dateable to the eighth century.

34 *Brahma Purāṇa* refers to Siddheśvara and Kapileśvara as early Śiva temples, while the *Virajā Kṣetra Māhātmya* places Iśāneśvara as the earliest. However, given the presence of Lakulīśa cult in the Bhubaneswar group of temples of the Bhaumakara period, one can say there were many Śaiva temples like in Bhubaneswar, which were dedicated to important Pāśupata teachers. Out of 18 commentators of the *Pāśupata Tantra*, Iśāna occupies the sixth position and Agasti occupies fifteenth position. Kapila was one of the successors of Kuśika, a disciple of Lakulīśa.

35 T. E. Donaldson, *Tantra and Sākta Art of Orissa* Vol. 1 (New Delhi: D.K. Printworld, 2002), 77.

36 *Epigraphia Indica,* Vol. XXVIII (1958):180–81.

37 *Epigraphia Indica,* Vol. XXVIII:184.

38 Ratnagiri, Udayagiri, Lalitgiri, Vajragiri, Kolanagari,Langudi and Solampur contain remains of Buddhist monasteries, *stūpas* and sculptures. Out of these sites, Ratnagiri, Udayagiri, Lalitgiri and Langudi had their origins in the early historical period while others came up the eighth century. Lalitgiri, Udayagiri and Ratnagiri saw massive expansion with the addition and alteration of monasteries, introduction of Buddhist deities and construction of temples within complexes. Other Buddhist sites in and around Jajpur, which can be dated to eighth/ninth centuries are Kuansa, Tarang Sagarapur, Kapila, Khadipada, Deuli, Tarapur, Erada, Kesariapur, Nathuavara, Kosalesvara, Bhelanga, Mugapada, Siddhesvarapur, Bilesvara, Jhadagan and Duburi hill. See Ekadashi Padhi, *Yuge Yuge Jajpur* (Cuttack: Chitrotpala Press, 2002), 50.

39 Trivedi, 'Further Excavations, 3.

40 Debala Mitra, 'Ratnagiri I', 198; T.E. Donaldson, *Iconography of the Buddhist Sculptures of Orissa*, Vol. 1 (New Delhi: IGNCA/Aryan Book,), 11.

41 *Epigraphia Indica* Vol. XV (1919): 1-8.

42 *Epigraphia Indica* Vol. XXXIII (1959): 263–274.

43 Chapter 4 Verse 17 of the *Virajā-kṣetra Māhātmya* states that to the east of the temple of Varāha is the entry point of the *Virajā-kṣetra.* Any devotee interested to go on a pilgrimage should start on the fourteenth day of the new moon of *Vaiśākha* or *Māgha* month by taking a dip in the *tīrthadvāra* (gateway) located east of the Varāha temple on the northern bank of Vaitaraṇī. Verse 21 elaborates that the pilgrim should go to goddess Śānteśvarī and worship her after taking the dip. Śānteśvarī is still worshipped as the presiding goddess of Solampur, soit constituted part of the pilgrimage field of *Virajā-kṣetra.* See Dash, *Jajpur*, 105.

44 Alexis Sanderson coined Śaiva Age to denote the preponderance of Śaiva-Śākta tantric religion from the sixth to thirteenth centuries. It also denotes that all other religions seeking patronage from kings were influenced by Śaiva-Śākta traditions. This dominance was explained by Sanderson primarily from the perspective of state protection rituals that Śaiva-Śākta Tantras provided in addition to other roles it performed. See A. Sanderson, 'The Śaiva Age—The Rise and Dominance of Saivism during the Early Medieval Period,'in *Genesis and Development of Tantrism*, ed. Shingo Einoo (Institute of Oriental Culture, University of Tokyo, 2009):41–349.

45 B. Bhattacharyya, *Guhysamāja Tantra or Tathāgataguhyaka,* Gaikaward Oriental Institute, Baroda, 1968 p. XXVII.

46 Benoytosh Bhattacharyya claims that Buddhist Vajarayoginī/ Vajravarāhī was how Chinnamastā was known by the seventh century. He cites the reference to the goddess in the Buddhist *Sādhanamālā*, the Brahmanical text *Tantrasāra* (seventeenth century) and *Chinnmastākalpa* of uncertain origin and concludes that the Buddhist and Hindu Chinnmastā are the same, identical in all details. However, these similarities in Buddhist and Brahmanical traditions in iconographic representation and modes of worship merely show fluidity in South Asian religion. See E.A. Bernard, *Chinnamastā: The Aweful Buddhist and Hindu Tantric Goddess* (New Delhi: Motilal Banarsidass, 2010).

47 R.L. Mitra, *The Sanskrit Buddhist Literature of Nepal* (Calcutta: Asiatic Society of Bengal, 1882), 269.

48 *Tāranātha's History of Buddhism in India*, translated by Lama Chimpa and Alaka Chattopadhyaya, ed. D.P Chattopadhyaya (Delhi: Motilal Banarsidass Publishers), 275-6

49 Sanderson, 'The Śaiva Age', p. 124.

50 U. Mishra, 'Dharanis from the Buddhist Sites of Odisha,' *Pratnatattva* Vol. 22(2016), 73–84.

51 Chapter 3 of *Vairocanābhisambodhi Sūtra* anticipates the often-cited criticism that Mantrayāna Buddhism incorporated practices from Śaivism and other orders. 'Lord of Mysteries, in future ages beings of inferior intelligence and no faith will, on hearing these explanations, be unable to accept them on faith because they have no intelligence, and their doubts will increase. If they merely hear them and remain set in their ways without practicing, they will harm themselves and harm others, and they will make statements such as "Non-Buddhists have such methods, but they were not taught by the Buddha". These ignorant people will produce such faith-and-understanding.' See *The Vairocanābhisambodhi Sūtra*, trans. R.L. Giebel (Berkeley: Numata Center for Buddhist Translation and Research, 2005), 57.

52 Sanderson, 'The Śaiva Age,' 144.

53 U. Mishra, 'Multiple Gods, Goddesses and Buddhas—Locating Buddhism in the Religious Dynamics of Early Medieval Orissa,' in *Imaging Odisha*, ed. H. Kulke (Bhubaneswar: Prafulla Pathagar, 2013), 194–210.

54 Śubhakarasiṁha, who studied in the Ratnagiri *Mahāvihāra* of Orissa, took *Mahāvairocana Sūtra* and *Sarvatathāgata Tattvasaṁgraha* to China. See *Mahāvairocana-sūtra*, trans. C. Yamamoto, Śata-Piṭaka Series 359 (New Delhi: International Academy of Indian Culture, 1990).

55 Ronald Davidson, 'Reflections on the Maheśvara Subjugation Myth: Indie Materials, Sa-skya-pa Apologetics, and the Birth of Heruka,' *The Journal of the International Association of Buddhist Studies,* Vol. 14, no. 2 (1991): 197–235.

56 David Gray, 'The *Cakrasaṁvara Tantra*: Its History, Interpretation, and Practice in India and Tibet,' *Religion Compass,* Vol. 1, no. 6 (2007): 695–710.

57 Richard Davis, *Lives of Indian Images* (Princeton: Princeton University Press, 1997), 263.

58 Debala Mitra, *Bronzes from Achutarajpur* (New Delhi: Agam Kala Prakashan, 1978), 84–5.

59 *The Nispannayogāvalī of Mahāpaṇdita Abhayankara*, ed. B. Bhattacharyya, Gaikwad Oriental Series 109 (Baroda: Gaikwad Oriental Institute, 1972), 334.

60 *Ekāmra Purāṇaṁ*, ed. U. Dhal, Chapters 25–32 (New Delhi: Nag Publishers, 1986).

61 Panigrahi notes, 'It is not unlikely that the war between the Śaivas and the Buddhists, of which the Asokan pillar converted into a Śiva *liṅga* provides us with archaeological evidence. Besides, there is a village in the neighbourhood of Khandagiri, which is known as Jāgamarā, meaning "the place where *jāga* or sacrifice was completed". The archaeological evidence, the tradition and the place-names thus combine to show that there was a religious struggle between the Śaivas and the Buddhists.' See K.C. Panigrahi, *Archaeological Remains in Bhubaneswar* (Cuttack: Kitab Mahal, 1961), 215.

62 Panigrahi, *History of Orissa*, 312.

63 Ibid.

64 Ibid.

65 Panigrahi, *Archaeological Remains,* 234–35.

66 Chapters 25–32 of the *Ekāmra Purāṇam* deal with the *Devāsura* war on the banks of Gandhavatī (identified with Gangua stream) over the destruction of sacrifices by demons. See Panigrahi, *Archaeological Remains*, 215.

67 G. Verardi, *Hardships and Downfall of Buddhism in India* (New Delhi: Manohar, 2011), 286–87.

68 Intermediate-level political elite such as *rāṇakas* and *sāmantas* patronised Buddhism when it penetrated tribal interiors in Odisha. See U. Mishra, 'Inscribed Buddhist Images and Copperplates from Odisha: An Analysis of the Social Background of Donors and Issues of Brahmanical-Buddhist Relation,' *Pratna Samiksha* Vol. 9 (2018): 69–94.

69 Verses 39 and 40 of Chapter 3 of the *Virajā-kṣetra Māhātmya* state that the *Virajā-kṣetra* extends up to five *kośas* (one *kośa* is two miles), and within this. is located Kilāteśvara, on the south Varuṇeśvara and on the western vertices of the inverted triangle of *Virajā-kṣetra* is located the Beleśvara temple. Kilāteśvara (also pronounced Khilātesvara) is located on the banks of the Kalindi river in the Alinagar village of Bhadrak, whereas Beleśvara is located five kilometers from Jajpur town near Kampagada.

70 *Akrāntam daityam jaṭharam dharmeṇa virajādriṇa Nabhikūpa samipetū devī yā virajā sthitā/tatra piṇḍādikrtsapta kulanuddharate narah/Mahendra giriṇā tasya pādau suniscalaau:Vāyu Purāṇa* II(44.85–86).

71 *Virajā-kṣetra Māhātmya*, Ch. 17, 180–84.

72 Ibid., Ch. 25, Verse 11.

73 *Ekāmra Candrikā*, (Bhubaneswar: Kedaranath Gaveshana Pratisthana, 1995), 3.

74 '*Boloi Jagannātha Nilagiribasi/ Bauddharūpe Nilakandare chanti isi// (Madhya Parva); Dvāpara Juge śeṣare Deva Jagannātah/Bauddharūpare Bije Karibe je ethi// (Sabhā Parva); Balabhadra Subhadrā o Kṛṣṇa tini rūpa/ Baudha rūpare hele emanta svarūpa// (Vana Parva); Jaya Niladrivihāri he Jagannātha/Bauddha rūpe Kaliyuge mahima bikhyāta// Kaliyuge rahibāku kichi dina icchā/ Bauddha avatāre nisce vihāribu.//*' See G.C. Tripathi, 'Jagannātha: The Ageless Deity of the Hindus', in *The Cult of Jagannatha*, eds. A. Eschmann, H. Kulke and G.C. Tripathi, 479.

75 Tripathi, 'Jagannātha', 477–90.

10

# Donors of Kurkihar Images: An Investigation into Their Socioeconomic Background

Sayantani Pal

Donation of images for the fulfilment of a vow is an age-old practice in South Asia. Initially, such practice was common among the Buddhists and the Jainas. Usually, donations were made at places of pilgrimage, private shrines or common religious centres.[1] Many Buddhist monasteries became a favourite location for such religious practices. Monasteries like Nalanda, Bodhgaya and Kurkihar attracted a number of devotees donating images, often inscribed with their names and other details like place of origin, ancestry, social background, etc. Many of these monasteries are located near, though set apart from, major pilgrimage centres. Again, Buddhist monasteries were often located near travel and trade routes encouraging the movement of people like merchants with their merchandise. Monasteries used to be a resting place for such people. This implies a range of interactions between the monasteries and the outside world. The surrounding villages, some of which were often granted to the monasteries for the supply of items of daily need, obviously became involved in this process of interaction. They could have housed the ateliers for the images that were manufactured and donated to the monasteries by devotees coming from elsewhere. Even craftsmen and other professionals were likely to be recruited from the neighbouring villages. Thus, the villages also came to share an intimate relationship with the activities inside the monasteries.

An investigation into the socio-economic background of the donors of inscribed images is a well-researched area and significant work has been done in this field.[2] However, an institution-wise study of the background of donors of inscribed images may help us further understand the pattern of patronage, the social base of the sacred establishment and the nature of its interaction with the outsiders. In this paper, an attempt has been made to understand the same with regard to the monastery at Kurkihar in Bihar. This monastery shows certain interesting features regarding the pattern of donation of images. For several centuries, it had a host of monk and nun visitors from different parts of South India, unlike any other monastery—even the great monastery at Nalanda.

Regarding image inscriptions, the availability of space is an important factor influencing the content of the text. How much space donors get to inscribe their details and which factors they consider to be important for preserving and proclaiming their identity to present and future residents and visitors of the establishment is the key to the understanding of the context of the inscriptions. For instance, persons travelling from distant places tried to mention the place of their origin since it would easily connect them to their country as well as the host of other visitors from their homeland who came before them.

Kurkihar is a village about 4.8 km north-east of Wazirganj on the Nawada–Gaya Road. Its present location is in the Wazirganj Block of the district of Gaya in Bihar. It is about 28 km from Gaya. Kurkihar first attracted the attention of scholars for its Buddhist remains. In the first half of the 19th century, M. Kittoe first brought it to notice. Later, in 1930, the metal images for which the place gained its popularity came to light. The site is located on the ancient road from Nalanda to Bodhgaya. It has been pointed out by C.B. Picron that Kurkihar was clearly at a nodal point with easy access to Gaya in the west, Bodhgaya in the south-west, and Rajgir and Nalanda to the north-east.[3]

Since the time of Kittoe, the name of the village has been associated by scholars with a place called Kukkuṭapādagiri mentioned by Chinese pilgrims. Both Fa Hsien and Xuan Zang have mentioned the 'Cock's Foot Mountain' or Kukkuṭapādagiri in the country of Magadha. It has been variously identified by several scholars, from time to time, with Murali hill, Sobhnath hill and Gurpa hill—all situated near Kurkihar. However, since the hills cover the entire area to the south of the Rajgir hills and around Kurkihar, it is difficult to identify Kukkuṭapādagiri with any particular hill.[4]

The dating of the inscribed images of Kurkihar has been largely done on the basis of palaeographic features. It is, therefore, difficult to establish a century-wise chronology and analysis of the data. In most cases, an eighth to ninth or ninth to tenth century CE dating has been prescribed by scholars.[5] Our chronology showing the pattern of donation through the centuries, therefore, would not be exact and absolute. Still, on the basis of the approximate dating of the images, an attempt may be made to understand the pattern of donation of images to the monastery.

It may be mentioned at the outset that on the basis of closeness to the Kurkihar stone sculptures, Picron has traced the images produced in the Kurkihar idiom, but transferred to nearby places like Bodhgaya, Gaya, Guneri, Itkhori and Nalanda. We shall, thus, take into account all the images produced in the Kurkihar idiom, and not only images found at Kurkihar.[6]

**Table 10.1: Century-Wise Analysis of the Pattern of Donation [Abbreviations: BSM: *bhūmisparśamudrā*; DCP: *dharmacakrapravartanamudrā*; AM: *abhayamudrā*; VM: *varadamudrā*]**

| Period | Total no. of donations | Donors | Images donated | Place of origin of the donor |
|---|---|---|---|---|
| 8th–9th century | 5 (all in stone) | 1 *bhikṣu*, 1 *bhikṣuṇī*, 1 *sthavira* | Mañjuśrī 1, Buddha in VM 1, Tārā 2, Rectangular slab with 9 figures 1 | Āndhra *viṣaya* 1, Colika *viṣaya* 1 |
| 9th century | 29 in stone | *sthavira* 6, *tailika* 3, *bhikṣu* 1, *vṛddha* 1, *dānapati* 1, *upāsaka* 1, *karaṇika* 2, *kāyastha's* daughter 1 | Avalokiteśvara 2, Tārā 3, Mañjuśrī 1, Buddha in BSM 12, Buddha in DCP 3, Buddha in AM 1, Buddha descending from Heaven 1, Rectangular slab with 9 figures 3, unidentified 1, Māyā giving birth to Buddha 1 | Cālika *viṣaya* 1, Kāñcī 1, Kalinga 1, Veṅgi 2, Malaya 1, Kāśi 1 |

| Period | Total no. of donations | Donors | Images donated | Place of origin of the donor |
|---|---|---|---|---|
| 9th century | 10 in metal | *sthavira* 1, *bhikṣu* 2, *paramopasaka* 1, *vaṇika* 1, wife of *grāmapradhāna* 1, *carmakāra* 1 | Buddha in BSM 6, Buddha in DCP 1, Vāgiśvara with Prajñāpāramitā 1, Balarāma 1, Viṣṇu 1 | Kāñci 4, Maddhu-grāma in Vāhiravana 1 |
| 9th–10th century | 3 in stone | *mahākṣapaṭalā-dhyakṣa karaṇika* | Tārā 1, Māyā giving birth to Buddha 1, Cundā 1 | none mentioned |
| 10th century | 21 in metal | *sthavira* 4, *upāsikā* 2, 2 wives of Gopālahina, 1 wife of Gopāla Mahiaru | Buddha in BSM 2, crowned Buddha 2, Tārā 5, Lokanātha 1, Vasudhārā 2, Umā-Maheśvara 2, Detached part of *prabhāmaṇḍala* 1, *Triratha* pedestal 1, Rectangular pedestal 1, bell 4 | Kāñcī 10 |
| 11th century | 17 in metal | *sthavira* 1, *param-opāsaka* 1, *upāsikā* 1, *bhikṣu* 1, wife and son of mahattama=2, son of suvarṇakāra 1 | 1 each – seated Lokanātha, Buddha in Vajraparyaṅka, Siddhaikavīra, Mañjuśrī, Standing four-armed Avalokiteśvara, Prajñāpāramitā, Surya, Viṣṇu, Vasudhārā; Buddha in abhayamudrā 6, Śyāmatārā 2 | Kāñci 2 |
| 12th century | 6 in metal | 1 *karmmakāra* | Crowned Buddha 4, Viṣṇu 1, Hārīti 1 | None mentioned |

*Source:* Author

Some of the stone images dated in Phase I, which begins from the eighth century CE, may be considered at the very beginning (Table 10.1).[7] They tend to indicate that donors from the south started coming from the early phase of the monastery. However, all of them were not from Kāñcī, wherefrom later South Indian monks came in large numbers. They were from Āndhra and Colika *viṣayas*. In the case of images, the practice was to inscribe the Buddhist creed on the stele, and together with this, the donor used to add his own details to the pedestals that were of different sizes. In the case of a Mañjuśrī image (see Image 10.1), the space was so limited that apart from his name, Yaśodhara, the donor had a very limited scope to provide more details.

**Image 10.1: Mañjuśrī, Kurkihar, c. eighth–ninth century CE**

*Credit*: Claudine Bautze Picron

Among the five donations, three are definitely from a monastic background (*bhikṣu, bhikṣuṇī* and *sthavira*). In the case of a Tārā image (see Image 10.2), the donor, Buddhacandra, from Colika *viṣaya* did not mention his status, although there is no shortage of space. He must be from a monastic background like the other donors close to his time and thus, did not feel it necessary to mention his status. But in another Tārā image, the donor, Guṇamati, did not fail to mention that she was a *bhikṣuṇī* (see Image 10.3). We may conclude that all the early donors are from monastic backgrounds. It may also be noted that all the donors had Sanskrit names like Yaśodhara, Kanakaśrībhadra, Guṇamati, etc.

**Image 10.2: Tārā, Kurkihar, c. eighth–ninth century CE**

*Credit*: Claudine Bautze Picron

**Image 10.3: Tārā by Guṇamati, Kurkihar, c. eighth–ninth century CE**

*Credit*: Claudine Bautze Picron

The ninth century saw the most prolific number of donation of images in stone, whereas, in metal, that wasn't the case (see Table 10.1). There were only 10 donations. Among the 29 stone images, three are dated to the period of Devapāla and Mahendrapāla (ninth century CE). The donors cover a wide social cross-section ranging from a *tailika* (oilman) or wife of a *tailika*, a *karaṇika* (scribe) or wife of a *karaṇika*, and the daughter of a *kāyastha*. It may be assumed that in cases where a woman donor mentions herself as the wife or daughter of someone, she must have been making the donation on behalf of her family and not independently, as was the case of the *bhikṣuṇīs*. The largest number of donations were made by the *sthaviras* (six donations). Interestingly, one slab with nine figures carries a long inscription saying the donation was made by a *sthavira*, with his wife and son. But one *carmakāra*, who was a friend of a Dhūpavāsani (?), was responsible for a perpetual endowment (*akṣayanīvī*). Although the relation of the leatherworker with the *sthavira* family is difficult to understand, the involvement of local craftsmen, such as leatherworker and oilman, who again made three donations, with the establishment is apparent. Craftsmen like them must have been closely associated with the monastic establishment as suppliers of daily necessities. The *karaṇikas* also made two donations. They could have been associated with the administration of the monastery. Interestingly, the *karaṇikas* and *kāyasthas* had Sanskrit names like Śrīdharacandra, Vijayacandra and Parvadatta. But their wives and the daughters had Prākṛt names like Sīdeka and Hārukā. Again, the *tailikas* had Prākṛt names like Muṣeka, while Puṣikā/ Eṣikā/ Ṣaṣīkā was the name of the wife of a *tailika*, and Tihuka was the son of *tailika* Māhū. The *sthaviras* always had Sanskrit names like Buddhapriya, Lokeśvara and so on. A stratified society, based on the use of language, clearly emerges out of this data. The learned class like those of the monks and clerical professionals occupied a higher rank, while those associated with physical labour like the *tailikas* were at a lower rank. Women customarily had Prākṛt names.

Among the donors, two of the *sthaviras* came from the south, namely from Cālika *viṣaya* (perhaps the same as Colika *viṣaya*) and Kañcī. Some other *sthaviras* did not mention their place of origin probably due to the shortage of space. Both of them had similar name endings—Prajñāprabha and Vimalaprabha—and must have been the disciples of the same preceptor. The Buddha images in *bhūmisparśamudrā* donated by them have the same attributes, but they differ in treatment. Among the deities, the image of Buddha in *bhūmisparśamudrā* predominates the donations (12 donations). Next is Buddha in *dharmacakrapravartanamudrā* (three donations). Together with other poses, the image of the Buddha dominates. Avalokiteśvara, Tārā and Mañjuśrī have been donated by two, three and one donors respectively. These three deities were popular throughout centuries. In respect to preferences for deities, no definite pattern emerged, since three of the *tailika* community donated Avalokiteśvara, Tārā and Buddha in *bhūmisparśamudrā*. The *sthaviras*, definitely, had preferences for Buddha in *bhūmisparśamudrā* and rectangular slabs with nine figures (two donations each). Among the 29 donors, seven came from outside—two from Veṅgi, one from Cālika *viṣaya*, one from Kāñcī, one from

Kaliṅga, one from Malaya and one from Kāśī. Others did not mention their place of origin. Interestingly, in an image of Māyā giving birth to the future Buddha, the donor's name Abhayacandra is inscribed twice, both on the left and right of the pedestal. Obviously, the sculptor did not have space to inscribe any other detail or even a full sentence.

In the case of the metal images of the ninth century CE, the donors from Kañcī predominate (four donations among 10). They were *sthavira* or *bhikṣu* in some cases. All were Varmans and thus, belonged to a single line of a succession of preceptors. Out of the four images donated, three were the images of Buddha in *bhūmisparśamudrā* and one in *dharmacakrapravartanamudrā*. Thus, their preference for Buddha images is clear. Other donors were *paramopāsakī*, *vaṇika*, *carmakāra* and wife of a village headman. All of them had non-Sanskrit names. The donation of a Balarāma image by the wife of a village headman from Maddhugrāma in Vāhiravana is interesting since, in this case, a Brahmanical image has been donated at a Buddhist monastery, perhaps from a village located near by. Being an influential person responsible for the administration of the village, he did not fail to mention the ruling king Devapāla. Cast images with intricate designs, often inlaid with silver or precious gems, were obviously valuable. Donation of such pieces by a merchant or a village headman is comprehensible. But how could a cobbler afford to make such a precious image? D.C. Sircar points out in this context that many cobblers of Bengal used to earn their livelihood by manufacturing musical instruments like the *mṛdaṅgam* and playing them during worship.[8] Thus, they could be wealthy as well. Interestingly, a cobbler also made a gift of the image of a Brahmanical god at a Buddhist monastery, such as the Āpaṇaka *mahāvihāra*. The Āpaṇaka *mahāvihāra* is referred to in inscriptions and manuscripts from the ninth to twelfth century CE. It was located in the vicinity of Kurkihar.

In the ninth/tenth centuries CE, the donation of stone images fell into decline but the donation of metal images carried on full-fledgedly (see Table 10.1). Among the three stone images, none are of the Buddha. One image of Cundā from Bodhgaya is akin to the Kurkihar idiom. It was donated by a *mahākṣapaṭalādhyakṣakaraṇika*. The selection of the goddess is, however, unusual for Kurkihar stone sculptors. But the donor, associated with the art of writing, would naturally be a devotee of the goddess linked with learning.

Among the metal images of the 10th century CE, there are 21 donations of which 10 are by those from Kañcī. Many were, as usual, *sthaviras*. They include the Varmans and the Siṁhas. Buddha/Vudhavarman was a prolific donor who donated an image of Buddha in *bhūmisparśamudrā* together with four bells. The other donors all had Prākṛt names. Two were *upāsikā* and two were wives of Gopālahina, and they made their donations at Āpaṇaka *mahāvihāra*. One of them was a resident there. Both donated the image of Vasudhārā, but the one donated by the resident woman of the *mahāvihāra* is of better workmanship. Another woman introduces herself as the wife of Gopāla Mahiaru, resident of Āpaṇaka *mahāvihāra*. She donated the image of Umā-Maheśvara. In the other four cases, the donors, all with Prākṛt names, have not given their details. They must be local residents who could afford to donate such precious images. The close association and patronage of the local residents of the *vihāra* were, thus, active in the 10th century CE. Naturally, the cast images were so small that space was much limited. Still, donors from the south never failed to mention the place of their origin. Thus, it seems that they were a close-knit community who made their identity strong in the land of Buddha.

In the 11th century CE, there are 17 donations of cast images (Table 10.1). Two are from Kāñcī; thus, gradually the presence of monks from the south decreased in number. Among the donors, there is a sole *sthavira* from Kāñcī, two *upāsakas*, one *upāsikā* and one *bhikṣu*. The wife and son of *mahattama* Dūlapa made two donations of Buddha in *abhayamudrā*, both dated to the time of reign of Vigrahapāla. The son of a *bhaṭṭa* (*brāhmaṇa*) donated a Sūrya image. The son of a *suvarṇakāra* donated the image of Prajñāpāramitā during the reign of Mahīpāla. So again in this century, we have local patronage, including patrons from affluent rural magnates like the *mahattama*.

Women donors and nine persons without details bear Prākṛt names. Among the deities, new images of Lokanātha, Siddhaikavīra and Śyāmatārā formed objects of donation. One interesting image of a seated Śyāmatārā mentions just one word, 'Kālitāru', which could well be the colloquial use of the name of the deity. This, again, indicates the dissemination of the concept of this Buddhist goddess among locals. The monastery definitely played a role in this process.

In the 12th century CE, the decline in donations is clearly visible (Table 10.1). Only six donations were made and among them, the image of crowned Buddha predominates. Apart from a Viṣṇu image donated by a *karmakāra*, the other donors, all with Prākṛt names, did not provide any details. All of them could be local residents. Thus, when the flow of patronage from the south died down, the monastery, as well as the metal workers, were maintained by local patronage, which included non-Buddhists too.

Although Brahmanical images formed a substantial part of the total donations, the *brāhmaṇas* themselves did not make any donation. The host of donors did not include rulers, high-ranking officials like *mahābalādhikṛta* and *mahāsenāpati* or persons from urban merchant classes like *śreṣṭhī*, *sārthavāha*, etc. Local donors were rather rural influential groups like *grāmapradhāna*, *mahattama*, or the learned class like *kāyastha* and *karaṇika*, together with rural craftsmen like *tailika*, *carmakāra*, *karmakāra*. It is more or less clear that the site had whole-hearted support and patronage from locals who donated images of not only Buddhist deities but also those they worshipped from different strands of belief—Viṣṇu, Balarāma and the major gods of the Brahmanical pantheon. This continued alongside donations by monks from the south. The harmonious coexistence of believers from the two different creeds goes against the religious atmosphere of early medieval India that had prompted the birth of images of aggressive Buddhist deities. We may mention in this context an image of the Buddhist goddess Aparājitā from the south of Bihar, dated ninth/tenth century CE. She is shown in a slapping gesture (*capeṭadānamudrā* on her right hand) while trampling Vighna or Gaṇapati.[9] The contribution of the villages surrounding the monastery of Kurkihar stands as a remarkable exception in this religious context of early medieval Bihar.

In view of the essentially rural profile of the monastery, the sheer craftsmanship of the donated images is significant. As pointed out by Susan Huntington, the metal images of Kurkihar display greater use of inlay of different colours of metal than Nalanda.[10] Such practices must have made the images more precious. We may consider here the two images of Tārā and four-armed Avalokiteśvara, both donated by *upāsikā* Duvajha. Both carried space for inserting gems; the *prabhāmaṇḍala* of Tārā was more intricate, showing the flame motifs as a continuous row of teardrop-shaped openings probably meant to hold gems. The metalworkers definitely excelled in their workmanship, and the formation of the Kurkihar idiom emphasises the excellence of the stone sculptors who could spread so much influence. Stella Kramrisch has pointed out that artistically, there is no difference in the treatment of Buddhist, Jaina and Brahmanical metal images, and they were produced in one centre.[11] Thus, the same atelier and same workmen produced them.

On the basis of a year-by-year analysis of 60 donative inscriptions of Kurkihar, it has been argued that 'Buddhist' was not an essential socio-religious identity for donors and that the monastery marginalised *varṇa-jāti* identity since it has been mentioned in only two cases among all inscriptions, that is *brāhmaṇa* and *carmakāra*.[12]

Regarding these observations, it may be pointed out that when a Buddhist made a donation at a monastery, there could hardly be any need to declare that he is a Buddhist. As far as our records are concerned, monks or lay worshippers in most cases have declared their identity. In cases when they belonged to the line of Kāñcī monks, they sometimes did not feel the necessity to mention it since their name endings told the story, such as Prajñāprabha mentioned that he was a *sthavira* but Vimalaprabha did not (both donated Buddha in *bhūmisparśamudrā*). In the case of Budhavarman, a *sthavira* from Kāñcī, while donating bells, incised his status and place of origin. But when he donated an image of Buddha in *bhūmisparśamudrā*, he simply mentioned his name and nothing more. There was a shortage of space too. Again, it was also not the responsibility of a Buddhist monastery to marginalise *varṇa-jāti* identity since they did not take any active role to alter or modify the Brahmanical social structure existing outside their establishment. A number of donors have mentioned their *jāti* status in our records, for example *carmakāra*, *suvarṇakāra* and so on. Admission to the *saṁgha* was not based on any caste preference.

Finally, the total number of donations in stone and metal show that among the 37 stone images, the monks donated eight images, while lay worshippers donated only one. Among the other donors, nine mentioned their identity, either in the form of occupational status or as wife of somebody. Others either did not mention their identity, or the inscriptions are illegible. Among the 56 donations in metal, the monks made 10 donations while lay worshippers made five donations. Twelve donors have clearly mentioned either their occupation, or, as the member of a family, they mentioned the head of the family.

Buddhist monks, therefore, made a number of donations but together with them, other occupational sub-castes and the local people joined hands to maintain the popularity of the site. Monks from the south definitely played the most important role in the making of the site, since the earliest donations were made by them. At the beginning of the eighth century CE, the participation of locals are not found since most of the donors were monks. But once it began, the site gained much popularity among the locals who were responsible for keeping the flow of patronage active until the last days of the monastery. Thus, it is only in the succeeding centuries that the monastery became popular and must have played a significant role in the livelihoods of local occupational groups.

In the beginning of this essay, we had noted the location of the *mahāvihāra* on the way from Rajgir to Bodhgaya, which would have surely attracted the movement of merchants and other outsiders. The name Āpaṇaka *mahāvihāra* for the monastery is also significant, since it is based on the term *āpaṇa*, meaning a shop or market. Therefore, one would expect the existence of a sizeable amount of merchant-donated images. However, in reality, such images are almost negligible at the site. The donors, apart from the Buddhists, were mostly local people and this reflects the character of the site.

Attempts have been made to understand the factors regarding the choice of the Kurkihar monastery by monks from the south. Picron suggests that from the fifth century CE, Brahmanical monuments began to supplant Buddhist constructions in the south.[13] Also, monk visitors to Kurkihar might perhaps have related to the belief in the presence of Mahākāśyapa hidden in a nearby hill, which implied the coming of Maitreya who will speak the *Dharma* anew in an unknown future. Hailing from a region where Buddhism was on the verge of disappearance, more than in the north, those monks might have felt some consolation in this belief. This movement of monks, thus, might have started centuries earlier, showing the progressive appropriation of Buddhist sites by Brahmanical temples in the south.

The itinerary of Xuan Zang refers to the visit of a monk from the south. Xuan Zang mentions the Ku-ku-t'a Saṅghārāma (Cock Monastery) in Magadha. He says it stood to the south-east of the 'Old City' of Pāṭaliputra.[14] Fa Hsien also agrees with Xuan Zang in placing the Cock Monastery to the south-east of Pāṭaliputra. To its north-west is an old monastery, which had the institution of the Gong-Call-Tope.[15] The gong was to be struck to call the learned together. Xuan Zang tells a story of conflict between the brethren of high character and great learning, and the Tīrthikas who had made the transmission of learning from the teacher to disciple a profession. At first, the Buddhists were defeated and monasteries forbidden to call meetings by gong-beating. After 12 years, Deva, a disciple of Nāgārjuna P'usa in South India, came to Pāṭaliputra and the Tīrthikas fearing defeat by his hand induced the king to order the gate-keepers to forbid any foreign monk to enter the city. Deva came in disguise, and beat the gong of the monastery in which he had slept. A public discussion followed and the Tīrthikas were defeated. The king and his ministers were pleased and raised the sacred structure as a memorial. This story establishes a connection between the monks of Magadha with those of the south. However, the visiting of monks from different parts of the south throughout a period of at least four centuries (eighth to eleventh century CE) remains inadequately explained. The explanation of Picron about anticipating or awaiting the future Buddha stands questioned in view of the negligible number (only five uninscribed stone images) of images of Maitreya from the Kurkihar monastery.

In fact, the importance of the Deccan and Far South in Indian Buddhism has been reflected in the accounts of Chinese pilgrims and in reference to the teachers living in these regions. The line of Varman and Siṁha *ācāryas* coming from the south to Kurkihar also bears clear testimony to this fact. Yet, Buddhist remains are comparatively less in the south. In the sixth and seventh centuries CE, the Pallava capital of Kanchipuram had a sizeable presence of Buddhists. Xuan Zang mentions 100 monasteries and 10,000 Mahāyāna monks in Kāñcī in the seventh century CE. Yet, Buddhist sculptures are fewer in number there. Since all of them are stone images of the Buddhas and there are no Bodhisattvas (as one would expect in a place dominated by Mahāyāna monks), it has been suggested that they were destroyed by anti-Buddhist saints between the eighth and the tenth centuries CE.[16] These anti-Buddhist activities might have played a role in the coming of large numbers of monks from Kāñcī. However, as we have already noted, the southern monks came from different parts, not only Kāñcī.

The monks, as we have seen, have made several donations of cast images. How could they afford to donate such precious pieces? Did they have their source of patronage in Kāñcī? Why did Kurkihar lose its attraction in the eleventh century CE when, at the nearby sites of Punawan and Hasra Kol, great activity of manufacturing images was taking place? Why did the artists of Kurkihar move to other places? These are some questions that remain unexplained by our analysis of donative images and patterns of patronage from Kukrihar.

## Endnotes

1 G. Sengupta, 'Donors of Images in Eastern India (c. 800–1300 AD)', *Proceedings of Indian History Congress* 43 (Kurukshetra: Indian History Congress, 1982): 158–164.

2 See papers of G. Bhattacharya in G. Bhattacharya, *Essays on Buddhist, Hindu, Jain Iconography and Epigraphy (Studies in Bengal Art Series)* (Dhaka: International Centre for Study of Bengal Art, 2000); G. Schopen, 'A Well Sanitized Shroud: Asceticism and Institutional Values in the Middle Period of Buddhist Monasticism', in *Between the Empires: Society in India 300 BCE to 400 CE*, ed., P. Olivelle (New York: Oxford University Press, 2006), 315–348; G. Schopen, *Buddhist Monks and Business Matters: Still More Papers on Monastic Buddhism in India* (Honolulu: University of Hawaii Press, 2004).

3 C.B. Picron, *The Forgotten Place: Stone Images from Kurkihar, Bihar* (New Delhi: Archaeological Survey of India, 2014), 15.

4 Picron, *The Forgotten Place*, 9.

5 Ibid.

6 Ibid.

7 Regarding the dating of the images, I have followed the chronology of C.B. Picron.

8 D.C. Sircar, *Pal-Sen Yuger Vamsanucharit* (Kolkata: Sahityalok, 1982), 174–175.

9 G. Bhattacharya, 'Ganeśa with a Dagger', in *Religion and Art: New Issues in Indian Iconography and Iconology*, ed. C.B. Picron (London: The British Academy, 2008),141–152.

10 S.L. Huntington, *The 'Pala-Sena' Schools of Sculpture* (Leiden: E.J. Brill, 1984), 102–105.

11 S. Kramrisch, 'A Note on the Metal Images of Kurkihar', in *Kurkihar, Gaya and Bodhgaya*, ed. S.K. Saraswati (Rajshahi: K.C.Sarkar, 1936), vii.

12 B.N. Prasad, 'The Socio-Religious Dimensions of Dedicatory Inscriptions on Sculptures Donated to a Buddhist Establishment in Early Medieval Magadha: Kurkihar, c. 800–1200 CE', *Journal of the Oxford Centre for Buddhist Studies* 7 (2014): 116–152.

13 Picron, *The Forgotten Place*, 18, fn. 91.

14 T. Watters, *On Yuan Chwang's Travels in India (A.D. 629–645)* (Delhi: Low Price Publication, 2004), 98.

15 Watters, *On Yuan Chwang's Travels*, 100.

16 R.L. Brown, 'The Act of Naming Avalokiteśvara in Ancient Southeast Asia,' in E.A. Bacus et al., *Interpreting Southeast Asia's Past: Monument, Image and Text: Selected Papers from the 10th International Conference of the European Association of Southeast Asian Archaeologists*, Vol. 2 (Singapore: Nus Press, 2004), 263–274.

# IV

# Social Imaginaries and the Ocular

11

# The Marriage Rite of Śiva-Pārvatī: Specimens of Early Medieval Indian Temple Art

Neha Singh

## Marriage: A Few Perspectives

Claude Levi-Strauss in his 1949 book, *Les Structures élémentaires de la Parenté* (*The Elementary Structures of Kinship*), regarded kinship as a universal system (not uniform everywhere) and marriage as one of the most important elementary structures of kinship in any society because it is through marriage that kinship ties are solidified or loosened.[1] Marriage, in the words of Levi-Strauss, is the 'archetype of exchange', an alliance that involves the gift of women.[2] The gift of women is ensured by the universal rule of the prohibition of incest and it prohibits marriage with the mother, sister or daughter, but more importantly, it obliges the mother, sister or daughter to be given as gifts to others. Prohibition of incest, hence, is a cultural construct rather than a natural one and its purpose is to widen the circle of kinship network for the gift of women through a marriage alliance. Marriage, according to Levi-Strauss, 'is thus a dramatic encounter between nature and culture, between alliance and kinship'.[3]

Levi-Strauss did not define marriage in itself but rather as a system within the kinship system, and hence, the definition. However, some scholars have attempted to define marriage per se. For instance, *The Journal of the Royal Anthropological Institute of Great Britain and Ireland*, in 1951, defined marriage as 'a union between a man and a woman such that children born to the woman are recognised legitimate offspring of both parents'.[4] It is apparent in this definition that marriage is the means to legitimise the progeny, though whether legitimation is social or legal is not made explicit in this definition. Further, it implies marriage as a union of heterosexual human beings. On the other hand, in 1971, sociologists like E.W. Burgess, H.J. Locke and M.M. Thomes provided a slightly less vague definition of marriage. In their words, marriage implies 'a ceremony, a socially sanctioned union of one or more men with one or more women, with a recognition of obligations to the community assumed by those entering this relationship'.[5] This definition also regards marriage as a union of heterosexual human beings. In addition, however, marriage is defined by these sociologists as a socially sanctioned phenomenon.

A combination of these two definitions is perspicuous in defining marriage provided in the Glossary of the book *Family, Kinship and Marriage in India*, published in 1993 and edited by Patricia Uberoi. Such an element is not surprising as the book is a part of the series, *Oxford in Indian Readings in Sociology and Social Anthropology*. 'Marriage is', as mentioned in the Glossary, 'a socially sanctioned relationship between a man and a woman, usually involving economic co-operation and residential and sexual cohabitation, and ensuring the legitimacy of the children born of the union'.[6] This definition too refers to marriage as a socially sanctioned union between heterosexual human beings, which also legitimises the children born of such a union. However, residential and sexual cohabitation is regarded as an occasional and not an accomplished occurrence.

Marriage, taking into consideration all these definitions furnished by social anthropologists and sociologists, can be regarded as an alliance, a union of heterosexual human beings, which is socially sanctioned, whereby the children born of such a union may be ascertained as legitimate. Furthermore, marriage occasionally implies residential and sexual cohabitation.

However, the marriage of Śiva with Pārvatī signifies another feature with regard to marriage within the context of Brahmanical tradition, that is, the marriage is monogamous. In a monogamous marriage, one man is married to one woman at one time.[7] Śiva is not married to Satī and Pārvatī at the same time. He marries them one after the other. His marriage to Pārvatī takes place after Satī dies at her father's grand Vedic sacrifice. On both these occasions, Śiva is a reluctant groom and does not readily agree to marry either Satī or Pārvatī. Even though Śiva is represented in the *Purāṇas* as being married twice, it is maintained that Śiva's spouse is actually one, for both Satī and Pārvatī are the human incarnations of Śakti. Śiva, for example, says to Pārvatī when they reach Kailāsa after the due completion of their marriage rites: 'I am reminding you although you know the previous birth. If you remember, speak out. In my divine sport you are always my beloved.'[8]

On the other hand, Satī and Pārvatī are born for no reason but to be Śiva's wives. This implies that Śiva's marriages to Satī and then Pārvatī are monogamous.

The *Purāṇas* provide an answer to why Śiva's marriages are monogamous. But before looking at that, a discussion on the reasons provided by Frederick Engels for the occurrence of monogamy will be useful, for it will provide a comparative understanding.

The fruits of Lewis Henry Morgan's anthropological work were put to use for the first time in order to provide a historical explanation of the origin of the family, private property and the state by Engels in 1942. His work[9] is based on Morgan's *Ancient Society*, which appeared in 1877.[10] Engels attempted to sharpen the theoretical implications of Morgan's work, dealing with four major topics—developmental stages in human history, 'the nature of primitive society with regard to property, rank, family forms and descent systems', the emergence of economically based classes and the state, and 'primate' social organisation and its significance—for insight into early humans.[11]

Engels explains the stages of the development of human society in terms of materialistic realities. He describes savagery, the earliest stage, as 'the period in which man's appropriation of products in their natural stage predominated'. The second stage, barbarism, is defined as 'the period in which man acquired methods of increasing the supply of natural products by human activity'. The third stage, civilisation, is the time when 'men learned to apply' more advanced methods to the process of production of natural products.[12] These stages, according to Engels, correspond with the three principal forms of marriage: group marriage during the period of savagery, pairing marriage during barbarism and monogamy in the course of civilisation.[13]

The monogamous family, according to Engels, developed out of the pairing family, and its marked prevalence was the sign that the stage of civilisation had begun.[14] In Engels's words, the monogamous family 'is based on the supremacy of the man' as the main purpose is to have children of undisputed paternity as they inherit their father's property as his heirs. Undisputed paternity demands the wife's sexual fidelity towards her husband. This feature makes the dissolution of marriage ties upon the wife's wishes an improbability and results in the manifestation of sexually monogamous marriages for women. However, Engels points out that such is not the case with the husband for 'the right of congeal infidelity' as well as the right to remarry remains secure for him.[15]

Engels proves his case by elucidating historical evidence from ancient Greece. He points out that unlike the wife, the husband could dissolve a childless marriage or take a second wife as well. Engels mentions the cases of two Spartan kings—Anaxandridas (around 650 BCE) and Ariston. King Anaxandridas had two wives, for his first wife was childless. King Ariston took a third wife and dismissed one of the first two childless wives.[16] Hence, asserts Engels, 'monogamy from the beginning' had the 'specific character of monogamy *for the woman only*, but not for the man'.[17] Monogamy, he continues, was not natural but based on the development of private wealth; 'on the victory of private property over primitive, natural communal property' and the subjugation of female sex by the male.[18] The crux of Engels's argument, thus, is that monogamy is not a given, but a social phenomenon existing due to the prevalence of private property. Social realities, thereby, are affected by economic conditions because they are interlinked.

However, the reason provided in the *Purāṇas* for the occurrence of monogamy is different from the one given by Engels. The former is narrated through a myth. In the *Śatarudra Saṁhitā* of the *Śiva Purāṇa*, there's a myth of the half-female incarnation of Śiva. The summary is as follows:

> Once the subjects created by Brahmā did not multiply, while much distressed he was with this, a celestial voice said:
>
> 'Carry on the creation produced by couples.'
>
> Brahmā realised that since no generation of women was formed by him creation by means of copulation was not possible. Hence, Brahmā began a penance while pondering over Śiva united with Śakti called Śivā. After a long period Śiva, being satisfied with Brahmā's penance, disposed himself in the form of half male and half female to Brahmā. On seeing this form of Śiva and Śivā, Brahmā eulogised with palms joined in reverence. Then, Śiva said to Brahmā,
>
> 'It is for the increase of the subjects that this penance has been performed by you now. I am delighted by that penance. I shall confer on you what you desire.'
>
> Consequently, Śiva detached the female half Śivā from his body. Brahmā pleased by seeing the detached Śakti from Śiva requested Śakti thus,
>
> 'O Śivā, the gods and others were mentally created by me. But they do not multiply themselves. Hence… hereafter I wish all my subjects flourish by making the creation originate from pairs.'
>
> Brahmā further said to Śakti that since all Śaktis originate from the great Śakti alone he would be obliged to be granted the power to create women by the great Śakti. Along with this boon Brahmā requested Śakti to be born as the daughter of his son Dakṣa, 'for the increase of the mobile and immobile beings through the Īśa (Śiva).' Hence, Śivā—the great Śakti—created another Śakti in her own image from the middle of her eyebrows. Looking at the created Śakti, Śiva spoke to her,
>
> 'O goddess, you have been propitiated by Brahmā through his penance. Lovingly become pleased with him and fulfill his desires.'
>
> Saying thus, Śiva merged with Śivā again and vanished from the scene. Thereafter, the creation became copulatory.[19]

This myth is regarded by Ellen Goldberg as the one in which 'the ideology of patriarchy is being birthed in' and given divine sanction for 'Śakti emerges from, and returns to, the male-identified god head (Śiva)'.[20] However, this myth expresses another feature as well. Firstly, it narrates how creation became copulatory. But more importantly, it defines monogamy as a given. In the myth, it is Śiva who is shown as possessing the female half. It is from Śiva that Śakti comes into being completely as an individual. Therefore, it is made explicit that Śakti belongs to Śiva and that she alone can be Śiva's better half, that is, spouse, for she alone is equal to him, though differently. Śakti is the eternal spouse of Śiva. Consequently, her incarnation as a mortal female is destined to attain Śiva as the husband. All this, though, also adds to the reverential status of Śiva as a god, for Śakti's sole purpose to incarnate is to be united with Śiva; Śakti, thus, exists for Śiva.

## The Marriage of Śiva-Pārvatī

### Prologue

Dakṣa refuses to see (take *darśana* of) Śiva. Being uninvited, Śiva too refuses to (give *darśan*) attend Dakṣa's sacrifice. Śiva says to Satī:

> Dakṣa is very well your father, dear. But he is my particular enemy. O gentle lady, those who go to another man's house without being invited attain disrespect which is more serious than even death.[21]

Though warned, Satī attends Dakṣa's sacrifice. However, as prophesied by Śiva, she invites disrespect at the hands of her host. Unable to reconcile the two opposing worlds—Dakṣa's and Śiva's—Satī sacrifices herself, in the hope that her death will bring the two together. This does happen, but Śiva's world destroys the world of Dakṣa (Brahmanical society). The death of Satī, therefore, does not actually bring Śiva closer to Dakṣa. Śiva, on the other hand, enters into deep meditation, until Satī reincarnates as Pārvatī—the daughter of Himavat and Menā—in the world of mortals and stirs desire in him.[22]

Himavat brings Pārvatī to Śiva, so that Pārvatī can serve Śiva who has come to perform penance at the Himalayan ridge Gaṅgāvatāra.[23] Pārvatī serves Śiva every day. However, Śiva, being in meditation, remains oblivious to her presence. Gods try to help but in vain. One example is of Kāmadeva's destruction by Śiva. Kāmadeva, having been instructed by Indra, reaches the entrance of Śiva's penance grove along with Rati (his wife) and Spring. Pārvatī arrives as well with two friends and begins to worship Śiva who is in deep meditation. Taking advantage of this moment, Kāmadeva shoots his flowery arrows at Śiva. Śiva's mind, as a result, is perturbed and his meditation disturbed. He sees Kāmadeva stationed on his left and his fury results in the discharge of a huge flame from his third eye. The flame reduces Kāmadeva to ashes. Pārvatī sees Śiva. But her scared friends immediately take her to her abode. Thereafter, gods appear before Śiva and inform him that Kāmadeva was sent to make Śiva amenable to marry Pārvatī. Śiva agrees to resuscitate Kāmadeva at a certain point in time but does not agree to marry Pārvatī.[24]

However, Pārvatī developed a desire for Śiva. She now not only wishes Śiva's *darśan* but also turn his gaze onto herself. Śiva's *darśan* instills desire in her to see him more and alone, and that Śiva too sees her with the desire to have her alone. But when Pārvatī goes to see Śiva the next day at Gaṅgāvatāra, she doesn't find him. Hence, she performs severe penance to attain Śiva and her tenacity finally wins him over. Śiva, pleased with her penance, appears before her and grants her the boon to be his bride. The marriage of Śiva and Pārvatī may be regarded as the Gāndharva kind, 'the mutual union by desire of a maiden and the bridegroom',[25] but it is actually the Brāhma type—a marriage rite that is captured in art in the form of Kalyāṇasundaramūrti.

## The Kalyāṇasundaramūrti

> ...in an age when paper and printing had not yet been developed, books were not easy to come by and in consequence, were available only to a limited number even among the educated few ... the temple sculptures ... virtually amount to a standing public announcement in the best possible technique.[26]

The iconographic representations of Pārvatī with Śiva are many. They are mostly represented together in art, but the one image, which explicitly expresses the nature of Pārvatī's relation with Śiva, is the Kalyāṇasundaramūrti, found roughly sixth century CE onwards in the south-western region of India. The Kalyāṇasundaramūrti represents the marriage ceremony of Śiva and Pārvatī. This theme is narrated elaborately in Puranic myths, but the elements portrayed in the iconography of the Kalyāṇasundaramūrti are rather concise, which is indicative of the artist's attempt to express only the most important aspects of the alliance.

**Image 11.1: The Kalyāṇasundaramūrti panel, Cave 29, Ellora, c. second half of the seventh century CE**

*Credit*: American Institute of Indian Studies

In this essay, I will attempt to analyse the 'public announcement' of socio-religious features of the Brahmanical tradition made through the Kalyāṇasundaramūrti to both the Brahmanical and non-Brahmanical masses in the early medieval period in India. I will examine the representations of the Kalyāṇasundaramūrti found in early medieval Brahmanical temples, beginning my discussion with the analysis of the iconographic depiction of the Kalyāṇasundaramūrti at Cave 29, Ellora (see Image 11.1). Thereafter, I will study other representations of this *mūrti* found in other Brahmanical temples of early medieval India. Finally, I will put forward my concluding remarks regarding this *mūrti*.

Sara L. Schastok in her work, *The Śāmalājī Sculptures and 6th Century Art in Western India*, while discussing the increasing importance of Skanda in Śaiva art, during the sixth century CE, states that the representation of Kalyāṇasundaramūrti at Ellora's cave temple 21 has to be explored within the context of the two other panels (one showing a conversation between Brahmā and Himavat, and another showing Pārvatī's *pañcāgni tapas*) carved on both the sides of the Kalyāṇasundaramūrti panel. The need for such an undertaking arises, in Schastok's view, from the fact that the whole north-western side wing of cave temple 21, which enshrines these panels, actually represents the Puranic myth of the birth of Skanda.[27] According to Schastok, the independent space provided for the representation of 'the myth of the birth of Skanda' in art at this cave temple is reflective of the increasing prominence of Skanda in the Śaiva pantheon. She further states that the reason no such pattern is found at cave temples 29 and 15 at Ellora is because these are chronologically late, and hence 'required no further interpretation at Ellora'.[28]

The case put forward by Schastok is validated by the evidence used by her. However, the Kalyāṇasundaramūrti is used in art not only to build up anticipation for the birth of Skanda. The reason is that there are numerous cases in which this *mūrti* isn't followed by sculptural representations of Skanda as a child or as the leader of the divine army. This suggests that the Kalyāṇasundaramūrti may have conveyed many other elements than merely being a sculpture created to anticipate the birth of Skanda. The following discussion, thus, will explore the other elements the Kalyāṇasundaramūrti may have conveyed.

The marriage of Śiva with Pārvatī is depicted in its final stage in the Kalyāṇasundaramūrti at cave temple 29 at Ellora. This could have been due to limited space the artist may have had within the sacred landscape of the cave temple. But the following discussion will make apparent that this iconographic representation depicts only the most important aspects of the divine marriage between Śiva and Pārvatī.

The depiction of Śiva and Pārvatī's marriage in art, like in the Puranic myths, conveys the significance of their alliance. The wedding is attended by almost all semi-divine beings visible in the upper zone of the Kalyāṇasundaramūrti panel at cave temple 29.[29] To the proper left, Varuṇa, Yama, Vāyu, Nandī, Īśāna and Vidyādhara can be seen, while to the proper right are shown the Vidyādhara couple, Indra and other celestial beings. The presence of these semi-divine figures as attendants evidently suggests the importance of this marriage at the cosmic level. It is lent more magnificence by the presence of Brahmā as the officiating priest, shown in the panel on Śiva's left, seated on the floor in the act of making offerings into the sacrificial fire.[30] The presence of Brahmā as the priest also conveys the *sastric* nature of this divine marriage.

Among the eight types of marriages classified in Sanskrit legal texts, the marriage of Śiva with Pārvatī as portrayed in the panel can be equated with the first type of *sastric* sanctioned marriage, that is, the Brāhma rite. The Brāhma rite is defined by Manu in the *Mānava Dharmaśāstra* as:

> The gift of maiden, (the father) having adorned and honoured (her) (with ornaments, etc.), and having himself invited (the bridegroom), to a man of Vedic learning and good character.[31]

This kind of rite is described in the myth of the marriage between Pārvatī and Śiva in the Śiva *Purāṇa*. In the *Pārvatīkhaṇḍa* of *Rudreśvara Saṁhitā* of the Śiva *Purāṇa*, Himavat, while giving his daughter Pārvatī to Śiva, says:

> O lord Śiva, I am giving this girl, my daughter to you as your wife. O lord of all, be pleased to accept her.[32]

In the panel, the act of Pārvatī being given away is apparent by the presence of her parents, Himavat and Menā, shown standing on her proper right, and more importantly by the placement of Pārvatī's right hand in the right hand of Śiva, i.e., in the act of *pāṇigrahaṇa* (the ceremony of taking hold of the hands).[33] *Pāṇigrahaṇa* is a crucial ritual in a Brāhma marriage rite. It symbolises the official observance of the bride being handed over to the groom.[34] According to Kumkum Roy, it marks the 'appropriation of the procreative powers of the woman' and hence, the *pāṇigrahaṇa* rite epitomises the creation of bonds of 'control, dominance and subordination'.[35] This being stated, the representation of this rite in the panel suggests that the marriage of Pārvatī with Śiva lends her a less prominent position than him as his wife.

Furthermore, this rite upholds other kinds of *sastric* sanctions. It is both *anulomic* or hypergamous and *savarṇic* or isogamous (of the same estate) in nature. *Anuloma* unions are those in which a female is given in marriage to a male whose social status is higher than the female and her family. Thus, females are 'married up'.[36] On the other hand, *savarṇic* or isogamous unions are 'the marriage of status-equals'.[37] These features are visible in the panel under discussion as well.

Pārvatī and Śiva are the central figures in the panel for the size of their representation is bigger than the other figures.[38] Both are adorned with many ornaments. Importantly, the figure of Pārvatī is smaller than Śiva, which indicates her physical strength being less than that of Śiva's. Pārvatī is shown as having two arms. In her left arm, placed closer to her chest, she holds a lotus,[39] which along with her lowered eyelids, reflects her coyness as well as surrender. The two arms mark the mortal aspect of her being. On the other hand, Śiva has four arms. His two upper arms are shown as having a flower and in *abhayahasta*, and his left arm rests on the tuft of his lower garment.[40] Śiva's posture, as well as his physical representation in the panel, thus suggests his mightiness and divine prowess. Pārvatī, then, is portrayed as less powerful than Śiva. She is married up. But the union is not a mismatch, for the halos (*prabhāvalaya*) behind the heads of both Pārvatī and Śiva prove the union is between compatible beings, that is, Pārvatī, though human, is eligible to be married to Śiva, the lord of the world. Hence, their marriage can also be termed as isogamous in nature. It is a union between two empowered beings, albeit 'not in identical ways'.[41]

This panel, thus, shows gender hierarchy between the divine couple Pārvatī and Śiva, that is, a different status is accorded to Pārvatī in comparison to Śiva primarily because of her gender. The panel also depicts the existence of hierarchy in the world of male divinities. This is obvious if one looks at the size of the gods' figures depicted on it. Size is literally used to express the hierarchical nature of the Śaiva Brahmanical pantheon, on whose basis the gods can be placed in descending order of divine status. Śiva comes first, next comes Himavat (in some cases Himavat is replaced by Viṣṇu), then Brahmā, and thereafter, beginning with Indra, other celestial beings can be slotted.[42] Here, it must be noted that the figure of Pārvatī is smaller than that of Śiva's alone. On one hand, it indicates that her status within the Śaiva pantheon is of more significance than that of Viṣṇu's or Brahmā's. On the other hand, this feature metaphorically suggests that for a husband (Śiva), his first priority is his wife (Pārvatī), and for a wife (Pārvatī), her husband (Śiva) is the ultimate authority to be concerned about.

**Image 11.2: The Kalyāṇasundaramūrti panel, Cave 1, Elephanta, c. mid-sixth century CE**

*Credit*: American Institute of Indian Studies

The panel in discussion hails from Ellora cave temple 29, which is dated approximately to the second half of the seventh century CE.[43] Similar representations of the Kalyāṇasundaramūrti can be found at Ellora cave temples 21 and 15 (dated approximately to the second half of the seventh century CE and early half of the eighth century CE),[44] and Cave I at Elephanta (Image 11.2) dated to the mid-sixth century CE.[45] However, the representations of Kalyāṇasundaramūrti in the structural temples of the Deccan during this period appear to have been provided a less prominent place. For example, in the Kasi-Visvesvara Temple at Pattadakal (dated to the last decades of the eighth century CE),[46] the scene of Pārvatī's marriage with Śiva in the presence of Brahmā and Viṣṇu is depicted on a small panel in the *padma-bandha* of the right hind pillar from the east of the *sabha-maṇḍapa*.[47] In the Mallikarjuna Temple as well, situated immediately to the south of the Kasi-Visvesvara Temple, the Kalyāṇasundaramūrti can be seen on the sculptural panel in the *padma-bandha* of the northern pillar of the *sabha-maṇḍapa*.[48]

This trend appears to have been followed in the structural temples built during the tenth and eleventh centuries CE in South India too. For instance, the marriage of Śiva with Pārvatī is carved on the four east-facing panels of the lower flight of the southern stairway leading to the vestibule at the Bṛhadīśvara Temple at Tanjavur. The figures of *gaṇas* on the three panels are depicted as turned toward the fourth panel, which depicts the marriage ceremony of Śiva and Pārvatī.

In the fourth panel Pārvatī is represented, as in most of the depictions of the Kalyāṇasundaramūrti, standing to the right of Śiva with her right hand placed in the right hand of Śiva, a seated Brahmā as the officiating priest and Viṣṇu and other celestial beings attending the ceremony.[49] The Kalyāṇasundaramūrti again finds space in stone on the lower left side of the outer face of the inner gateway of the Bṛhadīśvara Temple. However, in this representation Brahmā is absent.[50]

In contrast, the Kalyāṇasundaramūrti is elaborately represented on the structural temples of early medieval central India. However, the representations are not as elaborate as found in the cave temples of Ellora and Elephanta. For example, the image of Śiva's marriage with Pārvatī found 'in a small shrine situated on the northern side of the tank in Batesara valley, District Morena', dated approximately between 725 and 800 CE,[51] is not crowded by a host of celestial beings (see Image 11.3).

**Image 11.3: The Kalyāṇasundaramūrti panel, Batesar, Morena, c. 725–800 CE**

*Credit*: American Institute of Indian Studies

In the panel, apart from Pārvatī and Śiva, only six celestial beings are visible: Indra on his elephant mount is shown in the upper left corner; Sūrya, seated on a lotus, is visible in the upper middle section; a Vidyādhara figure is in the upper right corner; Brahmā, the officiating priest, is placed between the figures of Pārvatī and Śiva; on Śiva's left, perhaps, Viṣṇu is shown to stand holding a pitcher in his right hand; and similarly on Pārvatī's right, perhaps, it's Lakṣmī with a pitcher in her left hand.[52] The focus of the panel, yet again, is Pārvatī with Śiva in the act of *pāṇigrahaṇa*. Pārvatī is two-armed, with her left hand holding a mirror and right held by the four-armed Śiva, who stands on her left with a flower in the upper right hand, a trident in the upper left hand and the lower left hand resting on his waist. The figures are surrounded by lotus foliage.[53]

This kind of representation of the Kalyāṇasundaramūrti is followed with minor differences in the structural temples of the Chandella period at Khajuraho. The image of Śiva-Pārvatī's marriage can be seen in the northeastern niche in the *mahāmaṇḍapa* of the Kandariyā Mahādeva Temple[54] (Image 11.4) as well as in the northern vestibule niche of the Lakshmaṇa Temple.[55] At both the temples, dated approximately to the 10th/11th centuries CE,[56] in the Kalyāṇasundaramūrti are depicted a lion and Nandī below Pārvatī and Śiva respectively. This iconographic element is absent in the Kalyāṇasundaramūrti at Batesara. Another new element is the representation of 'four water jars (*maṅgala-ghaṭas*) placed one above the other on each side of the panel'.[57] Other than these, the Kalyāṇasundaramūrti composition contains similar features to the Batesara panel.

From this discussion, it seems that the difference in the placement of the Kalyāṇasundaramūrti in the structural temples of the Deccan, southern India and central India was region-specific. Another feature of more importance is the composition of the Kalyāṇasundaramūrti itself. Be it in the structural temples or in the cave temples, three figures appear to be central to the representation of this *mūrti*, that is, Pārvatī, Śiva and Brahmā. Much more significant are the ways in which these divine beings are portrayed consistently. Pārvatī is always with two arms. She is fragile and coy. Śiva, on the other hand, is four-armed and represented as physically larger than any other divine beings in the Kalyāṇasundaramūrti panels.

**Image 11.4: The Kalyāṇasundaramūrti panel (left), the Kandariyā Mahādeva temple, Khajuraho, c. 10th–11th centuries CE**

*Credit*: Sneha Ganguly

Finally, the persistent portrayal of Brahmā as the officiating priest also requires commenting. His presence, on one level, overtly suggests the *sastric* nature of this marriage, and on another level, conveys the importance this union has for the Brahmanical world. A marriage ceremony that has Brahmā, the grandfather of the Brahmanical pantheon[58] as the priest sanctifying it, marks the importance of the ceremony. Collectively, then, all the three figures portray in a very concise manner what the myths narrate on an extended scale.

After analysing the selected representations of the Kalyāṇasundaramūrti, it appears that it has threefold signification. First, through the representation of Pārvatī and Śiva in the act of getting married in the presence of Brahmā and other celestial beings, the preferred mode of marriage ceremony within the Brahmanical society is made apparent. Second, this kind of depiction is metaphorically indicative of the behavioural code of conduct expected from females and males in the context of Brahmanical modes of marriage. Third, this *mūrti* makes the place accorded to various divinities within the hierarchical order of the Brahmanical Śaiva pantheon evident. These three meanings were maintained in the representations of the Kalyāṇasundaramūrti throughout early medieval India.

## Endnotes

1 Claude Levi-Strauss, *The Elementary Structures of Kinship*, trans. James Harle Bell and John Richard von Sturmer, ed. Rodney Needham (London: Social Science Paperbacks in association with Eyre & Spottiswoode, 1970), 483.

2 Ibid.

3 Ibid., 489.

4 Patricia Uberoi, ed., *Family, Kinship and Marriage in India* (New Delhi: Oxford University Press, 2005), 237.

5 Ernest W. Burgess, Harvey J. Locke and Mary Margaret Thomes, *The Family: From Traditional to Companionship* (New York: Van Nostrand Reinhold Company, 1971), 5.

6 Uberoi, *Family*, 469.

7 Ibid., 470.

8 *The Śiva Purāṇa* Vol. II, Part II, trans. J.L. Shastri (New Delhi: Motilal Banarsidass, 1970), 707.

9 Frederick Engels, *The Origin of the Family, Private Property and the State: In the Light of the Researches of Lewis H. Morgan* (New York: International Publishers, 1981).

10 Engels, *The Origin*, 7.

11 Ibid.

12 Ibid., 13.

13 Ibid., 29.

14 Ibid., 125.

15 Ibid.

16 Ibid., 126–127.

17 Ibid., 126.

18 Ibid., 129.

19 *The Śiva Purāṇa* Vol. III, Part III, trans. J.L. Shastri (New Delhi: Motilal Banarsidass, 1970), 1075–1078.

20 Ellen Goldberg, *The Lord Who is Half Woman: Ardhanārīśvara in Indian and Feminist Perspective* (Albany: State University of New York Press, 2002), 116–117.

21 *The Śiva Purāṇa* Vol. I, Part I, trans. J.L. Shastri (New Delhi: Motilal Banarsidass, 1970), 407.

22 Ibid., 472.

23 *The Śiva Purāṇa* Vol. II, Part II, 512–516.

24 Ibid., 537–548.

25 Stephanie W. Jamison, *Sacrificed Wife/Sacrificer's Wife: Women, Ritual, and Hospitality in Ancient India* (New York: Oxford University Press, 1996), 211.

26 Y. Krishan, 'The Erotic Sculptures of India,' *Artibus Asiae* 34, no. 4 (1972): 339.

27 Sara L. Schastok, *The Śāmalājī Sculptures and 6th Century Art in Western India* (Netherlands: Brill Academic Publishers, 1985), 89.

28 Ibid., 89.

29 K.V. Soundara Rajan, *Cave Temples of the Deccan* (New Delhi: Archaeological Survey of India, 1981), 121.

30 Ibid., 121.

31 Quoted in Jamison, *Sacrificed Wife*, 211.

32 *The Śiva Purāṇa* Vol. II, Part II, p. 679.

33 T. A. Gopinatha Rao, *Elements of Hindu Iconography* Vol. Two,' Part I (Madras: Motilal Banarsidass, 1993), 341.

34 Jaya Tyagi, *Engendering the Early Household: Brahmanical Precepts in the Early Gṛhyasūtras, Middle of the First Millennium B.C.E.* (New Delhi: Orient Longman, 2008), 132.

35 Kumkum Roy, *The Power of Gender and the Gender of Power: Explorations in Early Indian History* (New Delhi: Oxford University Press, 2010), 228.

36 See Thomas R. Trautmann, *Dravidian Kinship* (New Delhi: Vistaar Publications, 1995), 273; Uma Chakravarti, *Gendering Caste: Through a Feminist Lens* (Calcutta: Stree, 2009), 54.

37 Thomas R. Trautmann, *Dravidian Kinship* (New Delhi: Vistaar Publications, 1995), 272.

38 Rajan, *Cave Temples*, 120.

39 Ibid.

40 Ibid.

41 Roy, *The Power of Gender*, 227.

42 Rajan, *Cave Temples*, 120–121.

43 P.R. Srinivasan, *Ellora*, World Heritage Series (New Delhi: ASI, 2007), 13.

44 Srinivasan, *Ellora*, 13.

45 M.K. Dhavalikar, *Elephanta*, World Heritage Series (New Delhi: ASI, 2007), 14.

46 A. Sundara, *Pattadakal*, World Heritage Series (New Delhi: ASI, 2008), 56.

47 Ibid., 58.

48 Ibid., 68.

49 Lalit M. Gujral, ed., *The Iconography of the Bṛhadīśvara Temple* (New Delhi: Aryan Books International, 2002), 17.

50 Ibid., 17, 28.

51 R.D. Trivedi, *Temples of the Pratihara Period in Central India* (New Delhi: ASI, 1990), 28.

52 Ibid., 28–29.

53 Ibid., 29.

54 Krishna Deva, *Temples of Khajuraho* (New Delhi: ASI, 1990), 183.

55 Devangana Desai, *The Religious Imagery of Khajuraho*, Project for Indian Cultural Studies Publication IV (Mumbai: Franco-Indian Research, 1996), 132.

56 Alexander Cunningham, *Four Reports Made During the Years 1862–65*, Vol. II (New Delhi: ASI, 2000), 420.

57 Deva, *Temples of Khajuraho*, 183–184.

58 *The Śiva Purāṇa* Vol. II, Part II, 864.

# 12

# Imagery of Love Making: Representation of the Erotic Body in the Temples of Early Medieval Odisha

Sujata Rakshit

*Śilpa* or art is an important marker of the world view of any culture. If we consider the art traditions in different parts of India as mirroring notions of femininity and masculinity prevalent in society, the sculptures in various regional contexts provide us with ample examples of such representations of gender. This essay focuses on the normative understanding of women and femininity as depicted in sculptures on the temple walls, particularly the representations that have been termed as *nāyikā*, *surasundarī* and/ or *alasākanyā* in prescriptive texts, such as the *Śilpa Prakāśa* (c. 10th century CE) and the *Śilparatnakośa* (c. 16th century CE). These representations find a prominent place on the temple walls in early medieval Odisha. The temples of Bhubaneswar, Puri and Konark belonging to the early medieval period came up at a time when various dynasties like Bhaumakaras, Somavaṁśīs and the Gaṅgas emerged as regional powers in Odisha. The dynastic inscriptions suggest that endowed lands and temples were scattered all over the semi-fertile and fertile zones of south-eastern, middle and northern parts of Odisha. The importance of the Mahanadi river in the growth of the agrarian economy can be seen through the growth of rural settlements in the riverine areas at the beginning of the early medieval period, which kept steadily increasing. The numerous temples that were constructed and the emergence of great pilgrimage centres of Bhubaneswar and Puri by the 11th century CE, that drew people from across the sub-regions of Odisha, were a product of the socio-economic transformations.

One of the means through which dynasties sought legitimacy was land grants to Brahmanical temples, with the *brāhmaṇas* as both the custodians and recipients of the grants. The development of art and architecture as seen through the numerous temples that were built at this time can be attributed to this process. The early medieval period saw the development of many regional cultures in the Indian subcontinent, particularly centred on the growth of temples and other religious institutions. The temple emerged as a result of the spread of the Puranic Brahmanical traditions, with a focus on the sectarian worship of Viṣṇu and Śiva, and at a later point of time Devī as well. But the temple was not merely a religious space; it also provided a visual canvas for the artistic and architectural traditions of particular regions to develop. While the broad architectural structure and themes for the visual presentation were drawn from the epic-Puranic mythology, local elements in the form of ornamentation and style developed. It is in this context that the numerous iconographic expressions of the female form in temples, mostly erotic in nature, may be considered as reflecting certain dominant notions about womanhood and femininity. Erotic sculptures in early medieval Indian temples introduced a visual spectacle. The possibility that such ideas emanated from Vedic rituals and folk customs has been suggested by some scholars.

Scholars have also highlighted the outstanding and grand architecture of the early medieval temples of Odisha, and the sculptures carved on them. These temples are known as the Kaliṅga type and considered part of the Nāgara architecture of North India. These sculptures reflect innovations in many details that attest to the development of artistic technique and style. What is especially distinctive is the profusion of erotic art on the external walls of the temple. The term erotic addresses a range of sexual expressions, from the gentle gestures of lovemaking to crude and extreme forms of sexual intercourse. Devangana Desai describes some elementary sexual motifs in the Indian sculptural context like the *mithuna* (amorous couple), the *maithuna* (copulating pair) and other erotic groups.[1] Besides the depiction of a heterosexual couple, there were also representations of a man or a woman with more than one partner, as well as alone, and also depictions of humans and animals in sexual congress. In the later period, the *mithuna* adorned temple gates and other places, possibly because of the influence of the Śākta cult. Tāntric influence cannot be denied as well, though it is generally accepted that Tāntric practices veered towards the esoteric. The temples of Paraśurāmeśvara (c. seventh–ninth century CE), Vaitāla, Liṅgarāja, Rājārānī and Mukteśvara (all dated to c. 9th–12th centuries CE) are remarkable for their indigenous character and exquisite sculptures. In these, the most significant common and decorative motifs are the female semi-divine figures, known as *nāyikās*. According to *Śākta* philosophy, femininity is considered the highest active principle of the universe.[2] Although some authors define such depictions as realism, others would argue that the role of the erotic symbols at Konark cannot simply be explained away by concluding that the temple was giving space to the non-religious, to allow us to think that the statuary was intended to be purely for aesthetic purposes.[3] There are still others like Ananda Coomaraswamy, the pioneering scholar on Indian art, who would see the imagery as marking the sublimation of the worldly desires of the devotee entering the temple, taking her to a higher spiritual and sublime plane.[4]

## Textual Description of *Mithuna*

The earliest art traditions primarily in Buddhist contexts depict two kinds of erotic images, the *yakṣī* and the *śālabhañjikās*, generally shown standing tall, and hanging on to the branch of a tree respectively. Coomaraswamy interprets the *yakṣī* figure as a non-religious celebration of fertility.[5] Similarly, the *śālabhañjikā* as the name itself denotes links the woman to the śāla tree, whose branch she is clinging to.[6] The voluptuous figure of the *śālabhañjikās* carved out on the *toraṇas* of Buddhist *stūpas* from the early centuries of the first millennium began to be depicted in different postures and spaces on the walls of early medieval temples, particularly in Odisha. According to the 10th century *Śilpa Prakāśa*, composed by Rāmacandra Mahāpātra Kaula Bhaṭṭāraka of the *Śākta Kaula sampradāya* (left-hand), the graceful female figures we find distributed on temple walls in Odisha are the *alasā kanyā*s (indolent or playful maidens in various poses decorating the exterior part of the temple), and in the plural sense, the whole sculptural panel containing the *nāyikā*s is called *alasā-bandha* or *nārībandha*.

Female sculptures were carved to portray liberation from material needs. To pay homage to femininity, the temple walls were carved with voluptuous sculptures within the *nārībandha* (panel of the maidens). The *Śilpa Prakāśa* says,

> *As a house without a wife, as playful enjoyment without a woman, so without (the figure of) women, art will be deficient and bear no fruit.*[7]

It has also been said that a temple is not only a house of the deity, it is also a spiritual powerhouse. The temple, through the depiction of *nāyikās*, is believed to have attracted the soul of the creator of the universe.[8] It is interesting that the text talks of art itself having a purpose, and it is in this context that the depiction of alluring and desirable women may be seen. The architects of early medieval Odishan temples followed the core directions and instructions of the *Śilpa Prakāśa* to decorate the temple walls with the *nāyikās*.[9] This *alasā kanyā* motif was possibly the most favoured as the text prescribed its portrayal on numerous places on the *vimāna* and *mukhaśālā*.[10]

Erotic sculptures in sacred architecture were not a new phenomenon. But in the evolved phase of temple architecture in the early medieval period across the Indian subcontinent, their appearance was more profuse and complex than in the earlier stages. Such profusion and intricacy can be seen in the erotic forms and postures of sculptures in the temples of Odisha. Erotic imagery serves the same auspicious function as other decorative motifs and may likewise be symbolic of what was either propitious or catastrophic or both.[11] Erotic imagery on the later temples must be perceived in the same manner as other portrayals of auspicious motifs, which beautify and protect the temple. According to the *Śilpa Prakāśa*, it is generally the magical power of sexual engagement that dominates these images, along with the underlying secret *yantras*.[12] In Tantrism, it is believed that passion cannot be suppressed, but one can get *mokṣa* by the satisfaction of earthly pleasures, coition being one of them. The *Śilpa Prakāśa* clearly explains the significance of erotic sculpture in the following verses:

> *Without Śiva and Śakti creation would be nothing but mere imagination. Without the action of Kāma there would be no birth or death.*

> *Śiva himself is visibly manifested as the mahāliṅga, and Śakti in the form of the Bhaga (womb). By their union the whole universe comes into being. This is called the action of love (kāma kriyā).*[13]

The decorative and symbolic motifs of earlier traditions of Indian art were being included in early medieval temple art, but with some new dimensions.[14] The ancient tree and woman motif, known earlier as *śālabhañjikā*, is introduced in the *Śilpa Prakāśa* as *gelaba nārī* (female figures intertwined with creepers and trees). More importantly, the erotic couples can be understood in early medieval times as constituting *mithuna* and *maithuna* motifs.[15] The intense pleasures from sexual union of all creatures of the universe cause happiness and salvation, according to the text.

In the *Śilpa Prakāśa*, couples can be comprehended as engaging in *mithuna* and *maithuna* acts. The text clearly explains the significance of erotic sculpture in the following verse:

> *Jagatastu mūlaṅ kāmah kāmād bhūtādi jāyante.*
> *Mūlabhūte tathā bhūtaṁ kāmena pravilīyate.*[16]
>
> Love is the root of the universe. From love, all beings are born. Primordial elements and all beings are reabsorbed again in love.[17]

In this analysis, sexual intercourse in the religion appears to have been considered as a part of life, and life was seen as neither separated nor possible without pleasure. It was intended for people to see the sexual imagery and associate it with the laws of nature, thus lending legitimacy to its worship. There were two primary blueprints or models – *yantras* – to be used in the temple, to facilitate the *kaula* ritual: the *yoginī yantra* and the *kāmakalā yantra.*[18] The actual meaning of these imageries on temple walls was believed to be hidden underneath the *kāmakalā yantra,* which is not revealed to those who are not initiated into the Tāntric tradition.[19] The idea behind these *yantras* was to depict through diagrams of intersecting triangles the presence of the goddess as both one and many, as well as her union with Śiva, who completed her multiform figure.[20]

To describe the eroticism in images, *Śilpa Prakāśa* introduces another description, which is called *Mithuna-bandha.*

*Śṛṇu mithunabandhāṅśca kena yantrādiniścayah.*
*Nānā mithunabandhā hi kāmaśāstrānusāreṇa.*
*Kevalaṅ kelih mukhyā hi na pāto na ca saṅgamah.*
*Kelih bahuvidhā śāstre kevalaṅ krīḍābhāvitā.*[21]

Here on what *yantra mithuna-bandha* is made. According to the *Kāma-Śāstras* there are different types of love-images.

Here only love-play is important; there should be no couples in lying postures, nor sexual union. There are many types of love-play in the *Śāstras*, which are mere frolic.[22]

So, while the text firmly recommends erotic sculpture to be displayed, it also specifies the type of imagery. It firmly disallows depiction of sexual intercourse or coital sex and suggests that the amorous couple instead be depicted.

For the most part, in early medieval Odishan temples, these images seem unrelated to any specific religious sects even though the temples are Śaivite in nature. At the beginning of the eighth century CE, erotic imagery was placed in the *bārāṇḍā* and was explicitly associated with Śiva, possibly relating to specific religious rituals. The main methodological problem with the Odishan temples is that it is difficult to determine the nature of the influence of the Pāśupata and Kāpālika sects due to the absence of inscriptional evidence. Despite some major differences in their doctrines and rituals, one can see the engagement of these two sects, which had been described collectively by medieval Sanskrit writers. That includes their unorthodox ascetic practices of sexual exhibition and ritual sex.[23] According to Donaldson, 'in some rituals, the idea of propitiation is absent, or minimised, and the worshipper is united with divinity through food, drink, sex, or mental ecstasy, communion rituals similar to Dionysian revels in ancient Greece and the belief in enthusiasm, the belief that a man through physical intoxication at first, later through spiritual ecstasy, could pass from the human to the divine'.[24] Although we have no *Kāpālika* texts, we can reconstruct their rituals from other Sanskrit texts, all of which state that they worship Bhairava and his consort (Cāmuṇḍā).

The central ritual of Tāntric communion is sexual intercourse. Woman and sexual union thus played a central role in Tāntric *sādhanā*. Basically, there are three scenes deviating from conventional lovemaking which, along with added figures, suggest the ritual nature of the activity — *yonī-abhiṣeka* (anointing the female genitalia), *puraṣcaraṇa* (preparatory rites) and *rajapāna* (drinking female discharge).[25] Semen and menstrual discharges are both offered as sacrifices in Tāntric rituals so the specific act here is relevant only with respect to identifying the particular text being illustrated. The ritual ceremony or *yonī-abhiṣeka* is another important motif in this context. A female sculpture is seen squatting with her legs apart, and a dwarf attendant is applying some substance (possibly *alaktaka*) to her vagina with a stick to prepare her for the ceremony. The role played by women of low caste and courtesans in Tāntric rituals is well known, and the more depraved and debauched the woman according to Brahmanical thinking, the more fit she is for the rite. This is also considered as a Tāntric motif. In all of the early scenes of fellatio, the kneeling female is depicted with rough features suggesting she is of low caste, possibly a *Ḍombi*, the favourite of Tāntric authors, and a fact that reinforces the ritual and casteist nature of the activity.[26] Part of this exaltation is a reaction against orthodox systems and the ideology of castes, while on a symbolic level, it is related to the Tāntric doctrine of the identity of opposites.

In the 10th century CE, with the Somavaṁśī rulers from the upper Mahanadi valley firmly entrenched in eastern Odisha, the Pāśupata and Kāpālika sects were gradually replaced in popularity by Śāktism and newly introduced religious sects, such as the Kaulācāras popular in central India. The popularity of erotic motifs can be seen in political articulations as well—Somavaṁśī Keśarī rulers glorify the pursuit of love and their domain is visualised as the pleasure garden of *Kāma*.[27] Whereas the earlier erotic friezes depicting Tāntric rituals appear to be an indigenous development, the pursuit of love extolled by the new rulers reflects the changing social and religious attitudes that were spreading throughout the Indian subcontinent at this time.[28] In the *Ananta Vāsudeva* temple, the *mithuna* motif is generally found in an *anurāha* niche of the upper *jāṅgha*, the other images in these recesses being *alasā kanyā*s and scenes from daily life.

## Early Medieval Temples of Odisha

Since the theme of this paper is erotic sculptures on the temple walls of early medieval Odisha, the data has been organised on the basis of where the temples are found.

The early medieval Odishan temples are divided into two groups: the early group of temples (seventh century CE to the ninth century CE) and the mature phase of temples (ninth century CE to the twelfth century CE). The geographical distribution of these groups is mostly across the eastern part of modern-day Odisha. The sculptures of the early and later phases of Kaliṅga architecture were similar in the temples built during the early medieval period. The main focus of the study is the temples of Puri, Konark and Bhubaneswar, and it is only in Bhubaneswar that the distinction of early and later phases is relevant. For instance, in the early group Paraśurāmeśvara, Rāmeśvara and Bharateśvara temples in Bhubaneswar, female sculptures are portrayed in a crude manner. The Vaitāla temple, built in the cusp of the later period, displays more gradual skilled sculptural representations. The Jagannātha Temple at Puri and Liṅgarāja Temple in Bhubaneswar belong roughly to the same time span and show a more evolved iconographic expertise. The Rājārānī and Mukteśvara Temples of Bhubaneswar, and the Konark Sun temple reveal that the sculptors had gained mastery in making complex and intricate sculptures. Slightly later than that period, the Ananta Vāsudeva temple of Bhubaneswar also proves the fine workmanship of sculptures in the early 13th century CE.

The main methodological problem in dividing these temples is that they cannot be categorised in terms of the early medieval historical geography. In the same time period, artists at the three specified sites of early medieval Odisha appear to have interchanged ideas related to sculpting a figure, using the *Śilpa* texts, particularly *Śilpa Prakāśa* and *Śilparatnakośa*, as their manuals.

## Early Phase (Seventh Century CE to Ninth Century CE)

In Odishan temples, the influence of the art and architecture of the post-Gupta period is seen in a large number of architectural and sculptural specimens found in Bhubaneswar and Puri. The temples of Bhubaneswar belonging to the early phase were constructed across the city at various points by the rulers of the Bhaumakara dynasty. The earliest temples of Odisha that can be dated to the seventh century CE are Śatrughneśvara, Bharateśvara and Lakṣmaṇeśvara situated in Bhubaneswar. These temples and their sculptures are mostly ravaged, hence we cannot use any material from here. But the Paraśurāmeśvara temple, constructed after the above-mentioned temples, has more refined and definitive sculptural details amongst this early group. Other temples we have studied here are Rāmeśvara, Bharateśvara, Śatrughneśvara, Vaitāla deūla and Swarnajāleśvara.

## Lakṣmaṇeśvara and Bharateśvara Temples

Amongst the early group of temples, Lakṣmaṇeśvara and Bharateśvara (sixth to seventh century CE) appear to be primitive in architectural patterns, design and sculptural presentations. In terms of iconography, *alasā kanyās*, *vinyasās*, dancers and erotic couples are seen on the *jāṅgha* and *śikhara*. Most of the sculptures were ravaged and the Archaeological Survey of India has renovated some.

## Paraśurāmeśvara Temple

This temple was built in the mid-eighth century CE. The elongated pillared hall of the main temple contains a plethora of sculptures. Female figures flank doorways and on the walls are exquisite examples of stone carvings. Musicians and dancers with flutes, cymbals and trumpets performing difficult twists of the body in the course of dance find representation. Amorous couples or *mithuna* scenes are vividly depicted on the *śikhara* of the temple. *Bandhana* or the space between two *jāṅgha* (upper and lower) is also full of *mithuna* and *maithuna* figures. There are also depictions of the *alasā kanyā* as prescribed by texts on the walls, doorways and lintels. On the back wall of the temple, an interesting sculpture is seen—a lady gently touching her own breast. Although there is no specific name for this *kanyā* in the text, it is clear from her depiction that she belongs to the generic category of *alasā kanyā*. Another sculpture on the side panel of the *Kārttikeya* niche on the same wall of the temple also shows such a *kanyā* holding a bunch of mangoes, while a dwarf figure is collecting them from her hand. In the *bāḍa* (wall portion) of the temple, the sculpture of mother and child (*mātṛmūrti*) depicts their various moods—mother lifting her child, mother breastfeeding her infant, the child in his/her mother's lap, etc. is portrayed on the panels. *Cāmarā* and other *nāyikā* figures are also present on the *śikhara* and *bandhana* of the temple. The placement of a *maithuna* couple engaged in sexual congress on the south flank of the major *vajra mastaka* design on the Paraśurāmeśvara temple can be seen. At the Paraśurāmeśvara temple, the *bāḍa* from the *gaṇḍi* (spire) demarcates the *bārāṇḍā* (recess), where the erotic sculptural panels are situated.[29] In the panel over the *bandhana*, as prescribed by the *Śilpa Śāstras*, amorous couples are seen making love to their beloveds in different poses (touching each other's chest, kissing, standing in a sensuous pose, etc.). A vertical column along the *śikhara* heading into the *bāḍa* with *mithuna* representations has been clearly projected, which also appears to conform to prescriptions. Beside the door jamb, two amorous couples can be seen standing proportionally with the *cāmarā*.

**Image 12.1: Mithuna, Rāmeśvara temple, Bhubaneswar, c. ninth century CE**

*Credit*: Author

### Rāmeśvara Temple

This ninth-century temple provides another example of sculptural masterpieces. There are sculptural panels showing both *mithuna* and *maithuna* on the upper and lower *jāṅgha* of the temple (see Image 12.1). Amorous figures are vividly shown depicting sexual intercourse that cover most of the carvings of the *śikhara*.

### Śatrughneśvara Temple

Both *mithuna* and *maithuna* are visible on the temple walls. Couples having private conversations have been sensuously portrayed. A lady seated on an *āsana*, with her legs apart and knees raised off the ground, is showing off her *yonī*. As mentioned earlier, it has been postulated that such depictions had a ritualistic or symbolic significance in Śaiva Tāntricism. The erotic motifs appear on the *pābhāga* (base mouldings), niche lintels and *gaṇḍi* of the temples. Other sculptures, such as a lady taking blessings from a bearded Śaiva *ācārya*, seem to validate this point.

## Later Phase (Ninth Century CE to Twelfth Century CE)

The ancient texts state that the *nāyika*s to be depicted in sculpture and literature are full of perfection and artistic in nature. The delicate beauty has been expressed in different ways to reveal intense feelings of love, emotion and tenderness. The most common female figures found in Odishan temples are in the context of sexual conjugations.

### Vaitāla Deūla

Śākta philosophy appears to have enveloped the temple. In the case of Vaitāla Deūl, the *bandhana* and niches of the temple wall are full of *mithuna* and *maithuna* figures. Both *mithuna* and *maithuna* motifs are found over the *jāṅgha* and *bandhana* of the temple. The *bandhana* between *bāḍa* and *śikhara* is horizontally carved with erotic figures—males and female engaged in erotic rituals, adolescent female figures and *alasā* images.

**Image 12.2:** ***Yonī-abhiṣeka*****, Rājārānī temple, Bhubaneswar, c. 11th century CE**

*Credit*: Author

## Rājārānī Temple

This eleventh-century temple in Bhubaneswar is a piece of sculptural marvel in early medieval Odishan temple architecture. The *garbhagṛha* of the temple is empty. The name Rājārānī has come from a particular type of local sandstone (Rajaraniya), which is believed to have been used in the construction of the temple.[30] *Mithuna* figures are also very prominent in this temple. A man holding his beloved affectionately, a bearded man provoking a *nāyikā*, a man removing the garment of a *nāyikā*, etc. are the noticeable sculptural forms. Extreme sexual acts, such as masturbation and fellatio, are also graphically depicted on the temple wall. The sculpture of *yonī-abhiṣeka* mentioned in the Tāntric context is an important motif of this temple (see Image 12.2). In the *pābhāga* of the temple, there are small erotic motifs depicted as well.

## Kedāreśvara and Gaurī Temples

These early medieval temples in Bhubaneswar consist of some magnificent sculptures of *nāyikās* belonging to the later phase of Odishan art, having the typical iconographical features. In Kedāreśvara temple, the treatments of *maithuna* sculptures are very vivid. Ithyphallic carvings of males are distinguishable among the female semi-divine sculptures. Scenes with highly ornamented amorous couples are also carved out splendidly. Gaurī temple, which is on the same premises, also provides a range of carvings of beautiful *nāyikās*. A woman touching her breast, *nāyikā* clasping her garment, etc. are portrayed on the *bāḍa* of the temple in an exquisite manner.

## Brahmeśvara Temple

The Somavaṁśī queen Kolāvatī Devī erected the Brahmeśvara temple in Bhubaneswar in 1060 CE.[31] Along with the *śikhara*, the *bāḍa* (temple wall including lower and upper *jāṅgha*) is replete with sculptures of amorous couples engaged in various sexual acts. A range of coitus practices has been depicted in this temple. Śākta-influenced motifs (Śaiva *ācārya* engaged in intercourse and other sexual congresses) too are prominent on the temple wall. Sculptures of lovemaking, including *mithuna* and *maithuna*, are very delicately carved in this early medieval Odishan temple.

## Liṅgarāja Temple

This late twelfth-century temple in Bhubaneswar is a typical specimen of Kaliṅga architecture. It is divided into four main architectural parts—*deūl* (sanctum), *jagamohana*, *nāṭamaṇḍapa* and *bhogamaṇḍapa*. In the temples described earlier, we have seen various attractive poses, gestures and moods of *nāyikas*. Most female figures are extremely charming and well proportioned. Such graceful and provocative figures have also been carved out by the sculptors of the Liṅgarāja temple. The decoration of the *jāṅgha* is fully intended to pay homage to female sculptures.[32] On the *śikhara* and *jāṅgha*, erotic motifs are prominently shown.

## Ananta Vāsudeva Temple

This late twelfth-century temple of Bhubaneswar provides an example of prolific sculptures amongst the early medieval Odishan specimens. Established by the Gaṅga princess Candrikā Devī, this temple situated on the banks of an artificial lake built by her, Bindusarobara, is a remarkable piece of art. Like the Liṅgarāja temple, Ananta Vāsudeva also has four distinct architectural parts in its ground plan. Exquisite *mithuna* and *maithuna* figures are found in the niches of *bāḍa*, *anurāha* and on the upper *jāṅgha*. The varied iconographic mastery seen in the sculptures is exceptional. The figures of the semi-divine females are more slender than in the previous temples of Bhubaneswar.

## The Sun Temple of Konark

This temple was constructed after the Liṅgarāja temple, but in no way inferior with regard to the merit of sculptural representation. The Sun temple is, in fact, considered as a majestic and supreme example of Kaliṅga art and architecture. It was erected to commemorate the victory of Narasiṁhadeva I (1238–1264 CE) over parts of Bengal.[33] Female figures and erotic couples are the most celebrated features of the Konark Sun temple. The usage of heavy ornaments and fine garments in the sculptures is clearly visible. The erotic group of sculptures dominates the upper and lower *jāṅgha* of the *jagamohana*.

**Image 12.3: *Liṅga Pūjā*, Konark Sun temple, Puri, c. 13th century CE**

*Credit*: Author

Amongst the *maithuna* figures, the male symbolises virile potency, be it an ascetic or a royal figure. In several cases at Konark, the male holds his *liṅga* while straddling a fire altar, again suggesting the sacrifice of semen. Here, the *yonī* can symbolise fire, and the woman herself is the altar. The motif can be understood as the female allowing the *liṅga* to penetrate, suggesting communion as well as sacrifice. There are numerous other themes suggesting Tāntric influence, including the motif of a priest engaged in sexual congress with several females. The earliest illustrations of erotic rituals generally appeared in the *bandhana* of the temple. These images are usually associated with *liṅga pūjā*, drinking or eating from a *kāpāla*, which illustrate the doctrine combining aspects of Pāśupata and Kāpālika *sādhanā* through the temple sculptures of early medieval Odisha (see Image 12.3).

In Konark, *mithuna* and *maithuna* figures can be seen in different ways and postures. The deliberate depiction of these fanciful *maithuna* figures cannot be judged without their artistic value. *Nāyikā*s have been sculpted into the spokes of the *cakra* (wheel) of the *ratha* (chariot), showing their engagement in daily lives.[34] However, most of them are depicted in the context of coital acts, like stimulating each other's sexual interests, having intercourse in different positions, etc. The portrayal of *rajapāna* is clearly visible from the sculptures in the *bāḍa* of the temple where a man is passing his tongue over the stretched genital of a *nāyikā* (see Image 12.4). A couple has been portrayed touching each other's genitals by their tongue.

**Image 12.4: *Rajapāna*, Konark Sun temple, Puri, c. 13th century CE**

*Credit*: Author

Amongst the *mithuna* figures, men snatching the garment from a *nāyikā*, hugging each other delicately, etc. are seen on the walls of the *jagamohana*. Again, unlike depictions of the *Śilpa Prakāśa* and *Śilpa Ratnakośa*, some *maithuna* or extreme sexual motifs are seen on the present temple's walls. Scenes of coitus in a group have frequently been identified in the Konark Sun temple. One of the sculptures portrays two *nāyikās* engaged in a sexual act with a man. In another, a *nāyikā* is holding the erect phallus of a male partner.

In a niche on the lower *jāṅgha* of the west wall of the temple, yet another extreme coital scene has been depicted. A man is penetrating his genital into the genital of a *nāyikā*, while she bends down and touches her tongue to another man's sexual organ. It has been noticed previously that a *nāyikā* herself is touching her breast with her hand (*svastana-sparśā*). Different from this, a *mithuna* motif has been identified on the *bāḍa* where a male partner is touching the right breast of a *nāyikā* to stimulate sexual urge.

Erotic imageries more varied and explicit than in the *Śilpa Śāstras* are found in the present temple. In some of the *maithuna* sculptures, it can be observed that male figures are carrying their beards. One can assume that these types of erotic motifs are directly related to Tantrism, which defines the existence of the Śaiva *ācārya* or the *gurus* of the particular sect. The *bāḍa* of this temple is mostly covered with carvings of sexual congresses. The borders of the projected niches on the *jāṅgha* are full of erotic motifs, in which couples are seen enjoying sexual pleasures. On the north wall of the *jagamohana* another striking sculpture has been found—a man is holding the hair of a *kanyā* and penetrating her from behind.

At the *nāṭamaṇḍapa* of the temple, several *maithuna* figures like on the *jagamohana* are noticed. The fact that frequently emerges after this study is that the sculptors engaged to engrave such motifs had average knowledge of the *Śāstras*. They were only sculpting the erotic figures according to their own imagination. Here, the sculptor's mind departs from the interpretation of the text that reflects the artistic agency of the sculptors.

**Image 12.5: *Maithuna*, Konark Sun temple, Puri, c. 13th century CE**

*Credit*: Author

## Jagannātha Temple

The imperial Gaṅga ruler Anantavarman Coḍagaṅga enlarged the monument and established the Viṣṇu cult in what until then was primarily a Śaivite region. The vicinity of Puri marked an important politico-religious and economic zone for the Kaliṅga state after Bhubaneswar. The temple of Puri is an early medieval structure of the Kaliṅga style of architecture. It was established by the Somavaṁśīs, but it is under the Gaṅgas that the cult of *Jagannātha* flourished and the deity became the main presiding deity of the political region of early medieval Odisha.

The main *śrīdeūl*, *jagamohana*, *nāṭamaṇḍapa* (dance hall) and *bhogamaṇḍapa* (hall of offerings) lie geometrically on the axis of the temple. The sculptures on the temple walls are similar to the ones in Bhubaneswar and Konark in the portrayal and style of carving. Erotic and semi-divine couples are shown on the upper and lower *jāṅgha* of the temple walls of the *śrīdeūl* and *jagamohana*. In the context of erotic figures, the doorjambs inside the shrine are fully carved with these miniature motifs. At the entrance of the main *garbhagṛha,* a small panel has been sculpted with miniature erotic figures in different postures, surrounded by floral motifs. The *maithuna* have been portrayed profusely on the lower and upper *jāṅgha* of the temple. On the upper *jāṅgha* of the *jagamohana,* again the sculpture of a *nāyikā* touching her breast is noticeable. The image of *rajapāna* is on the same sculptural panel.

The Liṅgarāja temple in Bhubaneswar and the Konark Sun temple, along with the Jagannātha temple in Puri reflect common sculptural traditions. Early medieval Odishan art was mostly influenced by the Tāntric sect, which motivated sculptural depictions across these three regions.

## Iconographic Interpretations

This particular portion deals with the iconographic features of female sculptures depicted on the temple walls of Bhubaneswar, Konark and Puri. These sculptural panels are divided into two phases—the early phase (seventh century CE to the ninth century CE), and later phase (ninth century CE to the twelfth century CE).

The sculptural canvas in Bhubaneswar provides us with the best example of Kaliṅga or Odishan art. The exteriors of temples, including the platforms, walls and towers, are the vistas where the sculptural tradition of Odisha can be identified. The devotees look at the temple first when they come near the building, and then, particularly during the ritual of walking around or circumambulation, they come in close proximity to the images and comprehend the meaning and symbolism of those sculptures. The temple now comes alive with the images.[35]

According to Stella Kramrisch, 'the coherence of its monumental shape is enriched by its carvings; nowhere else in India are the walls of the temple as intimately connected with their sculptures. The temple here is a work of monumental sculpture of which the single carvings form the intricate surface.'[36] The external surfaces of the Odisha temples have been, in large numbers, decorated and ornamented, in contrast to their interiors, which are mainly plain. The *Śilpa* texts do not mention any reason for this. But the interior of the *deūla* or sanctum is conceived as the *garbha* or womb of the cosmic being.[37] According to the primary concept of the womb, the walls have been left plain.[38] The plainness of the walls also emphasises the quiet and solemn atmosphere, which is required for the performance of the rituals of the deity.[39]

The interiors of the early medieval temples have been decorated with sculptures and ornamented with various vegetation and floral motifs.[40] But this practice could not become popular and therefore did not continue. The interiors of both the *mukhaśālā* and *vimāna* have been kept plain as far as possible.[41] A perfect agreement between architecture and sculpture has been achieved in the Odisha temples.[42] After the early period of unsure efforts, the Odisha craftsmen succeeded in achieving an orderly arrangement of the sculptural motifs and cult icons on the body of the temple.[43] They also succeeded in assuring the balance between magnificence and attractiveness, contributing to the monumentality and elegance of the temple.[44]

It has been already pointed out that the sculptural art of Odisha had travelled a long way from the time the Śatrughneśvara group of temples, the earliest extant temples, were erected. The temple sculptures followed the tradition established by the earlier sculptors.[45] The sculptures on the early group of existing temples appear to be the work of what C.L. Fabri observes as 'provincial artists'.[46]

Another important development in the early medieval period was the textual authentication of iconographic norms from the early period. Artists were forced to follow strict doctrines to carve god and goddess images. This helped to focus light on the basic iconographical expression of the sculptures.[47] Early medieval architecture and sculptures not only follow the strict version of sculpting but imbue canonical application to authenticate the texts through the representations. The images of women depicted on the temple walls were thus refashioned and appeared more mechanical than earlier ones.[48]

The sculptures in the temples of the early phase in Odisha are not so exquisitely treated. Their development and evolution have been understood as part of religious organisations of the time. They were mostly sculpted on the lower portions of the temple. Here, Vidya Dehejia states, 'Proportions are poor, images stocky and figures generally in rigid postures. The human body has an uncomfortable appearance with arms and legs seeming to be separate entities, flat and flabby, and attached to the body in an inorganic fashion without any depiction of underlying bone or muscular structure.'[49] The toes too look crude, which is not the case in sculptures of the later period. Likewise, the figures in sitting postures are disturbingly located.[50] Noticeably, the appearance and condition of sub-shrine deities are better than the rest of the figures. Dehejia states that these could have been done by the 'more advanced craftsmen' of the region.[51]

After the early constructions, the later phase temples show more prolific work in the context of carvings. A.N. Parida suggests that the images have been scooped out in deeper reliefs.[52] For this reason, the figures of *kanyās* have more sensuous and delicate manners.[53] This group of temples offers more exquisite and intellectually developed figures than the early temples group. Facial expressions and eyes are more prominent and gracious, the figures are more slender and charming. Along with the semi-divine and divine figures, the images of the *kanyās* are perfect. Talking about the images of this period, Debala Mitra said, 'The dignified self-composed figures of the deities with the expression of absorption are mellowed with warmth of spiritual grace and are elegant and refined.'[54] The treatment of organs and parts of the body on temple walls is also precise.[55]

In the context of the *maithuna* and *mithuna* sculptures of the early medieval temples of Odisha, the later phase is significant with regard to the profusion of such images.[56] According to K.C. Panigrahi, the sculptures of the later phase contain similar features of the Buddhist style depicted in Cuttack district (Ratnagiri).[57] Some later phase temples like Mukteśvara, Rājārānī, Liṅgarāja, Ananta Vāsudeva and the Sun temple are seen with huge ornamentation and decorations with elaborately carved female figures. The arrangement and proliferation of the sculptures reflect the perfection of artistic technique and regional style. These figures are carved in a profuse manner, which points at the skill and mastery of the artists.[58] Panigrahi noticed that the *kanyā* or *nāyikā* figures are the most exquisite and profuse, along with the divine figures, in the temples of early medieval Odisha.[59] The profusion and sculptural detailing is directly associated with the technique. The theoretical knowledge of beauty and aesthetics is also blended with the mechanism of the making of the sculptures.[60] Hence, one can state that from the earliest form of the images, which are less elaborate and profuse, to the most matured and refined stage, where the temple walls become abundantly decorated, we see the development of the Kaliṅga style of art and architecture.[61]

In the Liṅgarāja, Mukteśvara, Rājārānī and Brahmeśvara temples, the erotic motifs are separately carved in different niches. At Bhubaneswar group of temples, the Konark Sun temple and Puri's Jagannātha temple, the sculptures are placed hierarchically. According to K.S. Behera, the illustrations of the *Śilpa Prakāśa* can hardly be regarded as products of artistic merit.[62] Though the architectural description of the temple complex, in general, is correct, the illustrations of the architectural elements do not throw a clear light on the details that are now missing. In the lower and upper *jāṅgha* of the temple *bāḍa* (outer wall), the *nārībandha* not only shows the features of a woman, but this area is chiefly dominated by *mithuna* (erotic couples) in various poses. It could be said that the life of a human being has been portrayed within the chariot wheel (*cakra* of the *ratha*) of the Konark Sun temple. It could be that they wanted to depict the cycle of life metaphorically.

In the Bhubaneswar group of temples, the *nārībandha* is the prime space where the female semi-divine sculptures could be depicted. On the outer wall of the temple, the lower and upper *jāṅgha* are fully carved with female sculptures. According to the *Śilpa Prakāśa*, the *alasā yantra* should demonstrate the plan to situate a sculpture of a *nāyikā*.[63] This takes us back to our earlier observation that the voluptuous figure of the woman was as symbolic as the *mithuna* and the *maithuna* figures on the temple walls.

## Conclusion

This paper reveals the significance attached to women in the socio-religious context, as seen from the innumerable iconographic representations on temple walls. While the delicacy and beauty of the feminine form were at the centre of the sculptor's creation, it must be kept in mind that women here were being given space to evoke notions of fertility. Tantrism-influenced acts of copulation between male and female was seen as the simulation of the coming together of *Śiva* and *Śakti*, who, in turn, represented *Puruṣa* and *Prakṛti*. The Śakta tradition with its emphasis on the feminine principle also became dominant during this time and could have influenced the conspicuous feminine representations on the temple walls. The different images of the couples conform to ideas expounded in the prescriptive texts, while at the same time revealing the artist's flights of imagination. But more than anything else, it is in the evocation of beauty and aesthetics that the sculptures stand out. It has been pointed out in this paper that the pursuit of beauty and love were seen as important in early medieval society, and particularly the aspect of lovemaking was of socio-religious significance. The portrayal of men and women in the early medieval temples of Odisha reflected this ideology, which is also visible in the literary descriptions of the period.

## Endnotes

1 Devangana Desai, *Erotic Sculptures of India* (New Delhi: Tata McGraw-Hill Publishing, 1975), 7.

2 K.S. Behera, *The Liṅgarāja Temple of Bhubaneswar Art and Cultural Legacy* (New Delhi: Indira Gandhi National Centre For The Arts, 2008), 27–28.

3 Max-Pol Fouchet and Brian Rhys, *The Erotic Sculpture of India* (London: Lausanne Print, 1959), 145.

4 Desai, *Erotic Sculptures.*

5 Cited in M.L. Varadpande, *Woman in Indian Sculpture* (New Delhi: Abhinav Publications, 2006), 31.

6 Varadpande, *Woman in Indian Sculpture,* 11; U.N. Roy, *Salabhanjika in Art, Philosophy and Literature* (Allahabad: Lok Bharati Publications, 1979), 26.

7 Alice Boner, trans., *Śilpa Prakāśa,* First *Prakāśa,* 392–393; Sadasiva Rath Sharma (New Delhi: IGNCA and Motilal Banarsidass, 2005), 149.

8 *Śilpa Prakāśa,* First *Prakāśa,* 392–393, 149.

9 Vidya Dehejia, *Early Stone Temples of Orissa* (New Delhi: Vikas Publishing House, 1979), 69.

10 *Śilpa Prakāśa,* First *Prakāśa,* xiii.

11 T.E. Donaldson, 'Erotic Rituals on Orissan Temples,' *East and West* 36, no. 1/3 (September 1986): 75–100.

12 *Śilpa Prakāśa,* Second *Prakāśa,* 502–503, 307.

13 Ibid., 499–501, 305–307.

14 Ibid., xii.

15 Ibid. For a discussion on different kinds of erotic sculpture, see Devangana Desai, *Erotic Sculptures of India* (New Delhi: Tata McGraw-Hill, 1975).

16 *Śilpa Prakāśa,* Second *Prakāśa,* 499–500, 305–307.
17 Ibid., 306–307.
18 David Gordon White, *Kiss of the Yoginī: 'Tantric Sex' in its South Asian Contexts* (Chicago: University of Chicago Press, 2003), 94–95.
19 Donaldson, 'Erotic Rituals,' 307.
20 White, *Kiss of the Yoginī,* 95.
21 *Śilpa Prakāśa,* First *Prakāśa,* 548–550, 186.
22 Ibid., 186–187.
23 Donaldson, 'Erotic Rituals', 137–138.
24 Ibid., 144.
25 Ibid., 169.
26 Ibid., 137–138.
27 Ibid.
28 Ibid., 186–187.
29 Ibid.
30 Found on the entrance plaque of ASI in front of the Rājārānī Temple.
31 P. Acharya, 'Brahmeśvara Temple Inscription,' *JASB* 13 (1947): 70.
32 T.E. Donaldson, *Hindu Temple Art of Orissa,* Vol. 1 (Leiden: E.J Brill, 1985), 101.
33 E.I. Vol. XXIX, 16–17.
34 The Sun Temple of Konark is imagined as the *Ratha* of *Sūrya* (sun god), which is drawn by horses. The *ratha* has wheels, in which the cycle of life, daily lives and numerous postures of the *nāyikās* have been carved out.
35 Stella Kramrisch, 'Wall and Image in Indian Art', *Proceedings of the American Philosophical Society* 102, no. 1 (February 17, 1958): 7–13.
36 Stella Kramrisch, *The Hindu Temple,* Vol. I (Calcutta: University of Calcutta, 1946), 216–217.
37 Dehejia, *Early Stone Temples,* 31.
38 A.N. Parida, *Early Temples of Orissa: From the Sixth Century A.D. To The End of Somavamsi Rule* (New Delhi: Commonwealth Publisher, 1999), 41. The interior walls of the Vaitāla Temple have been carved with images of Saptamātṛkās, Vīrabhadra, Gaṇeśa and Bhairava. These images are not intended to fulfil a visual purpose. In Odishan temples, there is no concept of wall decorations. These figures are carved to be worshipped along with *Cāmuṇḍā,* the presiding deity of the temple.
39 Parida, *Early Temples,* 41.
40 Ibid. The ceilings of the Mukteśvara and Brahmeśvara temples are carved with inverted and fully blossomed lotuses. Except the temples of my study area, the existing *mukhaśālā* of the Kosaleśvara Temple has been carved exquisitely.

41 Parida, *Early Temples*, 41.
42 Ibid., 42–43.
43 Ibid., 43–45.
44 Ibid.
45 C.L. Fabri, *History of the Art of Orissa* (Bombay: Orient Longman, 1974), 31.
46 Ibid.
47 Parida, *Early Temples.*
48 Ibid.
49 Dehejia, *Early Stone Temples*, 62.
50 Ibid.
51 Ibid.
52 Parida, *Early Temples*, 45.
53 Ibid.
54 Debala Mitra, *Bhubaneswar* (New Delhi: ASI Publication, 1958), 24.
55 Ibid.
56 Parida, *Early Temples,* 45–48.
57 K.C. Panigrahi, *Archaeological Remains at Bhubaneswar* (Delhi: Orient Longman, 1961), 33–36.
58 Ibid.
59 Ibid.
60 Ibid.
61 Ibid.
62 K.S. Behera, 'Palm-Leaf Manuscript on the Architecture of Koṇārk Temple,' *Annals of the Bhandarkar Oriental Research Institute* 57, no. 1/4 (1976).
63 *Śilpa Prakāśa,* First *Prakāśa*, 151.

13

# Of Men, Stones and Stories: Revisiting the *Vīrakals* of South India

Malavika Binny

An analysis of South Indian *vīrakals* reveals several interesting facts about its contemporaneous society, the high emphasis on heroism being one among them. That chivalry (or *vīrya*) was understood to be one of the most important qualities to be possessed upon which a code of honour was built and almost religiously followed comes as no surprise taking into concern that some historians have referred to the state of the early historic period in South India as belonging to a heroic society with heroic chiefs ruling the polity.[1] While there have been several studies on memorial stones across India, a comprehensive survey of hero stones is yet to be undertaken.

Hero stones, as it is used in academic parlance today, has also become an umbrella term for most memorial stones, which have the depiction of a centrally positioned male figure and certain sepulchral or funerary connotations attached to them. Of course, the male figure may have female figures or figures of animals or deities on their sides (Image 13.1). Several types of memorial stones, such as *niṣidis*, *kīrti-stambhas*, *pāliyas*, *khatris*, *māsti* stones/sculptures, *chāyāstambhas*, and, in some cases, even megalithic monuments are often clubbed under the title hero stones. While all of them share certain features, such as the use of stone as the medium, association with death and commemoration, and elements of sacrality and worship, their purposes and cultural contexts vary dimensionally. While the *niṣidis* have been traced to Jain origins as monuments that memorialised the act of *sallekhanā* or *samādhi-maraṇa* of Jain monks, the *chāyāstambhas* of Andhra Pradesh depicts the life history of the person commemorated by them. This essay will focus on the particular genre of memorial stones called *vīrakals* or *vīragals* found across the South Indian states of Tamil Nadu, Kerala and Karnataka. These memorial stones, with their intimate connection to chivalry, continued to be produced in South India from the first century CE to as late as the fourteenth century CE. The earliest record of memorial stone is found in the *Caṅkam* literature of the first century CE and have been described by more than 25 poets.[2]

**Image 13.1: *Vīrakal*, Karnataka, 14th–15th century CE**

*Credit*: Project Saveeragallu by K.S. Lathasree

Studies on memorial stones in general and hero stones in particular have been numerous especially by scholars from South India. For instance, S. Settar and M.M. Kalaburgi have attempted to draw out connections between *vīrakals* and *vīrakāvyas* through a study of hero cults in Karnataka.[3] A.N. Upadhye has attempted to understand the role of *niṣidis* as memorial stones, concluding that these were post-mortem burials located where the person breathed his or her last, where religious rites were performed, or where bone relics were interned, and makes a clear distinction between *niṣidis* and hero stones. He also traces the origins of the hero stones to Jain *niṣidis*.[4] G.R. Kuppuswamy[5] provides a detailed analysis of the practice of providing land grants by local rulers in South India for the installation and maintenance of hero stones. Stuart H. Blackburn has compared the ideals of the Puranic hero to the local hero using Tamil folk ballads and hero stones with a strong reference to caste and class connotations.[6]

N. Vanamalai claims that 'the chronological range and qualitative differences in the iconographic and palaeographic representations open up a rare opportunity to make investigations and postulate hypotheses about the beliefs of the people who erected and worshipped the stones',[7] and uses data provided by hero stones to analyse the notion of heaven in folk beliefs and *bhakti*. D.R. Patil traces the evolution of North Indian memorial stones from rock edicts to monolithic pillars.[8] The historian argues that the installation of memorial pillars or hero stones had its origins in the Buddhist practice of relic worship, 'which, in turn, was derived from the funeral practices of the easterners or the *asuras* of the Vedic texts'[9] for northern, north-eastern and western India. Patil is however unsure whether the hero stones of South India owe its origins to the same practice. In a recent study on megaliths and graffiti, Y. Subbarayalu claims that the 'the tradition of raising hero stones in memory of dead warrior-heroes may also be an extension of the menhir tradition, as the earliest-inscribed hero stones are found to be shaped like menhirs tapering upwards....'[10]

But other historians and archaeologists like K.V. Soundara Rajan argue that there is little or no connection between the megaliths of South India and hero stones either in symbolism or cultural features. Using epigraphical evidence from other memorial stones and hero stones and through an extremely nuanced analysis of the scripts used in them, Soundara Rajan puts forward a chronological and geographical classification of hero stones and clearly proves they are different from the megaliths.[11] K. Rajan, in a detailed survey of memorial stones including hero stones, has attempted to trace the links between territorial divisions and memorial stones.[12] There have also been studies on hero stones and land grants[13] and also on the artists who engraved and inscribed the monuments, among several other studies on the same.[14]

*Vīrakal* or *vīragal* as they are known in different parts of South India are post-mortem memorials mostly commemorative in character and erected in memory of 'heroes'; a large number of *vīrakals* also have inscriptions on them and are associated with land grants to the community or family the hero belonged to. These monuments can range from a height of two to eight feet, some even up to 12 feet, and have single or multiple panels engraved upon them. In the single-panelled *vīrakal*, the hero is represented with his weapon, and his wife or wives and children may also be depicted alongside him (Image 13.1). A common theme that runs through multipanelled monuments is the event/s of the death of the hero, followed by his funeral and entry into the afterlife (Image 13.2). Both single and multipanelled *vīrakals* have the representation of the sun and moon on them, which could indicate both immortality and a grant in perpetuity. The association between *vīrakals* and other kinds of memorial stones and land grants have been worked out well by historians and there is considerable consensus on the practice of rulers providing grants for the upkeep and maintenance of the monuments. It may also be argued that the depiction of the sun and moon not only represents the notion of the hero's memory living on forever but also of the provision or land grant given in lieu of his sacrifice in perpetuity being iconographically represented on hero stones.

**Image 13.2: Multi-panelled *Vīrakal*, Bedkani. Uttara Kanada, undated**

*Credit*: Saurabh Saxena

There are several references to hero stones or *nāṭukals* in *Caṅkam* literature, especially in the *Akanāṉūru* and *Puṟanāṉūru*, which associate the monuments to the deaths of warriors in battles and cattle raids. *Puṟanāṉūru*, for instance, refers to a hero in a hero stone who looks at the plight of his patron's palace after his death and laments its fall into bad times. The hero stone is mentioned as installed far from the palace, decorated with *karantai* flowers,[15] which usually represent victory in war in early Tamil literature. *Puṟanāṉūru* also has references to memorial stones being erected for kings (*Puṟam* 221), of poets praying to hero stones (*Puṟam* 222),[16] hero stones being adorned with peacock feathers and offered toddy and rice (*Puṟam* 232, 260, 264), being inscribed with names of the fallen heroes (*Puṟam* 264), and worshipped (*Puṟam* 263, 329, 335). Certain verses also describe hero stones as being the only gods worthy of being worshipped (*Puṟam* 335).

*Akanāṉūru* refers to rows of hero stones in forests and along forest paths (*Akam* 67, 131, 387, 365), worshipped by villagers (*Akam* 289), offered *karantai* and *atiral* flowers, smeared with turmeric paste[17] (*Akam* 269, 289) and adorned with peacock feathers (*Akam* 131). *Kuṟal* and *Tolkāppiyam* also have references to hero stones; the latter, in its *Poruḷatikāram* section, describes the installation of hero stones as part of the funerary customs of warriors who die in battle or while defending the village from cattle-raiders. Along with the beating of drums and *piḷḷaiyāṭṭu* (a kind of dance), the fallen warrior is sent to the afterlife and commemorated by erecting a memorial stone.[18] The *Kuṟal* also has a fascinating verse in which a warrior boasts that he has turned all his foes into stones![19]

It can be argued from the evidence from *Caṅkam* literature that the institution of hero stones was fairly well established in the early historic period, and was one of the most popular rituals associated with the death of warriors. A special case can be made here for the warriors who were involved in cattle raids, as most of the verses in *Akanāṉūru* and *Puṟanāṉūru* on memorial stones dedicated to warriors allude to cattle raids of one kind or the other;[20] but one should not assume that the monuments were erected only in the event of cattle raids, especially in the later periods. Several hero stones have inscriptions mentioning heroes dying in battles, boundary disputes and while saving villagers from marauders and bandits. One of the defining features of a *vīrakal* in the early historic period, which distinguishes it from a *niṣidi* or a *chāyāstambha* is the element of aggression or physical violence associated with the monument. It may also be mentioned that *vīrakals* very rarely commemorate self-immolation or self-sacrifice in the devotion of any particular deity, unlike the *pāliyas* from peninsular and northern India. In fact, several verses from early Tamil historic literature indicate that the heroes in the stones were sometimes worshipped as the only gods by certain communities. *Puṟam* 335 says:

> *There are no flowers other than these four;*
> *Kuṛavam, taḷavam, kuruntam and mullai,*
> *There is no food other than these four;*
> *Vaṛaku with black stems, large-eared tiṇai,*
> *Small vined kōl, and spotted avaṛai* beans,
> *And there are no groups (kuṭis) other than (of) these four;*
> *Tuṭi* drummers, *pāṇars, paṟai* drummers and *katampans.*
>
> *There are no gods, other than the-*
> *Memorial stones of heroes who blocked enemies,*
> *(and) killed their elephants with/(who had) bright lifted tusks*
> *And were killed, to be worshiped with rice (or paddy) showerings!*[21]

K. Rajan argues that the memorial stones from Tamil Nadu mostly belong to the Pallava period that is from the fourth century CE to the ninth century CE. But the Pallavas did not use *vaṭṭeḻuttu* for their monuments, hence memorial stones were erected and used by certain ethnic groups.[22] His argument about later hero stones seems to extend to the earlier ones as well, as even in *Caṅkam* literature, commemoration through hero stones does not seem to be the only form of funerary arrangement and appears to have been practised only by certain communities who considered these monuments to be deities. There are several verses across *Caṅkam* literature on various other deities, such as Indra, Śiva, Vel and so on, depending on the *tiṇai* and the period. So, one may safely assume that there were communities for whom the hero stones were the only deities, while other communities followed other deities and had other forms of burial practices. N. Vanamamalai argues that it is with the practice of cremation that hero stones came to be located in the villages to which the heroes belonged.[23] *Maṇimēkalai* (fifth century CE), the famous Buddhist epic, in chapter six (66–67), refers to various kinds of burials, namely cremation (*cuṭuvōr*), post-excarnation burial (*iṭuvōr*), burying the deceased in a pit (*toṭukuḻip paṭuvōr*), rock chamber or cist burial (*tāḻvāyiṉ aṭaippōr*), and urn burial capped with lid (*tāḻiyiṟ kavippōr*).[24] It is clear that a number of burial practices were employed by the early historic people in South India and a majority of them continued post-*Caṅkam* period as well. It may also be argued that the practices might not have belonged to any one community and may have been shared by a number of groups, such as the ones in the stated verses (*tuṭi*-drummers, *pāṇars*, *paṟai* drummers and *katampans*). A differentiation between elite and common memorial stones, which some historians refer to,[25] might not hold good in light of textual evidence, although archaeological evidence records both elaborate and crude hero stones; this might have more to do with internal variation among communities than division within.

A pertinent question about *vīrakals* is whether these are sepulchral or commemorative in character as part of funerary arrangements. There is no archaeological evidence of any burial deposits having been found under or in the vicinity of *vīrakals* (though some of these monuments have been found near megalithic complexes), and there is also very little textual evidence suggesting any connection between direct burial or interment and hero stones, although they may be referred to as funerary monuments. *Tolkāppiyam*, regarded to be the oldest available treatise on Tamil grammar,[26] has a detailed description in its *Poruḷatikāram* section on the funerary practice of erecting a memorial stone. It elaborates five stages, which include *kāṭci* (the selection of an appropriate stone to serve as the memorial stone), *nīrpaṭai* (the cleaning and washing of the stone), *naṭukal* (the installation of the stone), *kālkōl* (the inscription of the stone with the hero's achievements and giving flowers and offerings) and *perumpaṭai* (extolling the stone, and maybe deifying it in the process).[27] One may assume that at best, the monuments were part of funerary rituals and without direct sepulchral association.

One of the most interesting aspects of *vīrakals* is their location. Almost all *vīrakals* found in Kerala were recovered from dense forests along the north-eastern boundary of the state, from places, such as Wayanad,

Pulppali, Sasimala and Attapady (Image 13.3).[28] A large number of *vīrakals* from Karnataka have also been found in forests. In the case of Tamil Nadu, numerous *vīrakal* clusters have been found outside villages or along the boundaries of villages and forests. The practice of installing *vīrakals* in clusters, which continues till date in Tamil Nadu and Karnataka, can also be traced back to early historic customs, as several verses from *Puṟanāṉūru* refer to these memorial stones being found in groups along forest paths. While a case can be made for hero stone worship being a custom of forest-dwelling groups, there are several references to hero stones of heroes who died protecting travellers from forest bandits and marauders.[29] There are also references to heroes who were in the service of patrons from fertile rice-growing areas, who later became commemorated trough *vīrakals* for their acts of bravery.

**Image 13.3: *Vīrakal*, Citalayam, Wayanad, 9th century CE**

*Credit*: Author

There have been attempts by historians to classify the monuments into 'greater or lesser religious traditions, involving gods in temples and immortal warriors (become godly) in the hero stones' or into 'metropolitan and tribal'.[30] It is also opined that hero stones are 'clearly an original and indigenous form, and is decidedly later than the main sepulchral megalithic tradition of Tamil Nadu, which is comprehensively involved throughout the entire state in its modes and cultural vestiges'.[31] It is certainly apt to point out that *vīrakals* are not as frequent and does not have the reach of megaliths and are more or less clustered in certain districts of Tamil Nadu, Karnataka and Kerala, but though they might have emerged from the same cultural complex as that of megaliths, unlike the megaliths, hero stones continued to be produced till the early modern period albeit greatly diminished in number. It is also to be noted that their provenance and indigeneity within the early South Indian cultural milieu have been fairly established. Back to the question of the location of the hero stones, the maximum references to hero stones in *Caṅkam* are in the context of the forests—the largest number of hero stones from Kerala and Karnataka have been found in forests. In the case of Tamil Nadu, 'it is seen that the provenance of the hero stones themselves is concentrated mainly on the border areas, full of hills, forests, narrow valleys and rivers, in the western part of North Arcot, the northern part of Salem and the present Dharmapuri District, and the northern part of Coimbatore District. No hero stone as such is found on the mainland of Tondainadu, the lower Kaveri valley of the Vaigai and Tamaraparani valleys.'[32]

Since early times, forests have been buffer zones between states, contiguous with or serving as versatile boundaries and marked by forest paths. These paths have several mentions in early Tamil literature, both in *Caṅkam* and post-*Caṅkam* literature. *Cilapattikāram* refers to the protagonists Kōvalan and Kaṇṇaki crossing the forest on their way from Pukār in the Cōḻa territory to Madurai in the Pandya territory. Similarly, *Akananūru*, *Puṟanānūru* and *Paripāṭal* have several references to forest paths and travel through the forest paths. R. Parthasarthy has argued that the forest served as the 'other' of society during the time of *Cilapattikāram*.[33] In this context, Soundara Rajan's observes that the worship of hero stones in the forest served as a different form of worship than the worship of other gods, such as Indra in temples, and that hero stones 'are one among the lesser vehicles current along with the greater religious tradition of Tamil Nadu in the *Caṅkam* period'.[34] M.S. Mate, on the other hand, argues that *vīrakals*, 'both in their plastic form and essential iconography are results of the classic as distinct from folk traditions'. The historian also opines that artistically and iconographically, hero stones form part of the classical Hindu tradition rather than folk tradition.[35]

Whether the forest served as the 'other' of the city and the village is beyond the scope of this essay, but the question as to whether hero stones served as an alternate form of worship by those who lived in the forests can be answered using textual evidence from the *Eṭṭutokai*. *Puṟanānūru* refers to kings being commemorated with hero stones (or having become hero stones) and has several references to villagers worshipping hero stones.[36] There are also references of hero stones falling into neglect in some verses; for instance, a salt seller's carts bruising hero stones along forest paths.[37] Similarly, there is mention of warriors sharpening their swords on memorial stones and names inscribed on the stones being forgotten by people,[38] but it must also be remembered that the practice continued in southwest India well into the medieval period. In light of internal evidence, it can be argued that the binaries of classical and folk or metropolitan and tribal may not be apt to describe *vīrakals*, as the monuments might be markers of exchange between the forest and the village. While people in the hill tract may have associated themselves with the worship of hero stones, it is clear that people from fertile tracts—not just the *Maṟavars* or the forest tribes—worshipped hero stones though they might not have belonged to the same religious complex. One may also be prompted to suggest that the monuments may have been a shared practice between both traditions, and the versatility of the medium is made clear by the presence of a large number of *vīrakals*, which have Jaina, Śaivite and Vaiṣṇavite images on the top panel, sharing the same or similar iconography on the bottom panels, including fighting/battle scenes, funeral pyres and female attendants in multi-panelled *vīrakals* (Image 13.2). Almost all of them also have images of the sun and moon on the top panel or on their back.

On the location of *vīrakals* in forests or along the boundaries of villages, there might have been ritualistic aspects regarding the installation of hero stones in the forest or along forest paths. There are several references of travellers and poets praying to hero stones, which point to them having served as wayside shrines, safeguarding transit through the forests. Surveys of hero stones have revealed the idea of heroes in the hero stones serving as guardian spirits of either the village or the villagers crossing the forest. Several historians have also pointed out the close connection between hero stones and land grants. As mentioned earlier, G.R. Kuppuswamy has also pointed out the practice of the provision of land-grants for the installation and maintenance of hero stones by local rulers, especially in South India. Land was also granted to meet the cost of the consecration, preservation and maintenance of the rites of the memorial to the hero's dependants as a reward.[39] Land grants given to villages to which the heroes belonged or where the hero stones are located have also been inscribed on the monuments.[40] One may even conjecture that hero stones served as boundary markers especially in the later periods owing to their positions on the boundaries of the village, and similarity to boundary stones of later periods. Medieval boundary stones in Kerala bear the same marks of sun and the moon, symbolising the use of the boundary in perpetuity, along with the royal symbol of the dynasty concerned.

Early *vīrakals* offer us a portal to understanding how early historic society perceived the dialectics of life and death and wove them into a process of monumentalisation, extolling the most desirable characteristic. In this case, it is of *vīra*—a self-sacrificial version of chivalry through it—with monuments in question being at varying degrees of divinity based on the social groups involved. When we move towards the early medieval period, the practice of installing *vīrakals* continued as a cultural institution and was observed by multiple ruling groups,[41] though several features change moderately both in style and meaning. One of the marked changes is in terms of stylisation; most early medieval to medieval *vīrakals* have three or four panels engraved into them, though single-panelled *vīrakals* continued to be produced up to the seventeenth century. While the early *vīrakals* would mostly depict the hero (or exceptionally the heroine) and his spouse, a weapon of choice and the sun and moon, the later ones were more elaborately carved with multiple panels, showing scenes that depicted the death of the hero, funeral pyre, the hero being welcomed or accompanied into the afterlife by *apsarās* holding fly-whisks or *kalaśas*, the hero seated alongside a deity, most commonly a Śiva *liṅga* (there may also be representations of Kṛṣṇa and *tīrthankarās*). The sun and moon remained, though elements of Vaiṣṇava, Śaiva and Jaina iconography found their way into the *vīrakals*. Several were added with a *kīrtimukha* or *jayamukha* along with a miniature *toraṇa*-like carving at the top. Historians have shown that most *vīrakals* from Karnataka depict 'the *toraṇa* with a *kīrtimukha*, apart from features like faceted pillars, etc., which are common to other regions as well'.[42] The deities in many Pallava *vīrakals* also have depictions of temple-like structures on the panels housing them. Curiously, very few *vīrakals* depict priests and the top panel usually only depicts the deity. There may be two possibilities in this context: one being the appropriation or the acculturation of the heroic cult into the larger Āgamic fold at a later time, and second being the practice becoming part of the cultural milieu and shared across religious traditions from a very early period, and communities continuing observing them albeit with modifications in stylistic aspects.

It is of interest that the human figures depicted on the hero stones do not register much changes in terms of attire and adornment, though the weapons clearly show the changes. *Vīrakals* with heroes holding rifle (?) guns, roughly attributed to the early 17th century CE, have been recovered from Attapady and Wayanad.[43] Similarly, some hero stones recovered from Goa and housed in the Goa State Museum represent ships and boats with rudders. The change registered on hero stones representing changes in technology (mostly military weaponry) is a point to ponder over and will in turn help in understanding the evolution of military technology in South India.

K.K.N. Kurup argues that the practice of erecting and worshipping hero stones disappeared gradually in the medieval period and was supplanted by the practice of *Theyyam*, a performing art, which also commemorates fallen heroes in battle.[44] While several aspects of the rituals associated with the installation of hero stones are similar to the performance of *Theyyam*, such as the presence of dance and music and location under shady trees, the difference in medium is conspicuous. Similarly, one can point out that other forms of dance and music that have non-Sanskritic elements are also part of other temple-based art forms, such as *Muḍiyēttu* and *Kaḷameḻuttu*, which have little to do with commemoration or worship of warriors who died in battles or cattle raids. Kurup also attributes the dwindling of hero stones in the late medieval period to the acculturation of folk cults into the Āgamic tradition, probably through the channel of *bhakti*.

Several hero stones belonging to the late medieval period and early modern period have been recovered in the past couple of years from northern Kerala and north-western parts of Tamil Nadu, which clearly demonstrates that the making of hero stones continued well beyond the medieval period. Two hero stones, now in the Thrissur Sakthan Thampuran Museum, depict warriors holding guns in attacking postures, indicating that they belong to a period later than the fifteenth and sixteenth centuries. While both *Theyyam* and *vīrakal* might have risen from the same cultural complex, one practice replacing another does not seem to have taken place. Erecting a stone as part of rituals in a grove or *kāvu*-based worship traditions especially *nāgakallu* or snake stones, which demonstrates alternate shrine-based worship other than the Āgamic forms, was prevalent among the castes that practised performing arts, such as *Theyyam*. This was also the case in Kerala. Though the stones bear slight resemblance to hero stones (granite stones are the medium for both), these votive stones, which are also worshipped, are not hero stones nor funerary or commemorative in character.

On the question of the iconographical details of hero stones registering only minor changes over long periods of time, it might be owing to a convention by artists or the makers of hero stones. There is much epigraphical evidence of artists who have inscribed their names along with names of their clans and villages on hero stones. It has been noted by historians and art historians that artists involved in the production of *vīrakals* did not usually travel from kingdom to kingdom or even from village to village.[45] Settar and F.A. Ganihar, however, provide evidence of certain exceptions where artists have moved to other areas for carving memorial stones, and there were instances where artists from far-off villages were commissioned to make hero stones.[46] In this context, the similarity amongst hero stones across regions is striking, especially as they are found across four South Indian states, not having fallen within the purview of the classical tradition and not subscribed to classical rules. It can be argued that installation of *vīrakals* may have become a social convention by the early medieval period. Both inscribed and non-inscribed *vīrakals* continued to be produced well into this period though certain meanings attached to the practice may have changed.

**Image 13.4a: *Vīrakal* showing musicians, Karnataka, 14th–15th century CE**

*Credit:* Project Saveeragallu by K.S. Lathasree

**Image 13.4b: *Vīrakal* showing a flutist with puckered lips, Karnataka, 14th–15th century CE**

*Credit:* Project Saveeragallu by K.S. Lathasree

**Image 13.5: *Vīrakal*, Near Whitefield, Bangalore, Karnataka, 13th–14th century CE**

*Credit:* Author

While in the *Caṅkam* period hero stones may have served as funerary and commemorative monuments, especially in favour of heroes who died during cattle raids, this purpose and attribution may have changed over the course of time. Hero stones came to be produced for those who may not have died in battle and for any hero who might have been important for the community as well; in sum, the practice was perhaps formulaic in the post-*Caṅkam* period. The installation of hero stones might have become associated with any kind of commemoration of those who had died. The images carved also registered changes, featuring depictions of performing artists, such as drummers, dancers and other musicians, and of men in different postures (Images 13.4a, 13.4b). Though these are also called *vīrakal*, the images do not bear any element of bravery. R.C. Agrawala, in an iconographical study of Govardhana pillars in Rajasthan, provides evidence of most memorial monuments having the image of Kṛṣṇa as Govardhanadhāra initially, but not having the particular image later albeit retaining the nomenclature Govardhana pillars.[47] It might be a similar case with *vīrakals*, which retained the name, though some of them, especially from Tamil Nadu and Karnataka, exhibited very prominent changes in imagery though similarity in style. In this context, it could be said that not all wives portrayed on hero stones committed *sati*, especially when there is no epigraphical evidence of *sati* involved; they might have simply suited an artistic pattern or convention to represent the wife as well. On modern ancestor memorials, for example, of the Dhangars in Maharashtra, the wife is also shown though she was possibly alive.[48] The representation of children along with the wife on *vīrakals* also suggests this was more a stylistic element rather than the representation of *sahagamana* or *sati* (Image 13.5). So, on one hand, the practice of installing hero stones may have been a social convention to commemorate ancestors or whoever was considered prominent in due course of time; on the other hand, in other areas, the images on the stones underwent change from aggressive postures to other representations, but retained the nomenclature *vīrakal.*

## Endnotes

1 Rajan Gurukkal, *Social Formations of Early South India* (New Delhi: Oxford University Press, 2012). Also, Rajan Gurukkal and M.R. Raghava Warrier, eds., *Cultural History of Kerala*, Vol. 1 (Kerala: Department of Cultural Publications, Government of Kerala, 1999).

2 K. Rajan, 'Territorial Division as Gleaned from Memorial Stones', *East and West* 51, no. 3/4 (December 2001): 359.

3 S. Settar and M.M. Kalaburgi, 'The Hero Cult: A Study of Kannada Literature from 9th to 13th Century,' in *Memorial Stones: A Study of Their Origin, Significance and Variety*, eds. S. Settar and Gunther D. Sontheimer (Dharwad: Institute of Indian Art History, Karnatak University; Germany: South Asia Institute, University of Heidelberg, 1982).

4 A.N. Upadhye, 'Nishidi—Its Meaning,' in *Memorial Stones: A Study of Their Origin, Significance and Variety*, eds. S. Settar and Gunther D. Sontheimer (Dharwad: Institute of Indian Art History, Karnatak University; Germany: South Asia Institute, University of Heidelberg, 1982): 45–46.

5 G.R. Kuppuswamy, 'Economic Factors Governing The Memorial Stones in Karnataka,' in *Memorial Stones: A Study of Their Origin, Significance and Variety*, eds. S. Settar and Gunther D. Sontheimer (Dharwad: Institute of Indian Art History, Karnatak University; Germany: South Asia Institute, University of Heidelberg, 1982): 307–312.

6 Stuart H. Blackburn, 'The Folk Hero and Class Interests in Tamil Heroic Ballads,' *Asian Folklore Studies* 37, no. 1 (1978): 131–149.

7 N. Vanamamalai, 'Herostone Worship in Ancient South India,' *Social Scientist* 3, no. 10 (May 1975): 40.

8 D.R. Patil, 'The Origin of Memorial Stones,' in *Memorial Stones: A Study of Their Origin, Significance and Variety*, eds. S. Settar and Gunther D. Sontheimer (Dharwad: Institute of Indian Art History, Karnatak University; Germany: South Asia Institute, University of Heidelberg, 1982): 47–58.

9 Ibid., 58.

10 Y. Subbarayalu, 'Megalithic Burials and Graffiti,' in *A Concise History of South India: Issues and Interpretations*, ed. Noboru Karashima (New Delhi: Oxford University Press, 2014).

11 K.V. Soundara Rajan, 'Origin and Spread of Memorial Stones in Tamil Nadu,' in *Memorial Stones: A Study of Their Origin, Significance and Variety*, eds. S. Settar and Gunther D. Sontheimer (Dharwad: Institute of Indian Art History, Karnatak University; Germany: South Asia Institute, University of Heidelberg, 1982): 59–76.

12 Rajan, 'Territorial Division,' 359–367.

13 Kuppuswamy, 'Economic Factors,' 307–312.

14 S. Settar and G.K. Vettickal, 'Artists of Memorial Stones in Karnataka: From Early Cālukya to the Kadamba Times (6th–10th Cent. AD),' 313–318; S. Settar and H.B. Sunkad, 'Vijayanagara; Artists of Memorial Stones,' 339–346; S. Settar and F.A. Ganihar, 'Artists of Memorial Stones: Cālukya-Hoysala,' in *Memorial Stones: A Study of Their Origin, Significance and Variety*, eds. S. Settar and Gunther D. Sontheimer (Dharwad: Institute of Indian Art History, Karnatak University; Germany: South Asia Institute, University of Heidelberg, 1982), 319–338.

15 *Puṟam* 261.

16 In *Puṟam* 222, the poet Pothiyār speaks to the memorial stone of King Kōperunchōlan according to Vaidehi Herbert. 'Sangam Poems Translated by Vaidehi,' last accessed 6 January 2019, https://sangamtranslationsbyvaidehi.com/ettuthokai-purananuru-201-400/.

17 The practice of smearing turmeric on hero stones continues in practice till date in Karnataka and Tamil Nadu. See Image 13.5.

18 *Tolkāppiyam, Puṟattiṇai* 33.

19 *Kuraḷ*, 771.

20 *Puṟam*, 260, 263.

21 *Caṅkam* poems translated by Vaidehi with modifications by the author of this essay.

22 Rajan, 'Territorial Division,' 363.

23 Vanamamalai, 'Herostone Worship,' 41.

24 E. Iniyan, 'Burial and Funerary Culture of Ancient Tamils (During 1000 BCE–250/300 CE),' *International Journal of Social Science and Humanity* 5, no. 12 (December 2015): 1069.

25 Vanamamalai refers to two kinds of hero stones—of the elites, such as the kings and chiefs, and those that belonged to common soldiers. See Vanamamalai, 'Herostone Worship,' 40–46.

26 Kamil Zvelebil dates the early sections of the *Tolkāppiyam* to the first or second century CE. See Kamil Zvelebil, *The Smile of Murugan: On Tamil Literature of South India* (Leiden: Brill, 1973).

27 For detailed reference to the process, see Subrahmanya Sastri's english commentary on *Tolkāppiyam* (Chennai: The Kuppuswami Sastri Research Institute, 2002): 42–43.

28 Some of the best-preserved *vīrakals* are housed in the Ambalavyal Museum in Wayanad. *Vīrakals* are also stored in museums across Kerala and Tamil Nadu.

29 *Akam*, 269.

30 Soundara Rajan, 'Origin and Spread of Memorial Stones,' 59–76.

31 Ibid., 72.

32 Ibid., 75.

33 R. Parthasarathy, 'Introduction,' in *Cilappatikaram: The Tale of An Anklet*, Iḷaṅkōvaṭikaḷ (India: Penguin Books, 2004), 15.

34 Soundara Rajan, 'Origin and Spread of Memorial Stones,' 74.

35 M.S. Mate, 'Hero Stones: The Folk and the Classic,' 79–82.

36 *Puṟam*, 221, 222, 263, 329, 335.

37 *Akam*, 343.

38 *Akam*, 297.

39 Kuppuswamy, 'Economic Factors,' 307.

40 G.S. Dikshit, 'Boundary Disputes and Hero Stones in Karnataka,' in *Memorial Stones: A Study of Their Origin, Significance and Variety*, eds. S. Settar and Gunther D. Sontheimer (Dharwad: Institute of Indian Art History, Karnatak University; Germany: South Asia Institute, University of Heidelberg, 1982); Kuppuswamy, 'Economic Factors'.

41 There are references to Cēra, Cōḻa and Pāṇṭiya rulers as well as Pallava, Kadamba, Gaṅga and Cālukya rulers in the inscriptions on hero stones.

42 Mate, 'Hero Stones,' 81.

43 The *vīrakals* that show the hero holding a gun are located in the Archaeological Museum of Thrissur in Kerala.

44 K.K.N. Kurup, 'Memorial Tablets in Kerala,' in *Memorial Stones: A Study of Their Origin, Significance and Variety*, eds. S. Settar and Gunther D. Sontheimer (Dharwad: Institute of Indian Art History, Karnatak University; Germany: South Asia Institute, University of Heidelberg, 1982): 243–254.

45 Settar and Ganihar, 'Artists of Memorial Stones,' 324.

46 Ibid., 319–338.

47 R.C. Agarwala, 'Govaradhana Pillars from Rajasthan: An Iconographic Study,' in *Memorial Stones: A Study of Their Origin, Significance and Variety*, eds. S. Settar and Gunther D. Sontheimer (Dharwad: Institute of Indian Art History, Karnatak University; Germany: South Asia Institute, University of Heidelberg, 1982): 151–155.

48 Gunther D. Sontheimer, 'Hero and Sati-Stone of Maharashtra,' in *Memorial Stones: A Study of Their Origin, Significance and Variety*, eds. S. Settar and Gunther D. Sontheimer (Dharwad: Institute of Indian Art History, Karnatak University; Germany: South Asia Institute, University of Heidelberg, 1982): 280.

# V

# Prescriptions and Representations

# 14

# The *Gaṇa* Who Consumed Himself: *Kīrtimukha* in North Indian Literature and Art, 400 CE–900 CE

Anisha Saxena

> 'When Rāhu spoke thus, a terrific being resonate like the thunder came out from the space between the eyebrows of the trident-bearing deity. He had a leonine mouth, with a moving tongue; his eyes shed fiery flames; his hair stood at its end; his body was dry and tough. He appeared to be the man-lion incarnation of Viṣṇu...'
>
> —*Yuddhakāṇḍa, Śiva Purāṇa*[1]

*Kīrtimukha* or *grāsamukha* is one of the most indispensable elements of North Indian art. A floating bodiless, jawless lion face with bulging eyes, ferocious teeth and fangs, horns, a full moustache and a tuft of hair rising from space between its eyebrows appears on Buddhist, Brahmanical and Jaina sacred structures alike. The earliest appearance of *kīrtimukha* as an architectural decorative motif can be dated to the early fifth century CE in North India under the Gupta artistic patronage. By the early medieval period, it had acquired a special, almost celebrated status and occupied *maṇḍovara* (temple walls), *vedibandha* (basal wall mouldings), *dvāra-śākhā* (door-jambs), *jālaka* or *vātāyana* (windows), *stambha* (columns), *toraṇa* (gateways), *śikhara* (spires), *mukuṭa* (crowns), *kaṭibandha* or *mekhalā* (belts), *mālā* (necklaces) and *aṁśumālā* or *paridhi* (aureoles) all over the Indian subcontinent and beyond.

Indian art, its motifs and symbols are not merely aesthetic designs; they are deeply rooted in religious philosophy and have layered meanings and associations.[2] *Kīrtimukha* is one such decorative motif and its origin can be traced to the Puranic texts. The *Yuddhakāṇḍa* of *Śiva Purāṇa* and the *Viṣṇukāṇḍa* of *Skanda Purāṇa* narrate the legend of a demon named Grāsa (devourer), who was born out of Śiva's glabella to swallow or devour the planet Rāhu. According to the legend, when Rāhu saw the ferocious being, he begged Śiva for mercy, and the great lord forgave him. Now, devoid of his purpose and meal, Grāsa told Śiva that hunger torments him and as he can no longer eat his intended meal (Rāhu), what should he consume? Śiva in good humor suggested that if hunger torments him, he should consume his own body. Being an upright follower of Śiva, Grāsa consumed his own body and limbs and was only left with his jawless face. Śiva, extremely pleased at this act of Grāsa, called him a great *gaṇa* (Śiva's goblin), provided him with the honour of being his doorkeeper and gave him a new name—*kīrtimukha* or the 'face of glory'. In architecture, *kīrtimukha* literally becomes Śiva's doorkeeper when the demon's face is carved on temple plinths, door-jambs, threshold and columns.

This essay takes on a detailed literary and art historical survey of *kīrtimukha* from the fifth to the tenth century CE, mapping its transformation from a fictional literary character into an architectural motif. Divided into two sections, the first part of the paper focuses on studying the literary accounts; both Puranic and architectural treatises are analysed in detail, discussing the legend of the origin of *kīrtimukha* and its treatment as a decorative architectural motif in various North Indian architectural texts. The second section undertakes an art historical investigation into the form, style and representation of *kīrtimukha* in architecture, sculpture and painting.

## *Kīrtimukha* in Literature

The story of the creation of *kīrtimukha* appears in the *Yuddhakāṇḍa* of *Rudra Saṁhitā* of the *Śiva Purāṇa* and the *Kārttikamāsa* of *Vaiṣṇavakāṇḍa* of *Skanda Purāṇa*. The *Purāṇas*, meaning old or ancient, refer to an assembly of extensive literature composed in Sanskrit and includes 18 *Mahā Purāṇas*, 18 *Upa Purāṇas* and a vast number of regional or local *Purāṇas*, *Sthala Purāṇas* as well as Jaina *Purāṇas*. Each *Purāṇa* comprises a number of chapters and sub-chapters known as *kāṇḍas*. The *Padma Purāṇa* classified the *Purāṇas* into three categories—*sāttvika*, *tāmasa* and *rājasa*.[3] Both the *Śiva Purāṇa* and the *Skanda Purāṇa* are considered *Mahā Purāṇas* and belong to the *tāmasa* category. The *Yuddhakāṇḍa* of *Śiva Purāṇa* is dated to the 14th century CE and the *Viṣṇukāṇḍa* of *Skanda Purāṇa* is dated between the eighth and the fourteenth century CE. The *Purāṇas* often borrowed chapters, stories and verses from each other and other Sanskrit literature.[4] Portions of the *Yuddhakāṇḍa* of *Śiva Purāṇa* are believed to have derived from sections of *Jñāna Saṁhitā*, *Padma Purāṇa*, *Brahmāvaivarta Purāṇa* and *Dharma Saṁhitā*.[5] The Skanda *Purāṇa*, in fact, is not considered a single text, but a collection of portions from other *Purāṇas*, and it's possible that the legend of *kīrtimukha* that appears in the *Skanda Purāṇa* was picked from *Śiva Purāṇa* or vice versa.

The *kīrtimukha* legend is closely associated with the legend of demon king Jalandhara and planet Rāhu.[6] According to the legend, a mighty demon called Jalandhara, who was born out of the confluence of Śiva's fiery rays that emerged from his third eye and the ocean, had become extremely powerful, and the gods became weary of his increasing powers. The demon was blessed by Brahmā that he could only be killed by his creator, Śiva and hence the gods hatched a plan where sage Nārada was sent to Jalandhara. After applauding his great power and prestige, Nārada told Jalandhara that a mighty demon like him deserves a beautiful wife and Śiva's wife Pārvatī is the most beautiful woman. Jalandhara, smitten by Nārada's description of Pārvatī's grace and beauty, sent Rāhu as an emissary to Śiva, asking him to surrender Pārvatī. When Rāhu told Śiva about Jalandhara's proposal, Śiva was filled with immense rage and a terrible being (demon) was born out of the space between his eyebrows. He had hard skin and with his tongue protruding, he ran towards Rāhu to kill (eat) him. On seeing the creature, Rāhu was terrified and ran, but the demon caught hold of him. Rāhu begged Śiva for his mercy, and Śiva told the being:

> 'Leave off this Brahmin Rāhu, the emissary who has sought refuge.
>
> O excellent Gaṇa, those who seek shelter shall be protected, not punished'...
>
> After leaving off Rāhu, the Gaṇa came near Śiva and pleaded to the great lord in piteous words...

> "O lord, I am tormented by hunger, so I am utterly emaciated, O lord of the gods, what shall be eaten by me? Please command me lord."
>
> ...On hearing these words of the being, the great lord of wonderful sports, eager to help his own persons, replied...
>
> "If you are badly in need of food, if hunger torments you, eat up immediately the flesh of your own hands and feet."
>
> On being commanded thus by Śiva, the being ate up the flesh from his limbs. He was then left only with his head.
>
> On seeing that being of terrible activities, left only with his head, the delighted Sadāśiva spoke smilingly...
>
> "O great Gaṇa, you are blessed since you carried out my behest, to the very letter. O excellent one, I am pleased with this action of yours.
>
> You shall hereafter be known by the title Kīrtimukha. You shall be my doorkeeper. You shall be one of my great Gaṇas, very heroic and terrible to all wicked persons.
>
> You are my favorite. In the course of my worship, you too shall be worshipped always by my devotees. Those you cannot worship you, cannot be pleasing to me."[7]

While the *Śiva Purāṇa* provides an excellent graphic description of the creation of *kīrtimukha* and his metamorphosis into a jawless, bodiless creature, the architectural text *Mānasāra* furnishes detailed instructions for architects and sculptors about how *kīrtimukha* should be carved as a decorative motif.

The *Mānasāra*, an architectural and sculptural text dated between the eighth and the twelfth centuries CE, states that the face of a *kīrtimukha* should be made smiling and should have two eyes and two ears. The eyes should be carved as they appear looking at all sides; they should be terrible and dazzling with fury and from the root of the space between the eyes should emerge a tuft of hair (*śikhā-mūla*).[8] The ears should be like those of a boar and the two horns like that of a ram.[9] One of the teeth should slightly resemble a projecting tooth and be attached to the root of the fang; the cheeks on the two sides should be smiling and straight and broad on the two foreparts. The face should be (painted) dark blue all over like the face of a female crocodile and the teeth and lips should be white.

The text instructs the architects about the placement of the motif on structures. While describing different kinds of temple porches, the author states that while creating the front porch of a temple, a *kīrtivaktra* (monumental face or jaw) should be carved in the shape of a projection.[10] Furthermore, the *kīrtivaktra* should be carved on the *stūpika* (miniature domes) and *śṛṅga* (spirelet) parts of the structure. The *Mānasāra* also instructs architects and sculptors to carve *kīrtimukha* on a variety of column bases. In the description of the types of column bases, the author says the 'face-like ornament' should be carved on the *śrī bandha* type of column base, which is fit for buildings created for *cakravartin* rulers and temples dedicated to Śiva and Viṣṇu. For the *mañcha-bandha* type of column base, the text states that two parts or rows of the column and the *antarita* (intervals) should be carved with the 'face ornament'.[11] Similarly, for the *śreṇi-bandha*, *padma-bandha*, *kumbha-bandha* and *kampa-bandha* types of column bases, which are suited for temples dedicated to all gods, the author instructs that two rows of 'face ornament' should be attached with *antarita*.[12]

*Aparājitapṛcchā*, a twelfth-century architectural text on western Indian style of *Nāgara* architecture states that the *Bhūmija* (a variety of *Nāgara* shrine) type of temple *pīṭha* (socle) should be divided into 22 parts or mouldings and one of the mouldings should be carved with *grāsapaṭṭi* (band of repeated *grāsa* faces).[13] Additionally, the *maṇḍovara* (wall) of the temple constructed over the *pīṭha* should have 44 mouldings and *grāsapaṭṭi* should be one of the mouldings; the *uḍumbara* (threshold) should be divided into three parts, the central part having a lotus and a projecting *kīrtimukha* carved on either side.[14]

The *Śilpa Prakāśa*, a Tantric text on Odishan temple architecture composed by Rāmacandra Mahāpātra Kaula Bhaṭṭāraka, is dated between the ninth and eleventh centuries and deals in detail with the architecture, iconography and symbolism of temples of Odisha, especially the *Vimānamālinī* type of Tantric temples. It refers to *kīrtimukha* as *vajra-mastaka*. The *vajra-mastaka* motif, which later transforms into the celebrated *bho* of Kaliṅga school of architecture, was placed on the *gaṇḍi* (spire) of Odishan temples; on the apex of the motif was placed a large *kīrtimukha*.[15]

The effortless transformation of *kīrtimukha* from literature into architecture as a fantastical creature provides insight into the minds of the composers of architectural texts, sculptors and architects of ancient

India who envisioned *kīrtimukha*, a great *gaṇa*, as the doorkeeper of Śiva and worthy of being worshipped alongside Śiva, to be carved on different parts of temples. The motif is predominantly exhibited with pearl festoons emerging from their mouths, a detail missing in the legend recorded in the *Purāṇas*, but later imagined and executed by artists erecting Brahmanical temples. This pattern of continuously recurring *kīrtimukha* faces with beaded pearl festoons emerging from their mouths and joining each other in a rhythmic, repeated pattern became one of the most popular motifs of Indian art and architecture in the Gupta and post-Gupta periods. The *kīrtimukha* motif was also combined with the *gavākṣa* (cow's eye or horseshoe arch) and placed on the apex of a *gavākṣa* or a *candraśālā*. V.S. Agarwal asserts that originally, the term *kīrti* signified an excavated *caitya* hall and later it was used to denote sacred and secular structures; *kīrtimukha* in the architectural sense referred to the opening of a window. 'The large window or opening with which the hollowing out of the rock started and which remained as the most conspicuous part of the whole operation, was naturally called Kirtimukha.'[16] Originally associated with Śiva and found on Śaiva structures, *kīrtimukha* in time became a universal architectural and sculptural decorative motif and was placed on sculpture and architecture irrespective of their religious associations.

## *Kīrtimukha* in Art

The first appearance of a fully formed *kīrtimukha* motif is dated to the mature Gupta artistic period. The motif appears as a *grāsapaṭṭaka*, *grāsapaṭṭi*, *grāsamālā* (band of repeated *kīrtimukha* or *grāsa* faces with pearl festoons emerging from their mouths) or as a *grāsakiṅkiṇika* (band of repeated *kīrtimukha* with bells suspended from their mouths) on Gupta sacred structures.[17] One of the earliest examples of *kīrtimukha* comes from a column located at Udayagiri Cave 19 or the Amrita Cave (425 CE) in Vidisha, Madhya Pradesh. The column is divided into several decorative registers and *grāsapaṭṭaka* appears on the top and bottom registers; the *kīrtimukha* faces appear to have been carved in accordance with the guidelines provided in the *Mānasāra*. They have prominent round eyes and noses, and moustaches (see Image 14.1). Fangs can be seen coming out of both sides of their mouths and a tuft of hair rises from their foreheads. A bunch of pearl festoons, consisting of carefully carved clusters of small beaded pearl strings, emerge from their mouths. As directed in the *Mānasāra* the hair of *kīrtimukha* stands at its end, almost reaching the upper register; the fangs and moustaches have also been carved in a manner pointing upwards, providing a sense of rhythm and harmony to the image.

**Image 14.1: *Maṇḍapa* pillar detail, Cave Number 19, Udayagiri, Vidhisha, c. 425 CE**

*Credit*: American Institute of Indian Studies

*Kīrtimukha* also becomes an essential element of Buddhist architecture and sculpture in the Gupta period. At Sarnath, several examples of *kīrtimukha* can be noticed. On a pillar fragment, dated to the late fifth century CE, *grāsapaṭṭaka* have been carved with *kīrtimukha* faces with round bulging eyes and cheeks and flaring nostrils, while the moustaches and tufts of hair have been carved stylistically curving upward, almost appearing like foliage. A single *kīrtimukha* appears as a crown embellishment on a standing stone image of Bodhisattva Padmapāṇi. Occupying the centre of the crown, the *kīrtimukha* has been carved with bulging eyes and a full moustache, and plain unbeaded festoons emerge from his mouth. Another *kīrtimukha* from Sarnath appears inside a *gavākṣa* in a door lintel showing scenes from the *Khantivādī/ Kṣāntivādī Jātaka* (500 CE–525 CE).

Some of the most exquisitely carved examples of Gupta period *kīrtimukha* appear from the site of Nachna in Panna district, Madhya Pradesh. Dated to early sixth century, the site is littered with loose architectural fragments, and among them appears a purple sandstone pillar fragment with intricately carved *grāsapaṭṭaka. Kīrtimukha* faces appear with round bulging eyes, prominent sharp noses and stylised moustaches; a tuft of hair protrude from their glabella. The horns of the creature effortlessly rise out of their foreheads and curve inwards, hanging like a bell, poignantly touching the tuft of hair. The moustaches have been carved stylistically, with the upper parts following the curving pattern of the horns and dropping like a bell, and the lower halves dropping downwards, reaching the large bunch of pearl festoons emerging from their mouths. The festoons have been carved delicately and intricately; the sculptors added a large bead in the centre of the festoon, which breaks their monotony and adds more grace to the design.

Another style of *kīrtimukha* appears on a *triśākhā* door-jamb (door-jamb with three jambs or *śākhā*) at Nachna in Uttar Pradesh. Carved on the bottom of the *stambhaśākhā* (pillar design *śākhā* or jamb), this small *kīrtimukha* appears to be creeping out of a window or an opening and has protruding ears, round bulging eyes, a prominent flat nose and cheeks, and a thick, curvy moustache; fangs can be seen coming out of his mouth.

At Bhumra Śiva temple (475 CE–500 CE), located 15 km from Nachna, *grāsapaṭṭi* appears on columns, and chains can be seen suspended from *kīrtimukha*'s mouth. Also at Bhumra, images of *gaṇas* (Śiva's goblins) in various postures have been carved on the *vedibadha* (basal wall mouldings) of the temple—among them appears a dancing *gaṇa* with a lion head, which may be a rare representation of *kīrtimukha* as *grāsa*, the demon with his body, before he consumed himself. According to a legend recorded in the *Śiva Purāṇa*, *kīrtimukha* was born as *grāsa*, with the face of a lion and 'appeared to be the man-lion incarnation of Vishnu'.[18] The artists at Bhumra, aware of the legend, might have chosen to add *kīrtimukha* as *grāsa*.

At Pipariya (510 CE–520 CE) in Madhya Pradesh, single large *kīrtimukha* faces appear on the square finial of the columns.[19] *Kīrtimukha* appears with a flat round nose, small eyes, thick lips and a clearly visible full jaw. He has sharp pointed fangs, which emerge from both sides of the mouth. His beard, hair and the tuft of hair on his forehead form a stylised curvy pattern, appearing like foliage. *Kīrtimukha* also appear at Gupta temples at Tigawa, Pipariya and Sakora. At the Mahasthan Buddhist Brick temple and the Gokul Śiva temple in Bogra, Bangladesh pottery tiles with *kīrtimukha* faces have been found.[20]

While the Guptas are credited with introducing *kīrtimukha* as an architectural decorative motif, it subsequently reached a new level of majesty and finesse in the early medieval period (600 CE–1200 CE). The *Nāgara* style of temple architecture, whose foundations were laid under Gupta patronage, developed a new vocabulary, style and grandeur in early medieval North India. Each geographical region developed its own artistic and architectural traditions marked with intense energy, vigour, innovation, and amalgamation of motifs, styles and design. Various styles of *Nāgara* architecture that flourished in North India adopted *kīrtimukha* as a decorative motif and it became a universal, inseparable aspect of architectural style, painting and sculpture.

The early medieval period is marked by the growth of a number of regional kingdoms and the rise of new economic, political and sacred centres.[21] There was a marked increase in the number of temples being constructed; new rulers patronised these grand sacred edifices in order to gain political and religious legitimisation. Temples became symbols of power and prestige for the rulers of regional kingdoms, who were often at war with each other. Temples also became centres of cultural and economic activities and were therefore patronised by guilds of artists and merchants.[22] Parts of north-western and north-central India witnessed the rise of a number of Rajput clans, each claiming *kṣatriya* status, and providing major encouragement to development architecture. Under the patronage of various Rajput kingdoms in western India (modern states of Rajasthan and Gujarat), there developed two different schools of architecture with their individual styles and vocabulary, namely the Mahā-Māru and Mahā-Gurjara styles. By the late tenth and early eleventh centuries, they came together and developed into the Māru-Gurjara school of architecture.[23]

The Candella kings who came to power in the Bundelkhand region of central India erected some of the most beautiful Brahmanical edifices in and around their capital Khajjuravāhaka (modern Khajuraho).[24] In eastern India, in the sixth and seventh centuries, under the patronage of the Pāṇḍuvaṃśī or Somavaṁśī kings who ruled from Sirpur (modern Chhattisgarh), the Mahākośala style of architecture developed.[25] The Mahākośala style is also credited with the later development of Kalinga architecture in Odisha, which thrived under the aegis of the Śailodbhavas.

The Ajanta Caves in western Deccan under the Vākāṭaka patronage emerged as a major Buddhist centre. Here, the *kīrtimukha* appears as a decorative motif in caves 1, 2, 4 and 19, all dated to the fifth century CE. At cave number 4, one of the largest *vihāras* at Ajanta, *kīrtimukha* faces are carved on the columns inside the cave.[26] These are large *kīrtimukha* faces, with protruding round eyes and noses; both the ears and horns have been prominently carved, and a bunch of beaded pearl festoons emerges from their mouths. The *kīrtimukha* that appears in cave 1 stylistically differs from the one in cave 4. Depicted with a prominent nose and a large open mouth with teeth clearly showing, pearl festoons emerge from behind the teeth. The tuft of hair rising out of his glabella is stylised and appears like foliage. Another variety of *kīrtimukha* has been painted in the palace scene on the wall outside the door of cave 1; the face painted inside a medallion appears with round eyes, a large round nose and an open mouth showing his fangs and teeth.[27]

Another beautifully painted *kīrtimukha* appears on the ceiling medallion of the Nidhī Shrinelet of cave number 2. It appears as a floating jawless face emerging from the clouds with an open mouth showing teeth and fangs. The face is painted deep green, his teeth and fangs in white, and horns, eyeballs, ears and lips are red; it has a curly beard and tuft of hair taking the shape of the clouds. In the courtyard of cave 19, *kīrtimukha* appears on the finial of the column—this is a plain large, smiling face, with bulging eyes, triangular pointed brows and a single unbeaded festoon emerges from his mouth.

Almost 100 km away from Ajanta, artistic activity began at Ellora under the Kālacuri patronage from about 550 CE. One of the most imaginatively carved examples of *kīrtimukha* comes from the facade of cave 10 or the Viśvakarma Cave. The central large *gavākṣa* window drops out of a *kīrtimukha* face. This central *gavākṣa* is flanked by two smaller *gavākṣas*, which also emerge out of the mouths of *kīrtimukha*; the smaller *gavākṣa* after the primary *candraśālā* or semi-circular arch breaks into a larger, elongated rectangular barrel-vaulted arch. At this point, artists were also splitting *kīrtimukha* faces into halves, each half placed above the rectangular barrel-vaulted arch next to the primary *candraśālā*. The entire motif is surrounded with a beaded pattern, reminiscent of the pearl festoons in *kīrtimukha*'s mouth. This style of splitting the *kīrtimukha*, as the architectural design progressed, is also noticed in Hoysaḷa architecture.[28]

From around the early seventh century, Ellora emerged as an important Brahmanical centre under the patronage of the Rāṣṭrakūṭa rulers. The famous rock-cut temple of Kailāśanātha was constructed during this period and *grāsapaṭṭaka* became a major decorative element in the entire scheme of the temple, covering columns both inside and outside the complex. At Ellora, *kīrtimukha* also appears as the *keyūra* (upper arm ornament).[29]

While the rock-cut edifices were being erected in the Deccan, parts of northwest, central and eastern India were being dotted with structural edifices dedicated to Brahmanical, Buddhist and Jaina gods and goddesses. The earliest examples of post-Gupta temples appear in central India, where a number of *maṇḍapikā* shrines (flat-roofed shrines) were built; in them appear beautifully carved *kīrtimukha* faces. At Śiva temple number 1 (650 CE–675 CE) in Mahua, Bihar, on pilasters at the entrance of the *garbhagṛha* (sanctum sanctorum), on the top octagonal neck appears *kīrtimukha* with pearl chains emerging from their mouths. *Grāsapaṭṭaka* also appears on the *vedibandha* of the temple.[30]

In north-western Rajasthan, at Makanganj temple number 2 (625 CE–650 CE), beautiful *kīrtimukha* faces with their tongues protruding are carved on the *śikhara*. At Śītaleśvara Mahādeva temple (689 CE) in Jhalawar, Rajasthan, in one of the earliest-surviving Pratihara temples in western Malava, sculptors created unique and exceptionally carved *kīrtimukha*.

On the pilasters outside the temple wall, large *kīrtimukha* appear with big round cheeks and flaring nostrils; they appear to be applying pressure on the pearl festoons, which emerge from their mouths. Inside the temple, three varieties of *kīrtimukha* designs can be noticed on the *maṇḍapa* columns. First, large fluid *kīrtimukha* faces appear as *grāsapaṭṭaka*'s with beaded pearl chains emerging from their mouths. In another variation, seated *gaṇas* playing trumpets appear alternatingly with *kīrtimukha*. In other columns, the *gaṇas* are replaced with *vyāla* (composite fantastic animal). On the round *raṅgmaṇḍapa* columns appear *grāsakiṅkiṇika* with elongated *kīrtimukha* faces, thick moustaches, round bulging eyes and long triangular stylised brows, carved much beyond the forehead almost reaching the tuft of hair, looking like horns. Festoons with a plain centre and beaded border emerge from their mouths, one part falling downward and the other ascending. This form of *kīrtimukha* with elongated, pointed brows became standard, appearing in temples constructed under the patronage of the Gurjara-Pratihara, and placed on the lowermost register of the *vedibandha*.

The Gurjara-Pratihāras came to power in western India around sixth century CE after defeating the Gurjaras of Nandipuri and Pratihāras of Jodhpur. Under their patronage, exquisite temples were erected in western India, but the *kīrtimukha* that appeared on the *vedibandha* lacks the grace and elegance of the Gupta-period *grāsapaṭṭaka*. The sculptors no longer took time to carve the beaded pearl festoons emerging from *kīrtimukha*'s mouth; the delicate carvings are replaced with plain unbeaded garlands. Sometimes, a bell or flower motif is carved between two *kīrtimukha* faces to break the monotony of the repeated pattern of *grāsapaṭṭaka*. In sharp contrast to the *kīrtimukha* faces that appear on the *vedibandha*, beautiful single *kīrtimukha* faces have been carved on the walls of temples and as sculptural ornaments. Two stone images of Jīvantasvāmi (Image 14.2a), dated to tenth century CE, stand in the courtyard of the Mahāvīra temple in Osian, Rajasthan. *Kīrtimukha* has been placed here as a belt buckle and crown ornament, though *kīrtimukha* has been carved in typical Gurjara-Pratihāra manner, with elongated triangular brows. The faces have been carved delicately and exhibit elegance and grace.[31]

**Image 14.2a: Standing Jīvantasvāmi, Mahāvīra temple, Osian, Jodhpur, c. 10th century CE**

*Credit*: Author

**Image 14.2b: Crown detail, Standing Jīvantasvāmi, Mahāvīra temple, Osian, Jodhpur, c. 10th century CE**

*Credit*: Author

**Image 14.2c: Girdle detail, Standing Jīvantasvāmi, Mahāvīra temple, Osian, Jodhpur, c. 10th century CE**

*Credit*: Author

Some of the most remarkable examples of *kīrtimukha* come from the Mahākośala style of architecture, which flourished under the patronage of the Śarabhapurīyas and the Pāṇḍuvaṃśi around Sirpur in Chhattisgarh.[32] At the Tāla Śiva temple (550 CE–557 CE) in Bilaspur, Chhattisgarh, large *kīrtimukha* faces appear on both sides of the *garbhagṛha* door, projecting almost 20 cm outwards.[33] The artists at Tāla imagined this powerful *kīrtimukha* as an organic being who effortlessness blends with the surrounding foliage. The *kīrtimukha* is carved with powerful round bulging eyes, with the inner eye carefully cut exposing bulging and stretching veins. The moustache, eyelids, brows, flaring nostrils and tuft of hair all take shapes of different twisting and turning leaves. This is a rare depiction of *kīrtimukha* as an organic being.

The Mahākośala style is believed to have influenced the Kalinga style of architecture, which flourished in Odisha under the patronage of the Śailodbhavas, who came to power in the second quarter of the sixth century CE.[34] The *kīrtimukha* in Kalinga architecture became synonymous with the decorative motif *vajra-mastaka*, which later transformed into the illustrious *bho*. According to *Śilpa Prakāśa*, the *vajra-mastak* motif repels evil spirits and protects the structure from lightning.[35] Most commonly often found on the *gaṇḍi* of the temple, it comprises a *kīrtimukha* placed at the apex with pearl strings dropping from his mouth, forming *caitya* medallions. Subsequently, the *vajra-mastaka* motif progressed, with *gaṇas* or *yakṣī* figures added on each side of the *kīrtimukha*. In the later *bho* design, bells can also be seen coming out of the *kīrtimukha* mouths apart from the pearl festoons. In addition to the *gaṇḍi*, the *kīrtimukha* or the *vajra-mastaka* motif is also found on temple door-jambs, crown mouldings and the apex of the *makara-toraṇa* (gateways emanating from crocodile mouths) and as a coiffure ornament.[36] Some of the best examples of the *vajra-mastaka* can be seen in the seventh-century Paraśurāmeśvara (Image 14.3) and Svarṇajāleśvara temples at Bhubaneshwar. In the tenth-century Mukteśvara temple, a completely developed *bho* ornament can be seen, with *kīrtimukha* flanked by *gaṇas* on either side.

**Image 14.3: *Vajra-Mastaka* detail, Paraśurāmeśvara temple, Bhubaneswar, c. 7th century CE**

*Credit*: American Institute of Indian Studies

In Kalinga architecture, *kīrtimukha* motifs with round bulging eyes and horns sometimes resemble the *makaramukha* (mouth of a crocodile) and it becomes difficult to differentiate between the two.[37] It is the same with Cālukya architecture, which flourished in the Deccan, and *kīrtimukha* occupied temple walls, plinths, spires, gateways and columns. Unfortunately, it is beyond the scope of this essay to discuss *kīrtimukha* forms and styles in Cālukyan or *Drāviḍa* style of architecture, where the motif is represented in its supreme power and majesty.

## Significance of Architectural Motifs in Indian Art

A mature Brahmanical temple built in early medieval and medieval India is a culmination of artistic expression and religious belief systems. While the interiors of the temples were deliberately devoid of ostentatious decoration—they were intended as personal spaces where devotees could be with their deities—the exterior acted as a canvas for artists depicting various Brahmanical gods, goddesses and minor deities, flora and fauna, and mortals engaged in various aspects of everyday life. The walls, pillars, gateways, platforms and spires were decorated with episodes from sacred texts and architectural motifs, *kīrtimukha* being one such motif.

In a way, a mature Brahmanical temple was a consolidation of a large number of architectural motifs and elements, each with profound cultural and religious symbolism and significance. It is imperative that each motif must be studied independently to understand its role in the larger scheme of Indian temple architecture. As art historians, we should engage in comprehensive studies of individual architectural motifs, investigating their origins in iconography and literature, mapping their iconographic journey, and understanding their aesthetic design and spiritual function.[38] Such an approach to the study of architectural motifs can also advance an understanding of the relationship between theory and practice in Indian art, and determine whether the origins of architectural motifs lay with the artists and sculptors, or the composers of architectural texts, and whether artists were aware of the rules prescribed in these treatises.

**Image 14.4: Reclining Buddha, Polonnaruva, Sri Lanka**

*Credit*: R. Mahalakshmi

In this essay, an attempt has been made to study the origin and evolution of *kīrtimukha* within the suggested methodological paradigm, discussing the origins and dissemination of *kīrtimukha* as an architectural motif in literature and art. *Kīrtimukha* is not merely an architectural decorative motif, it is an institution in itself. A motif deeply rooted in the Śaiva Puranic mythology, in time, it surpassed its original Śaiva character and found a place in non-Śaiva Brahmanical, Buddhist and Jaina structures. It also transcends geography, making its way into the art and architecture of the medieval South as well as Southeast Asian art. *Kīrtimukha* has been compared with the Chinese Ta'o T'ieh, a symbol found on Shang dynasty bronze vessels. Large *kīrtimukha* faces in spectacular form displaying power and wrath are found at temple entrances and gateways in Nepal, Java and Bali.[39] The Shishi and Bong ritual masks from Japan are also believed to be forms of *kīrtimukha*.[40] Sri Lankan artists employed the motif indiscriminately and it appears on Buddhist structures, sculptures, jewellery, crowns and pieces of furniture. In the reclining Buddha rock-cut image at the Gal Vihara in Polonnaruva, which is dated to 12th century CE, the artist transformed *kīrtimukha* into a textile decoration; it appears as a button on the bolster pillow, on which Buddha rests his head (Image 14.4).

## Endnotes

1 *The Śiva-Purāṇa* Vol. II, ed. and trans. J.L. Shastri (New Delhi: Motilal Banarsidass, 1970), 888.

2 The plan, elevation and every other architectural and decorative element of a Brahmanical temple are deeply rooted in religious mythology and philosophy. Each component is carefully designed and has symbolic meanings and divine associations. A Brahmanical temple begins with a square plan called the *vāstupuruṣamaṇḍala* (*vāstu* means site, *puruṣa* refers to the prime person from whom all originates and *maṇḍala* means a plan). It is the form from which the temple building rises. The square plan of the *vāstupuruṣamaṇḍala* is further divided into several sections, each section and direction are dedicated to specific deities. For details, see Stella Kramrisch, *The Hindu Temple Vol. I* (Calcutta: University of Calcutta, 1946), 7.

3 Ludo Rocher, *A History of Indian Literature: The Purāṇas Vol. II, Fasc. 3* (Wiesbaden: Harrassowitz, 1986), 20.

4 R.C. Hazra, *Studies in the Purāṇic Records on the Hindu Rites* (New Delhi: Motilal Banarsidass, 1975 [1940]), 7.

5 R.C. Hazra, 'The Problems Related to the *Śiva Puraṇā*,' in *Our Heritage*, Vol. I, Part 1 (January–June 1953): 65.

6 *The Śiva-Purāṇa*, 886.

7 Ibid., 886–888.

8 *Architecture of the Mānasāra,* Vol. IV, (ed.) P.K. Acharya (New Delhi: Munshiram Manoharlal, 1934), 215.

9 Ibid.

10 Ibid., 214.

11 Ibid., 186.

12 Ibid., 138–139.

13 L.M. Dubey, *Aparājitapṛcchā: A Critical Study* (Allahabad: Lakshmi Publications, 1987), 154–155.

14 Ibid., 169.

15 T.E. Donaldson, *Hindu Temple Art of Orissa*, Vol. II (Leiden: Brill, 1986).

16 V.S. Agarwal, 'Panch-Vaktra or Kīrtimukha Motif,' in *Studies in Indian Art* (Varanasi: Vishwavidyalaya Prakashan, 2003), 235–240.

17 Krishna Deva, 'Guptas and Their Feudatories', in *Encyclopedia of Indian Temple Architecture: Foundations of North Indian Style c. 250 BC–AD 1100*, Vol. 2, Part 1, ed. M.A. Dhaky (New Delhi: Princeton University Press [AIIS], 1988), 26.
18 *The Śiva-Purāṇa*, 888.
19 J.G. Williams, *Art of Gupta India: Empire and Province* (Princeton: Princeton University Press, 1982).
20 *Encyclopedia of Indian Temple Architecture*, 25.
21 B.D. Chattopadhyaya, 'Historical Context of the Early Medieval Temples of North India', in *Studying Early India: Archaeology, Texts and Historical Issues* (New Delhi: Oriental Blackswan, 2003), 153–171.
22 Chattopadhyaya, 'Historical Context', 164–166.
23 M.A. Dhaky, 'Genesis and Development of Māru-Gurjara Temple Architecture,' in *Studies in Indian Temple Architecture*, ed. Pramod Chandra (New Delhi: AIIS, 1975): 114–165.
24 Devangana Desai, *The Religious Imagery of Khajuraho*, Project for Indian Cultural Studies, Publication IV (Mumbai, 1996).
25 Krishna Deva, 'Pāṇḍuvaṃśīs of Śrīpura and Nalas', in *Encyclopedia of Indian Temple*, 219–227.
26 Walter M. Spink, *Ajanta: History and Development*, Vol. V (Leiden: Brill, 2007), 29.
27 O.C. Gangoly, 'A Note on Kīrtimukha: Being the Life History of an Indian Architectural Ornament,' in *Rūpam*, no. 1 (January 1920): 11–19.
28 Gerard Foekema, *A Complete Guide to Hoysala Temples* (New Delhi: Abhinav Publications, 1996).
29 Carmel Berkson, *Ellora: Concept and Style* (New Delhi: IGNCA and Abhinav Publications, 1992).
30 Krishna Deva, 'Minor Dynasties: Maṇḍapikā and Early Nāgara Traditions', in *Encyclopedia of Indian Temple Architecture*, 134.
31 Anisha Saxena, *Landscapes, Memory and History: Claims and Conflicts in the Constitution of Sacred Geographies in Western India*, PhD Dissertation submitted to the Centre for Historical Studies, Jawaharlal Nehru University, 2014, 97–111.
32 Krishna Deva, 'Pāṇḍuvaṃśīs', 219–227.
33 Williams, *Art of Gupta India*, 124–128.
34 Donaldson, *Hindu Temple Art*, 770.
35 Ibid.
36 Ibid.
37 Ibid., 771.

38 Dhaky has undertaken detailed study of various architectural motifs and elements of Indian temple architecture, exploring the origin and evolution of motifs in literature and architecture. Parul Pandya Dhar's *Toraṇa in Indian and Southeast Asian Architecture* is a brilliant study of one architectural element of Indian art; she also carefully discusses the evolution of *toraṇa* in Indian architecture and undertakes a detail discussion on the relationship between text and practice in the case of *toraṇa* in Indian temple architecture. Both Dhaky's and Dhar's works are a combination of intense fieldwork and detailed study of architectural and sacred texts. For details, see: M.A. Dhaky, *The Indian Temple Traceries* (New Delhi: AIIS, 2005); M.A. Dhaky, *The Vyāla Figure on the Medieval Temple of India* (Varanasi: Prithvi Prakashan, 1965); Parul Pandya Dhar, *Toraṇa in Indian and Southeast Asian Architecture* (New Delhi: D.K. Printworld, 2009).

39 Heather Elgood, *Hinduism and the Religious Arts* (New York: Cassell, 1999), 102.

40 Margaret Coldiron, 'Lions, Witches and Happy Old Men: Some Parallels between the Balinese and Japanese Masks,' in *Asian Theatre Journal* 22, no. 2 (Autumn 2005): 227–248.

15

# Buddhist Theory of Representation

Y.S. Alone

The present work is aimed at understanding the ideas of representation that existed in the Buddhist textual tradition. The aspects of representations are deeply rooted in the logic of *paṭīcca samuppāda* (Sanskrit *pratītya samutpāda*) (theory of dependent origination or interdependent origination) and the doctrine of *anatta* (*anātma*) (that is, the theory of non-soul). The textual account is vivid, and one can read ideas of representation through some of the cardinal *suttas* in the Pāli texts. The *Mahānidāna Sutta* of the *Dīgha Nikāya* explains the logic of the *paṭīcca samuppāda* in the form of the dialogue between Buddha and Ānanda (a disciple of Buddha). It explains the origin of problems through the idea of dependent/interdependent origination; for example, birth as the cause of death. In the fourth verse of the *sutta*, it is explained how dependent/interdependent are the types and qualities of existence:

> I have said: "Birth conditions ageing-and-death", and this is the way that should be understood. If, Ānanda, there were no birth at all, anywhere, of anybody or anything: of *devas* to the *deva*-state [*devatva*], of *gandhabbas* [*gandharvas*] ..., of *yakkhas* [*yakṣas*] ..., of ghosts [*bhūta*] ..., of humans [*manuṣya*] ..., of quadrupeds [*catuṣpada*] ..., of birds [*pakṣi*] ..., of reptiles to the reptile state [*sarīsṛp*], if there were absolutely no birth at all of all these beings, then, with the absence of all birth, the cessation of birth, could ageing-and-death appear?[1]

Though these are linguistic connotations, they are evolved and dependent on the types of characteristics. The linguistic connotations get evolved through the idea of characteristics that one object possesses and the manner in which it differs from another, and hence, representation is formulated on the basis of observed inferences. Buddha further explains the importance of *bhava* and *upādāna*. '"Clinging conditions becoming".... If there were absolutely no clinging: sensuous clinging, clinging to views, to rite-and-ritual, to personality-belief . . ., could becoming appear?' *Bhava* (place of existence/manifestation) is a category of manifestation whereas *upādāna* is a cause (that is, desire as a cause) for existence.[2]

Buddha explains, 'Feeling conditions cravings, if there were absolutely no feeling: feeling born of eye-contact, ear contact, nose-contact, tongue-contact, body-contact, mind-contact—in the absence of all feeling, with the cessation of feeling, could craving appear?' Ānanda replies, 'No *Bhante*.' Thereafter, the Buddha explains several types of *upādānas—kamma* (karma), *diṭṭhi* (*dṛṣṭi*), *sīlabbat* (*śīlavrata*), *attavāda* (*ātmavāda*) and so on. Desire is a cause for *rūpa taṇhā* (*tṝṣṇā*) (desire by sight), *sadda* (*śabda*) *taṇhā* (desire by sound/words), *gandha taṇhā* (desire by smell), *rasa taṇhā* (desire by taste), *sparśa taṇhā* (desire by tangibles), *dhamma taṇhā* (mind-subject desire), and that ultimately, desire is a cause of *vedanā* (feeling).[3]

Buddha denied the existence of soul and, therefore, there is no concept of soul in Buddhism—it is called *anattavāda (anattā = anātman)*. It emphasises that the fruits of the *buddhatva* (Buddhahood) lie in the existing body only. The *Mahānidāna Sutta* of the *Dīgha Nikāya* explains the no-soul doctrine and how Buddha refutes the existence of a soul, questioning its very existence and how one identifies it.[4] This is explained by questioning the experience of feeling. Buddha maintains that there are three *vedanā anubhava—sukha* (experience of feeling, happiness), *dukkha* (sorrow) and *adukkha-asukha* (no sorrow, no happiness); so, which is the soul? Therefore, *cetanā* (consciousness) becomes important, and its significance is traced in the *Mahāparinibbāna Sutta* of the *Dīgha Nikāya*.[5] Buddha also teaches his monastic fraternity the principles to be followed for the survival of the doctrine. He says as long as monks develop the perception of impermanence, non-self, impurity, overcoming desires, cessation of hate, anger, desire and discuss among themselves any matter, understand the *Buddhavacana* (discourses of Buddha) in the correct manner, refrain from doing wrong, etc., there will always be progress of the monks. In short, following these principles may be deemed as the way to carry forward the doctrine and maintain its spirit.

The Buddhist philosophy lays greater emphasis on *cetanā* (consciousness) and considers only two forms of knowledge or *pamāṇas* (*pramāṇas*): perception (*paccakha/pratyakṣa*) and inference (*anumāna*). The object of *paccakkha* is a unique particular, and the object of *anumāna* is universal.

Considering the nature of forms of knowledge, one has to investigate the problematisation of memory. Buddha emphasises how he expected his monks and nuns to memorise his discourses. Memory becomes important—to remember as well as understand the unique particulars associated with the representation. The idea of the memory of representation is evident in the *Mahāparinibbāna Sutta*. Two important aspects related to a memory are mentioned:

1. places related with the life of Buddha.
2. the building of memorials in the forms of *thūpa/stūpas*.

According to the *Mahāparinibbāna Sutta*, there are four *dassanīya/darśanīya* (to be seen physically) places for followers: Lumbini, where Tathāgata was born; Bodhgaya where Tathāgata got enlightenment or *samma* (*samyak*) *sambodhi*, Sarnath where Tathāgata gave the *dhammacakkapavattana* (first sermon) and Kusinara, where Tathāgata died—that is, *Mahāparinibbāna*.[6]

The text further talks about the construction of *thūpas* as a memorial for a certain class of people, *thūparahā*—Tathāgata *samma sambuddha* (fully enlightened universal Buddha), *pacceka sambuddha* (enlightened individual Buddha), *sāvaka* (disciple) of the Tathāgata and *cakkavattin* (*cakravartin*) king (universal ruler).[7] It is evident that the institution of the *stūpa* was legitimised in Buddhist practice and became an important means to keep the memory of a person. The narrative indicates that it was composed after the demise of Buddha. It may be observed that *Dīgha Nikāya* contains many important discourses and many philosophical explanations elaborated in it. The *Mahāparinibbāna Sutta* is the only narrative about his last journey, and it appears that many historical parts were retained and additions made to legitimise certain practices, as directed by the Buddha. However, *stūpas* were a part of the *śramaṇa* tradition; hence, they were adopted in Buddhism, and keeping one's memory alive appears to be part of ongoing practices. Textual accounts too point at the construction of *stūpas* when Buddha was alive. They demonstrate that the *Mahāparinibbāna Sutta* simply legitimised existing practices.

The *Bāhiya Sutta* in the *Udāna* of the *Khuddaka Nikāya* mentions the story of a person named Bāhiya.[8] He resided in Suppāraka *tīrtha* (Suppāraka is generally identified with Sopara on the west coast near Mumbai, but the mention of the word *tīrtha* is an interesting connotation and Suppāraka appears to be identified as a pilgrimage site). Bāhiya went to Sāvatthī/Śrāvastī, listened to a sermon by Buddha and developed detachment from a worldly life to become a monk. One day, Bāhiya was returning to the monastery after receiving alms when a bull crushed him to death. Buddha, also after receiving alms, was returning when he came to know of Bāhiya's death. He asked his followers to cremate the body to the sound of drum beats and build a *stūpa* over his ashes. Thus, it's clear that the erection of *stūpa* was practiced during Buddha's lifetime.

In the *Ratana Sutta* of the *Suttanipāta* of the *Khuddaka Nikāya*, Buddha is eulogised (in verse 3) as the best *ratna* (jewel) in *loka* (residing on earth) and *paraloka* (the other world).[9] Verses 15–17 of the same *Sutta* are an interesting composition. They state that Buddha is the best among all animals and human beings on earth and, therefore, salutations are offered to the Buddha, *dhamma* and *saṁgha*.[10] The genesis of the chant, *Buddhamsaraṇamgacchami*, appears to be taken from the *Ratana Sutta* and gets incorporated in a separate body of texts called *Khuddakapāṭha*.[11] *Dukamātikā* Verse 12, in the *Mātika* section under the main *Cūḷantaraduka* section in *Dhammasaṅgaṇī* of the *Abhidhamma Piṭaka*, mentions *lokiyādhammā* and *lokuttarādhammā* (things that are earthy/mundane, things that are non-earthy/supramundane).[12] Buddha being the propagator of *dhamma* (doctrine), the epithet of *lokuttarā*/*lokottara* gets associated with him. Nevertheless, the idea of Buddha being a historical person is constantly maintained in the textual tradition, and he is revered as the supreme human who evolved the theory of dependent/interdependent origination.

It is interesting to observe the way the Buddhist *vandanas* (chants) are composed. *Vandana* (chanting) is part of the *Khuddakapāṭha* of the *Khuddaka Nikāya*. Some of the *suttas* mentioned in the *Khuddakapāṭha* are also found in the *Dhammapada* and *Suttanipāta*, which indicate that the *Khuddakapāṭha* was composed after the *Suttanipāta* and *Dhammapada*. They all are part of the *Khuddaka Nikāya*. The main *vandana, Buddhamsaraṇamgacchami,* is recorded in this text. However, a later composition, which is not part of the standard *Khuddakapāṭha* text but exists in Sri Lankan tradition, states

*Buddham dhammam ca sangham sugatatanubhavā dhātavō dhatugabbhe*
*laṇkāyam jambudīpe tidasapuravare nagaloke ca thūpe.*

(To the Buddha, *dhamma, saṁgha*, I salute all the *stūpas* having the relics of the Buddha in Lanka, Jambūdvīpa, the 30th heaven and the nether world.)

*Sabbe buddhassa bimbē sakaladasadise kesa lōmādi dhātu*
*Vande sabbepi buddham dasabalatanuјam bodhicetyam namāmi.*

(Whatever are the forms of Buddha, the hairs and the bodily relics installed in the all ten directions, I salute them all.)

*Vandāmi cetiyam sabbam sabbathanesu patitthitam*
*Sāririka-dhātu-mahā-bodhi(m) buddharūpam sakalam sadā.*

(I salute/ pay respect to all the *caityas*, relics of the Buddha, Bodhi trees, they are all forms/representations of the Buddha.)[13]

The composition emerged after Buddhism was established in Sri Lanka, that is after third century BCE. The chant remained significant, and is followed in Sri Lanka and among the neo-Buddhist communities in India.

Another popular chant is:

*Yo sannisinno varabodhimūle, māram sasenām sujitam jinitvā*
*Sambōdhim āgacchi anantaññāṇo, lokuttamo tam panạmāmi Buddham.*

(The one who became enlightened under the Bodhi tree, the one who defeated Māra and his army, who is the best in the world, I salute to that Buddha.)[14]

This verse mentions Māra, and appears to be based on the *Mahākhandhaka* section of the *Mahāvaggo* of the *Vinaya Piṭaka*, as well as the *Saṁyutta Nikāya* (*Sagathavaggo* section), whereas *pañcasīlā* is derived from the verse found in the *Gahapati Vagga,* which is the fifth section of the *Nidānavagga* in the *Saṁyutta Nikāya.*[15] The verses in the *Khuddakapāṭha* have been taken from the actual *Nikāyas* and have been inducted into formal chanting. At the same time, the *Vinaya Piṭaka*, the earliest text among the body of Buddhist texts, mentions *Māravijaya*. It goes to show that early textual formulations are important to understand the early visual culture of the Buddhists.

The phrase *Māra sasenām sujitam jinitvā* (the one who conquered Māra) gets added emphasis in the pictorial representation. *Māravijaya* becomes a metaphor and is represented as the obstacle to the *nibbāna*. The pictorial representation of *Māravijaya* is one of the most popular themes in Buddhist monuments. *Padhānasutta* in the *Suttanipāta* describes various types of Māra's army.[16] It says Māra's first army is lust, second is discontent, third is hunger and thirst, fourth is desire, fifth is sloth and drowsiness, sixth cowardice, seventh doubt, and eighth hypocrisy and stupor. *Selasutta* in the *Mahāvagga* of the *Suttanipāta* mentions Sela (Shaila) the *brāhmaṇa* praising Buddha who had 32 *mahāpurisa lakkhaṇa* (*mahāpuruṣa lakṣanas*) and who ruled by the *dhamma* with seven jewels—*cakka-ratana, hasti-ratana, assa-ratana, maṇi-ratana, itthi-ratana, gahapati-ratana* and *pariṇāyaka-ratna* (wheel, elephant, horse, gems, women, householder and leader respectively).[17] In the *Vāseṭṭhasutta* of the *Mahāvagga* of the *Suttanipāta*, Buddha refutes the *varṇa* system and says that the difference between human beings is that of the substantive description/nouns and depends on his/her works or certain associations; thus the one who lives off cattle is a farmer and not a *brāhmaṇa*. Similarly, the one who lives on *sippa* (*śilpa*) will be considered a *sippi*, one depending on trade is a trader, one living off service is *pessā* (*preśya*), etc.[18] The idea of figural representation is also based on such identities.

In the *Mahānidānasutta* of the *Dīgha Nikāya*, Buddha, while explaining the theory of dependent origination, warns Ānanda: 'Do not say that, Ānanda, do not say that! This dependent origination is profound and appears profound. It is through not understanding, not penetrating this doctrine that this generation has become like a tangled ball of string, covered as with a blight: tangled like coarse grass, unable to pass beyond states of woe, the ill destiny, ruin and the round of birth-and-death?' He further says, 'If, Ānanda, you are asked: "Has ageing-and-death a condition for its existence?" you should answer: "Yes." If asked: "What conditions ageing-and-death?" you should answer: "ageing-and-death is conditioned by birth." … "What conditions birth?" ... "Becoming conditions birth."

... "Clinging conditions becoming." ... "Craving conditions clinging." "Feeling conditions craving." ... "Contact conditions feeling." ... "Mind-and-body conditions contact." ... "Consciousness conditions mind-and-body." ... If asked: "Has consciousness a condition for its existence? you should answer: "Yes." If asked: "What conditions consciousness?" you should answer "Mind-and-body conditions consciousness."'[19]

The theory is also explained in the *Desanāsutta* and *Vibhaṅgasutta* under the section *Nidānavagga* in the *Saṁyutta Nikāya*. The *Vibhaṅgasutta* also qualifies *bhava* (existence). It states,' There are these three kinds of existence: sense-sphere existence, form-sphere existence, formless-sphere existence.'[20] Consciousness is a key factor in understanding the phenomenon.

The *Mahānidānasutta* of the *Dīgha Nikāya* also explains the importance of the sensory organs as well as their positions. As there is a greater emphasis on the *pañcakhandhā* and *āyatana*—five sensory perception organs; the *khandhās* (*skandhā*) are *rūpa* (material qualities), *vedanā* (feeling), *saññā* (perception), *sankhārā* (coefficients of consciousness) and *viññāna* (consciousness).[21] The *Rāhula Saṁyutta* section of the *Nidānavagga* of the *Saṁyutta Nikāya* mentions dialogue between Buddha and Rahul. Buddha asks Rahul, 'Is the ear ... the nose ... the tongue ... the body ... the mind permanent or impermanent?' Rahul answers, 'Impermanent, venerable sir.'[22] Thus, emphasis on the nature of understanding differing perceptual realities and the mind-consciousness as impermanent show constant nature of change. The *āyatana* (sensory organs/positions) of *cakkhu*/*cakṣu* (sight), *sot*/*śrotra* (hearing), *ghān*/*ghrāṇa* (smell), *jivh*/*jihva* (taste), *kāy*/*kāya* (body), *man*/*mana* (mind) are important to our understanding of perception and inference. The *Mahānidānasutta* explains the seven stations of consciousness and two realms, which are the realm of unconscious beings and the realm of neither-perception-nor-non-perception.[23]

The term *āyatana* is understood as realms. But *āyatana* is a position of the sense organs. It hints at how mental constructs consist of reading or perception and in fact, reading/perception is also a mental construct. Buddha also explains eight liberations, in which fifth is consciousness (infinite consciousness). By transcending the sphere of infinite consciousness, thinking, 'There is nothing,' one enters and abides in the sphere of nothingness (emptiness). That is the sixth. By transcending the sphere of nothingness, one reaches and abides in the sphere of neither-perception-nor-non-perception. That is the seventh. By transcending the sphere of neither-perception-nor-non-perception, one enters and abides in the cessation of perception and feeling. That is the eighth liberation.[24]

The three modes of perception or *pamāṇa* (*pramāṇa*) are direct perception (*paccakkha*/*pratyakṣa*), inference (*anumāna*) and wrong direct perception or wrong inference, which results in the wrong perception (*abhava*). Thich Nhat Hanh explains different realms of mind consciousness, quoting *Abhidhammakosasāra* of Vasubandhu. He describes inference through five sense organs, sixth as mind consciousness and *manas*, the seventh consciousness, and writes, 'When we "perceive" something we are actually remembering or comparing it with a past experience or feeling that is already present in the form of a seed in our store consciousness.'[25] Thus, perceptual readings are based on the sensory organs and their holistic reading is the result of mind consciousness (*manoviññāṇa*), and *manas* becomes integral to the rising of mind-consciousness. *Ālayaviññāṇa* (stored consciousness) is the ground or base of the seventh consciousness.

Later philosophical analysis extensively discusses philosophical ideas that originated in *Nikāya* literature. According to Satkari Mookerjee, Dharmakīrti observes that 'the object of perception is the reality, which is immediately revealed to the mind and not such other ideas as generally (*sāmānya*), quality (*guṇa*), action (*kriyā*), substratum (*dravya*), or name (*naman*), which are not part of the presented sense-data but are supplied by imagination (*vikalpa*).'[26] Furthermore, 'external reality can never be an immediate object of perception but can at best be mediately known—in other words, it can only be inferred by its supposed likeness presented in the idea.'[27] It is evident Buddhists pitched the concept that the condition of likeness depends on its idea, so it could be said the idea of representation is about the idea through which a perceptual form is read and perceived.

Such theoretical conceptions/tools became a part of the analysis of mind and perception, and integral to the theory of *paṭiccasamuppāda*, or dependent origination. The object of perception is not reality in itself but an image we create. Stored consciousness also becomes active in mental formation, creating images through the existing realms of stored consciousness. Manifestation of images brings us to ideas of representation. As the object of the mind is thought/ ideas/ imagination, its resultant category is mind consciousness. In the *Mahānidānasutta*, Buddha's discourse on *anattāvāda* is an important marker. He denied the existence of soul and *anattāvāda* propagates inference through mental constructs, so the representation of the body in the form of any *kāyā* is construed as object representation.

Anxiety about the existence of Buddha appears around the early centuries of the Common Era. It is evident from *Milindapañho*; in the fifth section of the *anumāna pañha* (*praśna*), Milinda asks Nāgasena, 'Have you seen the Buddha? Has your teacher seen the Buddha?' Nāgasena answers, 'No, his highness.' Milinda responds, 'Oh monk, neither you nor your teachers saw the Buddha, that means there was no Buddha and there is no evidence of the Buddha.'[28]

To this Nāgasena poses a question to the king: 'Have you seen your ancestral kings? Have your court-people seen them?' When Milinda answers in the negative, Nāgasena counters, saying, 'Then there is no evidence of the existence of kings.' Milinda retorts: 'No, we do see the things/objects that are used by earlier kings such as parasols, crowns, shoes, swords, expensive beds, etc.' Nāgasena replies, 'Likewise, we too can understand about Buddha and confirm that Buddha is a historical figure. There are many things that still survive by which inference can be drawn that Buddha was existing:

1. Four *smṛtiprasthāna* (various memories): *kuśala* (good), *akuśala* (bad); *doṣa-yukta* (with fault), *doṣa-rahita* (without fault); *kṛṣṇa* (black); *śukla* (white),
2. Four *samyakpradhāna,*
3. Four *ṛddhipāda* (*yogasiddhis*),
4. Five sense organs,
5. Five *bala,*
6. Seven *bodhyānga* and
7. *ārya-aṣatāṇgika-mārga.*

Nāgasena, in reality, quotes *Mahāparinibbānasutta* as it mentions Buddha telling Ānanda how he explained his *dhamma* to people, which is to be learnt by all.[29] Nāgasena further describes the concept of the *Dhammanagara*, that is establishment of the *nagara* (city) having various components/facets of the teaching of *dhamma*, of *nibbāna-nagara*, and all categories of people. There's teaching about *Bodhyāṇga-ratana sati* (*smṛti*) (mindfulness), *dhamma vicaya* (investigation of doctrine), *viriya/vīrya*, *pīti/prīti* (joy), *passaddha* (*praśrabdha*) (tranquility), *samādhi* (concentration) and *upekhā* (equanimity), which monks use to kill ignorance in people, and mention of the constituents of Buddha's enlightenment, which contains *buddhavacana* (discourses of Buddha), *sarīradhātu* (body relics), objects used by Buddha, *caitya* and *saṁgha* ratana. The *Dhammanagara* section of the *Milindapañho* is considered a later addition as it is not mentioned in the Chinese version. However, this may be based on a mere assumption, as the Chinese version of the text itself refers to another version of the text. There is every possibility that this section of the text might have been lost and hence the surviving text has no mention of the subsequent section of the text.[30]

It may be observed that the *Mahāpadānasutta* of the *Dīgha Nikāya* sets conditions to become Buddha. To become Buddha, a Boddhisattva acquires *dasa-bala* (10 powers) in successive lives: *mudita* (joy), *vimala* (purity), *pabbākara* (brightness), *accimati* (intelligence of fire) and *dujjaya* (difficult to conquer). Then, he fully understands the connection of the relative and the absolute, so he becomes *abhimukha* (12 *nidāna*) in his sixth life, followed by *dūraṅgama* (going far off), where he knows the *dhamma* (righteousness), *acala*, *sādhumati* and, lastly, *dhammameghā*. Through this journey, he practices *dasapāramitā*.[31]

B.R. Ambedkar observes, 'The Jātaka theory is based upon the Buddha having the highest degree of purity as the essence of his being. The Avatāra theory does not require that the God should be pure in his making. All that the Brahmanic theory of Avatāra says is that God saves his followers by taking different forms although the God may be very impure and immoral in his conduct.'[32] The *Jātakas* have the components of the 10 *pāramitas* (perfect virtues). It may be added that the *Cariya Piṭaka*, a part of the *Khuddaka Nikāya* has only seven *pāramitas*. Hence, the *Mahāyāna* conception of the seven *pāramitas* has its genesis in the actual *Theravādin* tradition.

The concept of manifestation is divided into two categories, the *laukika* and *alaukika*. *Laukika* manifestations are physical in nature, having existence, whereas, *alaukika* are emotions, adjectives, Brahma and soul.

The *laukika* inference is considered as righteousness, so there is constant emphasis on the physical nature of the object, but at the same time, parts of *alaukika* become an integral part of representations.

There are 32 *mahāpurisa lakkhaṇa* mentioned in the *Mahāpadānasutta* of the *Dīgha Nikāya.*[33] It envisages the body type representation and constructs mental images of great persons. It also mentions the two types of life, *dhamma* and *cakkavattin*. The *Selasutta* in the *Suttanipāta* describe the body of Buddha as golden, born beautiful and having white teeth, etc.[34] The *Buddhacarita* mentions the personality of Buddha as follows:[35]

> *Pralaṁbabāhurmṛgarājajavikramo mahārṣabhākṣah kanakojjvaladyutiḥ*
> *Viśālavakṣā ghanadumdubhisvanastathāvidho'pyāśramavāsamarhati* || 8.53

> 'With his long arms and lion-gait, his bull-like eye, and his beauty bright like gold, his broad chest, and his voice deep as a drum or a cloud, should such a hero as this dwell in a hermitage?' (Book VIII: *Aṁaḥpuravilāpo* [Lamentations in the Palace, verse 8.53])

*Selasutta* of the *Majjhima Nikāya* and the *Suttanipāta* describe Buddha having 32 *mahāpurisalakkhaṇa*, and also mention a golden body. Here, the *brāhmaṇa* called Sela says, 'Perfect your body, shining well, well-born, lovely to look at, blessed one, you have a golden complexion, you have white teeth, you are vigorous. The characteristics of a well-born man, they are on thy body, the signs of a great man, the marks of great man, all are present in your body.'[36]

The *Ratanasutta* of the *Suttanipāta* categorically mentions that whoever exists in the sky and on this earth, the Tathāgata is revered by all and we respect the Buddha. It also adds *dhamma* and *saṁgha* as other two respectful entities.[37]

The concept of the 24 *Ādi*-Buddhas is elucidated in the *Buddhavaṁsa*, which is part of the *Khuddaka Nikāya.*[38] The narrative begins with the quest of Sumedha to become enlightened/Buddha, going on to describe the different conditions to become Buddha and how each Buddha had achieved that mark. The concept of *Ādi*-Buddha appears to have been initiated to provide pre-Buddha, that is pre-Śākyamuni-Buddha antiquity. The *Ādi*-Buddhas are also called *Mānuṣa* Buddhas.

The *Mahāpadānasutta* of the *Dīgha Nikāya* mentions the names of the *Ādi*-Buddhas and their respective trees of enlightenment—Vippassī (trumpet-flower), Sikhī (white-mango), Vessabhū (*sāl*), Kukusandha (acacia), Konāgamana (fig) and Kassapa (banyan), and the present Buddha (*assattha*).[39] The total number of past Buddhas mentioned in this narration is six (i.e. out of 24 mentioned in the *Buddhavaṁsa*). It also mentions the four reasons for renouncing the world by the *Ādi*-Buddhas. On the other hand, the *Saṁyutta Nikāya* briefly mentions how these *Ādi*-Buddhas became enlightened only after realisation of *paṭiccasamuppāda*. The *Nidāna Saṁyutta* of the *Nidānavagga* of the *Saṁyutta Nikāya* briefly describes this in the *Vippassīsutta* (no. 4) that the Buddha along with other *Ādi*-Buddhas, that is Sikhī (*Sikhīsutta* no. 5), *Vessabhūsutta* (no. 6), *Kukusandhasutta* (no. 7), *Konāgamana* (no. 8), Kassapa (no. 9), *Gotamasutta* (no. 10), got enlightened after understanding *paṭiccasamuppāda*.[40] All the six *Ādi*-Buddhas are briefly mentioned in a single line along with the present Buddha; thus, making the total of seven Buddhas, as in the *Dīgha Nikāya*). It appears there is a legitimisation process to push tradition to the remote past. This appears to have happened in the post-Buddha period.

**Image 15.1: Sanchi *Toraṇa*, north gate showing *Mānuṣī* Buddha *stūpas*, Sanchi, c. first century BCE**

*Credit*: Author

**Image 15.2: Ajanta Cave 17, entrance doorway, *Mānuṣī* Buddhas, c. late fifth century CE**

*Credit*: Author

Representations of *mānuṣī* Buddha *stūpas* are at the Sanchi *toraṇa* (Image 15.1) as well as at the Ajanta Cave 17 doorway (Image 15.2). The emergence of Buddha images has to be traced to historical contexts. The textual tradition has preserved the description of Buddha whereas the visual tradition, based on the available body types of ascetics, conceptualised the Buddha image. A.K. Coomaraswamy cites the example of the Bikkhu Bala image as conceptualisation based on the *yakṣa* images and demonstrated how Buddha pictures followed similar conventions.[41] However, a sculptural panel from the second century BCE on the railing pillar at Bodhgaya shows the body type observed in the later images of Buddha and Bodhisattva. It is a small relief depicting an unidentified scene (Image 15.3) of a small human figure standing in front of the hut along with an animal and a woman.

**Image 15.3: Bodhgaya relief, c. 2nd century BCE, Bodhgaya Museum, Gaya**

*Credit*: Sneha Ganguly

Going by the debate between the Buddhist and Brahmanical camps, it appears that *sadda-pamaññā* (*śabda-prāmāṇya*) became an important subject between the two. However, in case of the historical existence of Buddha, the *sadda* is not considered as *pāmāṇa* but the memories, teachings and followings of the *dhamma* along with seven *ratanas* are.

While analysing Indian philosophical developments, Rahul Sankrityayan categorised Buddhist philosophical schools as part of the *a-īśvarvādidarśan*, that is no-god philosophy. According to him, Nāgārjuna considers two meanings of *paṭicca-samuppāda*: evolution or emergence through cause and momentariness.[42] It may be observed that the idea of everything momentary gave rise to different kinds of interpretations as well as speculative metaphysical thinking. However, Nāgārjuna's *Dhāraṇī* literature propels ideas of personification and representation of mental faculties in the form of Boddhisattva and its imagery.

The existence of certain qualities of character became the issue of debate between the Buddhists and *Brāhmaṇas* who also accept the concept of *pratyakṣa* (perception) and *pramāṇa* (evidence) but reaffirm *śabda-prāmāṇya*. It is evident in the debate between Buddhists and the *Nyāya-Vaiśeṣikas*. Pradeep Gokhale points out that Nāgārjuna's extremism of momentariness is not accepted by other philosophers such as Asaṅga, Vasubandhu, Dignāga, Dharmakīrti and Śāntideva.[43] Ambedkar quotes Asaṅga who explains *śūnyatā* as follows:[44]

> 'All things are produced by the combination of causes and conditions and have no independent noumenon of their own. When the combination is dissolved, their destruction ensues.
>
> The body of a living being consists of the combination of four great elements, viz., earth, water, fire and air, and when this combination is resolved into the four component elements, dissolution ensues.
>
> This is called the impermanence of a composite entity.
>
> Impermanence of the living individual is best described by the formula, being is becoming. In this sense, a being of a past moment has lived, but does not live nor will he live. The being of a future moment will live but has not lived nor does he live; the being of the present moment does live but has not lived and will not live. In short, a human being is always changing, always growing. He is not the same at two different moments of his life.'

Gokhale states that 'Buddhists do not accept *śabda* as *pramāṇa*. They accept only two *pramāṇas* viz. *pratyakṣa* (perception) and *anumāna* (inference). There are only two forms of knowledge (*pramāṇas*): perception and inference. The object of *pratyakṣa* is a unique particular and the object of *anumāna* is a universal. Out of them only a unique particular is real because it has causal efficacy, whereas universals are unreal insofar as they are only mental constructs and do not have causal efficacy. *Pratyakṣa* is defined as cognition devoid of both mental construction and illusion, and a mental construction is defined as that the object of which is expressible in language. The cognition of a unique particular being devoid of mental construction is not expressible in language.'[45]

Dharmakīrti observes in his *Nyāyabindu* in the *svārthānumanasūtras* that inferences are of two types, *svārthānumana* and *parārthānumāna*. He stresses on the *svārthānumāna* that is constantly emphasised, as it is an indicator and associated with knowledge and not the *parārthānumāna.*[46] What Dignāga and Dharmakīrti argue is based on earlier positions found in the tradition of the Buddhist discourse. While explaining deficiencies in Dharmakīrti's exposition on language and its importance to understand as a subjective meaning-making process, Gokhale says, 'Another question can be raised about the role of *vivakṣā* in a linguistic activity. *Vivakṣāi* after all is the desire of a person to form a convention or to say something. But both these activities take place in an interpersonal, that is, social context. Forming a convention is not the matter of one person's desire but that of interpersonal agreement. Similarly, making a statement is also an interpersonal phenomenon. Though Dharmakīrti in *Santānāntarasiddhi* asserts there are other persons, he does not attach sufficient importance to this fact in his theory of language.'[47] It is important to observe that forming conventions is deemed as interpersonal agreement. Perhaps such a situation indeed existed and hence there are common grounds of agreement as to how image too is to be represented from the point of view of collective consciousness. In the early Buddhist monuments, many symbols are used, and such a phenomenon can be understood through various ways in which metaphors existed in the textual tradition. These metaphors are self-explanatory and visuality of such symbols becomes part of pictorial representations. While there is a process of historicisation in text, a similar method is observed in the visual tradition. Who made the first Buddha image has been approached from the viewpoint of who passed the goalpost first. Such an approach becomes too reductive and it is difficult to imagine there is resistance to represent the image as a human personification. As discussed, the conventions and body types already existed in the visual tradition and they need to be taken into account to see how we understand representation and how Buddhist philosophical doctrine helps us to comprehend the entire idea of representation. Susan Huntington observes that 'Scenes showing devotion to *shariraka* relics housed within the *stupas* and to *paribhogika* relics, primarily in the form of sacred trees, abound in early art. Indeed, reverence to *stupas* (and the relics housed within) and to trees comprise the most common subject in this corpus of art.'[48]

Accounts in the *Milindapañho* clearly indicated how new sets of questions were being raised in the context of the existence of the Buddha, as has been discussed earlier in the context of the conversation between Nāgasena and king Milinda, and therefore, the politics of image representation needs to be correlated. Klemens Karlsson eloquently presents the entire historiography with regard to early Buddhist art, in which he also includes observations by Frank Reynolds and Charles Halle about the possible chronology of the texts, and also questions the biography of Buddha being composed only in the Christian era.[49] As far as chronology of texts such as *Buddhacarita* is concerned, it is evident it belonged to the first and second centuries CE, whereas pictorial representation of the scene of the *māhābhinikkhamana* (great renunciation) at Sanchi is of the first century BCE. It shows prince Siddhartha leaving Kapilavastu in the presence of all others indicating that there were multiple textual records, and Aśvaghoṣa might have used them to write the biography of Buddha. On the other hand, A.K. Narain, John Huntington and Joe Cribb deal with the body of material obtained from various places, including coins, etc., and delve into the origins of the Buddha image.[50] Largely, the discussion veers towards the Gandhāra, the Mathura binary and the role of the Greek tradition. Huntington deals with the corpus of textual sources with an *a priori* approach, and hence it becomes problematic to follow his reading of the texts. While later textual tradition is extensively dealt with, early ones remain unexplored in these works. As we have argued in this paper, the idea of representation in its theoretical formulations, evident in the early Buddhist literature, need to be understood while dealing with the early Buddhist visual culture.

## Endnotes

1 Maurice Walshe, trans., *The Long Discourses of the Buddha: A Translation of the Dīgha Nikāya*, (Boston: Wisdon Publication, 1995 [1987]), 224. Also see, Bhikkhu Jagdish Kashyap, ed., *Dīgha Nikāya*, trans. Rahul Sankrityayan (Delhi: Gautam Book Depot, 2010 [1935]), 110–111.

2 *The Long Discourses of the Buddha*, 224.

3 Ibid., 224–225.

4 *The Long Discourses of the Buddha*, 223–230; *Dīgha Nikāya*, (in Hindi), 110–116.

5 *The Long Discourses of the Buddha*, 239–240; *Dīgha Nikāya*, (in Hindi), 126.

6 *The Long Discourses of the Buddha*, 263–264.

7 Ibid., 264–265.

8 Prasad Balmiki, ed., *Bāhiyasutta* no.10 of *Bodhivarga* section of *Udāna*, trans. (in Hindi) Bhikkhu Jagdish Kashyapa (Delhi: Samyak Prakashan, 2013), 29–31.

9 Lawrence Khantipalo Mills, trans., *Sutta Nipāta* (suttacentral.net, 2015), 76.

10 Ibid., 78–79.

11 Ānandajoti Bhikkhu, ed. and trans., *Khuddakapāṭha (Khuddakanikāya I) The Short* (Srilanka, 2014), https://www.ancient-buddhist-texts.net/English-Texts/Short-Readings/Short-Readings.pdf.

12 '*Cūḷantaradukam*', verse no. 12, in *Dhammasaṅgaṇī* of the *Abhidhamma Piṭaka*, published by Vippassana Research Institute, Igatpuri, Nasik, Maharashtra.

13 https://thebuddhistcentre.com/system/files/groups/files/03%20Buddha%20Puja%20in%20Pali%20Telugu%20and%20English.pdf.

14 *Collected Wheel Publications* 4, no. 47–60 (Kandy: Buddhist Publication Society, 2008), 194–195.

15 For the *Mahākhandaka*, see https://www.ancient-buddhist-texts.net/English-Texts/Great-Chapter/Great-Chapter.pdf, 23; for *Saṁyutta Nikāya*, see, '*Māra Saṁyutta*', in *The Connected Discourses of the Buddha: A New Translation of the Saṁyutta Nikāya*, trans. Bhikkhu Bodhi (Boston: Wisdom Publication, 2000), 195–220. For the discourse on conduct, see '*Nidānavagga*', *The Connected Discourses of the Buddha*, 579.

16 Bhikkhu Dhammarakhita, ed. and trans., '*Padhānasutta*', in *Suttanipāta* (Delhi: MLBD, 1983), 106–109. Also see, K.R. Norman, trans., *The Group of Discourses (Suttanipāta)* (Oxford: Pali Text Society, 2001 [1992]), 5–13.

17 Bhikkhu Dhammarakhita, '*Selasutta*', in *Suttanipāta*, 155–156; *The Group of Discourses*, 69–76.

18 '*Vāseṭṭasutta*', *Suttanipāta*, 158–172; *Group of Discourses*, 78–84.

19 *The Long Discourses of the Buddha*, 223.

20 *The Connected Discourses of the Buddha*, 535, 726.

21 *The Long Discourses of the Buddha*, 224–225.

22 *The Connected Discourses of the Buddha*, 694–697.

23 *The Long Discourses of the Buddha*, 228–229.

24 Ibid., 229.

25 Thich Nhat Hanh, *Understanding Our Mind* (Delhi: Harper Collins and India Today Group, 2009 [2006]), 125.

26 Satkari Mookerjee, *The Buddhist Philosophy of Universal Flux* (Calcutta: University of Calcutta, 1935), 337.

27 Ibid., 338.

28 Bhikkhu Jagadish Kashyap, trans., *Milinda Praśna* (Nagpur: Sugata Book Depot, 1995 [1937]), 404–426.

29 *The Long Discourses of the Buddha*, 231–277.

30 Vikas Singh, *Milindpañho Me Bhartiya Sanskriti* (Delhi: Vidyanidhi Prakashan, 2016), 18.

31 Ibid., 18.

32 B.R. Ambedkar, *The Buddha and His Dhamma* (Bombay: Siddharth College Publication/Peoples Education Society, 1957), 78.

33 *The Long Discourses of the Buddha*, 205.

34 Bhikkhu Dhammarakhita, '*Selasutta*', in *Suttanipāta*, 155–156.

35 Edward B. Cowell, ed. and trans., *The Buddha-Carita, Or Life of Buddha By Aśvaghoṣa* (Oxford: Clarendon, 1894), 103.

36 Bhikkhu Dhammarakhita, '*Selasutta*', in *Suttanipāta*, 155–156.

37 Bhikkhu Dhammarakhita '*Ratanasutta*', in *Suttanipāta*, 56.

38 Rev Richard Morris, ed., *The Buddhavaṁsa* (London: Pali Text Society, 1882), 37–38.

39 *The Long Discourses of the Buddha*, 200.

40 *The Connected Discourses of the Buddha*, 536.

41 A.K. Coomaraswamy, 'Origin of Buddha Image', *The Art Bulletin* 9, no. 4 (1927), 287–329.

42 Rahul Sankrityayan, *Darshan Digdarshan* (New Delhi: Kitab Mahal, 2007 [1944]), 533–539.

43 This was a personal communication from Pradeep Gokhale, an expert on Buddhist philosophy.

44 Ambedkar, *The Buddha*, 209.

45 Pradeep Gokhale, 'A Realist Buddhist Approach to Language and Verbal Testimony: An Exploration', *Journal of Buddhist Studies* 11 (2013), 111–128.

46 G.C. Pande, trans., *Nyaya Bindu of Acarya Dharmakirti with Dharmottara's Commentary* (Varanasi: Central Institute of Tibetan Studies, Sarnath, 1995), 35–39.

47 Gokhale, 'A Realist Buddhist', 111–128.

48 Susan Huntington, *Lay Rituals in Early Buddhist Art of India* (Amsterdam: Royal Netherlands Academy of Arts and Sciences, 2012), 18.

49 Klemens Karlsson, 'The Formation of Early Buddhist Culture', in *Material Religion* 2, no. 1, Jonkoping University and Stockholm University (2005), 68–96.

50 A.K. Narain, 'First Images of the Buddha and Bodhisattvas: Ideology and Chronology', *Studies in Buddhist Art of South Asia*, ed. A.K. Narain (Delhi: Kanak Publication, 1985), 1–21; John Huntington, 'Origin of the Buddha

Image, Early Image traditions and the Concept of Buddhadarsanapunya' in *Studies in Buddhist Art of South Asia*, ed. A.K. Narain (Delhi: Kanak Publication, 1985), 23–58; Joe Cribb, 'A re-examination of the Buddha images on the Coins of King Kaniṣka: New Light on the Origins of the Buddha Images in Gandhara Art', *Studies in Buddhist Art of South Asia*, ed. A.K. Narain (Delhi: Kanak Publication, 1985), 59–87.

# About the Editor and Contributors

## Editor

**R. Mahalakshmi** is Professor, Centre for Historical Studies, Jawaharlal Nehru University, New Delhi. Her research interests include the development of state, society, religion and art in ancient and medieval India, Nepal and Sri Lanka, and she has made presentations and published several articles related to these themes. Her book *The Making of the Goddess: Ko<u>r</u>ravai-Durgā in the Tamil Traditions* was awarded the best book by a woman historian by the Indian History Congress in 2013. She has also authored *The Book of Lakshmi* and co-edited *Colonization: A Comparative Study of India and Korea* with Vyjayanti Raghavan, in addition to articles in peer-reviewed journals and books. She has been co-investigator in an international project on 'India and Korea: A Comparative Study of Colonialism', and was Visiting Scholar Institut für Kunst-und Bildgeschichte, Humboldt University, in early 2018. She is the Secretary of the Indian History Congress, 2018–2021. She has delivered the Presidential addresses of the Historiography Section of the Andhra Pradesh History Congress, 2018–2019, and the Ancient Section of the Punjab History Conference, 2019–2020. She has also been invited to deliver the Erudite Lecture, Kerala History Congress and the prestigious Mamidipudi Venkatarangaiah Memorial Lecture (2018), in addition to talks in national and international conferences and seminars. She is currently in the process of finalising a ten volume series as General Editor on *Goddesses in South Asia*.

## Contributors

**Anisha Saxena** is Assistant Professor, Department of Social Sciences and Philosophy, Onondaga Community College, Syracuse, New York. She is an art historian and historian of South Asia and had worked on contested sacred geographies in India for her PhD thesis. She is in the process of converting her doctoral thesis into a monograph. She has published articles on architecture of medieval India, and religious cults and practices in regional contexts.

**Dev Kumar Jhanjh** is a doctoral candidate, Centre for Historical Studies, Jawaharlal Nehru University, New Delhi. He had received the prestigious DAAD Research Fellowship for the year 2018–2019, which enabled him to conduct his research at the Martin Luther University, Halle, Germany. He is the recipient of the Professor Vijay Kumar Thakur Memorial Prize for his research paper, 'Akṣaśālika, Akṣaśālin and Suvarṇakāra as the Engravers of Copper Plate Charters of Odisha (c. 7th–11th Centuries CE)', presented at the 78th session of the Indian History Congress in December 2017. He has published articles on state and society in early medieval India in prestigious journals and edited volumes.

**Malavika Binny** is Assistant Professor, Department of History, School of Liberal Arts and Basic Science, SRM University, Amaravati, Andhra Pradesh. She was the recipient of the Elamkulam Kunjan Pillai Memorial Young Historian Award instituted by the Kerala History Congress in 2017. She was also awarded the Erasmus Mundus IBIES Fellowship in 2015 in the course of her doctoral studies at JNU. Her research interests include histories of science, gender history, intellectual history and critical theory. She has a published on aspects of the history of bioprospecting, *Āyurveda*, *Vāstuśāstra* and gender in premodern and early modern India.

**Megha Yadav** is Assistant Professor, Department of History, Bharti College, University of Delhi. Her thesis, titled 'Divine Feminine in Tantric Buddhism, c. 6th century–12th century CE' focused on Tibetan Buddhism. She has presented papers in international and national seminars and conferences, and has published articles on gender and Buddhism. She is currently working on a monograph based on her thesis.

**Neha Singh** is an independent researcher. Her doctoral thesis focused on 'Śiva's *Kuṭumba*: Literary and Iconographic Representations in Early Medieval Northern India' and she is in the process of converting it into a monograph. Her research work combines an interest in the study of social history with that of mythology and mythography.

**Niharika K. Sankrityayan** was a postdoctoral fellow in the School of Humanities and Social Sciences, Indian Institute of Technology, Mandi, and worked on the project 'Sixteenth Century Renaissance in South India' from 2015 to 2018. Her areas of interest include early medieval South Asian art and architecture, with a specific focus on Brahmanical iconography and religious traditions.

**Sayantani Pal** is Associate Professor, Department of Ancient Indian History and Culture, University of Calcutta. She specialises in the field of epigraphy. Her area of research is the history of early Bengal on which she has done her doctoral thesis. She has published articles on palaeography and early medieval society and economy in various journals and is currently working on a monograph.

**Sneha Ganguly** is doctoral candidate, Centre for Historical Studies, Jawaharlal Nehru University, New Delhi. Her thesis focuses on the representation of the *asura* in literature and iconography from the mid-second millennium BCE to the mid-second millennium CE. She has worked as a researcher in an interdisciplinary University of Delhi Innovative Project (2012–2013) on 'Preserving our Cultural Heritage; The Monuments of Delhi: Zafar Mahal', and the findings were subsequently published in 2013. She has also interned with Indian National Trust for Art and Cultural Heritage (INTACH), the India City Walks in collaboration with Chhattisgarh Tourism, and the Rashtrapati Bhavan Museum.

**Suchandra Ghosh** is Professor, Department of Ancient Indian History and Culture, University of Calcutta. She specialises in epigraphy and numismatics. She was trained in early Indian scripts and her research interests include the political and cultural history of early India, regional history (southeastern Bengal and Assam), India's linkages with early southeast Asia, and Indian Ocean Buddhist and trade networks. She has been the recipient of the Charles Wallace Visiting Fellowship, United Kingdom, The Empowering Network for International Thai and ASEAN Studies (ENITAS) Scholarship, Chulalongkarn University, Bangkok, Lowick Memorial Grant for Oriental Studies by the Royal Numismatic Society, London, and visiting fellowships from the Fondation Maison des Sciences de l'Homme, Paris. She is the President of the Ancient India section of the 80th Session of the Indian History Congress, 2019. She has several national and international publications in both books and journals. Her own books include *Exploring Connectivity: Southeastern Bengal and Beyond* and *From the Oxus to the Indus: A Political and Cultural Study (c. 3rd century BCE – 1st century BCE).*

**Sujata Rakshit** has worked on Brahmanical iconography in early medieval Odisha. Her areas of interest include the iconographic traditions of premodern India, religious processes and gender studies. She is currently teaching undergraduate courses in Ramanujan College, University of Delhi.

**Umakanta Mishra** is Assistant Professor, Department of History, Ravenshaw University. His specialisation includes Buddhist archaeology, religious interactions and pre-Islamic Southeast Asian art. His monograph, *Vajrayana Buddhism: Study in Social Iconography,* focuses on the interpretation of Tantric ideas and icons in Buddhism. He has recently excavated the Chalcolithic site of Talagarh, Odisha.

**V. Selvakumar** is Associate Professor, Department of Epigraphy and Archaeology, Tamil University, Tanjavur. Earlier, he was with the Centre for Heritage Studies, Tripunithura, Kerala, from 2003 to 2007. He completed his doctoral research and post-doctoral research from Deccan College, Pune. He was an Nehru Trust for the Indian Collections at the Victoria and Albert Museum (NTICVAM) Visiting Researcher at the Centre for Maritime Archaeology, Southampton University. His research interests include the archaeology of India, particularly prehistory, heritage management, maritime history, history of science and technology, and ecocriticism. He is the President of the Archaeology section of the 80th Session of the Indian History Congress, 2019.

**Virendra Singh Bithoo** is Assistant Professor, College of Vocational Studies, University of Delhi. He completed his doctoral thesis on 'Science and Society in Varāhamihira's *Jyotiṣaśāstra*'. His MPhil research was on 'Goddesses in Early Medieval Rajasthan: Geographical Spread, Iconography and Mythology'. He is currently working towards publishing his MPhil dissertation and doctoral thesis.

**Y.S. Alone** is Professor, School of Arts and Aesthetics, Jawaharlal Nehru University, New Delhi. He has published several research papers on Ancient Indian art, critique of modern Indian art, popular neo-Buddhist visual culture, and the interpretative framework of B.R. Ambedkar in the social sciences. He has presented research papers at national and international art history and social sciences seminars/conferences as well as lectured widely in India and abroad. His recently published book *Early Western Indian Buddhist Caves: Forms and Patronage* examines the development of Buddhism through detailed field survey, inscriptional analysis and artistic oeuvres. He is currently engaged in the conceptual formulation of 'protected ignorance'.

# Index

T

It is an occasion of great pleasure to welcome in advance the release of the volume *Art and History: Texts, Contexts and Visual Representations in Ancient and Early Medieval India*. This anthology of essays written by an array of scholars, collectively demonstrates new strategies of reading history into the art heritage of our past. Hopefully, in future studies, this collection will help breakdown the conventional barrier between art history and history. The anthology covers a wide field, spatially and thematically, and its inclusive character hopefully will suggest directions for cross-regional comparisons in future research.

**B.D. Chattopadhyaya**, Professor (retired), Centre for Historical Studies, Jawaharlal Nehru University, New Delhi

This volume is an ambitious attempt to gather together a number of studies in the admittedly very large area of art (mainly sculpture) and thought (mainly religious) up to c. 1200 AD. The volume constitutes a thought-provoking inroad into the history of Indian art. The editor's introduction surveys almost every aspect of the theme, including a critical survey of the previous work on history of the Indian art. By its width and depth, the book will surely long serve as an important work of reference for all present and future students of the field.

**Irfan Habib**, Professor Emeritus, Aligarh Muslim University

This is a collection of articles by different scholars dealing with the interface between art and various aspects of historical development and underlines the importance of visual representations as a source of History. It emphasises their relevance to historical research and is an indispensable reading for historians and researchers.

**D.N. Jha**, Professor (retired), Department of History, University of Delhi, Delhi

As a historian, I am delighted about Prof. Mahalakshmi's comprehensive volume as we historians are often still too reluctant to contextualise the visual representations and symbolic elements of our texts. The present volume provides an overdue selection of excellent exemplary studies of understanding historical context from visual material.

**Hermann Kulke**, Professor Emeritus, University of Kiel

